The Erotics of Talk

Women's Writing
and Feminist Paradigms

CARLA KAPLAN

New York   Oxford
OXFORD UNIVERSITY PRESS
1996

Oxford University Press

Oxford   New York
Athens   Auckland   Bangkok   Bogotá   Bombay
Buenos Aires   Calcutta   Cape Town   Dar es Salaam
Delhi   Florence   Hong Kong   Istanbul   Karachi
Kuala Lumpur   Madras   Madrid   Melbourne
Mexico City   Nairobi   Paris   Singapore
Taipei   Tokyo   Toronto

and associated companies in
Berlin   Ibadan

Copyright © 1996 by Carla Kaplan

Published by Oxford University Press, Inc.,
198 Madison Avenue, New York, New York 10016

Oxford is a registered trademark of Oxford University Press

Library of Congress Cataloging-in-Publication Data
Kaplan, Carla.
The erotics of talk : women's writing
and feminist paradigms / by
Carla Kaplan.
p.   cm.   Includes bibliographical references and index.
ISBN 0-19-509914-1; ISBN 0-19-509915-X (pbk.)
1. American literature—Women authors—History and criticism—Theory, etc.
2. Feminism and literature—United States—History—20th century.
3. Jacobs, Harriet A. (Harriet Ann), 1813–1897. Incidents in the life of a slave girl.
4. Hurston, Zora Neale. Their eyes were watching God.
5. Brontë, Charlotte, 1816–1855. Jane Eyre.
6. Walker, Alice, 1944–   Color purple.
7. Women and literature.   8. Narration (Rhetoric)
9. Literary form.
I. Title.
PS147.K37   1996   810.9'9287—dc20   96-7135

1 3 5 7 9 8 6 4 2

Printed in the United States of America
on acid-free paper

For my parents,
Rosalyn and Bernard Kaplan,
and for John

Acknowledgments

I have encountered much generosity during the course of writing this book, and it is a great privilege to have many people and institutions to thank. For responses, discussions, suggestions, and support, I am grateful to Ann Ardis, Houston A. Baker, Jr., Richard Brodhead, Hazel Carby, Erin Cramer, Cathy Cohen, Deirdre David, Lynn Enterline, Judith Kegan Gardiner, Gerald Graff, Margaret Homans, Coppélia Kahn, Suzanne Keen, Jane Marcus, W. Douglas Payne, the late Julie Rolston, Linda Peterson, Mo Sila, Lynn Wardley, Laura Wexler, Ruth Yeazell, and all the members of the faculty colloquia of the Women's Studies program at Yale. For her timely help I thank my research assistant, Deborah Karush. Thanks also to Lindy for the photograph and to Tracy for the inspirational years of girl talk.

For reading many drafts with great enthusiasm and urgently needed insights, I am especially grateful to Lynne Huffer, Nina Miller, and Louise Yelin.

I also thank Yale University for a Morse fellowship, during which most of this book was written, for a grant from the A. Whitney Griswold Fund, which facilitated necessary travel, and for a Women's Studies Research Grant, which helped me complete the project.

Much of the writing of this project was completed while I was an Associate Fellow at the Oregon State University Center for the Humanities. I am grateful to Peter Copek for making it possible for me to be there and especially grateful to Patty Paulson for making it such a wonderful place to be. I wish it were still possible to thank her in person.

During the final stages of this project I received support from the Schomburg Center for Research in Black Culture and the Aaron Diamond

Fund of the National Endowment for the Humanities, for which I am deeply grateful.

At Oxford University Press I have been especially fortunate in my editors. Elizabeth Maguire's intellectual faith, encouragement, and good spirits illuminated many dark moments. And I greatly appreciate the grace under pressure of T. Susan Chang, with whom it has been such a pleasure to work in the earliest and also the final stages of the project. I also want to thank Elda Rotor for all her assistance and consideration and Stephanie Sakson for her copyediting.

My deepest debt is to John Brenkman, who offered his encouragement, insight, editorial acumen, sense of humor, and example of perseverance. This book is dedicated to him for all the many enthusiasms and the joys of daily conversation that make it all possible.

ॐ

Chapter One appeared, in slightly different form, in *Listening to Silences: New Essays in Feminist Criticism*, ed. Elaine Hedges and Shelley Fisher Fishkin (New York: Oxford UP, 1994). Chapter Two appeared in *The Yale Journal of Criticism*, Volume 6, No. 1 (Spring 1993); reprinted by permission of the Johns Hopkins University Press. Chapter Two also appeared, in slightly shorter form, in *Provoking Agents: Gender and Agency in Theory and Practice*, ed. Judith Kegan Gardiner (Urbana: University of Illinois Press, 1995); Chapter Four appeared in *American Literature*, Volume 67, No. 1 (March 1995). Portions of the Conclusion appeared, under the title "The Language of Crisis in Feminist Theory," in *"Turning the Century": Feminist Theory in the 1990's*, ed. Glynis Carr (Lewisburg: Bucknell University Press, copyright 1992 by Associated University Presses). I am grateful to the above publishers for permission to reprint.

Contents

The Erotics of Talk

A language is first and foremost someone talking. But there are language games in which the important thing is to listen, in which the rule deals with audition. Such a game is the game of the just. And in this game, one speaks only inasmuch as one listens, that is, one speaks as a listener.

—Jean-François Lyotard

"Conversation":

1. The action of living or having one's being in *a place or* among *persons.*

2. The action of consorting or having dealings with others; living together: commerce, intercourse, society, intimacy.

3. Sexual intercourse or intimacy.

4. Occupation or engagement with *things, in the way of business or study; the resulting condition of acquaintance or intimacy with a matter.*

5. Circle of acquaintance, company, society.

6. Manner of conducting oneself in the world or in society; behaviour, mode or course of life.

7. Interchange of thoughts and words; familiar discourse of debate.

8. A public conference, discussion, or debate.

9. An "At Home"=Conversazíone.

10. To converse, talk, engage in conversation.

—Oxford English Dictionary

Introduction: In Search of an Ideal Listener

Talk is like a structural midden, a refuse heap in which bits and oddments of all the ways of framing activity in culture are to be found.

—Erving Goffman[1]

Women's number one grievance about . . . men is that they "don't listen."

—Susan Faludi[2]

Being listened to is one of the few real aphrodisiacs left.

—*Ms.* Magazine[3]

In Search of an Ideal Listener

Let me begin with two stories about women's search for an ideal listener.

The first is by Henry James and sets out to describe the discursive desire of feminists. In *The Bostonians*, James presents his image of what Mrs. Farrinder, a strident radical feminist, wants in a listener. Facing a sympathetic roomful of women, Mrs. Farrinder finds that she has nothing to say:

> . . . she could only deliver her message to an audience which she felt to be partially hostile. There was no hostility there; they were all only too much in sympathy. "I don't require sympathy," she said with a tranquil smile. . . . "I only rise to the occasion, when I see prejudice, when I see bigotry, when I see injustice, when I see conservatism, massed before me like an army. Then I feel—I feel as I imagine Napoleon Bonaparte to have felt on the eve of one of his great victories. I MUST have unfriendly elements—I like to win them over.[4]

Olive Chancellor, another radical feminist, spies Basil Ransom and wonders if he might suffice for an unfriendly element; she offers him up as such to the still silent Mrs. Farrinder, "who expressed an earnest hope that if he were opposed to the principles which were so dear to the rest of them, he

3

might be induced to take the floor. . . . 'I should be so happy to answer him,' said Mrs. Farrinder, with supreme softness. 'I should be so glad, at any rate, to exchange ideas with him.'"[5]

James intends this as a portrait of perversity. The forms of talk and social exchange that "normal" people long for, James implies, are conversations, not battles. It may be one thing to be *willing* to fight, but only radical feminists, unnatural women like Mrs. Farrinder and Olive Chancellor, could be perverse enough to *desire* such an exchange of words.

James's misrepresentation is both fascinating and telling. On the one hand, his description is shot through with anxiety about women's speech, particularly an anxiety about the discursive passions of women. (In this, of course, James is hardly alone. Other modernist writings, like Hemingway's, for example, are filled with anxiety about women's love of talk, women's facility with words, women's passion for conversation: "he would have liked a girl if she had come to him and not wanted to talk. . . . that was the thing about French and German girls. There was not all this talking. . . . It was not worth it. . . . He would not go through all the talking. He did not want one badly enough."[6]) On the other hand, James misses what I am suggesting is one of the most recurrent features of modern women's writing: expressions of a longing for conversation, for "forms of talk," as the *Oxford English Dictionary*'s definition of "conversation" suggests, in which one can be "among persons," "living together," with "intimacy," "engagement," a "circle of acquaintance, company, society," an "interchange of thoughts and words"—conversations, in short, in which one can feel, quite simply, "at home."[7] Without question, women—perforce—engage in a kind of contestatory politics of voice all the time. But that is hardly to say that this is all they want.

My second story, by Gloria Naylor, is also about a search for an ideal listener under conditions in which no such person can be presupposed. Where Mrs. Farrinder can see rhetorical possibilities in such a situation, what this narrator wants is very different, a kind of discursive interrelation I call an erotics of talk.

Mama Day opens in the chorus-like voice of a narrator who speaks for an island community of descendants of African slaves in a town called Willow Springs. This preface begins with the legend of ex-slave and conjure woman Sapphira Wade, whose story "everybody knows, but nobody talks." Sapphira Wade is legendary because she resisted and survived. She became a subject, rather than an object of exchange, by killing her master, by marrying him, or by persuading him to deed her and his other slaves his land, which becomes Willow Springs. All that is known, with certainty, is the date of 1823: the year when all the land in Willow Springs shifted from his name to hers. 1823, or 18 & 23 as it is more properly known, is a signifier that in Willow Springs stands for everything from violence to seduction, persuasion to coercion, cowardice to courage, oppression to resistance, cunning to foolishness, catastrophe to good fortune.[8] Whether it signifies the moment when a black female slave committed murder, married a white man, or snookered her master, 1823 stands for the complex histories—and tortured options—of African American slaves.

The problem is not one of reconstructing the facts of 1823. That story can be told a myriad of possible ways, and none of them is right and none of them is wrong. The problem that the preface raises instead is whether there is anyone out there capable of *listening* to such stories, of understanding them, grasping what 18 & 23 means, how many things it means, how all of its different meanings not only fit together but belong together, why it is so important.

Things don't look good. The preface describes an eminently modern individual, "Reema's boy," a university student who comes "hauling himself back from one of those fancy colleges mainside, dragging his notebooks and tape recorder and a funny way of curling up his lip and clicking his teeth, all excited and determined to put Willow Springs on the map" (7). Reema's boy wants to get the story of Sapphira Wade down. He wants to preserve what he knows to be important history before it is lost forever. But he leaves empty-handed because he doesn't know how to ask the right question and has even less of an idea of how to hear its answer. "Reema's boy couldn't listen . . . or he woulda left here with quite a story," the preface concludes (10).

If Reema's boy is a pathetic figure, a parodic send-up of the literary or cultural critic as anthropologist, his mission is not comic. The presence or absence of an ideal or at least competent listener—of someone who understands—becomes a matter of life and death for Cocoa, the novel's main character. And her fate is in the hands of her husband, George, a man who, like Reema's boy, doesn't know how to listen. George, another modern, university-educated man "from beyond the bridge," tries to understand Willow Springs, a female world that runs on its own laws and in its own time. But he fails because he would rather die than learn to listen. And in dying he nearly kills his wife.

This is the fate that hangs in the balance for the town of Willow Springs and the legend of Sapphira Wade. The reader, by definition a person "from beyond the bridge," in all likelihood university-educated, perhaps in possession of notepad and tape recorder, is faced with the challenge of learning to be the ideal, or at least apt, listener that both Reema's boy and George fail to be. The survival of what may be one of the most important stories of American history—the story of female slave resistance and endurance—depends on that success. Will we prove up to the task? Will we fail, like Reema's boy? Will we die trying? Who, or what, will we bury with our own failure? How should we approach the problem? Why should we even bother?

The search for an ideal listener may be particular to our own cultural moment. According to some theorists, in fact, this search is modernity's defining problematic. Modernity is distinguished, Walter Benjamin argues, by an atomization and social disintegration so profound as to make exchange with one another seem impossible. "It is as if something that seemed inalienable to us, the securest among our possessions, were taken from us," Benjamin writes, "the ability to exchange experience."[9] In Charles Taylor's view, the prevailing discourse of modernity, in both the private and the public spheres, is one of recognition: an overwhelming appeal to the idea of an ideal listener. Conditions of modernity, Taylor argues, have inflected dialogue and conversation with a particular urgency. If feudal society, for example, told people exactly who they were—for better or worse—such clarity about social positions has never been a feature of modernity. But this does not mean that such clarity is no longer sought. The modern emphasis on identity and its discursive construction increasingly strives to join the public sphere, which no longer provides fixed and immutable social roles, to the private sphere, where recognition has often been consigned:

> On the social plane, the understanding that identities are formed in open dialogue, unshaped by a predefined social script, has made the politics of equal recognition more central and stressful. It has, in fact, considerably raised the stakes. Equal recognition is not just the appropriate mode for a healthy democratic society. Its refusal can inflict damage on those who are denied it, according to a widespread modern view. . . . Not only contemporary feminism but also race relations and multiculturalism are undergirded by the premise that the withholding of recognition can be a form of oppression. . . . And so the discourse of recognition has become familiar to us on two levels: First, in the intimate sphere, where we understand the formation of identity and the self as taking place in a continuing dialogue and struggle with significant others. And then in the public sphere, where a politics of equal recognition has come to play a bigger and bigger role.[10]

This "bigger role" does not result from increased intimacy, reciprocity, respect, and equality. On the contrary, the desire for the recognition promised by dialogue and conversation increases in direct proportion to the diminishment or fading of intimacy, reciprocity, respect, and equality. "What has come about with the modern age is not the need for recognition but the conditions in which the attempt to be recognized can fail," Taylor writes.[11]

This leads me to one of the questions at the heart of this book: *How does women's writing—where the stakes of recognition have always been particularly high—reflect that potential failure and rewrite the perennial quest for an ideal listener in light of it?*

The modern emphasis on identity and its discursive construction helps explain also why dialogue also comes to the fore in poststructuralism. Poststructuralist models of the mediation of language and discourse in the intersubjective formation of self-identity cannot help but privilege intersubjective discursive exchange. If modernists confront atomization and alienation as conditions to be answered or ameliorated by the recognition dialogue and intersubjective exchange promise, poststructuralists interrogate the very construction and conception of identity, questioning its groundedness: what, if anything, grounds our self-identity, our sense of being? Is the practice of dialogue and conversational exchange somehow a grounding one for poststructuralists? If the idea of an ideal listener answers to modernist yearnings to escape isolation, is there a poststructuralist yearning to which it answers as well?

A second question at the heart of this book is how feminist criticism, as an enterprise which has always privileged conversational themes and dialogic methods, reflects and responds to the peculiarly modern search for an ideal listener. *How does feminist criticism, taken as a whole, understand itself as a textually mandated listener and how does it establish its relation to its most cherished texts? What constructions of self-identity have its paradigms allowed?*

Interestingly, both James and Naylor project the search for an ideal listener as relatively problem-free. Mrs. Farrinder does not mind speaking to antagonists; indeed, she finds them ideal. And Naylor, quite cleverly, presents a presumption of readerly ideality which is really a provocation and a performative: "Reema's boy couldn't listen, like you. . . . Reema's boy coulda listened . . . the way you been listening" (10).

But the search for an ideal listener is no idle matter. If, as Lyotard claims, in a "language game of the just . . . the rule deals with audition,"[12] ideal listening is no easy thing.

Sapphira Wade's truly ideal listener, for example, would *not* presume she knows how to listen at the outset. She would be sensitive to how differences of "footing" or status may alter not just the context of speaking but also what is said.[13] And most important, she would recognize that the act of dialogic exchange, in and of itself, may not be sufficient to put speaker and listener on the footing they need to make their conversational exchange both meaningful and satisfying. The outcome of any conversational exchange, however strong its appeal, is always variable and contingent. It can never be presupposed at the outset or theorized purely in the abstract. Which means that we cannot take for granted whether speaking out will work. Or how it might fail.

Theorizing Cultural Conversation

In social theory and feminist philosophy, the models of cultural conversation which have proved most influential for feminists seeking to theorize the uses of dialogue and the possibilities of speaking out are those of Richard Rorty and Jürgen Habermas.[14] But both have also been challenged for presuming the transformative power of discourse itself, without attending sufficiently to the differing "footings" of its participants.

Richard Rorty, for example, proposes that we adopt conversation, or "cacophony and disorder," as a model for cultural practice and social change. "Conversation," Rorty argues, is "the ultimate context within which knowledge is to be understood." Certainty, philosophical or otherwise, must, hence, be "a matter of conversation between persons." For Rorty, "keeping a conversation going [is] a sufficient aim of philosophy," and wisdom consists in "the ability to sustain a conversation," not the provision of universal "truth" or creation of a metadiscourse to justify and legitimate the way things are.[15] As a cultural model, Rorty's conversationalism allies itself with both the work of feminist poststructuralists and the demand for a plurality of voices and social vocabularies that we now associate with multiculturalism.

But Rorty's model can no more explain how we get from here to there than can James's. Rorty fails to address the questions of access and footing, the ways in which our social positions inflect the very possibility of getting in on the conversation, let alone helping to sustain it or finding that endeavor worthwhile. Nancy Hartsock offers a strong version of the feminist critique of Rorty's model in her contention that "conversation on Rorty's terms would only reinforce previous power relations." Insofar as we are not "all in a position to participate as equals in a conversation," she argues, then a conversational model of cultural change "is, in fact, dangerous to those of us who have been marginalized."[16]

Hartsock's critique of Rorty's gender-blindness is right on the mark, but she reaches hyperbolic conclusions. Just as she shows that there is no reason to presuppose that getting in on the conversation will prove liberatory, so is there no reason to presuppose that doing so will necessarily prove "dangerous." If talk, as Erving Goffman maintains, is "a structural midden, a refuse heap in which bits and oddments of all the ways of framing activity in culture are to be found," we do need, as Hartsock suggests, to be more critical about presuming that merely getting in on the conversation or helping to sustain it (something for which women, as many linguists point out, have always taken more than their share of responsibility[17]) will guarantee the reframing we seek. But at the same time, we need to acknowledge that opting out of the conversation because of its dangers is hardly a solution. Even our silence, after all, would be part of the cultural conversation, not a move outside of it or a transcendence of it.

The problem is not only, as Hartsock claims, that "Rorty ignores power relations."[18] Both Hartsock and Rorty construct a false opposition between celebrating dialogue as emancipatory and liberatory on the one hand and vilifying it as dangerous and oppressive on the other. Rather than attend to categories of difference such as gender and race, or better yet concretizing practices of cultural conversation, Rorty theorizes the transformational effects of language purely in the abstract. But Hartsock, after attending to these very categories of difference, also generalizes and universalizes the efficacy of conversation. Neither abstraction can suffice. Only by engaging actual cultural conversations—social struggles, texts, readings, discourses, collective enterprises, debates, and so on—can we determine how "cacophony and disorder" come out: when getting in on the conversation serves liberatory purposes, when it proves dangerous, and how we might negotiate the shifts between these two—never mutually exclusive—extremes.

The enterprise of feminist criticism over the past twenty years or so provides one of the best models we could find of an ongoing and sustained cultural conversation. And whereas this enterprise used to be described in primarily harmonious terms—as a collaboration, an exchange, a dialogue—

now it is increasingly lamented as cacophonous, disordered, fragmented, and chaotic, the death knell of a formerly coherent project. *Has feminism's cacophony proved productive or destructive? What, if anything, should we do with all that noise?*

The theoretical tensions I have been discussing in Rorty's model are, if anything, even more evident in the work of Jürgen Habermas, whose theory of social discourse, or "communicative ethics," many feminists (myself included), find more compelling than Rorty's.

Habermas's argument, like Rorty's, proposes an anti-foundational "cacophony" in its assertion that "communicative ethics," as a procedural norm of truly participatory democracy in which everyone would have a "voice," must replace our conception of disembodied, putatively transcendental, and universal norms of justice and the social good. A "communicative ethics" provides the ground for a critique of existing norms and institutions not by appealing to a transcendental set of values, but by adherence to a process—hence Habermas's emphasis on the "procedural"—by which both social norms and "normal" discourse can be challenged and adjudicated.[19] A just norm, a fair social policy, a legitimate social practice, consequently, is one which is determined to be so on the basis of a non-coercive communal stipulation, or what Habermas calls an "ideal speech situation," a "situation of dialogue free of external pressures and internal distortions, in which participants would respond to the force of the better argument alone."[20] Because such procedures, clearly, can operate only under social conditions in which everyone has a voice and is able to express it freely, both institutions and individuals need a commitment to consensus, or at least to the principle of fruitful disagreement. "Institutions become criticizable once it can be shown that they, for example, structurally pre-empt a social group's participation on a par with others in such discursively mediated interactions, John Brenkman writes."[21]

We recognize that such commitments are not always present, but this does not license us, on Habermas's account, to behave as if they don't count:

> As a matter of fact we can in no way always (or even often) fulfill those im-
> probable pragmatic preconditions, from which we nevertheless begin in com-
> municative everyday practice, and indeed, in the sense of a transcendental
> necessity, *must* begin. For this reason, socio-cultural life-forms stand under
> the structural limitations of a communicative reason which is *simultaneously
> denied and laid claim to.*[22]

This is a crucial hedge in Habermas's theory. And it goes to the heart of a circularity in his argument. Habermas seems to place us under the imperative—whether as individuals or groups, regardless of who "we" happen to be[23]—to behave as if an "ideal speech situation" exists when it manifestly does not.

While Habermas's "communicative ethics" presents a very productive blueprint for social relations, its slippage from a diagnostic account of how things are to a programmatic model of how they should be appears to be grounded in a presumptive view of the inherent character of discourse itself. In taking little account of gender or race, his "normative ideal of self/other relationships" leaves open the question of how such a blueprint might be realized under given social conditions, how discourse might transcend or help transform its own inscription in social axes of subordination such as those based on gender, race, class, sexuality, or abledness. As Iris Marion Young points out, "only if oppressed groups are able to express their interests and experience in the public *on an equal basis with other groups* can group domination through formally equal processes of participation be avoided."[24]

Even more than Young, Nancy Fraser is interested in a critical recuperation of Habermas and shares his conviction that a commitment to the ideal of rational consensus need not be incommensurate with the considerable social obstacles to its realization and practice.[25] The critical weak spot in Habermas's model, for Fraser, is its gender-blindness. She points out that dialogic competency has itself been gendered. "Capacities for consent and speech, the ability to participate on a par with others in dialogue . . . are capacities that are connected with masculinity in male-dominated classical capitalism; they are capacities that are in myriad ways denied to women." Hence, for example, femininity comes to be conceptually opposed to citizenship or to civic life in the public sphere. Because these sorts of gendered conceptions structure all aspects of social life, merely moving from "normatively secured contexts of interaction" (based in taken-for-granted conventions and cultural traditions) to "communicatively achieved ones" (based on "explicit, reflectively achieved consensus, consensus reached by unconstrained discussion under conditions of freedom, equality, and fairness") will not intrinsically make the public sphere more amenable or accessible to women. "An emancipatory transformation of male-dominated, capitalist societies, early and late, requires a transformation of these gendered roles and of the institutions they mediate."[26]

Discourse alone, in other words, cannot suffice as both the means *and* the outcome of the transformational goals we seek. I agree with both Young and Fraser that we need to be asking not only how everyone might participate in the the cultural conversation but also how everyone might acquire the necessary respect to do so in a meaningful way. But Young and Fraser's accounts also participate in the circularity they pinpoint: communicative ethics can help transform unequal social relations; transformed social relations are prerequisite to communicative ethics. This circle can only be broken by looking at actual conversational practices, strategies, and social-political-discursive outcomes, not at abstract formulations of the dialogic alone.

Women's writing and feminist criticism seem tailor-made for such investigation. *How do different women's writings negotiate this circular imperative? Do the women writers feminism celebrates propose getting in on the conversation or getting out of it?*

In literary and cultural studies, the model of cultural conversation that has proved most influential has clearly been that of Mikhail Bakhtin. Indeed, it sometimes seems as if the project of literary criticism today has become synonymous with a search for the "dialogic": identifying multivocality or "heteroglossia," documenting a text's multiple discourses and the "cacophony and disorder" between them, discovering conflicting discourses.[27] Bakhtin's dialogics provides an indispensable map of cultural conversation, especially when we remember that Bakhtin was not particularly interested in sentimentalizing conversation or resolving cacophony. But whereas what Bakhtin offers us is principally descriptive, his theory of textual dialogics has often been taken to be programmatic, as if the mere identification of "heteroglossia" is itself a cause for celebration and proof of liberatory or subversive counterforces. Mapping the presence of and conflict between multiple textual voices is only one task; it cannot answer in advance the question of what conclusions we might draw about the particular forms taken by their presence and interaction, cannot answer the difficult questions about how—in concrete instances of dialogic exchange—conflicting agendas are negotiated and "footings" are rearranged.

The tendency to universalize and abstract the social efficacy of the dialogic is, of course, hardly the exclusive province of rhapsodic Bakhtinianism. To the question of what will be the medium of reframing and restructuring the cultural conversation, many narrative theorists answer: "talk itself." Hans Robert Jauss, for example, writing from the perspective of reception aesthetics and drawing on the philosophy of Hans-Georg Gadamer, maintains that the "dialogical character" of narrative resides in its power "to create an interlocutor capable of understanding."[28] "Every conversation," Gadamer writes, "presupposes a common language, or, it creates a common language. . . . To reach an understanding with one's partner in a dialogue is not merely a matter of total self-expression and the successful assertion of one's own point of view, but a transformation into a communion, in which we do not remain what we were."[29] Ross Chambers argues that narratives "seduce" their readers into "a suspension of conversational turn taking," a "tactic" that buys the narrator "room to maneuver," room to transform the reader's desire and thus room for the text to "*change its other.*"[30] All of these theories share the presumption that narrative exchange can be the means of the very social transformations it seeks to reflect and represent. Hence, the mere presence of the dialogic, the copresence of both text and reader, is itself a cause for celebration.

The Ethics of Feminist Criticism

While some critics posit that all reading strives for a conversation by trying, as Jonathan Culler puts it, to identify a narrator who can be imagined as "speaking" to the reader,[31] or by making textual understanding correspond, in Gadamer's words, to "the model of the conversation between two persons,"[32] or by answering what Peter Brooks describes as the "desire to be heard, recognized, listened to" driving all narrative,[33] the conversational paradigm has had a *particularly* strong purchase in feminist criticism, where the act of interpretation is often conceived as an "intimate conversation" between "the woman reader and the woman writer,"[34] a "dialogic" collaboration, an "empathic" imperative.[35] The theoretical problems I have been raising may be particularly acute for literary critics, whose work necessarily entails both an arrangement of multivocalities and the discernment and discovery of buried voices. But how much greater is that challenge for those, like feminist critics, who mostly deal in texts that have been dismissed, misunderstood, or neglected?[36]

Recognizing the numerous mechanisms that either deny voice to women or render their discourse meaningless, a feminist *politics of voice* often aims to rescue what has been silenced and disregarded. As Susan Lanser puts it:

> few words are as resonant to contemporary feminists as "voice." . . . Book titles announce "another voice," "a different voice," or resurrect the "lost voices" of women poets and pioneers; fictional figures ancient and modern, actual women famous and obscure, are honored for speaking up and speaking out. . . . Despite compelling interrogations of "voice" as a humanist fiction, for the collectively and personally silenced the term has become a trope of identity and power: as Luce Irigaray suggests, to find a voice (*voix*) is to find a way (*voie*).[37]

This recuperative imperative is inextricably linked to the now-discounted (and no longer practiced) practice of consciousness-raising: its effort to construct spaces of conversation free of coercion and inherited conventions, its rendering of women's responsibility to one another as an exchange of personal narrative, its assumption that women can and should identify with one another and with each other's stories.[38] Adrienne Rich's poetry, for example, which had such a profound influence in the late sixties and seventies, is replete with the voices of other women: Elvira Shatayev, Marie Curie, Paula Becker, and Clara Westhoff, "a woman dead in her forties," "the alleged murderess walking in her cell."[39] To identify with other women was then understood as a form—or ethic—of accountability: creating a dialogue between women who, for historical and social reasons, could not be present in the room to share their experiences and stories. "We identify with all women," the Redstockings manifesto read. "We define our best interest as that of the poorest, most brutally exploited woman."[40]

This politics of voice is a welcome antidote to the cruel disregard for others the right-wing keeps urging upon us. But it may also mirror the difficulties and circularities I have cited above. *Does searching for the "voice" of women's writing and attempting to "give voice" to silenced or disregarded texts take for granted that merely getting in on the conversation is cause for celebration? Have feminist theories that insist on the primacy of cultural reframing collided with methodologies that privilege textual talk?*

More than any other political movement, feminism has politicized the values of the intimate sphere, differentiated various possibilities of intimacy, and drawn attention to the importance of intersubjective exchange and dialogue. It has revealed the intimate sphere to be not only a safe, familiar space, but sometimes also a monstrous place: constricting, oppressive, and brutal. Has this insight always been sustained when it is feminist intimacy (or empathy, collaboration, or dialogism) itself which is under scrutiny? Feminist recuperations of women's subversive "voice" have not always acknowledged the myriad ways—even between women—that communication may *fail* and that failure may be symbolized. Feminist criticism has often looked to women's writing to mirror feminist criticism itself, wanting to see its own project of discovering lost female voices affirmed by the texts it recuperates. This drive to establish a relation to women's literature that is "intimate," "dialogic," or "empathic," to establish that the feminist critic is the ideal listener the text has been waiting for, to prove, as Roland Barthes puts it, that the text "*desires me*,"[41] may provide an outlet for a female erotics that is otherwise repressed, but it may also lead to identifications with narrators or authors which cannot be borne out, which are based on false assumptions or unrealistic hopes.

How can we preserve the ethical imperative of feminist criticism without falling prey either to essentialism or to sentimentality?

Listening to Women's Writing

Goffman proposes that no form of talk is as self-effacing, humiliating, or damaging to one's social standing as talking to ourselves: displaying our lack of a proper and appropriate interlocutor. "Extended self-talk," Goffman writes, "if discovered, reflects badly on the talker."[42]

Lunatics and children talk to themselves. Schizophrenics and cast-offs talk to themselves. Homeless people and drunks talk to themselves. Hence, the compulsion to produce a listener is not only a strong one, but is also motivated by a number of negative associations. And an important form of social power is the performative power to turn speakers into "self-talkers" by denying them a hearing. "A summons [to talk, to respond] that is openly snubbed," Goffman writes, "can leave us feeling that we have been caught engaging in something like talking to ourselves."[43] Such performatives not only mute the speech of those who are transformed into self-talkers, they render their very subjectivity suspect by associating them with those whom society has already effectively marginalized. And it is not enough to have *some* kind of interlocutor. We can be considered guilty of self-talk merely by addressing others like ourselves, by being caught in such devalued discourses as "girl talk" or "gossip,"[44] by being caught in a "hen party" of supposed meaninglessness.

Given this, one might expect a speaker's lack of social power to correlate directly with her willingness to compromise, to accept any legitimizing listener at all so as not to be transformed into a "self-talker." The consequences of "self-talking" are grave. Social norms mandate intersubjectivity, but failing to provide its necessary conditions social values also tend to blame the victim herself by accusing her, in effect, of failing to engage with others, a failure that becomes proof of her inadmissibility to the public sphere. Hence, one might expect to see behavior more like Mrs. Farrinder's desire to speak to her male antagonists, especially insofar as their presence as interlocutors, if not the substance of their response, would mark her address as valid. But is this what we find?

One response to being caught out without an appropriate listener is the attempt to procure one at all costs, but another is to performatively dramatize the failure, inaccessibility, or ineptitude of potential listeners. Thus "self-talk" becomes a form of refusal, a critique of the double bind.[45] "Self-talk," as Goffman astutely points out, whether in the form of silence, muttering, gossip, or girl talk, can function to disrupt our very sense of sociality by suggesting that we have no basis for mutual recognition. "Self-talk" poses a "threat to intersubjectivity; it warns others that they may be wrong in assuming a jointly maintained base of ready mutual intelligibility among all persons present."[46] Refusing to behave like Mrs. Farrinder can be a way of challenging "normal" social relations, what Luce Irigaray has described as the "goods" refusing to go to "market," or "commodities among themselves."[47] And refusing to behave like Mrs. Farrinder can take any number of forms: leaving the room, engaging Basil Ransom differently, speaking to Olive Chancellor instead, dramatizing the difficulty of all of these options.

The established feminist paradigm of searching for "voice" cannot, as I will argue in all of the chapters which follow, give us an adequate purchase on all of these strategies, on the range of ways black and white women's writing of the nineteenth and twentieth centuries has negotiated—or performed—women's difficult "footing" and variously both gotten in on and opted out of the cultural conversation. The feminist enterprise of recovering the textual voice of women's subversion has provided many rich insights and restored many valuable texts. But as I reread them, our own classic texts raise difficult questions about how we can make such subversive voices speak.

A metaphorics of feminism's intimate conversation with its women's texts has held sway across a surprisingly broad spectrum of critical positions. And this study is concerned in part with why that would be so. Yet while talk between women does loom large in many of the texts that have become feminist classics (which I think has a great deal to do with why they are chosen in the first place), does an "intimate," "empathic," and "dialogic" model really obtain in the women's literature in which feminist criticism finds it? Does it really explain the subversiveness so often sought?

Do the classic stories and novels of feminist criticism affirm the protocols of women's conversation they are taken (even perhaps, selected) to model, or do they call into question the very presuppositions of collaboration and sisterhood for which they have been serving as paradigms?

The Erotics of Talk

All of the stories and novels considered here are now feminist classics. Each has been recuperated by feminist readers intent on uncovering a subversive voice buried under misreadings and neglect, with the exception of *The Color Purple*, which is itself a recuperation of Hurston's politics of voice in *Their Eyes Were Watching God*. Each has been taken as a model of "coming to voice" and moving from culturally imposed silence to speech. But electing classics on the basis of their politics of voice obscures the presence of a competing topos in women's literature, one that it will be my project to map. This topos is the search not for a voice, but for a listener capable of hearing that voice and responding appropriately to it. Within many individual texts, this topos takes the form of a repeated and structuring metaphor—a performative trope—I call *the erotics of talk*.

In distinguishing a *politics of voice* from an *erotics of talk*, I have in mind the difference between the imperatives that drive Mrs. Farrinder to speak out against those who oppress her and the narrator of *Mama Day* who longs for a recognition, reciprocity, and understanding that seems to be always receding. An erotics of talk, we might say, is a utopian desire for the "ideal speech situation" which pointedly does not exist and which must be imagined more tangibly than in Habermasian theory. Whereas a politics of voice can celebrate the transformational power of argument and counternarration, an erotics of talk may imagine what happens to such narratives in the absence—a continued, continuing, and prolonged absence—of able and competent interlocutors. What happens, in short, when Reema's boy can't learn?

An erotics of talk may be a form of refusal or of "self-talk," opting out of Mrs. Farrinder's situation and turning to Olive Chancellor instead. It may be an attempt to dramatize the difficulty of being Mrs. Farrinder. An erotics of talk might be understood as wish fulfillment fantasy: a desire to be reassured that exchange between people is still possible, that we are not merely alone, speaking to ourselves, talking into the empty wind of a world from which meaningful and satisfying interrelationship has been eradicated. It is a figure for the representation both of desire and what thwarts desire. It is a performative that questions the status of performativity itself.

An erotics of talk, in other words, is a figuration for both personal desire and social critique, "a mode of discourse which projects normative possibilities unrealized but felt in a particular given social reality,"[48] a political allegory. The woman narrator who longs for an ideal respondent who never comes or who finds that respondent under only the most limited and temporary circumstances, holds a critical mirror up to the failures of her fictional world and the reader's world as well. Such mirroring says, of both the private and the public sphere, that "it does not have to be this way, it could be otherwise."[49] As a utopian figuration of a better world, an erotics of talk is a kind of poetic justice, a "political language"[50] for personal and social equality. As Audre Lorde has argued, the erotic is a kind of ethical geiger counter which we can use to determine "which of our various life endeavors bring us closest to that fullness. . . . As women, we need to examine the ways in which our world can be truly different."[51]

The feminist revision of Habermas's communicative ethics is most fruitfully read, I'd suggest, as a call to foreground desire. In Habermas's presupposition that cultural conversants will be committed not only to argument and its resolution but also to expressing universal and shared interests that lead to consensus, feminist philosophers like Young, Fraser, and Seyla Benhabib find a lingering adherence to ideas of impartiality and universality that inhibit difference, that inhibit the standpoints and perspectives of what Benhabib terms the "concrete other." Proceeding from real desires and needs, they suggest, means that participants need not bracket their particularity in the interest of a universality that will inevitably prove either false or coercive.[52]

Taking desire as a privileged entry point into cultural conversation, my trope of an erotics of talk can be used to map the textual inscription of those forms of intimacy, reciprocity, equality, recognition, and respect for difference which do not find realization under the prevailing conditions of modern social organization but which are nevertheless—or all the more—longed for and desired in so much women's writing and in feminism itself: a "possibility of intimacy," as Anthony Giddens puts it, which is also "the promise of democracy" because of intimacy's "imperative of free and open communication," its implicit demand for an "open forum."[53]

Since I have been emphasizing textual inscriptions of oppression and resistance, perhaps I should say a word more about the erotics of an erotics of talk, about why I have chosen to call this structuring trope an erotics of talk rather than either a poetics or a politics of talk, terms which might seem to apply just as well. I might say, along with Giddens, that the erotic is itself a communicative medium, empowered to both revitalize social interaction and mark our social "failure" to provide an "open forum" and that therefore it is only logical to talk about an erotics of talk.[54] But I am also suggesting that this figure makes particular sense for women's fiction.[55]

It has become relatively commonplace for narrative theorists to argue that desire is the driving force behind all narration. Narrative desire, on Peter Brooks's account, for example, is the desire to "seduce" or "captivate" a listener, to transform a listener, if necessary, from antagonist to conversational partner. "Narration," Brooks writes, is:

> a form of human desire . . . that seeks to *seduce* and to *subjugate* the listener, to *implicate* him in the *thrust* of a desire that can never quite speak its name— never quite come to the point—but that insists on speaking over and over again its movement toward that name. . . . Narrative may first come to life as narration, as the inchoate intent to tell. . . . It is in essence the desire to be heard, recognized, understood, which, never wholly satisfied or indeed satisfiable, continues to generate the desire to tell, the effort to enunciate a significant version of the life story in order to *captivate* a possible listener."[56]

Brooks's model accords well with those of other narrative theorists, such as Robert Scholes, who describe narrative's movement as that of the "sexual act . . . the fundamental orgastic rhythm of tumescence and detumescence, of tension and resolution, of intensification to the point of climax and consummation."[57]

This rhetoric of "seduction," "captivation," "thrusting," "subjugation," "tumescence and detumescence" reveals the understanding of desire upon which their conception of narrative exchange is based as fundamentally male and heterosexual. It also suggests that narrative desire, in their view, takes shape as a battle or a contest.

An erotics of talk invites us to interrogate those assumptions and to ask: *Is a masculinized, heterosexual, martial model of narrative desire really the only one available?*

Lesbian theorists, perforce, have been particularly sensitive to the hypostatization of desire along one unitary, putatively universal model, to how, in Teresa de Lauretis's description, narrative theory "ends up 'dehistoricizing the subject and thus universalizing the narrative process.'"[58] The familiar model of desire and fulfillment, "tumescence and detumescence," Judith Roof points out, is not only male and heterosexual, it is also static. What is needed in its place, she argues, is a "more dynamic interplay of desire and narrative than the models imply. If desire is shaped differently according to gender and sexual orientation, then it may differ in respect to other criteria as well. As the terms multiply, so do the operations of desire."[59] An erotics of talk suggests an alternative economy of sexual desire. It may, to borrow a phrase from Rachel Blau DuPlessis, cut "the Gordian knot of both heterosexuality and narrative convention."[60]

This trope of an erotics of talk has been an important (if overlooked) structure not only for women's writing, but also for feminist criticism. The desire to have women's texts mirror the feminist critical enterprise, the desire to prove oneself the text's ideal listener, may also be a desire to be the text's ideal lover, a blurring of the line between the erotics and the heroics of the critical enterprise. The erotic dimension of American feminist criticism has often gone unremarked. But in its privileging of dialogue, American feminist criticism often draws close to French feminism and contests what many perceive as a strict divide between the erotic, metaphoric, speculative, and celebratory energies of feminist theories such as Luce Irigaray's enormously influential manifesto for conversation, "When Our Lips Speak Together," and Hélène Cixous's "The Laugh of the Medusa" and a materialist, political, empirical, less playful, and less optimistic American tradition.[61] Just as we need to see French feminist metaphors for textual and interpretive erotics as profoundly and inescapably political, so American feminist paradigms of the dialogic and the collaborative need to be seen as an erotics as much as a politics.[62] The erotics of American feminist criticism, often expressed through its conversational metaphorics, is a critical legacy that we need to both recuperate and investigate.

To investigate the kinds of conversations women's writing imagines itself to be having with its readers alongside the conversations feminist criticism has imagined itself to have with its texts, I have divided my study into two sections: "The Politics of Recuperation" and "The Erotics of Talk."

In "The Politics of Recuperation" I work through the protocols for recovering the subversiveness of lost "voices" to trace out how they are tied to historically situated practices such as consciousness-raising, how they inscribe a politics of identification that privileges sameness over difference, and what kind of an erotics this politics may entail. The texts I analyze in this section all privilege silence over speech, even as they engage in a "politics of voice" that involves contesting hegemony. Failing to find or perhaps even to fully imagine the ideal listeners they seek, these narratives lean toward forms of resistance that involve disengagement and withdrawal. Representing the cultural conversation as an argument, these texts call into question the value of getting in on the "talkin' game," even when they may succeed, as Zora Neale Hurston contends women do, in getting "de best" of it.[63]

The texts I consider in Part II, "The Erotics of Talk," represent more success in finding, imagining, or projecting ideal listeners. But even here, such success appears delimited. The romantic paradigm I trace from *Jane Eyre* through *Their Eyes Were Watching God* to *The Color Purple* uses the trope of an ideal listener as the sine qua non of sexual and individual desire. Insofar as that imagined ideal listener is *both* gendered and limited (either to one person or one instance of fulfilling exchange), finding one's ideal listener/lover works to criticize the cultural conversation these texts both emulate and disrupt. Representing the cultural conversation as antithetical to, rather than an embodiment *of*, the values of recognition, reciprocity, equality, and intimacy, these texts seek out forms of intersubjectivity that can reinforce the divide between the private and public spheres, that seem to imagine conversation, as Goffman describes it, as a form of "idling," of escape from the face-to-face encounters of everyday life.

Each chapter of this study emphasizes a different keyword that I use to foreground different forms of talk: *silence, contract, romance, dialogue,* and *exchange.*

Chapter One considers how silence plays a part in women's texts which have served as allegories for feminist reading and investigates how feminist criticism has theorized silence, paradoxically, as both oppression and its resistance. In rereading the classic stories of Isak Dinesen, Charlotte Perkins Gilman, and Susan Glaspell against the grain of the identifications they have been taken to exemplify, I attempt to recover a politics of desire underwriting both their politics of voice and that of feminist criticism as well.

Chapter Two extends this focus on silence and the dangers of what Hurston calls the "talkin' game" by considering how Linda Brent, the female slave narrator of Harriet Jacobs's narrative, attempts to enter into the cultural conversation without conceding its discursive and social rules. This chapter's keyword, "contract," opens up questions about our own abilities to "contract" with a text, about common understandings of reading as a "contractual" exchange in which the reader uncovers the text's subversive agency.

Chapter Three sets the tone for the second section by considering Jane Eyre's struggle to narrate her own story, to explain and vindicate her life, to participate in what she calls "the joyous conversational murmur" as a model for the narrative desire—the romance, in effect—which also drives the other texts I consider in this section. My keyword here is "romance" because I am beginning to consider the trope of an erotics of talk not only as a search for an ideal listener but also as a way of rewriting the romance itself.

The keyword in Chapter Four is "dialogue" because my reading of *Their Eyes Were Watching God* is concerned not only with the representations of dialogue within the text but also with the way in which critical practice, once *it* is refashioned as a romantic dialogue, can work to occlude the very politics it seeks to reveal.

The keyword of Chapter Five is "exchange," and here I reverse my own method to consider not a text that fails to live up to the paradigms it is taken to embody but rather one that does exactly that: *The Color Purple*. I close with a novel that conforms to exactly the "collaborative," "empathic," "dialogic" model my other texts are taken to exemplify, a text that invites its reader to be its ideal listener, the lover it desires. Instead of affirming some of our most cherished paradigms, however, this text also suggests why they may need revision and for what they might be, more profitably, exchanged.

Stipulations:[64] "Can We Talk?"

I have chosen the texts studied here because they have already been established by feminist critics as a canon; my discussion of them does not represent an (additional) argument for a particular women's tradition, a female aesthetic, or a women's language.

This study is by no means a blanket indictment of feminist criticism or an attempt to stand above its history and practices and criticize it, as it were, from "on high." The methods and paradigms that I criticize here are not only ones that I have learned, they are ones that I use and teach. And no doubt will continue to do so.

I am, of course, not making a case against "speaking out" or "talking back." I teach and do both.

If feminist criticism has engaged in some sentimentalizing acts of self-mirroring, it is worth remembering that this is a gesture that many women's texts do invite.

No claim is made here to have covered all the classic texts of the feminist canon or all the classics of feminist criticism. Rather, I have tried to focus on those which foreground forms of talk between women in particularly interesting ways.

I am not out to decanonize the texts I discuss. I talk about them here because it seems to me that the way they talk about talk is worth discussing. I hope my readers will agree.

I

THE POLITICS OF
RECUPERATION

Our task, of course, is to choose *the texts that proffer (often only covertly) the subversive voice we find representative of the age.*
—Richard H. Weisberg

1

Reading Feminist Readings: Recuperative Reading and the Silent Heroine of Feminist Criticism

Nothing less than our sanity and survival is at stake in the issue of what we read.

—Judith Fetterley

Silent Heroines

I pulled and she shook. I shook and she pulled, and before morning we had peeled off yards of that paper.

—Charlotte Perkins Gilman,
"The Yellow Wallpaper"

In this chapter I want to consider the ways in which classic feminist texts may disrupt the very paradigms they are thought to endorse by focusing on three of the most well-known stories in the feminist canon: "The Yellow Wallpaper," "A Jury of Her Peers," and "The Blank Page." Let me briefly rehearse their plots.

"The Yellow Wallpaper" tells the story of a woman forcibly shut out from all forms of creativity and of conversation with anyone other than her husband, a man who is incapable of real dialogue. These restrictions, modeled on Weir Mitchell's infamous methods, are ostensibly intended to cure her of a "nervous" condition. The protagonist refuses them by inventing a fictional conversant—a woman, like herself, trapped in a world that will not let her live her own life. She increasingly identifies with this other woman and seeks to free her, a liberatory exercise that takes the form of "reading" her in the wallpaper text of her room.

In "A Jury of Her Peers" two women find themselves faced with the task of reading the life story of a third: a neighbor who has been accused of the gruesome murder of her husband. By deciphering details that the men in the story dismiss, the two women readers uncover not only the story of the murder, but the motive behind it as well. Identifying with the accused and empathizing with her motives, the women readers erase the evidence they find rather than strengthen the case against their female neighbor.

In "The Blank Page" a female storyteller describes a convent gallery in which the blood-stained marital sheets of local princesses are displayed as evidence of their consummated marriages, mute testimony to the exchange of women and the marital virginity it prizes.[1] The storyteller's tale lovingly describes how all the female visitors to the gallery are fascinated with the one blank sheet and how they read into its blankness a myriad of possible stories of rebellion and escape from the confining fates—marriage or the convent—available to women.

These stories are frequently invoked as allegories of feminist reading, manifestations of the need to recuperate women's silenced voices and draw them back into the cultural conversation or, at least, bear witness to their excision from it.

Before going on to read these allegories of feminist identification (and its limits), I want to sketch something of the history of the politics of recuperation—the sense, common to much feminist thinking of the seventies and early eighties, that the most important work of feminist scholarship lay in reclamation and recovery to be achieved by identifying with lost and silenced women. These stories both confirm and dispute this imperative. I want to look at this recuperative paradigm in two different registers: the literary historical, which I will attempt to sketch out through a few exemplary texts, and the literary critical, which I will explore through a number of influential readings of the three fables themselves. While revisionist recuperation has left an invaluable legacy of analytical tools,[2] it has also bequeathed us a number of problems and left us with a seeming impasse. By seeing our way through that impasse, recuperation itself can perhaps be recuperated.

ॐ

Thirty years ago Tillie Olsen presented a passionate case for feminist criticism as a corrective to cultural silencing. Delineating the "unnatural" silences characteristic of all creative endeavor but particularly definitive of women's writing, Olsen described

> the unnatural thwarting of what struggles to come into being, but cannot ... *hidden* silences; work aborted, deferred, denied—hidden by the work which does come to fruition ... censorship silences ... the silences where the lives never came to writing. Among these, the mute inglorious Miltons: those whose waking hours are all struggle for existence; the barely educated; the illiterate; women. Their silence the silence of centuries as to how life was, is, for most of humanity.[3]

In describing women's silences, Olsen built on an already established feminist tradition, drawing on Virginia Woolf's explorations of women's silence and its material conditions. Women, Woolf wrote, dine on "prunes and custard"[4] rather than the "partridges and wine" (23) that invigorate (male) thinking and conversation; have served for "centuries as looking glasses . . . reflecting the figure of man at twice its natural size" (35); are the subjects of literature and history but rarely its authors. Discouraged where men are encouraged, when women did write it was often defensively, in forms not suited to them, with a "lack of tradition" and "a scarcity and inadequacy of tools" (80).

Since the appearance of Olsen's *Silences*, feminist criticism has continued to build on this recuperative paradigm of recovering lost, silenced, misunderstood, or devalued women's voices. Attempting to map what Woolf called the "infinitely obscure lives" and works of silenced women (Woolf 93), the task of feminist criticism seemed to lie in three connected fields: 1) exposing the mechanisms of cultural silencing, 2) revaluing dismissed or ignored women's writing, and 3) recovering alternative forms of women's creative expression. "There is a whole literature to be re-estimated, revalued," Olsen wrote. "Others now forgotten, obscured, ignored, will live again for us."[5]

Much of the now classic feminist criticism of the seventies and early eighties took its political imperative from the need to write women back into what Adrienne Rich famously described as the "book of myths / in which / our names do not appear."[6] If revision was "an act of survival,"[7] criticism was coming to be understood as an act of salvation. I do not think it is simply the vantage point of historical hindsight (nor, to speak autobiographically, a younger feminist's idealistic nostalgia for missed moments) that lends so much criticism of the seventies and eighties[8] its aura of shared mission and purpose. There is something heroic—often self-consciously so—about much of the criticism of this period, the sense of being involved in struggles which, to quote Rich again, "help to change the lives of women whose gifts—and whose very being—continue to be thwarted and silenced."[9] "As women," Rich concludes, "we have our work cut out for us."[10]

The rescue of thwarted, silenced, marginalized women, from history or from critical traditions, women like Lilith or Medusa, H.D.'s Helen, Judy Grahn's "common" women, Freud's (or better, feminism's) Dora, Woolf's Judith Shakespeare, as well as actual writers such as Susan Glaspell, Harriet Jacobs, and Zora Neale Hurston, gave to feminist criticism what I would call its archeological imperative: "the recovery and cultivation," as Patrocinio Schweickart put it in 1986, "of women's culture." It also often imparted a sense of the heroic, an image of misunderstood, abandoned, neglected women, finally rescued and released by their stronger, bolder daughters, and the belief that the work of feminist criticism, in Schweickart's words again, is a "heartwarming task: that of recovering, articulating, and elaborating positive expressions of women's point of view, of celebrating the survival of this point of view in spite of the formidable forces that have ranged against it."[11]

Just as Schweickart's celebratory language of the eighties may strike an anachronistic note today, the recuperative paradigm itself, with its concerns for women's "voices" and female "experience," its grounding in sameness and identification, and its rendering of feminism as intergenerational bonding must seem even more dated. How, after all, can Olsen's gynocritical project of reclamation and tradition-building on behalf of women possibly be squared with the poststructural argument that categorical appeals to or on behalf of "woman" or "women" undermine a viable feminist politics because "woman" is a "regulatory fiction" that reifies existing structures of domination?[12] Is it true that, as Elaine Hedges warns, "the post-structuralist project to problematize and displace identity is difficult to reconcile with the feminist project to reclaim it"?[13] What place is there in what has become, for many, a postidentitarian, postidentificatory feminism for an enterprise tacitly founded on both identity and identification? How might we rethink the need for recognition—which suffuses both the private and the public spheres—in ways that do not also presuppose identification? How might we use our various fables to destabilize rather than restabilize our various and multiple identities but, at the same time, widen the possibilities for an expanding discursive community?

Throughout the seventies and early eighties it was possible for many feminists to rest fairly comfortably with a politics of identification. Indeed, identifying with other women seemed to be not only possible but also an important ethical commitment, a way, as Rich put it, of ensuring "accountability." But in the wake of poststructural challenges to "identity," "experience," "narrative," "woman," and the authenticity of "voice" and, perhaps even more important, in the wake of challenges posed by lesbians and women of color to the exclusionary practices within white American feminism's putative unity and homogeneity, the sorts of assumptions to which Olsen, Woolf, or Rich's "revisionary rereading" seem to subscribe may appear theoretically single-minded.

In a recent retrospective, Ann Rosalind Jones argues that the practice of consciousness-raising and its concomitant ethics of listening and "empathetic analysis" formed the basis for the particular hermeneutic feminist literary criticism developed. "It's certain," she compellingly argues, "that the phonocentric emphasis in American feminist criticism, the celebration of the 'real woman's voice,' came partly out of the consciousness-raising process: we wanted to speak, we constructed occasions to speak, we heard ourselves quavering out difficult sentences, we waited to hear a supportive response."[14] Anita Shreve's history of the consciousness-raising movement provides a summary of the protocols used by most practicing consciousness-raising groups. They include letting each woman speak "as long as she likes or needs to without fear of interruption," sitting in a circle to "help women listen to each other," and, importantly, admonishing the participants to "never challenge anyone else's experience."[15] The recuperative paradigm reinforced these cultural practices and their ethics.

"None the less," Jones relates, "there were crucial silences in that group. We were all white, all middle-class, and all (at least at the moment) hetero-sexual."[16] The relationship between speech, silence, and a sense of sameness is complicated here. The very silences Jones laments were also partly re-sponsible, she implies, for the feelings of safety and solidarity that empow-ered these women's speech. They felt comfortable, surrounded by others like themselves, able to identify with one another, sure of a sympathetic response. This was conversation as "girl talk," an "intimacy" of "being in place or among persons," a "familiar discourse," "an 'at home.'"

Consciousness-raising, as Jones is quick to point out, was hardly "per-manent." Shreve correlates its demise to "a changing political climate, expanding career opportunities for women, shifting priorities on the part of the Women's Movement, and . . . a subsequent lack of a sponsor."[17] But I would suggest that its collapse as a privileged cultural practice had at least as much to do with an increasing (and hard-fought) awareness of the ex-clusionary politics of American feminist "sisterhood" and with attempts to open feminist circles up to a proliferation of feminism*s*, to turn from simple solidarity to coalition politics and new, more complex understandings of identity politics, to open up challenges to the category of identity itself.

But the recuperative paradigm which consciousness-raising did so much to foment hardly died in consciousness-raising's wake. Should it have? Citing a tendency toward critical self-celebration, reliance on the problematic cate-gories mentioned above ("experience," "identity," "voice," and "identifica-tion" in particular), and a sentimentalizing self-understanding of "women's culture," many critics, no doubt, would say yes.

But while essentialism and identification are shaky grounds for femi-nist theory and politics, it is not so clear that recuperation need ground itself in either. In fact, a critique of identification and identificatory poli-tics, as I hope to show, can be as enabling to the important work of recu-perating women's literature as it is disabling.

And there should be no doubt that recuperation is still important work. In fact, it is perhaps most important, today, to the very groups of women—lesbians and women of color in particular—who are likely to challenge its identificatory premises. Much of the initial tradition-building work of locating, reevaluating, and reprinting women's texts (work that fueled so much of white American feminism through the seventies and early eight-ies) is still under way for the texts of lesbians and women of color. Olsen's concern for "hidden silences, work aborted, deferred, denied—hidden," for "censorship silences," for "the silences where the lives never came to writ-ing" still very much obtains, as pressing as it was twenty years ago when Alice Walker—among others—argued for the work of recuperating black women's texts.

Alluding to Woolf's incarnation of "a witch being dunked, of a woman possessed by devils, of a wise woman selling herbs, or even of "a very remarkable woman who had a mother" as signs of "a lost novelist, a suppressed poet, of some mute and inglorious Jane Austen, some Emily Brontë who dashed her brains out on the moor or moped and mowed about the highways crazed with the torture her gift had put her to" (50–51), Walker figures black female artists as "Crazy Saints . . . crazy, loony, pitiful women . . . our mothers and grandmothers" who "saw visions no one could understand . . . driven to a numb and bleeding madness by the springs of creativity in them for which there was no release."[18]

Those who did find release, Walker writes, did so in "wild and unlikely places": cooking, gardening, sewing, church singing, the blues. So when we look for their "texts," Walker writes, we must learn to look "close" and "low." Walker describes a quilt, made by "an anonymous black woman in Alabama, a hundred years ago":

> Though it follows no known pattern of quilt-making, and though it is made of bits and pieces of worthless rags, it is obviously the work of a person of powerful imagination and deep spiritual feeling. . . . If we could locate this "anonymous black woman from Alabama," she would turn out to be one of our grandmothers—an artist who left her mark in the only materials she could afford and in the only medium her position in society allowed her to use.[19]

Walker's use of "we" here, her fusion, on the one hand, of white and black feminist traditions and her specification, on the other, of other black women as her knowing, sympathetic, identifying audience, raises a number of questions. Whose enterprise should this recovery of "Crazy Saints" be? Whose grandmother is Walker locating? And who is equipped to recognize her text and hear her "voice"? Is such recognition a simple matter of categorical identity: of being black and female, for example? Or is such recognition contingent upon some uncategorically defined set of skills, upon what Sally Munt, for example, describes as lesbian readers' particular ability to read both "between the lines [and] from the margins"?[20] Can it be learned? And how have we—(and here I mean feminist critics)—been learning and teaching it?

To take up some of these questions, I want to begin with examples of feminist literary history that work from the recuperative paradigm I have associated with Olsen, Woolf, and Rich and that exemplify the uses to which recuperative readings may be put and the premises upon which they may depend. In rereading three of the most recuperated and privileged stories in the feminist canon I will be deploying the recuperative paradigm, in a sense, against itself to suggest new readings of these already often-read stories and to seek a recuperative practice based on a new paradigm that both complicates recuperation and takes it in a new direction. Rather than pronounce what has comprised the core of so much feminist work a theoretically, historically, or culturally bankrupt enterprise, I hope to contribute to its revitalization—to eroticize it in effect—by suggesting new paradigms less dependent on what Helena Michie calls the idioms of the "therapeutic," the "utopian," and the "familial."[21]

"Fantastic Collaboration" and the Politics of Identification

Once begun, liberation and identification are irreversible.

—Paula Treichler

In 1984, in a discussion of the critical recuperation of Sappho, Susan Gubar advanced the notion of "fantastic collaboration."[22] "Fantastic collaboration," as Gubar explains it, is an apt description of feminist recuperation and an antidote to the Bloomian "anxiety of influence" with which male writers supposedly confront—and battle—the precursors of their literary tradition.

Feminist literary history cannot help but be concerned with silences, absences, double messages, and palimpsestic texts. Its focus, in part, must be on the ways in which writers are silenced and force their way back into the cultural conversation through surreptitious means. As an investigation of the various "forms of talk" that comprise the literary historical record, it must be attentive to the traces of "muttering," screaming, or double-talk that signal the presence of previous contestations, attentive to the fact, as Walter Benjamin puts it, that "there is no document of civilization which is not at the same time a document of barbarism," a testimony to the battles of competing "voices."[23] While it is right, in this sense, to describe the work of feminist literary history as a "fantastic collaboration," need this work be premised on presumptive sameness or identification between women? Once connected, must liberation and identification remain inseparable?

Where a dialogic theory of literary tradition might see any address as a gamble and culture, therefore, as a site where struggles over recognition and identity are waged—"the very form of a work of art shows its character as *addressed*"[24]—Harold Bloom provided a literary historical account of this wager in which he viewed each address as an inevitable failure. This was so, on his account, because it was psychologically necessary for each addressee to misread the "voice" of his predecessor so as to carve out his own authentic space. Misrecognition, for Bloom, became an explanation of literary greatness and originality. Literary history became a pageant of "heroic warfare," "a literary Oedipal struggle," in which a writer becomes great "by somehow invalidating his poetic father" in "fierce power struggles."[25] In response, feminist scholars reversed Bloom's paradigm to argue that *women's* culture, at any rate, is one site where women's bid for recognition can succeed.

The influential theory of intertextuality that Susan Gubar and Sandra Gilbert develop in *The Madwoman in the Attic* takes its point of departure from Bloom's theory of "heroic warfare." The woman writer, they argue, "the daughter of too few mothers," could not afford such battles (although for her too they are part of creation). Hence, she suffers not from an "anxiety of authority" but rather from an "anxiety of authorship."[26] Rather than replicate the male writers' battles by attempting to overthrow her female precursors, the woman writer, Gilbert and Gubar argue, turns to other women as allies in a literary battle she wages not with them, but against her Oedipal *fathers*. The "female precursor . . . far from representing a threatening force to be denied or killed, proves by example that a revolt against patriarchal literary authority is possible."[27]

Where Bloom assumes that there must be a battle, and that recognition can take only a contestatory, negative form, Gilbert and Gubar seem to assume that, for women, there must be sisterhood and that recognition will always win out. Can either position advance a politics of difference that aims for recognition but acknowledges contestation? Rather than assume that identity is a fixed and stable construction to be either recognized—or misrecognized—by others, can we imagine a critical practice and a vision of literary tradition more open to the idea that identity is a fluid and interobjective phenomenon, constructed out of a dialogic—contestatory—process, a critical practice that nuances "recognition" accordingly?[28]

In their influential rereading of literary history, Gilbert and Gubar establish a pattern that is taken up again and again in subsequent feminist revisions of intertextuality and literary history. An initial delineation of a historically grounded difference—the difference between men's and women's cultural relation to writing and publicity in this case—gives way to an ahistorical assumption of identicality and identification among the members of the newly reconstructed group: women writers, for example. Classic feminist narratives often seem to represent just this assumption of conflict between men and women but cooperation between women: freeing the woman in the wallpaper, protecting a female neighbor from the law, honoring the evidence of a woman's escape from her fate. And this pattern of presumption is particularly pronounced in the work of other feminist literary historians who work, like Gilbert and Gubar, from an anti-Bloomian poetics of intertextuality.

Elaine Showalter's recent work, for example, repeats this pattern in the context of another refutation of Bloomian textual warfare:

> To a striking degree, American women writers have rejected the Oedipal metaphors of murderous "originality" set out as literary paradigms in Harold Bloom's *Anxiety of Influence*; the patricidal struggle defined by Bloom and exemplified in the careers of male American writers has no matricidal equivalent, no echo of denial, parody, exile. Instead, Alice Walker proclaims, "each writer writes the missing parts to the other writer's story."[29]

Showalter's reference to Walker here is striking, for Walker often serves as a launching pad for celebrations of female textual identification, of harmony in the literary historical dialogue.

Christine Froula's "The Daughter's Seduction: Sexual Violence and Literary History" (1986), for example, begins with the cultural silencing that makes for woman's lack of "freedom to tell her stories."[30] In her search for a "radical cure of the hysterical cultural text that entangles both women and men" (633) Froula turns to the work of Maya Angelou and Alice

Walker, work which she reads as a kind of allegory for the act of critical recuperation in which she herself is engaged. Angelou's "powerful memoir," Froula writes, "*rescues* the child's voice . . . by telling the prohibited story" (637, emphasis mine). *The Color Purple* Froula considers an even "more powerful cure" of "one daughter's hysterical silence" (637) and Celie a "hero . . . who recreates the universe by telling her story to the world" (644).

A politics of identification grounds Walker's novel, as I will argue in Chapter Five, as well as Froula's essay. As Froula points out, Celie's "identification" with other women—her mother, Sofia, Shug, and Mary Agnes—"saves her from silence" (638), presumably as an identification with Celie can "save," "cure," or "rescue" the reader or critic. But this identification goes much further. By the end of the novel, a divided and conflictual community of black men and women has become a homogenous, utopian family in which there is neither conflict nor difference. On this model, people "save" each other not by preserving one another's particularity and difference, but by converting everyone into a version of oneself, someone with whom it is not necessary to fight or disagree.[31] Is this truly something we would want to celebrate?

Another influential essay of feminist literary history which depends upon Walker's claim that "each writer writes the missing parts to the other writer's story" is Deborah McDowell's "'The Changing Same': Generational Connections and Black Women Novelists" (1987). McDowell demonstrates how Iola in Frances Harper's *Iola Leroy* and Celie in Walker's *The Color Purple* break cultural silences. Like Froula, McDowell views Celie as an allegory for her own feminist practice, a heroine who reincarnates earlier, silenced women, giving them life and voice. A "revisionist mission," she writes, is the "common center" of black women's literature.[32]

The black woman writer's relationship to her black female precursors, McDowell contends, "begins with thinking back through and reclaiming her female ancestors."[33] This process, she argues, is collaborative and nonconflictual:

> Bloom's linear theory of the Oedipal war between literary fathers and sons does not obtain among black women writers, many of whom reverently acknowledge their debts to their literary foremothers. Unlike Bloom, I see literary influence, to borrow from Julia Kristeva, in the intertextual sense, each text in dialogue with all previous texts, transforming and retaining narrative patterns and strategies in endless possibility. The pattern of literary influence . . . is also distinct from that among black men . . . [characterized by] formal relations . . . [which are] largely adversarial and parodic. . . . Therein lies a fundamental distinction between Afro-American male and female literary traditions.[34]

Yet McDowell also challenges this "revisionist mission" as an inherently limited project. Recovering women's silenced experience and identity by revising stereotypes and correcting misrepresentations, on her account, "is at once the greatest strength and the greatest weakness" of early women's texts. "It results without exception in the creation of static, disembodied, larger-than-life characters."[35]

There is nonetheless a tension within McDowell's essay between a generalized, identificatory politics and a critique of the politics of identification, even though she narrows the scope of her identificatory poetics to black women and generates her vision of their collaborative, intertextual dynamics from a concrete set of historical particulars. In constructing her own poetics of black women's intertextuality along counter-Bloomian lines, McDowell repeats the pattern found in Showalter and Froula's arguments. An initial gesture of differentiation, distinguishing black women's literary history from black men's or white women's, gives way to presumptions from which differences and conflict seem suddenly to fade. In this sense, McDowell's intertextual "dialogue" also idealizes and sentimentalizes an imagined community of women, what one critic calls an "imaginary feminism."[36]

"Imaginary feminism" in itself is not the problem. Neither is the kind of utopian thinking these critics engage in. Imaginary projections of sisterhood, solidarity, unity, and identification can operate *proleptically* in very productive ways. However, idealizing the gap between a contestatory and a collaborative aesthetic can jeopardize feminist literary history when it occludes those texts that fail to fit either the anti-Bloomian paradigm of a collaborative, sisterly, dialogic or the Bloomian paradigm of agonized warfare. In hypostatizing either side of this dialectic we may, as Jane Marcus puts it, "get carried away with our mission as liberators."[37]

Another way to put this would be to say that feminist revisions of Bloom have been too dependent on Bloom. It is often claimed that his "theory of influence" was important to feminist theory because it subverted the "static notion of a fixed or knowable text"[38] and thereby opened the way for a recognition of what Barbara Herrnstein Smith would later call "contingencies of value." But feminism hardly needed Bloom to make this point, which was already being advanced by feminists such as Annette Kolodny. It is really Bloom's heroics, I suspect, that have proved most seductive. If the Bloomian critic's misreadings make him a Poet—the highest honor Bloom can bestow and the form of identity, in his view, that every reader seeks—the feminist critic's "revisionary rereading" cannot help but make her a "fantastic collaborator," writing "the missing parts to the other writer's story." To my mind, a romantic conception of literary tradition offers no clearer explanation of the conditions of changing reception it takes as its starting point than does an agonistic, antagonistic one.

Understanding critical intervention or "collaboration" as a kind of cultural heroics was not, in fact, a feature of Gilbert and Gubar's original polemic with Bloom, although no other American feminists have been so badly caricatured as advocates of illusory and essentialistic notions of sameness and identification.[39] On Gilbert and Gubar's account, it was not the modern critic's sympathetic or collaborative "rescue" of precursor texts that defined feminism's heroics. Instead, Gilbert and Gubar located heroism in the efforts those precursors made to resist cultural silencing and leave a legacy, however coded and disguised it sometimes may have been. "If contemporary women do now attempt the pen with energy and authority," they wrote, "they are able to do so *only because* their eighteenth- and nineteenth-century foremothers struggled in isolation that felt like illness, alienation that felt like madness, obscurity that felt like paralysis."[40]

A still somewhat open question for Gilbert and Gubar—namely, how to narrate a story of conflict and discontinuity as well as collaboration and continuity—has become codified, in its most extreme forms, into a set of prescriptive ethics largely drawn from object-relations theory to shape a literary history that elides difference in favor of a chain of mother-daughter identification and indebtedness. While grounded in the crucial insight that "unreadability . . . [is] historically contingent,"[41] identification-based models of feminist reading often end up taking for granted that the modern reader has a kind of epistemological privilege that was not only, implicitly, impossible for other readers, but that also gives her, in the metaphorics and rhetorics of many accounts, a maternal relation to the texts she recuperates.

This is not to say that there isn't much that *is* genuinely heroic about the recuperative enterprise, the legacy of reading and rewriting silence inherited from Olsen, Woolf, Rich, Walker, and others. But the rhetoric of heroism that often attaches itself to this enterprise raises the suspicion that recuperative readings may be at least as attached to self-representation as to a recovery of "the other." There is a danger, I am suggesting, in any recuperative reading (including of course my own) that we will merely read, as Susan Lanser puts it, to have "our own image reflected back to us."[42] Particularly in those texts that are most often taken to mirror the practice of feminist criticism itself, constructing such textual mirrors may actually obscure the critical self-reflection these texts are meant, presumably, to provide.

(Re)Reading (Over)Reading

irresistible metaphorics

—Nancy K. Miller

In turning to three of the most overread stories in the feminist canon, I want to begin with the problem of "overreading" itself: a strategy for reading between the lines, deciphering silence, decoding double-talk, and filling in gaps to correct and compensate for the double silence of repressed expression and critical misunderstanding that we might identify with all revisionary, recuperative work. "Overreading," Nancy K. Miller writes, "self-consciously responds to the appeal of the abyss." As a form of what Annette Kolodny calls "revisionary rereading," "overreading" accomplishes two objectives; it unsettles available interpretive paradigms and it constructs a "new object of reading, women's writing." It reads women's writing "as if it had never been read."[43]

It is impossible, of course, to read "The Yellow Wallpaper," "A Jury of Her Peers," and "The Blank Page" as if they had never been read. Instead, I want to begin by reading the history of feminist readings of these stories, focusing in particular on the way these stories serve as allegories for an empathic, identificatory feminist criticism.

The narrator of "The Yellow Wallpaper" frees the woman trapped in the paper by learning to overread her "repellant," "uncertain," "outrageous," "lurid," "irritating," "isolated," "pointless," "defiant," "torturing," "strangled" text. The storyteller in "The Blank Page" has been trained as an overreader. She knows how to "hear the voice of silence" and to ensure that "silence will speak."[44] The two women in "A Jury of Her Peers" find themselves reluctantly but inescapably overreading. They "*understand*" a woman's text that the men in the story are unable to see and they "*know*" that to read and recognize it is itself a subversive activity.

By depicting a woman reader's unraveling of a mute and coded female "text," each story represents patriarchy's stake in silencing women and the need to expose and challenge such silencing. As such, these stories allegorize overreading and offer feminist criticism an "irresistible metaphorics" for its own imperatives. It is through stories like "The Yellow Wallpaper," Lanser has recently argued, that "American feminist criticism has constituted its terms."[45] It is, Gilbert and Gubar argue, "a paradigmatic tale . . . of female confinement and escape . . . *the* story that all literary women would tell if they could speak their 'speechless woe.'"[46] Elaine Hedges writes that

> rediscovering lost women writers, reclaiming the experience of anonymous women, reexamining the image of women in literature, and rereading texts in order to discern and appreciate female symbol systems—many of the major approaches that have characterized feminist literary criticism in the past decade have . . . found generous validation in the text of "A Jury of Her Peers." The story has become a paradigmatic one for feminist criticism."[47]

"For feminist critics of American literature," Elaine Showalter adds, "'A Jury of Her Peers' has been taken since the mid-1970s as a metaphor for feminist reading itself."[48] As a representation of "the voice of silence" and the imperative to ensure that "silence will speak," "The Blank Page" also provides a paradigm and mirror for feminist (over)reading and fantastic collaboration.

Although I agree that these stories provide a paradigm of feminist criticism as fantastic collaboration, they also suggest why such collaboration *is* fantastic, or fantasmatic. They both practice and parody feminist recuperation. Each warns against the very politics it seems to endorse, suggesting dangers, impasses, and problems inherent in a critical practice grounded too securely in a politics of identification. My own recuperation of these parables will seek out their critiques, as well as their endorsement, of the enterprise of fantastic collaboration.

Identification, in Fetterley's argument, accounts for the feminist "pleasure of the text" of "The Yellow Wallpaper." "It provides the woman reader with the gratification of discovering, recovering, and validating her own experience."[49] Even critics who see the narrator's identification as limiting or dangerous tend, along with Fetterley, to see the feminist paradigms encoded in this story in terms of problems and possibilities of identification.

"The Yellow Wallpaper" describes the constraints of "the sociocultural situation confronting women in the late nineteenth century."[50] Denied "work," "society," "stimulus," imagination, writing, or conversation, the protagonist of "The Yellow Wallpaper" initially defies prohibitions by writing in secret—"a great relief to my mind."[51] But "having to be so sly about it, or else meet with heavy opposition" (25) eventually proves too exhausting. "The effort," she declares, "is getting to be greater than the relief" (32).

Denied all other outlets, she becomes obsessed with the wallpaper in her room, a pattern she originally finds "repellant, almost revolting" (26), but which comes to resemble a woman behind bars. As she transfers her own passion for communication and recognition to this woman, she becomes a devoted reader, or overreader. And as she does so, she finds that "life is very much more exciting now than it used to be" (35).[52]

Her reading observes certain fundamental feminist critical precepts: that women's voices may appear in surprising texts (quilts, gardens, wallpaper, blankness); that women write between the lines of dominant discourses, hiding subversive "patterns" behind more acceptable ones ("this wallpaper has a kind of sub-pattern in a different shade" (30)); that such palimpsests demand specially trained and sympathetic readers (feminists who know how to (over)read); and that women's silence, blankness, or absence must be translated back into visibility or audibility by a reader whose reading is also a rewriting.

The narrator's impulse was originally compensatory, a substitute for other "work" and a hedge against boredom. But reading quickly develops its own urgency: saving the woman trapped in the suffocating wallpaper. The more willing the narrator is to see behind the dominant pattern, the more "the woman behind it is as plain as she can be" and the more clearly the dominant "pattern" becomes "bars" (34). From that point on, both are committed to fantastic collaboration, and the narrator devotes all her energy to unburying this coded female text.

The work of collaboration should strike a familiar note for those who remember the agonizing exhilaration of moving through the stages of consciousness-raising. First, the recognition of the violence of oppression: "she is all the time trying to climb through," "but nobody could climb through that pattern—it strangles so; I think that is why it has so many heads. They get through, and then the pattern strangles them off and turns them upside down, and makes their eyes white!" (38). Second, the danger of denial and the need to resist it: "if those heads were covered or taken off it [the wallpaper] would not be half so bad" (38). Third, a commitment to a new vision that changes everything: "I can see her out of every one of my windows!" (38). And fourth, an altered, sometimes obsessive, sense of the whole: instead of blaming the victim for her own oppression—"I don't blame her a bit" (38)—the narrator becomes increasingly alienated from and hostile to anyone who seems to have any part, however passive, in perpetuating the trap: "it does not do to trust people too much" (39).

As the narrator moves closer and closer to liberating this trapped figure, her actions seem to be more and more motivated by sisterly affection. "As soon as it was moonlight and that poor thing began to crawl and shake the pattern, I got up and ran to help her. I pulled and she shook, I shook and she pulled, and before morning we had peeled off yards of that paper" (39).

But sisterly identification is also associated with madness. "The narrator," Hedges argues, "both does and does not identify with the creeping women who surround her in her hallucinations."[53] To identify completely would be to become what the repressive woman-hating society wants her to be: creeping, hidden, inarticulate, helpless. She wants, as Hedges points out, both to liberate and to destroy this "tragic product of her society."[54] Haney-Peritz also observes that identifying with the woman in the wallpaper means identifying with precisely the representation of woman that the narrator seeks to resist.

> The narrator's identification with the wallpaper's shadow-woman seems to have turned her into the woman of John's dreams, for not only did the shadow woman first appear while John was sleeping, but the narrator also suspects that when all is said and done, she is what John really desires, the secret he would reveal if he were given the opportunity to do so.[55]

Yet, although the narrator's madness, as Hedges puts it, can "be read as a victory or a defeat"[56] and in many ways "the heroine . . . is destroyed,"[57] this is nonetheless read as a heroic story. The narrator, at whatever personal sacrifice, succeeds in passing on another woman's story, giving voice to what the dominant culture would keep silent and therefore, as Froula might say, curing both herself and other women. "Born of an hallucination," Catherine Golden writes, "her identification leads the narrator to free herself from the restrictive pattern of her own society and this liberation is conveyed on paper through her pronoun choice . . . [the] fusion of identity with the subtext of the wallpaper."[58]

Compelling as these various insights are, the heroic reading of the narrator's chilling sacrifice leaves important aspects of the reader-heroine relationship unexamined. The narrator's reading not only represents critical interpretation but also parodies it as a dangerous practice. Her madness raises the question so often at issue in scholarly debates: has she, like many an anxiety-ridden scholar, simply invented—or imagined—her topic so as to have something to work on? Gilman provides a brilliant depiction of feeling mocked by one's subject of analysis: "It [the paper] is dull enough to confuse the eye in following, pronounced enough to constantly irritate and provoke study, and when you follow the lame uncertain curves for a little distance they suddenly commit suicide—plunge off at outrageous angles, destroy themselves in unheard of contradictions . . . all those strangled heads and bulbous eyes and waddling fungus growths just shriek with derision!" (26, 40). And she also paints a painfully funny parody of the narrator's inability to "sleep much at night" (but sleeping "a good deal in the daytime") as her obsession with her subject grows and the deadline by which she must either complete her research or resign herself to failure approaches. Her determination "that nobody shall find out but myself!" (35) captures a classic moment of scholarly possessiveness, paranoia, and jealousy. "I don't want anybody to get that woman out at night but myself," she reports. She resolves that "no person touches this paper but me,—not *alive*!" (40); "there are things in that paper that nobody knows but me, or ever will" (32). Like most critics, she wants to "astonish" her intended audience and, like many, she will do violence to her subject, if necessary, to control it: "I've got a rope up here . . . if that woman does get out, and tries to get away, I can tie her!"(40). I take this parody as a serious warning about the dangers of the feminist overreading the story so vividly portrays. The reader—even if she sacrifices her "self" for her subject—is not necessarily more of a hero than John, the narrator's husband, or Jennie, his sister. The subject of all this heroics—the trapped woman—may find herself as imperiled and entrapped by her reader's own obsessions as she is rescued or released by them.

"A Jury of Her Peers" raises many of the same caveats about the potential hazards of the overreading it depicts. Here too, the "text" in question is a woman. Minnie Foster is in jail for the murder of her husband, and as the story opens the sheriff and county attorney are trying to find (read) the "motive" for the crime. Without good evidence of motive, they fear, the jury may not convict. The kitchen is filled with motive and evidence that the men are unable to read.

> "You're convinced there was nothing important here?" the county attorney asked the sheriff. "Nothing that would—point to any motive?" The sheriff too looked all around, as if to re-convince himself. "Nothing here but kitchen things," he said, with a little laugh for the insignificance of kitchen things.[59]

Whereas the men fail to (over)read any meaning in "kitchen things," these supposedly trivial details reveal to Mrs. Peters and Mrs. Hale the bleakness of Minnie Foster's life.

Mrs. Hale is quick to read the kitchen as a set of signs of haste, disruption, subverted order:

> Her eye was held by a bucket of sugar on a low shelf. The cover was off the wooden bucket, and beside it was a paper bag—half full. . . . Her eye was caught by a dish-towel in the middle of the kitchen table. Slowly she moved toward the table. One half of it was wiped clean, the other half was messy. Her eyes made a slow, almost unwilling turn to the bucket of sugar and the half empty bag beside it. Things begun—and not finished. (378)

The more they look around the kitchen, the more evidence Mrs. Peters and Mrs. Hale discern. Most tellingly, they discover Minnie Foster's quilting, an unmistakable sign of her determination to create and of her aggression toward her husband:

> Mrs. Hale was looking at the fine, even sewing, and preoccupied with thoughts of the woman who had done that sewing, when she heard the sheriff's wife say, in a queer tone:
> "Why, look at this one."
> She turned to take the block held out to her.
> "The sewing," said Mrs. Peters, in a troubled way. "All the rest of them have been so nice and even—but—this one. Why it looks as if she didn't know what she was about!"
> . . . Martha Hale now scrutinized that piece, compared it with the dainty, accurate sewing of the other blocks. The difference was startling. Holding this block made her feel queer, as if the distracted thoughts of the woman who had perhaps turned to it to try and quiet herself were communicating themselves to her. (873–74)

Like the evidence found in the kitchen, this sewing depicts an ordered life, disrupted by some untoward event. It tells the women that whatever Mrs. Foster did or didn't do, something was done *to her*. It is evidence of anger and upset. And it is testimony to the difficulty of both self-expression and self-definition; clearly Mrs. Foster didn't know what she was "about." After they discover this evidence of anger, they immediately find its cause: Minnie Foster's pet canary, its neck wrung, evidently by Mr. Foster. Minnie, the sheriff's wife remembers, used to be "kind of like a bird herself. Real sweet and pretty, but kind of timid and—fluttery. How—she—did—change."

What is thoroughly obscure to the men is painfully clear to the women. "Why do you and I *understand*? Why do we *know*—what we know this minute?" Mrs. Peters asks (384). Glaspell implies that given their experiences *as women* they cannot help but understand. And they not only sympathize but collaborate. As soon as Mrs. Hale finds the tell-tale evidence that might convict Minnie Foster, she moves to erase it:

> A moment Mrs. Hale sat there, her hands folded over that sewing which was so unlike all the rest of the sewing. Then she had pulled a knot and drawn the threads.
> "Oh, what are you doing, Mrs. Hale?" asked the sheriff's wife, startled.
> "Just pulling out a stitch or two that's not sewed very good," said Mrs. Hale, mildly.
> "I don't think we ought to touch things," Mrs. Peters said, a little helplessly.
> "I'll just finish up this end," answered Mrs. Hale, still in that mild, matter-of-fact fashion.
> She threaded a needle and started to replace bad sewing with good. For a little while she sewed in silence.

Mrs. Hale sews in silence; she literally sews silence into the text, replacing Minnie Foster's talking stitches with safer, speechless ones.

As with "The Yellow Wallpaper," this rendition of female overreading is generally read prescriptively, as a program meant for women readers to follow. But overreading endangers Minnie Foster as surely as it recognizes her. Simply put, it proves her guilt. The only way to save Minnie Foster is to say nothing, to *refuse* to create a "revisionary rereading." Her story must be left silent and untold. The actions that are called for here—pulling the tell-tale quilt stitches and hiding the dead bird "that would make certain the conviction of the other woman"—are ones that hide Minnie Foster's story, not ones that bring it to light.

In fact, overreading appears here as an ethically suspect attempt to compensate for the more important social actions these women failed to take. Reading correctly but doing nothing—materially and practically—to change Minnie's life is worse than irresponsible. It is criminal. "'Oh, I *wish* I'd come over here once in a while!' she [Mrs. Hale] cried. 'That was a crime! That was a crime! Who's going to punish that?'" (384). Identifying with Minnie Foster unravels the feminist subtext behind all three women's lives, but it does not give them a feminist politics of social transformation. To free Minnie Foster—and it is clearly too late to make amends—they needed to do more than identify with her or listen to her story. There is a kind of poetic justice in this story, but it is *only* poetic justice and Minnie Foster, clearly, will continue to suffer. Mrs. Hale and Mrs. Peters needed to take their understanding back out into the public sphere, where their men determine who will and will not have a phone (a source of contention between Mr. and Mrs. Foster), how women, like Mrs. Foster, will live out the conditions of their lives.

"The Blank Page" also contains a trapped heroine for whom identificatory reading is too little, too late. The story begins with a Carmelite order of nuns in the mountains of Portugal who produce, preserve, and exhibit the blood-stained bridal sheets of royal princesses. Among these "portraits" is one "canvas" before which "the story-tellers . . . draw their veils over their faces and are dumb." Before this canvas, "the old princesses of Portugal—worldly wise, dutiful, long-suffering queens, wives, and mothers—and their noble old playmates, bridesmaids and maids-of-honor have most often stood still. [Here] . . . old and young nuns, with the Mother Abbess herself, sink into deepest thought" (1423). This canvas is blank, an anonymous, unstained sheet of framed white linen, "snow white from corner to corner," which the convent sisters, with "eternal and unswerving loyalty" have included along with the others in their gallery.

As Susan Gubar in her classic essay on this story has suggested, where an unsympathetic reader would see emptiness and silence, the women who come to the gallery are prototypical overreaders. They recuperate a multiplicity of meanings from the blank canvas: perhaps she ran away or renounced sexuality, perhaps she was not a virgin when she married, perhaps she was rejected by the prince, perhaps she died or was killed before the marriage could be consummated. The very absence of a story, Gubar argues, makes this sheet so subversive. "The resistance of the princess," she writes, "allows for self-expression; for she makes her statement by not writing what she is expected to write."[60]

Although it might seem that this story presents overreading and recuperation in a positive light, the most precious, revered, protected, and coveted "subject" in this story is not this heroine's text at all. Paradoxically, it is silence itself that is most revered. "Who," asks the "old coffee-brown, black veiled woman who made her living by telling stories" (1418),

> tells a finer tale than any of us? Silence does. And where does one read a deeper tale than upon the most perfectly printed page of the most precious book? Upon the blank page. When a royal and gallant pen, in the moment of its highest inspiration, has written down its tale with the rarest ink of all—where, then, may one read a still deeper, sweeter, merrier and more cruel tale than that? Upon the blank page (1419).

This affirmation of silence is double-valenced. It affirms the importance of later, recuperative readers. It suggests that they are necessary and that the story, in every way, depends on them. But it also suggests that trying to tell silence's story may be a presumptuous, hazardous, even cruel endeavor. Why cruel? As soon as the reader rewrites the tale, it becomes her own. A story about her. About her own reading, her own life. An allegory, in short. In a sense, this gives the feminist reader a stake in the cultural silencing of women, the condition that makes her intervention necessary. Silence gives the critic/reader her reason for being. For this reason, she may always be in danger of re-silencing—in one form or another—the "other woman" she saves, thus ensuring her own continued place.

There are alternatives, I believe, to such heroic cruelties. In the concluding section, I want to suggest two different means of opening the recuperative paradigm up to a more fluid model of intersubjective exchange. First, I want to suggest that the politics of identification has an occluded counterpart: desire. Desire, I am suggesting, might allow us to listen to each other, through the mediation of the text, without assuming, as identification tends to do, that we already know what the other is saying. Second, incorporating a dialectic of desire and identification into a heterogenous rather than homogenous model of discursive communities opens a space in which concrete others can reveal their particularity, not only a place in which generalized others can affirm and confirm their similarities.

Ecstatic Excavation

The reading of women's texts by women might have been and might still be eroticized.

—Judith Fetterley

Gubar, like Fetterley, has suggested that for certain writers revisionary re-reading is a "euphoric coupling in which the other is bound to the self as a lover,"[61] and that the practice of feminist recuperation or "excavation" is a potentially erotic one.[62] Although Gubar investigates this erotics only where there is manifest lesbian content, the formulation suggests that feminist classics might be read not only for their politics of identification but also for their textual erotics, that the homoerotics of classic women's writing and classic feminist paradigms remains to be recuperated.

In suggesting a homoerotic reading of these stories, or what Gubar might call an "ecstatic excavation,"[63] I risk accusations of appropriating lesbianism as a merely metaphorical sign for nonlesbian sorority. Let me begin, then, with what I hope will be the less controversial strand of my thesis: that each of these stories, insofar as it invites our collaboration, asks us to collaborate in a critique of what one critic calls "heteronormativity," asks us to join in a resistance to compulsory heterosexuality that we might call "heterocritical" if not explicitly queer.[64] In each of these stories, a desire that life with a man has thwarted is revived and reinscribed as yearning for another woman or for women. It is the meaning of that displacement and the quality of that yearning that need to be examined.

"The Yellow Wallpaper" depicts a woman's imprisonment in a bed-room. Although she seeks "work," "society and stimulus," air and exer-cise, her husband locks her in, "shut[s] the window" (25), forbids exer-cise, and laughs at her. "One expects that in a marriage," she remarks (24). The narrator longs, at first, for a room of her own "downstairs that opened on the piazza and had roses all over the window and such pretty old-fashioned chintz hangings!" But recognizing that she seeks to shut him out, "John would not hear of it. He said there was only one window and *not room for two beds*, and no near room for him if he took another" (26, emphasis mine). Beds loom large in this story. The room in which the nar-rator has been confined contains a "great immovable bed" nailed down to the floor and contrasted with the nonthreatening single bed of the "pretty" room downstairs. At one point, in her effort to get to the woman in the wallpaper the narrator tries to move the bed in her room but finds that "this bed will *not* move! I tried to lift and push it until I was lame, and then I got so angry I bit off a little piece at one corner—but it hurt my teeth" (40). At another point in the story she describes the "great bedstead" as "fairly gnawed" from frustration and fury (40). As the signifier and the site of her sexual relationship with her husband the bed is a logical, if ineffectual, outlet for her rage.

Her husband is not alone in compelling heterosexuality. He is joined by the narrator's brother, who "is also a physician, and also of high stand-ing, and he says the same thing" (25). Other doctors, like Weir Mitchell, concur. "But I don't want to go there at all. I had a friend *who was in his hands once*, and she says he is just like John and my brother, only more so!" (30, emphasis mine). As the narrator's attention and longing increasingly turn toward the woman in the wallpaper, she becomes a parody of John, a possessive and jealous lover who doesn't "want anybody to get that woman out at night but myself" (38): "If that woman gets out and tries to get away, I can tie her!"; "I am determined that nobody shall find it out but myself!" (35). And John, of course, is the obstacle to her attainment of this love object. She wants to be free of him: "I wish he would take another room!" (38). As gatekeeper and policeman for patriarchy, he becomes simply the malevolent, generic "that man" who locks her in and, in effect, locks the other woman out.

"A Jury of Her Peers" investigates compulsory heterosexuality through depictions of gendered justice and reading. Toward the end of the story, the county attorney declines to scrutinize the things Mrs. Hale and Mrs. Peters have set aside to bring to Mrs. Foster in jail, remarking that "Mrs. Peters doesn't need supervising" because as a sheriff's wife, she is "married to the law" (385). His comment echoes his earlier remark, in answer to the sheriff's question of whether "'anything Mrs. Peters does'll be all right'": "'of course Mrs. Peters is one of us'" (376). What Mrs. Peters comes to recognize, however, is that "*the* law" is *their* law and she is *not* "one of them." Destroying evidence to save Mrs. Foster is an act of resistance to collaborating with "the(ir) law."

Minnie Foster's crime is linked even more explicitly to compulsory heterosexuality. She kills her husband in bed, reversing the symbolism by which she has been "tied" to his bed and "killed" in their marriage. Even her claim to have slept right through the murder—because she was on the "inside" of the bed and "didn't wake up" (374)—defamiliarizes compulsory heterosexuality and renders it both comic and absurd.

The story is filled with male violence and gender antagonism. The men make fun of the women for their interest in "trifles." They deride Mrs. Foster's homemaking. The women bristle at their ridicule and bitterly defend Minnie Foster against their nasty jibes. Cruelties abound to animals as well as women. Besides Minnie Foster's dead bird, Mrs. Peters remembers something that happened when she was a girl: "'my kitten—there was a boy took a hatchet and before my eyes—before I could get there—' she covered her face an instant. 'If they hadn't held me back I would have'—she caught herself, looked upstairs where footsteps were heard, and finished weakly—'hurt him'" (383).

In this context, when the women decide that the key crime is not Minnie Foster's murder of her husband, not even his oppression of her, but rather *their* abandonment of her to him (letting "her die for lack of life"), they deliberately step outside of the signifying system of compulsory heterosexuality, a system that depends upon making women's ties to one another incidental and insignificant. Ending the story with the women's pun on Mrs. Foster's quilting, "we call it—knot it" (385), stresses this move outside, this refusal of complicity in the oppression of another woman or the administration of male justice.

This resistance to compulsory heterosexuality and discovery of sororal alternatives to it are even more explicit in "The Blank Page." What the other two stories imply through tropes of beds, justice, the law, and retribution, "The Blank Page" articulates through a plot that directly ironizes and undermines heteronormativity. Exhibiting the bloodstained sheets as testimony to the consummation of royal marriages, the convent sisters seem complicit with a social order that demands virginity from the women it exchanges between men. But placing a blank sheet "in the midst of the long row" demonstrates both the possibility of alternatives—somehow this woman did not adhere to the script written for her—and the cultural denial of such alternatives—we can say no more than "somehow" because her sheet is blank. The story's convent setting (often the *only* choice available to women who sought to resist marriage) reinforces this counternarrative.

Storytelling itself is linked to resisting heterosexuality. The narrator's storytelling, like Scheherezade's, avoids both male sexuality and death, which it thereby links. Her stories began as responses to male seduction narratives: "tales of a red rose, two smooth lily buds, and four silky, supple, deadly entwining snakes" (1418–19). And storytelling was taught to her as a refuge from male sexuality: "it was my Mother's mother, *the black-eyed dancer, the often-embraced*, who in the end—wrinkled like a winter apple and crouching beneath the mercy of the veil—took upon herself to teach me the art of storytelling" (1419, emphasis mine). Telling her story as she does to a "sweet lady and gentleman" slyly introduces dissonance into the romantic dyad, suggesting to the woman in particular that there are cultural signs which may not be evident to her but which she might well contemplate. Storytelling, as Hannah Arendt points out, becomes a way of making so-called private experience public, of rendering the experiences of "private life" visible and therefore open to debate and public discussion.[65]

"The Blank Page," moreover, embeds a story of female love within its narrative of resistance to heterosexual marriage. A "very old highborn spinster " who had "once, a long time ago, been playmate, friend and maid-of-honor to a young princess of Portugal" (1422) comes to the gallery as a "loyal friend and confidante" to "sigh" and remember. Her story demonstrates how "old playmates" and friends, once they become "bridesmaids and maids-of-honor," are often left alone, abandoned to their memories and nostalgia:

> Slowly, slowly a row of recollections passes through the small, venerable, skull-like head under its mantilla of black lace, and it nods to them in amicable recognition. The loyal friend and confidante looks back upon the young bride's elevated married life with the elected royal consort. She takes stock of happy events and disappointments—coronations and jubilees, court intrigues and wars, the birth of heirs to the throne, the alliances of younger generations of princes and princesses, the rise or decline of dynasties. The old lady will remember how once, from the markings on the canvas, omens were drawn; now she will be able to compare the fulfillment to the omen, sighing a little and smiling a little (1422).

As a reader, the spinster serves to reflect the story's own implied reader, suggesting that not merely identification but desire may ground recuperation.

In each of these three stories, the reader is asked not so much to collaborate by identifying with victimization and silencing, but by desiring other women, or at least by identifying with that desire. Collaboration in each story hinges upon and embraces an erotically charged, passionate connection between women: the narrator and the woman behind the wallpaper, the abandoned spinster's longing for her long-gone princess-friend, even Mrs. Peters and Mrs. Hale's moments of ecstatic merger with the absent Minnie Foster.

By (re)reading these longings for merger, fusion, and contact as something more than identification have I "conflated identification and desire"?[66] In a recent critique of the "representation of lesbianism within feminist theory," Teresa de Lauretis faults feminism for such collapses. In much feminist theory, she argues, there is a "sweeping of lesbian sexuality and desire under the rug of sisterhood, female friendship, and the now popular theme of 'the mother-daughter bond.' In all three parts of the rug, what is in question is not desire, but identification."[67] Drawing on psychoanalytic categories to draw out the stakes of this "confusion," de Lauretis argues that "the distinction between object-libido and narcissistic or ego-libido is crucial here, for one is sexual and has to do with desire, *wanting to have (the object)*, the other is desexualized and has to do with narcissistic identification, *wanting to be or be like* or seeing oneself as (the object)."[68] De Lauretis warns against blurring this distinction and thereby contributing to a tendency to de-eroticize writing and at the same time to erase lesbian representation altogether.

Following recent critiques of this model, I want to take the opposite tack. Blurring this distinction, as these stories so deftly demonstrate, can also work quite productively to generate the very visibility de Lauretis has in mind. In all three of these texts a collapse or blurring of the dynamics of identification and desire works to suggest the dialectical relationship at work between identification and desire at work, presumably, in all acts of critical interpretation.[69]

Diana Fuss, in a recent essay on "Fashion and the Homospectatorial Look," argues that identification and desire are not on opposite ends of a spectrum but that identification is the product, or result, of desire. She writes:

> For Freud, Lacan, and Kristeva, desire and identification are mutually interdependent but counterdirectional trajectories in which identifying with one sex is the necessary condition for desiring the other. To identify with *and* to desire a person of the same sex is, in this logic, a structural impossibility. But such a symmetrical, rigid, chiasmatic relation between terms may disguise the ways in which any identification *with* an other is secured through a simultaneous and continuing desire *for* that other . . . the desire to be *like* can itself be motivated and sustained by the desire to *possess*: being can be the most radical form of having. Identification may well operate in the end not as a foreclosure of desire but as its most perfect, and most *ruthless*, fulfillment.[70]

Fuss's insight is particularly relevant to the questions I have raised about the feminist readings of these three stories. On the one hand, none of them explicitly raises the possibility of a lesbian reading. On the other hand, the reading models they suggest blur the line between identification and desire even as they seek to sharpen it. Fuss suggests that heterosexuality is maintained not by eschewing homosexuality, but by marshaling it and putting it to use. Recuperating those uses may help us break down this debilitating constraint that we may *only* either want or want to be like one another.

Identification, as Judith Kegan Gardiner has pointed out, is sometimes treated as feminism's cardinal sin. Critics such as Toril Moi and Catherine Belsey, Gardiner protests, become "particularly moralistic on this issue; they do not deny that readers identify with texts but condemn them for doing so."[71] And indeed, it is true that reading is pretty much unthinkable without different forms of identification. The same might be said of political activism. Or of identity. There is no point either defending or attacking identification in and of itself. The question, rather, is *how* we identify and what we do with the shifting relations that identifications—and the inevitable *dis*identifications they engender—always entail, with the erotic, intellectual, and emotional excess which inevitably follow in identification's wake.[72]

An exclusive focus on identificatory reading oversimplifies the "collaborations" and disidentifications these texts project between themselves and their readers. By the same token, a posture of heroic "rescue" obscures what may be the critic's own erotic investments in the texts she recuperates, the erotic excess that is part of critical recuperation itself. Incorporating desire into the recuperative process, as I will be seeking to do particularly in Part II, "The Erotics of Talk," helps to foreground the fact, as is so clear in "The Yellow Wallpaper" and "The Blank Page," that no reading has access to *the* meaning of the story and that all readings are stories of readerly desire. The integration of desire (which need not demand sameness) into a literary politics of identification (which does) allows for difference as well as sameness, for disidentification and conflict as well as collaboration and cure. It reminds us that we need not, as Hedges argues, be always "pursuing and finding in the text, as the narrator does in the wallpaper, only our own image reflected back."[73] Finally, foregrounding desire as part of the recuperative process mitigates against some of the more solipsistic, self-celebratory dangers of the recuperative paradigm. Insofar as the critic recuperating a woman's text identifies its heroine or its author *as herself*, she rescues not another woman, but an aspect of her own being. If the other woman can only be seen—and saved—insofar as she represents a version of oneself, then perhaps we *can* only save, liberate, or help ourselves, one of the messages of nineties-style self-help ideology which I would be particularly loath to see feminism adopt.

None of these emendations solves the limits of the recuperative paradigm. On the contrary, foregrounding desire may be an effective way to keep those limits more clearly in view. The need to use recuperative strategies to move beyond recuperation, beyond poetic justice, was Woolf's message in what may well be the most famous instance of feminist recuperation: her influential evocation of Judith Shakespeare. Judith Shakespeare's true recuperation, Woolf insisted, could never be effected by interpretive intervention, readerly identification, or critical desire alone. Judith Shakespeare "would come," Woolf wrote, "only *if* we worked for her . . . as for her coming without that preparation, without that effort on our part, without that determination that when she is born again she will find it possible to live and write her poetry, that we cannot expect, for that would be impossible."[74]

Opening the recuperative paradigm up to desire as well as identification provides for a larger, and to my mind more interesting, set of readings. It preserves a set of analytical tools crucial to a critical social vision and its concomitant transformations. That such strategies might, however, perform that transformative work on their own remains, as Woolf, Gilman, Glaspell, and Dinesen suggest, "impossible." In fact, making a space for those who've been erased, creating a heterogeneous public sphere that is both inclusive and open to contestation, especially contestation by the most marginalized and delegitimated speakers, often seems, as I will argue in the next chapter, an impossibly—if at the same time a necessary—utopian dream.

2

Recuperating Agents: Narrative Contracts, Emancipatory Readers, and *Incidents in the Life of a Slave Girl*

Reader, my story ends with freedom; not in the usual way, with marriage.[1]

—Linda Brent [Harriet Jacobs], *Incidents in the Life of a Slave Girl*

Freedom, Slavery, and Contract

In this often-noted concluding line, Harriet Jacobs's narrator, Linda Brent, rejects the marriage contract and, more generally, the conventions regulating women's lives and literature. By opposing freedom and marriage she undermines the nineteenth-century ideology of marriage as woman's "sacred absolute," the means of her personal fulfillment and the proper end of her life.[2] By suggesting, moreover, that freedom does not have the "usual" meaning for black slave women that it has for free white women, she challenges us to think about freedom and agency as specific and contextual, not as abstract and universal, to think about freedom, as she puts it, "not in the usual way."

But what would it mean for us to think about freedom or agency "not in the usual way"? Brent's "freedom" at the end of the narrative is complex and ambiguous. Although "free"—"as free from the power of slaveholders as are the white people of the north" (201)—she remains unfulfilled. "The dream of my life is not yet realized," she writes (201). "I do not sit with my children in a home of my own. I still long for a hearthstone of my own, however humble" (201).

This dream embraces both sides of a double desire. On the one hand, a home of her own represents a refuge, not only from social conventions

47

but also from the social relations entailed in her obligation to serve the northern white woman who has helped obtain her freedom. "God so orders circumstances as to keep me with my friend Mrs. Bruce. Love, duty, gratitude also bind me to her side. It is a privilege to serve her who pities my oppressed people, and who has bestowed the inestimable boon of freedom on me and my children" (201). Brent's "dream" of a "hearthstone" counterposes idyllic isolation to the social world which "binds" her. Such a dream represents freedom as social escape, concretizing that line of liberal ideology which understands the individual's freedom as autonomy, as freedom *from* (tyranny, domination, involuntary rule). In Brent's childhood, her grandmother's "snug little home," the reward of "perseverance and unwearied industry," had realized those ideals of refuge and escape: "We longed for a home like hers. There we always found sweet balsam for our troubles" (17). This home shields Linda Brent for the seven years that she hides in its garret to escape her master's sexual abuse, and it provides a daily refuge from the many forms of oppression and harassment which plague other blacks, free and slave. During the "muster," for example, which local whites use as an excuse to rob, beat, and terrorize blacks, her grandmother's home allows Brent to taunt the "country bullies and poor whites." She reports how annoyed they were "to see colored people living in comfort and respectability" and how she deliberately laid out the house "as neatly as possible. I put white quilts on the beds, and decorated some of the rooms with flowers. When all was arranged, I sat down at the window to watch" (63). While other black families suffer beatings and looting, Brent's family "came out of this affair very fortunately; not losing anything except some wearing apparel" (66). Her grandmother's home, then, is not just a conventional, gendered symbol of sentimental nineteenth-century domesticity. It affords considerable freedoms.

Brent's desire for a home of her own also signals that other conception of freedom central to liberal ideology, one which understands the individual's freedom in terms of rights: as freedom *to* (contract, exchange, trade—in short to engage in the whole array of social relations and practices constitutive of civil society). Brent passionately describes the pain of exclusion from this rights-based conception of freedom. "Never should I know peace till my children were emancipated with all due formalities of law" (138). Her efforts are thwarted because, as she is quick to point out, "there was no protecting arm of the law for me to invoke" (138). She is excluded from possessive individualism.[3] "A slave, *being* property, can *hold* no property," she reminds us (6), including property in one's own person, that supposedly inalienable fulcrum upon which both liberal and patriarchal conceptions of the individual, freedom, and agency rest.[4] As Carole Pateman explains it, under liberalism, ownership makes individuals free and equal. Each individual is both "naturally complete in himself" (55) and the owner of "property in his own person" (55). Therefore, he can engage in contracts with others on a mutual basis. A home of Brent's own, then, might seem to provide just the access to personhood—through possession and possessive individualism—which national law, regional slave codes, the Dred Scott case, the Fugitive Slave Act, and dominant ideology would otherwise deny.[5]

But reading Brent's desire as an endorsement of liberal ideology would be mistaken.[6] Her position is considerably more complex, as are the insights her solutions offer to a feminist theory of cultural conversation. With neither the means to escape "the law," nor any protection within it, Brent remains caught between both poles of a contradictory and equally inaccessible ideal. What does it mean to embrace both sides? How, by whom, and through what mediations can Brent's dilemma be resolved?

By introducing the category of gender into a critique of social contract theory, Pateman's important work on the sexual and social contract helps illuminate the practical and philosophical conundrum Jacobs's narrator faces. From the seventeenth century on, a rights-based conception of individual freedom and agency (or freedom *as* agency) has taken contract as its basis. "Contract is seen as the paradigm of free agreement" (6). Contract offers itself as the point of mediation between the seemingly conflicting ideals of freedom as autonomy and as rights. The possessiveness of free and equal individuals allows for "free agreement" in the form of exchange— "exchange is at the heart of contract" (57)—and conventions function so that the "free and equal" individual can "recognize the others as property owners like himself . . . mutual recognition by property owners is achieved through contract" (56).

Contract, as a balanced, voluntary exchange between individuals, mediates human relationships, derives its meaning from them, and also— importantly—presents itself as having the power to change them (like the theories of narrative transformation we have looked at earlier). Contract, perhaps not surprisingly then, generally appears as a progressive form of social relations:

> Classic social contract theory and the broader argument that, ideally, all social relations should take a contractual form, derive from a revolutionary claim. The claim is that individuals are naturally free and equal to each other, or that individuals are born free and equal. . . . The assumption that individuals were born free and equal to each other meant that none of the old arguments for subordination could be accepted. (39)

The problem, Pateman argues, is that contract reinforces subordination. "The genius of contract theorists," according to Pateman, "has been to present both the original contract and actual contracts as exemplifying and securing individual freedom" (8). Contract perpetuates domination because it is based on two fictions, universal freedom and the equality of individuals: "in contract theory universal freedom is always an hypothesis, a story, a political fiction" (8). This fiction is maintained, in the face of undeniable social domination, by positing a moment, or moments, in which individuals agree to domination (in exchange for safety or other goods). As free and equal individuals, the argument goes, their domination could have resulted only from their voluntary submission.

Introducing gender and race exposes the circularity of this logic by unmasking the neutral contractarian "individual" as a free, white male and so-called "universal" freedom, therefore, as a highly contingent state.

And here, Patemen explains, individual contracts come in. Where the conditions of universal freedom and equality of individuals do not exist—which is to say, most of the time—it is the task of discrete, individual contracts to provide them. But how is it that contracts produce their own preconditions? How do they override difference, inequality, and domination? When institutionally secured forms of oppression are at play between contracting parties, won't the contract tend to reinforce rather than transcend or transform those inequalities?

A critique of the social contract and its coercive capabilities is, as Benhabib explains, at the heart of communicative ethics. "Only those norms and normative institutional arrangements are valid, it is claimed, which individuals can or would freely consent to as a result of engaging in certain argumentative practices."[7] The question is whether or not practices of contracting can help provide for that legitimation.

Pateman argues that not only do individual contracts fail to provide their own preconditions in freedom and equality, but that contract in fact depends upon excluding many people from its equalizing, emancipatory machinery. Hence, her implicit suggestion is that the only option available to the excluded is a wholesale rejection of all contracts, a position more or less homologous to arguing that we should opt out of the cultural conversation because we cannot enter it as equals.

Incidents in the Life of a Slave Girl often seems to join in the suggestion that anyone who is not a free, white male cannot take advantage of a form of mediation within which he or she is categorically disadvantaged at the outset. One of the narrative's most impassioned passages is a powerful rejection of contract. Here, Brent describes her unhappiness upon receiving a letter from her white friend and employer Mrs. Bruce,

> informing me that my new master was still searching for me, and that she intended to put an end to this persecution by buying my freedom. I felt grateful for the kindness that prompted this offer, but the idea was not so pleasant to me as might have been expected. The more my mind had become enlightened, the more difficult it was for me to consider myself an article of property; and to pay money to those who had so greviously oppressed me seemed like taking from my sufferings the glory of triumph. I wrote to Mrs. Bruce, thanking her, but saying that being sold from one owner to another seemed too much like slavery. (199)

Without Brent's knowledge, Mrs. Bruce undertakes her purchase.[8] Brent experiences what might seem to be merely her entry into contract—by becoming "property in her own person"—as a psychological explosion. "'My brain reeled as I read these lines," Brent reports: "'The bill of sale!' Those words struck me like a blow. So I was *sold* at last! A human being *sold* in the free city of New York! . . . I well know the value of that bit of paper; but much as I love freedom, I do not like to look upon it" (200).

But while Jacobs demonstrates her categorical exclusion from pre-vailing ideas of personhood and individuality, she also indicts slavery by exposing its *denial* of contractual human relations. In other words, while she rejects contracts to which she cannot be a fully equal and voluntary party, she does not reject the ideals to which such contracts allude. Unlike Pateman, who would reject contracts because she rejects the ideology of contract, Brent rejects contracts because, I believe, she endorses and even longs for the ideals and ideologies of individuality embodied by the idea of the social contract.

This position is a precarious one, particularly because writing seems to inevitably entail contracts. In response, Jacobs, I will argue, at once fore-grounds narrative contracts and, paradoxically, avoids them. She makes her own dilemma a complex performative, as do other writers I will look at later.

Incidents in the Life of a Slave Girl has been the object of an important recent critical recuperation. Along with a handful of other texts by marginalized writers, it has emerged as an exemplar of textual resistance and subversion. But some of the critical maneuvers of that recuperation have actually occluded Jacobs's modes of resistance and subversion, ultimately reinscribing her within the very contractual mediations she seeks to avoid and expose. Jacobs, as the final section of this chapter will show, attempts a difficult, complex, and often precarious task. Like a number of modern African American women writers, she seeks to create a new black narrative position, one founded in a rejection of both the attestory position of slave narrators and the seductive one typical of white women's romances. This position aims to avoid being drawn into narrative contracts which can nei-ther grant her freedom nor change her status.

Recuperating Harriet Jacobs

A critical recuperation of Jacobs's text has been necessary to restore its authenticity and recognize the complex socio-political conditions of its production. In spite of authorial insistences such as "Reader, be assured this narrative is no fiction" (1), earlier critics, such as John Blassingame, insisted that "the work is not credible."[9] More like a sentimental seduction novel than a documentary account, too well written to have been authored by a slave, too sensational (particularly in its treatment of the sexual exploi-tation of slave women) for historical accuracy, the book was often assumed to be a novel, modeled on Richardson's *Pamela* and written by Jacobs's editor, white abolitionist Lydia Maria Child. Jean Fagan Yellin's dramatic discovery of Jacobs's letters, in 1981, restored the text's historical authen-ticity and inaugurated its critical reappraisal.[10]

This reappraisal has centered on Jacobs's strategic use of the constrain-ing literary conventions within which she worked. In her clear-sighted re-sistance to domination, her remarkable insistence on fairness and principles, and her thoughtful critique of existing moral and political ideologies, Jacobs has become, for many readers and critics, proof that human agency can still

be affirmed under even the most seemingly relentless and repressive conditions. "Jacobs' narrator," Yellin writes, "does not characterize herself conventionally as a passive female victim, but . . . was an effective moral agent"
("Introduction," xxx).

The celebration of Jacobs's agency has often rested on valorizing the
act of writing itself as a signal achievement of personal power. The conditions slave narrators faced make any published and self-authored account a
remarkable achievement. Historically, (il)literacy was used as a measure of
slaves' (in)humanity.[11] More specifically, the attestory, juridical position
of slave narrators, denied traditional modes of literary—and social—
authority, generated the use of certain literary forms which strategically
authenticated and legitimated their discourse. Such forms included modes
of disavowal—elaborate apologias for putative inarticulateness such as
Brent's request that her readers "excuse deficiencies in consideration of circumstances" (3–4); disclaimers of artistry such as the opening assertion "this
narrative is no fiction"; third-person testimonials to credibility such as
Child's introduction to Jacobs' narrative or Jacobs's inclusion of letters by
Amy Post and George W. Lowther attesting to her reliability and good
character; and the inclusion of what James Olney describes as a "bewilder-
ing array of documents": reproduced letters, bills of sale, transcriptions of
courtroom proceedings, newspaper clippings, marriage certificates, wills,
extracts from legal codes, sermons, speeches, and letters, all meant to at-
test to the reality the narrative describes.[12]

What attitude toward literacy might such strategies induce? For Jacobs,
literacy is not a transcendent value. It is a social practice deeply inscribed
by the forms of power and authority which it mediates and in which it is
situated.[13] Taught to read and write by her first mistress, Brent finds that
literacy opens her to new forms of assault as well as new avenues of response
when Dr. Flint uses clandestine letters to communicate his sexual desires.
Writing her own story, Brent asserts, is a painful experience, which she
undertakes only to aid abolition, and specifically to protest the Fugitive Slave
Act, enacted in 1850 and in effect as Jacobs writes. Brent describes her
earnest "desire to arouse the women of the North to a realizing sense of
the conditions of two millions of women at the South, still in bondage,
suffering what I suffered, and most of them far worse," and insists, "I have
not written my experiences in order to attract attention to myself; on the
contrary, it would have been more pleasant to me to have been silent about
my own history" (1–2).

Brent neither idealizes literacy nor treats it as the measure of her worth,
but her modern readers have been more sweeping. Minrose Gwin, for
example, sees it as a way "to control and dominate, in language, those who
controlled and dominated her."[14] Valerie Smith argues that by writing
Jacobs "seized authority over her literary restraints in much the same way
that she seized power in her life."[15] "By creating Linda Brent, by writing
and publishing her life story," Yellin argues, "Jacobs gained her victory."[16]

These readings are part of the broader enterprise of critical recuperation which seeks to rewrite the history of cultural resistance and elaborate

our understanding of how literary struggles are both sites and modes of social struggle. Situated within an archeology of literary history, this recuperative enterprise has located and resuscitated scores of texts by African American and women writers. Equally important, its methods have taught us to read silence, decipher madness, recognize and decode the unofficial documents of our culture: quilt stitches, everyday practices, the inscriptions of and on the body—the "lost arts," as Alice Walker describes the work of marginalized and illiterate artists.

But this recuperative enterprise has also fostered a sentimentalization of the marginal, the oppositional, and the subversive, not to mention a very particular privileging of writing and narrative as subversive and oppositional practices.

In "The Affirmative Character of Culture," Herbert Marcuse claimed that anyone who tried to imagine genuine cultural "oppositionality" was inhabiting a "fool's paradise."[17] Separated off as an independent realm of value and experience, "affirmative culture," as Marcuse argued it, answers "the concern for the individual's claim to happiness" and the "historical demand for the general liberation of the individual" by providing illusory satisfactions and, thereby, making an insufferable social order seem bearable; it is in this sense that cultural expression, in Marcuse's view, affirms the social order it appears to contest. "This is the real miracle of affirmative culture," Marcuse wrote, "men can feel themselves happy even without being so at all."[18]

Even while feminist and African American scholarship has posed an alternative to "affirmative culture" in the works of blacks and women and has rejected Marcuse's refusal to attribute greater social agency to cultural production, it has also wandered into his "fool's paradise" by reversing his proposition. How much difference is there, after all, between arguing, as Marcuse did, that no cultural artifact can offer true opposition and liberation and arguing, as so much recent criticism has implied, that no text can *fail* to do so? *Incidents in the Life of a Slave Girl*'s skepticism about the value and status of narrative, as I hope to show, challenges the optimism these abstractions convey.

In what follows I will be seeking to analyze some limits of emancipatory reading which assumes, a priori and in the abstract, the subversivity or "transformational" power, as Chambers calls it,[19] of all writing. Recuperative readings of *Incidents in the Life of a Slave Girl* present a two-sided problem. They define agency too narrowly—as subversive "acts." But they also define it too broadly, attributing it to narration, narrativity, or discourse per se and often, in so doing, tacitly affirming problematic models of individuality, subjectivity, and cultural conversation. My quarrel here is not so much with particular critics as with specific critical maneuvers which celebrate literature as a "talking cure" for social ills. This notion often exacerbates the impasses it describes and frequently substitutes the critic's own agency for the textual agency supposedly being restored. Typically, this includes one or more of the three following approaches to recuperating textual agency: locating it in the acts described, locating it in the act of narration itself, and locating it in the relationship between the narrator and the implied reader. In these last two cases particularly, notions of social and sexual contract which Jacobs explores and exposes often remain at the heart of theories of narration.

Emancipatory Reading

Incidents in the Life of a Slave Girl is structured around a series of disappointed expectations of imminent freedom. In the opening chapter Brent relates what she calls the "unusually fortunate circumstances" of her childhood: loving parents, a family home, an extended family, a kind and caring mistress, a father who was allowed to hire out his skills as a carpenter. All this comes to an end when Brent is twelve and her "kind mistress sickened and died." Although promised that this mistress's will would free her, Brent is instead "bequeathed" to the mistress's niece, "a child of five years old." At this point she becomes subject to the child's father, her new master Dr. Flint.

The rest of Jacobs's account details her attempts to evade Flint's sexual harassment, which begins when she approaches adolescence:

> a sad epoch in the life of a slave girl. My master began to whisper foul words in my ear. . . . He tried his utmost to corrupt the pure principles my grandmother had instilled. . . . My soul revolted against the mean tyranny. But where could I turn for protection? No matter whether the slave girl be as black as ebony or as fair as her mistress. In either case, there is no shadow of law to protect her from insult, from violence, or even from death; all these are inflicted by fiends who bear the shape of men. (27)

To avoid Flint's advances Jacobs ultimately takes three actions which she rationalizes, justifies, or explains in terms of relative conceptions of freedom. These acts have been the focus of a number of critical interpretations which argue that Linda Brent undermines structures of domination through strategic subversions which assert her own agency.

First, she enters into a sexual liaison and has two children with a white man in the town, Mr. Sands, a decision she describes as a "desperate" "plunge into the abyss" (53). Insisting on her own responsibility for this act, she asserts, "I knew what I did and I did it with deliberate calculation" (54):

> It seems less degrading to give one's self, than to submit to compulsion. There is something akin to freedom in having a lover who has no control over you, except that which he gains by kindness and attachment. . . . He was a man of more generosity and feeling than my master, and I thought my freedom could be easily obtained from him. . . . I also felt quite sure that they [her two children] would be made free. (55)

Second, Brent takes refuge in the garret of her grandmother's house, a "dismal hole . . . only nine feet long and seven wide" (113). Insisting again upon her own responsibility, Brent chooses freedom from sexual harass-

ment over the freedom from material discomfort she could obtain by becoming Flint's mistress:

> It seemed horrible to sit or lie in a cramped position day after day, without
> one gleam of light. Yet I would have chosen this, rather than my lot as a slave,
> though white people considered it an easy one; and it was so compared with
> the fate of others. . . . On the contrary, I had always been kindly treated, and
> tenderly cared for, until I came into the hands of Dr. Flint. I had never wished
> for freedom till then. (115)

As she makes clear, her "choice" is paradoxical; true freedom eludes her
either way.

Third, after five years in the garret, Brent writes a series of letters to
Dr. Flint, postmarked from New York and Boston to trick him into believing that she is a fugitive in the North. "I resolved," she writes, "to match
my cunning against his cunning" (128). Even when Linda's letters seem to
incite Flint's desire to recapture her, she is optimistic about them: "the letters
will do good in the end. I shall get out of this dark hole some time or other"
(131). And with Flint convinced that she is in the North, it does prove safer
for Brent occasionally to slip downstairs and exercise her atrophying muscles.
Since these letters cannot be answered by Flint, they are also an outlet into
play, one-way communications that parody the letter-writing exchange they
imitate.[20]

These acts form the basis of a surprisingly coherent set of readings. "The
affair with Sands was as much an act of subversion as of surrender," William Andrews concludes[21] with reference to Jacobs's assertion that "it seems
less degrading to give one's self, than to submit to compulsion." Valerie
Smith argues that "even the act of choosing her own mode of confinement
constitutes an exercise of will, an indirect assault on her master's domination."[22] She echoes Houston A. Baker, Jr.'s view that "the slave girl chooses
'retreat' as a strategy, the new position that she occupies is very much a
'loophole'—a hole in the wall from which she wages effective combat."[23]
Jean Yellin sees in Brent's letters "a sophisticated version of a power reversal in which the slave controls the master" ("Introduction," xxvi). She echoes
Andrews, among others, who asserts that Jacobs's "experiments in writing
let her play the role of a slave trickster lodged in the interstices of a social
structure that she pries apart with her spying eyes and ventriloquist voice."[24]

It is of course true that many writers bury subversive plots or elements
beneath more ostensibly orthodox ones.[25] And I would certainly put in this
category Brent's liaison with Sands, her self-imprisonment in the garret,
and her letter-writing, particularly as all of these activities so self-consciously
undermine and parody the narrative conventions of romance, slave narratives, and epistolary fiction. But do we really want to call a black slave
woman's "desperate" plunge into an affair with a free white man an "act of
subversion"? Even if we agree that any act of choice is also an "exercise of
will," do we really want to label a slave woman's desperate self-imprisonment an "*assault* on her master's domination"? In what sense is this miser-

able, wasting, wasted seven-year period a form of "*effective combat*"? Do her letters really effect a "*power reversal*"? Do they "*pry apart*" the social system? Is this justice or poetic justice—and how significant is the difference between them?

While I am in sympathy with much of what motivates these conclusions, they obviously make me uncomfortable. First, by identifying Brent's agency solely with the rebelliousness of these acts the critic assumes that their liberatory meanings override their self-defeating or submissive ones: the sense of "desperate" plunge in Linda's affair, of self-imprisonment and living death in the garret, of false choices, in short. Where does the authority for such a judgment come from? And what kind of position do we put ourselves in to make it? Second, not only do these conclusions seem to me to risk suggesting that power is easily subverted and reversed, but they also risk occluding the very impasse this narrative represents. Jacobs is at great pains to dramatize Brent's *inability* to "subvert" her status, "*assault*" her master's domination, wage "*effective*" combat, or "reverse" the power structures which bind her. This inability is the lived meaning of slavery for Linda Brent. It is this narrative's strongest indictment. To define agency as simply the act of writing is to miss the point of Brent's performance.

One of the more remarkable (and lucky) features of Brent's struggle with Dr. Flint is the fact that he does not rape her, although clearly he could: "do you know that I have a right to do as I like with you,—that I can kill you, if I please?" (39). Flint, in effect, insists that Linda consent to his coercion. He demands not simply her body, but also her consent; he wants her to legitimate his domination over her. This Linda refuses to do. "You have no right to do as you like with me," she answers Dr. Flint (39). Linda exercises agency here by refusing to consent, just as elsewhere she does so by refusing to act. Insofar as we attempt to locate Brent's agency in specifically rebellious acts, making any meaningful rebellion of hers tantamount to *acting*, her refusal of consent and justification, which often takes the form of seeming to refuse to "act," may remain invisible. Defining agency more narrowly, as certain kinds of acts, may also miss the point.

While acting remains, of course, crucial to agency, it is the discursive construction of action, the *narration* of resistance rather than its *narrated acts*, which allows us to register Jacobs's resistance. Anthony Giddens, in *The Constitution of Society*, argues that "acts" cannot be identified except in reference to their discursive construction. Acts are the reflexive and discursive construction of those aspects of lived experience which we seek— for pragmatic and particular purposes—to define and designate as such out of a whole array of human activity. Giddens writes:

> To be a human being is to be a purposive agent, who both has reasons for his or her activities and is able, if asked, to elaborate discursively upon those reasons (including lying about them). . . . Human action occurs as a *durée*, a continuous flow of conduct, as does cognition. Purposive action is not composed of an aggregate or series of separate intentions, reasons and motives . . . is not a combination of "acts": "acts" are constituted only by a discursive moment of attention to the *durée* of lived-through experience.[26]

Following Giddens, it is Jacobs's discursive *construction* of acts, including the broad array of activity from which they are selected, which constitutes her purposive behavior and her agency.

To be judged competent as an actor or agent, according to Giddens, is to be able to give an account of one's own actions, a self-justification or explanation which legitimates one's life and choices. "The capability of specifying such reasons discursively . . . is expected by competent agents of others—and is the main criterion of competence applied in day-to-day conduct—that actors will usually be able to explain most of what they do, if asked."[27] On this account, agency is attestory.

This raises important questions for any recuperative enterprise. Typically, the recuperative critic operates on behalf of a writer who is marginalized, silenced, undervalued, misunderstood, or underattended, and who is represented by the critic as in desperate need of a sympathetic listener. The critic then sets out to revalue the writer's work by revealing what previous—politically motivated—misreadings have elided or taken for granted. Such work restores important texts, helps us to reshape the canon, maps the lines of ideological struggle along which canons have been laid out. But in authorizing him or herself as the ideal listener for whom that text has been waiting, the critic also takes possession of a juridical position.

The shift, then, from Brent's narrated acts to Jacobs's act of narration, may be a troubling one. Not only because it seems to require us to talk about the author as well as her narrator, but because it reminds us that we, as readers, are implicated in the problem we are analyzing. Narration, or writing, has no fixed status in Jacobs's text. It derives its meaning from the human interactions it mediates: our own, in this case. This raises an important methodological question for recuperative work: what will it mean for us to recover or recuperate Jacobs's agency when we, as readers, are problematically and unavoidably implicated in the process of its construction?[28]

The problem of locating and perhaps even of restoring Brent's agency becomes particularly troubling when we recognize, as I think we must, that structurally we parallel Dr. Flint. The narrative offers just two representations of writing: first, the "bit of paper" which "frees" Linda, but sends her reeling with an even stronger sense of unfreedom; and, second, her fraudulent letters to Flint. As the addressee of Brent's letters, Flint therefore is the narrative's only represented reader. He parodies the convention of an implied reader who is also an ideal reader. But because (like God in Alice Walker's *The Color Purple* or Pheoby in Hurston's *Their Eyes Were Watching God*) he is the text's *only* representation of a reader, we are forced to ask about ourselves in relation to him. How ideal are we? How competent? What forms of authority and power do we bring to this text? How do we inscribe it with those as we read? The letter-writing exchange parallels our reading. And it is pointedly nondialogic. It parodies writing as a form of communication, as a coming together of writer and reader, as the frequently invoked writer-reader "contract."

Narrative Contracts

The assumption that literature involves reader/writer contracts is so commonplace as to appear merely descriptive. Northrop Frye, for example, can refer to it as simply an "accepted postulate" that "the contract agreed upon by the reader before he can start reading, is the same thing as a convention."[29] But just as the term "convention" has been denaturalized as a set of particular knowledges and historically situated contingencies which vary enormously from one "interpretive community" to another,[30] so the idea of the literary contract needs rethinking. Do narratives really work like contracts between writers and readers? And if so, what grounds them and makes them binding? How are they broken? How are they adjudicated and enforced? By whom? With what authority?

A convention, in the literary sense, is a tacit agreement, an implicit understanding as to form, genre, purpose or other expectations. As Raymond Williams has argued, "in normal use convention is indeed the opposite of formal agreement." And yet this more common meaning of "implicit agreed method"[31] makes sense only by incorporating and alluding to the idea of formal agreement, the ideal of a collective ratification which, as many critics have shown, is most frequently evoked just when it is most glaringly absent.[32] In what sense has the idea of the literary contract evolved from social and legal ones? In what ways does it allude back to them to ground and legitimate itself?

Jonathan Culler's discussion of the novel in *Structuralist Poetics* illuminates how a theory of narrative contract drawn from the social and the legal may work. Culler discusses how the "mimetic contract" works to generate intelligibility and recognition by building up "descriptive residue . . . gesturing towards a world in which he [the reader] can identify" and assuring "the reader that he can interpret the text as about a real world." Culler draws here from Greimas's category of "*syntagmes contractuels*" to argue that narrative is shaped by thematic and structural contracts, specifically by the narrative movement between implicit and broken contracts.[33] But if here Culler's discussion of narrative's contractual nature is explicit, and, I would suggest, relatively unproblematic, elsewhere contract plays a more implicit role.

Culler's account of the novel as "communication about a world" between a narrator and imaginary reader who "share the same world to which the language of the novel refers" (195–96) reiterates what I am taking to be a prevailing—if not always acknowledged—model. According to Culler, the novel shares, across an array of subgenres and stylistic/structural innovations, an essentially conversational dynamic. Readers deploy a wide range of strategies of "recuperation" to identify, imagine, or construct narrators, so as to answer the dialogic question of who is speaking to whom, such that even the most unlikely and radically innovative texts resemble conversations.

This insistence on conversational models (less Culler's own perhaps than his diagnosis of critical and theoretical pieties) helps us to grasp the homology between a conversational fictional model and a contractarian social one.

As we have seen, contracts depend, at the moment of contracting, on a consensual exchange between equals. And contract theory, as we have also seen, encounters the fact of inequality as its most pressing dilemma. It resolves this dilemma through the double fiction that we are always already equals (because our apparent inequalities are themselves the products of previous contracts), and that the contract itself, as the medium of transaction between the two parties, not only regulates an exchange between parties, but is also the medium of their transformation—however momentary—into equals. A homologous theoretical dilemma arises from maintaining that the novel mediates between parties who "share the same world to which the language of the novel refers." Not only is this rarely the case, but, as we know, novels are often written explicitly in and about the gap or conflict between those worlds. And whereas both sides of a homologous double fiction are available to resolve this narrative dilemma, one view seems to have lost currency in recent years: namely, that we all do share the same world (because good literature is universal). But corresponding to the fiction that contract mediates the transformation *into* equals of contracting parties is the idea that narrative not only mediates between non-equals, but mediates a transformation whereby the narrator and reader are equalized through the narrative "transaction." I would argue that this fiction, unlike that of literary universality, is gaining currency.

Taken to its extreme, the occlusion of the divisions and differences between different readerships (historical and otherwise), can lead to seeing all narrative as an intrinsically oppositional practice. Ross Chambers, for example, describes narrative as a "transactional" or "contractual" practice that "mediates human relationships," "has the power to change human situations," and is therefore an "'oppositional practice' of considerable significance" (4, 7, 212). It is the job of progressive-minded critics, Chambers suggests, to reconstruct the mechanisms of that transformation and reveal how texts transform the power relationships they code between themselves and their readers. Chambers's position is, in some ways, extreme. But it resonates with a great deal of contemporary criticism.

The key mechanism of this transformation Chambers calls "seduction." "Narration as seduction," he argues, wins narrative authority from "a situation from which power is itself absent. . . . The narrator, who is situationally condemned to operate without preexistent authority and *to earn the authority to narrate in the very act of storytelling*, must be a master of certain 'tactical' devices" (214, emphasis mine).

Such seduction, for Chambers, is contractual: narration

> depends on social agreements, implicit pacts or contracts in order to produce exchanges that themselves are a function of desires, purposes, constraints. . . . It is only on the strength of such agreements [or contracts] that narratives can exert their impact and produce change. . . . No act of narration occurs without at least an implicit contract, that is, an understanding between narrator and narratee, an illocutionary situation that makes the act meaningful and gives it what we call a "point." (4, 9)

Writers and their readers contract to exchange the narrator's authority for the reader's interest. Like the original contract which posits an exchange of civic obedience for protection, this reader/writer contract functions to naturalize narrative as a social process while it guarantees one possible outcome as a constitutive feature *of* that process. Like classic social contract theory, the claim that narrative equalizes social relations seems revolutionary, but also like classic social contract theory, it obviates the need for any explanation of persistent inequalities.

Even work which foregrounds the divisions and differences of different readerships can fail to explain how they are breached. Important feminist work on Jacobs, for example, has examined her use of literary conventions to break social contracts. According to Valerie Smith, slave narrators "not only grant themselves significance and figurative power over their superordinates, but in their manipulation of received literary conventions they also engage with and challenge dominant ideology. . . . Jacobs inscribes a subversive plot of empowerment beneath the more orthodox, public plot of weakness and vulnerability."[34] Jacobs found no available literary form for the story she needed to tell: as a woman she broke with many of the conventions of the traditional slave narrative; as a black slave she broke the taboos of nineteenth-century sentimental women's writing. Consequently, Smith argues, she uses silence as a protest and indictment: "By consigning to the narrative silences those aspects of her own sexuality for which the genre does not allow, Jacobs points to an inadequacy in the form."[35] "*Incidents*," Yellin writes, "transforms the conventions of literature. . . . Formal problems suggest that new forms were needed, new characters, new narrative voices, if literature was to express the fullness of Jacobs's new point of view and her new content."[36] Hazel Carby's reading of *Incidents* focuses on its "dissection of the conventions of true womanhood. . . . The narrative of Linda Brent's life stands as an exposition of her womanhood and motherhood, contradicting and transforming an ideology that could not take account of her experience."[37]

These readings convincingly delineate the narrative strategies Jacobs developed to address her situation as a fugitive slave woman and author. They shift the ground from narrated acts to problems of narration, and they draw attention to the important ways that literary conventions index social ideologies. Breaking with patterns of slave narratives, Brent's story does not end with freedom. Reversing patterns of nineteenth-century women's literature, Brent prefers a loss of sexual purity and virtue to death. Her sexual struggle does not resolve social conflict. Nor does it enable her—through marriage—to change her class status.

But these readings also raise an important question. Don't modern readers pose the very same problem of authority and legitimation that obviated Jacobs's use of available conventions? How do contemporary readers recognize a "subversive" plot which, presumably, slipped past many others? If contemporary feminist scholars can recognize the unsaid meanings of silences which other readers failed perhaps even to notice—and it is important to acknowledge such gains—have those now-spoken silences, then, lost their power to indict? Does our new understanding signal the arrival of the "new forms" which Jacobs suggested would be needed? How, in short, can a recuperative reading recover these silences, indictments, and subversions without assuming its own position of historical and epistemological privilege? "Sympathy" or "identification" with the narrator might seem to be an obvious answer, but as feminist readings like Nelson's and Carby's point out, cultural assumptions about "sympathy" and "identification" are part of what Jacobs puts under interrogation.

In place of sympathy or identification, a critic like Chambers might suggest that "seduction" is the answer. Some texts are simply more seductive than others. Not all texts are equally "seductive" to all readers at all historical moments. The question, for his analysis, is not one of historical privilege or even of relative knowledges, but is merely a matter of mutual attraction, a kind of successful coming together, if you will, of reader and writer through the "contractual" mediations of the text. Chambers fails to notice how categories like gender or race inflect this formula. What kind of charge, after all, would "seduction" carry in the context of a black slave woman's story, addressed to northern white women, of her master's failed seduction? In Jacobs's context, is a seductive contract really possible, let alone in her interest? Is she empowered to enter into contracts—literary or social—on her own behalf at all?

Where feminist critics have focused, in the main, on Jacobs's rupture of literary conventions and social contracts, Baker makes a case for Jacobs's use of contract. He contends that the slave narrator's challenge was to master the "economics of slavery" (3) through the "ironic transformation of property by property into humanity" (36), a transformation enacted discursively. The slave narrator must "negotiate the economics of slavery" (37) and free himself by engaging in acts which redefine him as an individual. As an example, Baker offers Frederick Douglass's marriage certificate. "What Douglass's certificate of marriage . . . signifies," Baker argues, "is that the black man has repossessed himself in a manner that enables him to enter the kind of relationship disrupted, or foreclosed, by the economics of slavery" (48).

Baker argues that Brent, like Douglass, negotiates through economic exchanges with Sands which commodify herself and her children. Thus she becomes a possessive individual, or "at least provides the necessary conditions for such a conversion to occur" (54).[38] Although, Baker argues, "gender produces striking modifications in the Afro-American discursive subtext," "gender does not," he concludes, "alter a fundamentally commercial set of negotiations represented as liberating in the black narrative" (50, 54). But Baker's example of Douglass's negotiation could hardly be more inflected *by* gender. It is marriage, after all, that engenders contractarian individuality. It establishes male possessive individuality through the exchange of women who mediate social relations not by being possessors of property but by being property. The entry into individuality available to Douglass necessitates a woman's exclusion from it, and would not be available *to* her. While for Brent, also, marriage is a relationship "foreclosed by the economics of slavery," it can only signify a deeper inscription into that economics, not a pathway out of it.[39] As for her self-commodification via Sands, Jacobs, we might remember, expressly rejects the strategy of "ironic transformation of property by property into humanity" that Baker identifies with Douglass when she attempts to avoid her own purchase and self-possession. The efficacy of contract, in other words, like "seduction" on the narrative register, is inflected with Jacobs's gender. What may be "represented as liberating" for Douglass doesn't offer Jacobs any measure of freedom at all.

Gender, in other words, *does* alter those "negotiations represented as liberating in the black narrative," as Baker puts it. Douglass accepts, as Baker so deftly demonstrates, the available modes of freedom: mercantile freedom, freedom through literacy, freedom as a possessive individual. In so doing, Douglass fights his way into contractarian ideology and the rights that this entails. And Baker, quite rightly, celebrates this. But Brent, as we have seen, *refuses* available modes of freedom: mercantile freedom, freedom through marriage, freedom as a (self-)possessive individual. And in so doing, Brent exposes her own categorical exclusion from that ideology and from those rights, an exposure which depends, in large part, upon her deconstruction of "negotiation" itself, narrative "negotiation" not excepted.[40]

Narrative Resistance

Robert Stepto writes that while African American narrators may long for ideal readers and the pleasures of narrative "conversation," they may be more likely to find themselves in un-ideal discursive situations, facing readers who are unsympathetic, uncomprehending, even antagonistic. The texts of the African American tradition, Stepto argues, "are fully 'about' the communicative prospects of Afro-Americans writing for American readers, black and white, given the race rituals which color reading and/or listening." Insofar as these "race rituals" work to limit and constrain those "communicative prospects," African American writers develop, Stepto compellingly argues, "a discourse of distrust." In African American storytelling texts, unreliability is located not with the narrator or author, but with the reader.[41] And the reader is "told off" for being so untrustworthy:

> . . . acts of creative communication are fully initiated not when the text is assaulted but when the reader gets "told"—or "told off"—in such a way that he or she finally begins to *hear*. It is usually in this way that most written tales express their distrust not just of readers but of official literate culture in general.[42]

On Stepto's account, this distrust does not mean that such narrators fail, as some narrative theorists put it, to "captivate," "seduce," or transform" their readers. On the contrary. African American texts, Stepto argues, "*coerce* authors and reader (or if you will, texts and readers) into teller-hearer relationships" and transform their untrustworthy readers into conversational partners through argumentation itself.[43] The African American narrator, Stepto maintains, "tells off" unreliable readers—much as Mrs. Farrinder is ready to "tell off" poor Basil Ransom—and hence converts them into reliable listeners, capable of conversational intimacy and pleasure, of satisfying the text's desire, as Brooks put it, "to be heard, recognized, understood."

Stepto's compelling account helps us locate the reader as the constitutive feature of Jacobs's narrative strategies and her handling of literary conventions. But it raises rather than resolves the question of whether or not Jacobs believes she can "tell off" her reader, whether or not she believes doing so will transform her, whether or not she puts her stock in this particular kind of poetic justice.

Elizabeth Fox-Genovese writes:

> imagined readers shape the ways in which an autobiographer constructs the narrative of her life . . . [and] there is little evidence that black women autobiographers assumed that any significant number of other black women would read their work. . . . Black female autobiographers wrote to be read by those who might influence the course of public events, might pay money for their book, or might authenticate them as authors. . . . The tension at the heart of black women's autobiography derives in large part from the chasm between the autobiographer's intuitive sense of herself and her attitude toward her probable readers.[44]

Brent makes frequent reference to her implied readers as "the women of the North" (1) and often addresses them directly, as when she asks that "you happy free women, contrast *your* New Year's day with that of the poor bond-woman" (16), or when she states that

> the degradation, the wrongs, the vices that grow out of slavery, are more than I can describe. They are greater than you would willingly believe. Surely, if you credited one half the truths that are told you concerning the helpless millions suffering in this cruel bondage, you at the North would not help to tighten the yoke. (29)

Her attitude toward this reader is expressed through her strategies of address, particularly her technique of presenting information a northern white woman would be unlikely to know as if she is merely stating the obvious. Frequently, Brent deploys this tactic just when she is presenting information most crucial to a sympathetic understanding of slave life. "We all know that the memory of a faithful slave does not avail much to save her children from the auction block" (7), she declares in a passage designed precisely to show her readers how little slave loyalty was valued by slave owners. At another crucial point she remarks that "the reader probably knows that no promise or writing given to a slave is legally binding; for, according to Southern laws, a slave *being* property, can *hold* no property" (6). As Brent elsewhere suggests, these are just the sorts of things her reader would *not* know. Indeed, it is largely to try and *explain* such things that the narrative is written: "O virtuous reader! You never knew what it is to be a slave; to be entirely unprotected by law or custom; to have the laws reduce you to the condition of a chattel, entirely subject to the will of another" (55). On another occasion, when her son Benjamin finally contrives to join his fugitive mother in the north, Brent asks, "O reader, can you imagine my joy?" and quickly answers herself, "No, you cannot, unless you have been a slave mother" (173).

Why, then, pose, like the narrator of *Mama Day*, as if this reader knows things she does not, feels things she doesn't feel, understands things she apparently couldn't possibly understand? Stepto suggests that when the (white) reader (of the African American text) is "told off" it is for his or her own good. The "instructional nature" of the "discourse of distrust" resides in teaching the reader how to read the African American tale.[45] The formula goes something like this:

> [The] narrative depicts a black storyteller's white listener socially and mor-
> ally maturing into competency [as a reader]. In thus presenting a very par-
> ticular reader in the text, the basic written story squarely addresses the issue
> of its probable audience while raising an issue for some or most of its readers
> regarding the extent to which they can or will identify with the text's "reader"
> while pursuing (if not always completing) their own act of reading.[46]

Brent's strategies of address do not follow this formula. She does not go to the trouble of "telling off" her reader and expecting—or even invit-ing—her to change. Instead, she encourages the implied reader to regard herself as already ideal and competent, even in the face of massive evidence to the contrary. Rather than tell her off, Brent invites her reader to con-gratulate herself for moral gestures this reader is spared from having to make.[47] Consequently, the text is spared having to facilitate the reader's transformation. Whereas Chambers argues that narrative "has the power to produce change, and first and foremost to change the relationship be-tween narrator and narratee" (74), Jacobs's presumption seems to be that narration lacks this power, that the reader will not change, and that the mechanics of the narrative encounter are insufficient to the task of moral transformation. In place of a "discourse of distrust" she substitutes a pro-foundly more skeptical distrust of discourse. The inadequacies of literary form and convention she points to turn out to be inadequacies in her reader. And it is harder, she suggests, to invent new readers or improve available ones than it is to invent new forms or modify old ones. That an ideal reader might be aware of this ironization of narrative transaction does little to mitigate distrust. The difference between implied and ideal readers, for Jacobs, is a product of history, circumstance, race, or gender, not of the narrative itself. These are differences that she does not trust—or even ask—her narrative itself to ameliorate.

What we might call Jacobs's radical narrative skepticism is evident not only in her ironic treatment of "transactional" discourse and mockery of the reader's capacity for change (the narrative's capacity *to* change the reader), but also in her treatment of silence as a gendered form of kind-ness, respect, and fineness—or "delicacy"—of feeling.[48] Her kindest white friends, for example, are represented as exhibiting the "delicate silence of womanly sympathy" (162), and as being careful "not to say anything that might wound my feelings" (161). Her daughter, Ellen, is praised "for the delicacy she had manifested towards her unfortunate mother" in not speak-ing aimlessly of painful subjects (189). Even more important, silence is also racially coded. Whereas white silence is presented as shameful and cowardly, black silence is valued, privileged, and protected. Whereas whites are called upon to speak out against the outrages of the Fugitive Slave Act—"Why are ye silent, ye free men and women of the north? Why do your tongues falter in maintenance of the right?" (30)—the ability to keep silent is an index, among blacks, of trustworthiness and reliability. Brent's children's good character, for example, is established by their ability to maintain a "prudent," "cautious," and "cunning" silence about their mother's presence in the garret above them. Upon leaving her good friend Peter, who has helped to engineer her escape, Brent relates that "we parted in silence. Our hearts were all too full for words!" (156). There is much in the narrative to suggest that we take Brent at her word when she insists, on the very first page, that "it would have been more pleasant to me to have been silent about my own history" (1) and repeats, on the very last page, that "it has been painful to me to recall the dreary years I passed in bondage" (201).

But of course recall those years she does by telling her own and her family's history. "What tangled skeins are the genealogies of slavery!" she declares (78), and much of our work as readers involves putting together the complicated puzzle of her family history. It is, indeed, difficult to piece together the nearly impossibly complicated relations—of blood and status— among Brent's family members. The shifting status of "free" blacks is evoked from the first page of the narrative, when Brent describes the family background of her maternal grandmother, "the daughter of a planter in South Carolina, who, at his death, left her mother [Brent's maternal great-grandmother, his slave and forced concubine] and his three children free with money to go to St. Augustine, where they had relatives. It was during the Revolutionary War; they were captured on their passage, carried back, and sold to different purchasers" (5). (See figure next page.)

The status of Brent's own children is particularly complicated. They are eventually bought by Sands, but under the name of their own grandmother, Aunt Marthy, and are therefore technically her property, although, being black, she could neither sell nor free them. Sands, despite numerous promises, fails to free them. Instead, he sells Ellen, Brent's daughter, to his cousin as a "waiting maid," whereupon Ellen becomes *her* property. All the while, the children may still technically be the property of Dr. Flint, since at the time they were sold they were legally the property of his young daughter who did not concede to the sale.

Brent's own status is no less complicated. Although a fugitive slave, she considers herself free because she has escaped north. But the Fugitive Slave Act virtually negates that freedom. At the end of the narrative she is made free only through *purchase* by her friend Mrs. Bruce. Often, Brent "verily believed myself to be a free woman" (161) only to discover that she is still bound.

Racial status and gender politics come together in her family's sexual history. Three generations of women have all had children by white men, whether through rape, coercion, or, as in Brent's case, strategy. The puzzle in this history is Brent's maternal grandmother, the "Aunt Marthy" who judges Linda so harshly for her liaison with Sands. Both of Brent's parents are termed "mulattoes," implying that both have mixed parents. Brent's aunts

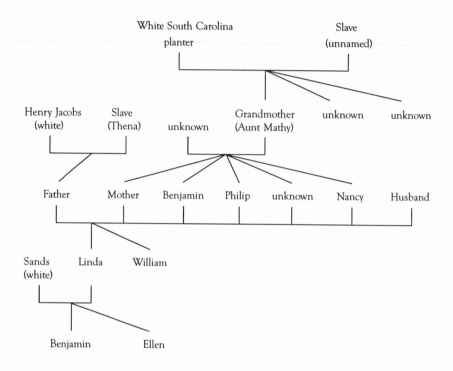

and uncles are extremely light; in fact Benjamin is described as "nearly white" and escapes slavery by passing (6). Aunt Marthy, this suggests, may also have had her children, including Brent's mother, by a white slaveowner. A narrative silence surrounds this grandfather, in spite of the extensive attention otherwise devoted to establishing family history. How is this peculiar silence explained? Only through Brent's very odd claim that she does "not remember all the particulars." This silence is less a memory lapse than a denial—to the reader—of information, information which would support her own claims of "tangled skeins" but which might titillate her readers at her grandmother's expense, shame her grandmother, or expose another family member to ridicule or derision. This use of silence suggests that thinking about freedom "not in the usual way" may entail imagining what it would be like not to have to give an account of yourself or your family to others, what it would be like to be freed from the juridical, attestory, or seductive position characteristic of slave narratives. What it would be like *not* to have to seduce your readers, even if this means not doing so at your own expense.

Of course, Jacobs's options for representing and engaging in communicative exchanges are not limited to those between narrators and readers. Internal dialogues, William Andrews has argued, play an important role in exposing the power relations which inflect the production and reception of slave narratives. I agree with his claim that "dialogue in slave narratives tells us something about the negotiation of power that goes on in discourse, whether between a master and a slave or a black autobiographer and a reader."⁴⁹ But I question his celebration of dialogue as a "liminal phase" of indeterminacy, power, and "freedom, even for slaves that would seem to be most powerless."⁵⁰ Andrews contends that *Incidents* is the most "'dialogized'" of antebellum black autobiographies," and that Brent's "repeated 'dialogic' struggles with Flint testify to the power she could and did exercise against his attempts to manipulate and dominate her."⁵¹

But what is the nature of Jacobs's reconstructed dialogues? In whose favor *are* they resolved? There are eight passages which, broadly speaking, might be called dialogues between Linda Brent and Dr. Flint, but of these, only three can properly be called reconstructed dialogues; most of Brent's responses are summarized, not rendered in direct speech. Moreover, many of these dialogues end violently. In one, Dr. Flint learns that Linda is pregnant again and cuts off all her hair and beats and harangues her until she faints at his feet (77). In another, he learns that Sands has tried to buy Linda and the children and hurls Benjamin across the room, nearly killing him (81). All the remaining "dialogues" end in unresolved silence. A number of times, Brent refuses to consent to Flint's desires. When he demands that she go to the cottage he has built for her, she replies, "'I will never go there. In a few months I shall be a mother'" (56). And, again, later, "'No, sir'" (83). In each of these instances Brent acts out an imaginary scenario of not responding, of being outside of attestory or seductive roles.

Moreover, in almost every instance Brent addresses her responses *not* to Flint at all, but to the reader. Following, for example, a lengthy expostulation by Flint on why Brent should submit herself to him, Brent asks, "Reader, did you ever hate? I hope not. I never did but once; and I trust I never shall again. Somebody has called it 'the atmosphere of hell'; and I believe it is so" (40). In having Brent address her reader—a reader she has already represented as a failed listener—rather than her interlocutor, Jacobs establishes a discursive triangle which makes any dialogue, in Andrews's sense, clearly impossible: the participants—Brent, Flint, and the reader— do not exist on the same plane, let alone within the same temporal register. While Brent may speak, in other words, she does so in a way which avoids exchanges or direct response.

There are two instances in which, as Andrews claims, Brent answers Flint back: telling him, in one, that he has no right to do as he likes with her (39) and stating, in the other, that she has sinned against God and herself but not against him (58). Here the "verbal battle" is over Flint's demand that Brent not only become his mistress, but, perhaps more important, that she consent to being so. In this, Flint implies that she could also *not* consent, that she has, in other words, real consent to either give or withhold. When she does refuse, she exposes Flint's rhetoric—he never means her to have that real consent—and makes any further conversation between them impossible. That is why their exchanges can end only in violence, silence, or in turning to the reader. Even when she is being most seemingly "dialogic," then, Brent is also exposing and attempting to refuse her categorical disadvantages within the verbal exchange. This refusal of dialogue is continuous with her refusal of consent and is part of her larger effort to avoid all contracts and exchanges in which she is definitionally disadvantaged.

But if Jacobs was so resistant to narrative, dialogic, or contractual exchanges, one might ask, why did she write and publish her story? Surely writing for publication means entry into a whole range of contractual practices, both market and metaphoric. The answer to that very important question lies in two seemingly contradictory but mutually constitutive moments. On the one hand, she suspects that any contract between whites and blacks is an impossible relation, expressed in the precept that "promises made to slaves, though with kind intentions and sincere at the time, depend on many contingencies for their fulfillment" (134). On the other hand, she hopes that contractual exchanges—of all types—will offer some kind of self-empowerment, expressed in her avowal that "never should I know peace till my children were emancipated with all due formalities of law" (138).

For Brent, then, as I believe for us, contracts remain compelling, performatively if not substantively. And there are many good reasons for this. Not only do they represent power, or at least its possibility, but they also represent an ideal of equal and equalizing social and civic relations.[52]

Perhaps it should not be surprising that Jacobs seems, at times, to cling to contracts. She is, as I have suggested, at a terrible impasse. Narration fails her as a mode of social transformation, yet remains one of her few available tools. Contracts fail to alter her status or provide her real freedom, yet they remain her only meaningful hope for both protection and change.

Where does this leave us as readers and critics, particularly if we turn to this text, as I believe we still should, as an exemplar of resistance and rebellion? We seem to have little in our critical repertoire that could ameliorate this impasse. We could, of course, argue that Brent's ambivalence about narrative, writing, and dialogue is only a feature of her particular historical situation and that better, more sympathetic readers would render it superfluous. But given the extent to which Jacobs parodies—even as she seems to invite—the collapse of ideal and implied readers, this solution risks obscuring the tragic conditions which make Jacobs ambivalent and wary in the first place. Although Brent does eventually get out of her miserable attic hideaway, Jacobs does not escape the impasse this narrative so brilliantly renders. And that is the narrative's point. Her inability to do so suggests that we take further—or future—action on her behalf.

Brent's efforts to avoid consenting to or participating in her own nearly overwhelming disempowerment lead her to refusals of engagement or contract which can look like passivity, like an unwillingness to fight back. But what counts as fighting back is partly what's at stake here. And many forms of "verbal battle," we must remember, insofar as they are already coded as juridical and attestory, are objects of Brent's rebellion rather than its tools. One of the costs of refusing to consent and of trying to place limits on the universality of contract may be this high a degree of self-constriction and restraint, a self-constraint, in this case, as deliberately, if as tragically, chosen as the garret in which she imprisoned herself.

II

THE EROTICS
OF TALK

The fight for Eros is the political *fight.*

—Herbert Marcuse

We need an erotics of art.

—Susan Sontag

Seduction is often carried on by means of erotic talk.

—Jane Gallop

3

Girl Talk: *Jane Eyre* and the Romance of Women's Narration

we talk, I believe, all day long . . .[1]

—Jane Eyre

a cult text of feminism . . .[2]

—Gayatri Spivak

"Speak I Must"

If freedom for Linda Brent means freedom from having to give an account of herself, it would seem to mean the opposite for Jane Eyre. From childhood on, Jane struggles to narrate her own story, to explain and vindicate her life, to exercise her voice and participate in the "joyous conversational murmur" (198).

The opening pages of the novel dramatize Jane's narrative conditions by immersing her in negations. She is denied activity ("there was no possibility of taking a walk that day"), banished ("dispensed from joining the group"), and muzzled ("'be seated somewhere; and until you can speak pleasantly, remain silent'" (39)). She is told that to argue with Mrs. Reed would be to "cavill" and to "question," the very unpleasant and unnatural behavior with which she has been charged. Understandably, then, Jane feels herself to be "'always suffering, always browbeaten, always accused, forever condemned'" (46).

Yet she talks back. Jane experiences her first moment of self-narration, in conflict with the official version of her life given by Mrs. Reed, as a moment of "un-hoped for liberty," "the first victory I had gained," "the strangest sense of freedom, of triumph, I ever felt" (69). "*Speak* I must," Jane resolves, vowing to Mrs. Reed that

71

I shall remember how you thrust me back—roughly and violently thrust me back—into the red-room, and locked me up there, to my dying day, though I was in agony, though I cried out, while suffocating with distress, "Have mercy! Have mercy, Aunt Reed!" And that punishment you made me suffer because your wicked boy struck me—knocked me down for nothing. I will tell anybody who asks me questions this exact tale. People think you a good woman, but you are bad, hard-hearted. *You* are deceitful! . . . If any one asks me how I liked you, and how you treated me, I will say the very thought of you makes me sick, and that you treated me with miserable cruelty. (69, 68)

In spite of her extreme youth, her habits of quiescence and submission (re-sistance was "a new thing for me," she readily admits (44)), her need to be loved and approved, even if only by her oppressors, Jane stands up for her-self and for fairness.

Is it any wonder, then, that *Jane Eyre* would come to occupy a posi-tion of privilege in the feminist canon,[3] that it would be read as a "revolu-tionary manifesto of the subject,"[4] and that Jane's value as a feminist hero-ine would be "figured in the ability to tell (if not direct) her own story"?[5] The story of Jane's voice, Sandra Gilbert and Susan Gubar have argued, is "a pattern for countless others . . . a story of enclosure and escape . . . of the difficulties Everywoman in a patriarchal society must meet and over-come."[6] Reading Jane's voice as a "challenge [to the] limits on female authority" and "the trope par excellence of power,"[7] a tradition of femi-nist criticism has constructed its romance with *Jane Eyre* by reading it as a model of resistance, not only to "the Victorian conception of woman's place,"[8] but to "women's fate within the symbolic order."[9]

In addition to this politics of voice, however, an erotics of talk also informs—and complicates—the entire novel. *Jane Eyre* is a paradigm of the narrative desire for intimacy and recognition which drives the plots of many women's novels and which is grounded in the insight that human life has a "fundamentally *dialogic* character."[10] In Charles Taylor's words, "discov-ering my own identity doesn't mean that I work it out in isolation, but that I negotiate it through dialogue . . . with others. . . . My own identity cru-cially depends on my dialogical relations with others."[11] When Jane laments her "isolation—this banishment from my kind!" (361), she acknowledges that to be shut out of human dialogue, to be silenced, isolated, and spoken for by others is to be denied identity and being. "Dialogic interaction," Mikhail Bakhtin writes, "is indeed the authentic sphere where language" and therefore the possibility of self-expression "*lives.*"[12]

But even if the structure of all language (and therefore of subjectivity as well) is fundamentally dialogic—because, as Bakhtin would have it, every utterance exists only in relation to other utterances—it does not follow that this dialogic relation is always defined by equality and mutuality or that every exchange makes good on its subject-affirming potential. On the contrary. There is no guarantee that any given utterance will succeed as either self-expressive or other-responsive. Conditions of inequality, in fact, virtually guarantee that it will not. Many women's novels articulate, as I have been showing throughout Part I, a desire for a form of exchange that is always receding, always missing its mark, even as it is always representing itself as possible, as in the case of contracts, for example. What Hans-Georg Gadamer calls a "true conversation," in which neither partner dominates, controls, coerces, or instrumentalizes the other, in which the partners "do not talk at cross purposes,"[13] is an object of narrative desire to the very extent that it is not a feature of everyday lived experience. Mapping this dynamic means locating sites of social failure overwritten by utopian desire.

The texts I discussed in Part I do not anticipate the fulfillment of such desire. Although the heroines of those stories may overcome silence, they do not find apt, let alone ideal, listeners to counteract the coercions and exclusions of the public sphere, conversations that might embody those ideals which the intimate sphere is meant to provide but may not.

The texts I turn to now are not terribly optimistic about such outcomes either. But they are more willing to entertain and imagine what Habermas calls ideal speech situations than are the texts I discuss in Part I. The form this imagination takes—its erotics of talk—ties the image of an ideal listener to the romantic quest for an ideal lover, recasting the classic romantic quest (which conventionally promises a happy ending) *as* a search for just this form of receding, elusive, seemingly impossible completion. When that ideal listener is gendered as another woman, as is the case in differing degrees in all of the three texts I will discuss in this section, the trope of an erotics of talk becomes a way not only to mediate between the different forms of discourse traditionally relegated to the public and private spheres, but also to reflect critically upon the norms and ideologies of heterosexual romance even as the form of romance gives shape to that inquiry.

Romance is double-edged. It requires, as various feminist critics have noted, that women's anxieties about gender inequality be both aroused and allayed. In Janice Radway's words, "romantic fiction originates in the failure of patriarchal culture to satisfy its female members."[14] Therefore, it must interpolate a critique of heterosexual gender norms into its compensatory formula of fulfillment if it is, ultimately, to do the work of normalizing and affirming heterosexuality itself. On this account Jane's longing for an ideal interlocutor is an index of patriarchal culture's failure to meet her needs, not only for intimate recognition, but, as Anthony Giddens suggests, for "free and equal relations" in the public sphere as well.[15] A happy, chatty, satisfying marriage to Rochester apologizes for gender and class inequality by suggesting that even women and poor governesses *can* find "fuflfillment" within the status quo.

It is my contention that Brontë inserts a pause into the inevitable machinery of this compensatory formula, that she both projects and questions this kind of poetic justice. This novel's erotics of talk provokes anxieties about the political and the personal order which are not ultimately allayed by its romantic resolution. In fact, a significant tension is built into what seems, at first blush, a, perhaps *the*, classic happy ending. Jane does provide a model of "voice," as feminist critics have argued, but important discursive desires remain nonetheless unmet.

In distinguishing *Jane Eyre*'s erotics of talk from its politics of voice, I am not recapitulating the long-standing claims for the differences between an American feminism presumed to be politically engaged but theoretically naive, particularly in its search for a "female voice," and a French or post-structuralist feminism presumed to be more alert to female pleasure and the erotic possibilities of language, but unable to account for subversion beyond the discursive realm.[16] Instead, I am interested in how Jane's private search for discursive intimacy and, through it, the novel's invest-ment in an erotics of talk that casts dialogue as mutuality, rather than con-testation or power politics, needs to be mapped against the public quest for a rebellious voice celebrated by most feminist readers of the novel.

In 1967, Kathleen Tillotson argued that *Jane Eyre* "has the least rela-tion to its time" of comparable Victorian novels. It is not, she argued, "a novel of contemporary life . . . such social commentary as it may offer is oblique, limited, incidental. It is both in purpose and effect primarily a novel of the inner life, not of man in his social relations; it maps a private world."[17] But Jane's erotics of talk does map profoundly social desires as well as pri-vate ones. The desire for discursive intimacy which I will be tracing through the trope of an erotics of talk is a map of a public sphere which, like Atlantis, Jane imagines buried beneath the unequal gender, class, and sexual rela-tions of Victorian England.

This vision of intimacy sometimes works against the grain of the novel's more obviously subversive politics of voice as a covert critique of the inad-equacies of social relations in the public sphere. Jane's seemingly private desire, every bit as much as her rebellious public ones, "speaks the language of revo-lution," to borrow Giddens's phrase for how ideas of intimacy encode our responses to transformations in the public sphere.[18] Unlike the contestatory voice of rebellion Jane successfully wields, Brontë's erotics of talk refuses to compensate for the failures of the public sphere. It reaches toward a vision of social relations marked as unrealizable under the forms of social organiza-tion she documents and even, at times, seems to celebrate. A difficult ques-tion, to which I will return at the end of this chapter, has to do with how we might view and understand Jane's evolution into a writer who, like Brontë, must address her narration to that very heterogeneous—and failed—public.

The imperatives of a politics of voice and an erotics of talk are frequently at odds. When Jane says "speak I must" and then vows to tell her own story at whatever cost, she expresses the novel's politics of voice and speaks to the importance of self-articulation and self-determination. When, however, she reports on the quality of her marital bliss, it is an erotics of talk she describes: "we talk, I believe, all day long: to talk to each other is but a more animated and an audible thinking. All my confidence is bestowed on him, all his confidence is devoted to me; we are precisely suited in charac-ter—perfect concord is the result" (476).

Conversation is that "paradise of union" (284) to which Jane aspires. A romance with conversation is at the heart of *Jane Eyre*. "I could never rest in communication with strong, discreet, and refined minds, whether male or female, till I had passed the outworks of conventional reserve, and crossed the threshold of confidence, and won a place by their heart's very hearthstone," Jane confides (400).

Although Jane's disempowered, delegitimated narrative position—"all said I was wicked" (44); "I was silent. Mrs. Reed answered for me" (64)—might reasonably lead her to the same distrust of discourse we have seen Harriet Jacobs exercise, she remains hopeful. Nothing seems to shake her longing to talk, her desire for narrative and story, her belief in the possibilities of exchange. Indeed, while the novel's opening establishes Jane's exclusion from the symbolic order, it also establishes her love of narration, figured in her turning to a book to compensate and console her for being shut out of the family conversation. Thomas Bewick's *History of British Birds* might seem like dull reading for a young girl, but if we were to look at it, we would find, interspersed among its descriptions of birds and their environs, engravings of storm-tossed seas, shipwrecks, rocky promontories, drunken men urinating and vomiting, drownings, lynchings, abandoned graveyards, devils of all sorts, and a variety of monstrous predators: just the sort of thing to excite an under-stimulated imagination. "Each picture told a story," Jane relates; "with Bewick on my knee I was then happy: happy at least in my way" (41).

Jane measures human relationships by a yardstick of narrative exchange. Bessie is loved for her "remarkable knack of narrative" (61) and because sometimes she "told me some of her most enchanting stories" (72). Jane likes Mary Ann Wilson because she "had a turn for narrative" (109). Her cousins, Diana and Mary Rivers, appeal to her not only because they are good-natured and educated, but because "they could always talk; and their discourse, witty, pithy, original, had such charms for me, that I preferred listening to, and sharing in it, to doing anything else" (420). As a governess, Jane feels isolated and lonely at Thornfield because she cannot find companions who are "of a descriptive or narrative turn" (142). Mrs. Fairfax, unfortunately, can neither tell stories nor converse: "there are people who seem to have no notion of sketching a character, of observing and describing salient points, either in persons or things: the good lady evidently belonged to this class; my queries puzzled, but did not draw her out" (136).

Jane is not above trying to squeeze story from a stone. She first encounters Helen Burns reading a book. "I, too, liked reading," Jane remarks, in a masterful instance of understatement.[19] Helen is "sitting on a stone bench" (81) near a "stone tablet" about which Jane has been trying, somewhat unsucessfully, to spin out an interesting story:[20]

> Lowood Institution.—This portion was rebuilt A.D.—by Naomi Brocklehurst, of Brocklehurst Hall, in this county . . . I read these words over and over again. I felt that an explanation belonged to them, and was unable to penetrate their import. (81)

Trying to wrest a conversation from Helen proves nearly as difficult. Helen is as stonily resistant to satisfying Jane's need for narrative as is the tablet: "'You ask rather too many questions,'" Helen tells her. "'I have given you answers enough for the present. Now I want to read'" (83). Jane is sorely disappointed.

Some of the more gothic moments of the novel become most intelligible when viewed through this investment in discursive exchange. When Jane is on the verge of sacrificing herself to St. John's missionary ideals, for example, she is saved by a famous moment of transcendent dialogue with Rochester. "'Jane! Jane! Jane!'" she hears, and answers, "'I am coming. . . . Wait for me! . . . Where are you?'" (445).[21] This moment of romantic mysticism, which changes the direction of Jane's life and ensures not only her survival but also her happiness, is not merely an authorial sleight of hand. It also gives dramatic shape to a tropological conceit that has informed the ethos of the entire novel by providing an "ethical framework for a democratic personal order." "Revelation to the other," Giddens observes, "is a binding aspiration of democratically ordered interaction" because it establishes the "cluster of prerogatives and responsibilities that define agendas of practical activity," "the rights and obligations" which "define what intimacy actually is."[22]

The story Jane tells is not simply the story of her movement from victim to agent, orphan girl to familied heiress, governess to wife; it is also the story of her own longing to talk, to find someone to credit her version of her life, to sympathize with her trials and listen as a friend. It is, ultimately, the story of the growth of a writer, someone who can extend the gesture— or invitation, if you will—of her own, assured voice to an unknown and unpredictable other (the reader). Jane's desire for discursive intimacy is shaped by protest against her place in the social order and by a concomitant vision of social change. When describing why it would grieve her to leave Thornfield, she recounts how conversation with Rochester has compensated for dehumanization and brutalization:

> I grieve to leave Thornfield: I love Thornfield: I love it, because I have lived in it a full and delightful life—momentarily at least. I have not been trampled on. I have not been petrified. I have not been buried with inferior minds, and excluded from every glimpse of communion with what is bright and energetic and high. *I have talked, face to face*, with what I reverence, with what I delight in—with an original, a vigorous, an expanded mind. (281, emphasis mine)

The grammar of this passage is remarkable, particularly in its repeated use of first-person, subject-verb constructions. Reiterated no less than ten times, this repetition of the pronoun "I" dramatizes, as Brenda Silver puts it, that "social discourse [is] necessary for an ontological affirmation of self."[23]

Jane then makes one of the novel's most spectacular declarations of "self," a direct parallel to her childhood resolution "speak I must": "I am not talking to you now through the medium of custom, conventionalities, nor even of mortal flesh: it is my spirit that addresses your spirit; just as if both had passed through the grave, and we stood at God's feet, equal—as we are!" (281) Jane proclaims to Rochester. Just as the declaration "speak I must" embodies the novel's politics of voice, this resolution to talk as equals embodies the "ethical framework" of its erotics of talk.

Celebratory as both of these orations may be and celebrated as they have *been* by generations of feminist readers, they are also represented as utopian, exceptional moments. They are etched with impossibility. When Jane speaks back as a child, her action is underscored as other-worldly: "it seems as if my tongue pronounced words without my will consenting to their utterance: something spoke out of me over which I had no control" (60). "The fact is, I was a trifle beside myself; or rather *out* of myself, as the French would say," Jane coyly confides (44). The imagined world in which she and Rochester can communicate as equals is also represented as an *other* world, beyond life itself: "as if both had passed through the grave." Both outbursts do project the discursive ideals toward which Jane will strive. But such ideals may, nonetheless, be represented by Brontë as substantially unrealizable.

Prevailing feminist paradigms read Jane, in Elaine Showalter's words, as a "heroine of fulfillment."[24] But this reading eclipses the novel's erotics of talk (even if, as I will argue later, it may clandestinely covet and even mimic it by imagining not only that Jane finds her ideal listener/lover but that Brontë does as well—in us). The occlusion of the novel's erotics is important on two counts: first, because Jane's achievement of her discursive ambition is uneven; and second, because Brontë's romantic (and discursive) model is not as strictly (or simply) heterosexual as it may appear.

It is my contention that, as in the case of Jacobs's slave narrative, *Jane Eyre* raises doubts about the workings of poetic justice. Under conditions in which a writer feels that the only—or the best—form in which she can press for justice is in literature, she may look to represent justice in textual terms. Poetic justice, then, internalizes—rather than necessarily challenging—a gap between the literary and the political. *Jane Eyre* also raises related doubts about the possibility of discursive satisfaction for women. Neither celebrating discourse's putative subversiveness nor, conversely, assuming that women are denied all access to discourse can illuminate these doubts.[25] Jane's discursive satisfaction recedes in the novel in part because the demands of speaking out come into conflict with desires for a conflict-free intersubjective exchange: a clash, in short, mapped as one between the novel's politics of voice and its erotics of talk. But the social conditions Jane faces as a speaker also have much to do with why such desires remain utopian. Jane has vowed to liberate herself by telling her story to "anybody who asks me." The problem is that hardly anyone *does* ask. And when they do ask, the request is not often based in the sort of intimacy Jane desires, but in the kind of judgmental, juridical, even tyrannical position that Linda Brent resisted to the point of forgoing (or imagining forgoing) speech and narrative altogether.

"If Any One Asks Me"

Three moments of self-narration, all fairly early in the novel, demonstrate how a practice of successful discursive contestation is no guarantee of intersubjective exchange. Talking back gains Jane little, beyond a sense of personal strength, confidence, and "self-esteem" (55). It does not alter the unequal power relations which must be transformed before a democratizing, subject-affirming dialogue might be achieved. Insofar as equality is both prerequisite to and a measure of the discursive intimacy Jane seeks—"equal as we are"—the failure of that democratization calls into question whatever success may be won by narrative exchange.

Jane's "first and only opportunity of relieving [her] grief by imparting" her tale of "miserable cruelty" comes with Mr. Lloyd, the "good apothecary" who has been called in to see to Jane's health after her confinement in the red room. As so frequently befalls Jane, Bessie insists upon interposing her own official version of events: "I dare say she is crying because she could not go out with missis in the carriage"; "she had a fall" (55). The "shrewd" and "hard-featured yet good-natured" Mr. Lloyd contrives to get Bessie to leave the room with the pretense of reprimanding Jane. "You can go down," he offers to Bessie when the bell for the servants' dinner rings, "I'll give Miss Jane a lecture till you come back" (55). As soon as Bessie has reluctantly retreated downstairs, Mr. Lloyd gives Jane the opportunity to speak: "the fall did not make you ill; what did then?"

The sympathetic Mr. Lloyd invites Jane to talk and he seems to be asking, as Jane hoped someone would, to hear her story. But reassuring as his bedside manner may appear, he nonetheless responds to Jane's account of the "cruel" treatment she suffered when she was "knocked down" and "shut up in a room," by accusing her of being a "baby" and declaring her account "nonsense." She maintains that she has many reasons to be unhappy, and Mr. Lloyd invites her to "tell me some of them." When Jane answers this prompting by trying in her "meagre" and "bungling" way to explain what it is like to be an orphan in a mean-spirited family, Mr. Lloyd counters that she has "a kind aunt and cousins" (56). Insisting that "John Reed knocked me down, and my aunt shut me up in the red-room," she is answered by the rejoinder that Gateshead Hall is "a very beautiful house" and that she ought to feel "very thankful to have such a fine place to live" (56). "It is not my house, sir; and Abbot says I have less right to be here than a servant," Jane essays. "'Pooh!'" he responds, "'you can't be silly enough to wish to leave such a splendid place'" (56).

Jane is indeed "silly" enough to want to leave and Mr. Lloyd, it is implied, is "good" enough to recommend that she be sent away to school. It is his conclusion that "'the child ought to have a change of air and scene.'" Her "'nerves,'" he determines, are "'not in a good state'" (57). Mr. Lloyd cannot grasp that Jane's nerve, her resolve to fight back, and to protect herself is the healthiest thing about her. Mr. Lloyd in effect does "lecture" to Jane after all. Rather than respond to her own perceptions, he treats her as if she is merely "muttering," speaking incoherently, childishly, and foolishly, almost as if she'd been talking to herself.

The second time Jane tells her story she also fails to realize the intimacy she seeks. If anything, it seems to alienate and antagonize her interlocutor. Here, Jane has been debating what she describes as Helen's "doctrine of endurance" (88), countering it with her own ethos of reciprocity, based in the precept that one need only be "good to those who are good to you" (89):

> "If people were always kind and obedient to those who are cruel and unjust, the wicked people would have it all their own way; they would never feel afraid, and so they would never alter, but grow worse and worse." (89–90)

When Jane declares that she "must resist those who punish me unjustly" (90), Helen challenges Jane to explain this "heathen" and "savage" view (90). To explain why it would be "'impossible'" for her to "'love Mrs. Reed'" or "'bless her son John,'" Jane responds by proceeding to "'pour out, in my own way, the tale of my sufferings and resentments'" (90).

Helen's reaction is hardly sympathetic. First, Helen "said nothing" (90). When Jane presses a response, Helen replies that Jane misunderstands Mrs. Reed's attempts to help her—"'she dislikes your cast of character, as Miss Scatcherd does mine'" (90). Life is "'too short to be spent nursing animosity, or registering wrongs,'" she tells Jane (90). It is better to think of eternal rest than to fret over earthly injustice. With that, Helen stops talking altogether to "converse with her own thought" instead (91), just as earlier she stopped talking with Jane to read.

Telling her story to Helen has failed to provide Jane with either an "ontological affirmation of self," as Silver puts it, or a democratized mirror of the public sphere. It does not win her a place by the "heart's very hearthstone." Indeed, Helen chides Jane for her desire for intimacy after Jane confesses that "'to gain some real affection'" she would "'willingly submit to have the bone of my arm broken, or to let a bull toss me, or to stand behind a kicking horse, and let it dash its hoof at my chest—'" (101). "'Hush, Jane!'" is Helen's disgusted retort, "'you think too much of the love of human beings'" (101).

When Jane next attempts to win both justice and "real affection" with her story, the hazards of this double imperative become even clearer. Once again her self-narration has a good outcome practically, but it fails to provide the emotional intimacy Jane seeks. Following Mr. Brocklehurst's decision to banish her from sociality and his admonition to her classmates to "'avoid her company, exclude her from your sports, shut her out from your converse'" (98), Miss Temple invites Jane to defend herself:

> "Well, now, Jane, you know, or at least I will tell you, that when a criminal is accused, he is always allowed to speak in his own defence. You have been charged with falsehood; defend yourself to me as well as you can." (102)

Jane's defense is to tell "all the story of my sad childhood" (103). And her efforts are rewarded by Miss Temple's declaration that "'to me, Jane, you are clear now'" (103).

Two things complicate Jane's apparent success. First, Miss Temple requires outside corroboration before she will clear Jane formally: "'if [Mr. Lloyd's] reply agrees with your statement, you shall be publicly cleared from every imputation,'" she promises (103). Second, and more important, the intimacy which follows from this exchange occurs not between Miss Temple and Jane but chiefly between Miss Temple and Helen Burns. In Miss Temple's embrace, Helen's nearness, and the "feast" which Miss Temple improvises, Jane does receive some of the nourishing contact she has been seeking. But she spends most of the evening as a listener, observing "a conversation [which] followed between [Miss Temple] and Helen, which it was indeed a privilege to be admitted to hear" (105).

It is Helen, not Jane, who finds her voice and becomes a speaker in a scene remarkable for the passionate overtones of Miss Temple and Helen's relationship and for Jane's sense of eavesdropping on such passion:

> They conversed of things I had never heard of: of nations and times past; of countries far away; of secrets of nature discovered or guessed at: they spoke of books: how many they had read! What stores of knowledge they possessed! Then they seemed so familiar with French and French authors. . . . Miss Temple asked Helen if she sometimes snatched a moment to recall the Latin her father had taught her, and, taking a book from a shelf, bade her read and construe a page of Virgil. . . . The bell announced bedtime; no delay could be admitted; Miss Temple embraced us both. . . . Helen she held a little longer than me; she let her go more reluctantly. It was Helen her eye followed to the door; it was for her she a second time breathed a sad sigh; for her she wiped a tear from her cheek. (105)

Miss Temple's weeping ostensibly has to do with her awareness of Helen's impending death. But we could hardly ask for a more vivid picture of the erotics of talk than the fervor in which Helen's transformed beauty—"a beauty neither of fine colour nor long eyelash, nor pencilled brow, but of meaning, of movement, of radiance" (105)—is generated by yearning and Miss Temple's sighs and tears by pining and desire. Jane has "passed the outworks of conventional reserve" and rendered her own version of her life. While her storytelling makes her a witness to "real affection," it still does not bring her to the "heart's very hearthstone."

Perhaps it is unreasonable on Jane's part, as Michel Foucault might suggest, to look for intimacy under juridical conditions. Insofar as her story is adduced as attestation by those with more power and narrative authority than she herself possesses, Jane is positioned disadvantageously, much as Linda Brent is in Harriet Jacobs's *Incidents in the Life of a Slave Girl*.[26] Indeed, published only two years after Frederick Douglass's influential *Narrative of the Life of Frederick Douglass, an American Slave, Written by Himself* appeared, *Jane Eyre* often bears striking resemblance to slave narratives, from its use of "Currer Bell's" reassuring preface, a direct parallel to Lydia Maria Child's authenticating preface for Jacobs's account or William Lloyd Garrison and Wendell Phillips's endorsements of Frederick

Douglass's story, to the various and subtle mechanisms Jane must deploy to try to win her reader's trust and to earn herself the stamp of reliability. She also faces a similar challenge to that faced by slave narrators: not only to gain legitimacy and authority as a speaker, but also to locate a competent, legitimate, and qualified audience, an audience with whom it would be possible to satisfy the imperatives of "true conversation."[27] "Jane's progress in the novel," as Rosemarie Bodenheimer writes, "has to do with finding a fit audience for whom she can give a proper shape to her own story."[28]

Jane, interestingly enough, seems not to view the double imperative of self-defense and intimacy as necessarily at odds, as Linda Brent, the narrator of "The Yellow Wallpaper," or Minnie Foster of "A Jury of Her Peers" clearly do. Indeed, where Linda Brent resists being forced to tell her story under conditions of inequality, and the narrator of "The Yellow Wallpaper," the princess of "The Blank Page," or Minnie Foster all elect not even to try, Jane welcomes opportunities to defend herself as chances to seduce, perhaps even to create, an ideal and sympathetic listener. Where Linda Brent and others recoil from conflicts with superordinates, Jane craves their recognition and hence embraces contestation.

In this context I want to advance an alternative reading of what is probably, among feminist critics at least, the novel's most frequently cited passage:

> Anybody may blame me who likes, when I add further that . . . I longed for a power of vision which might . . . reach the busy world, towns, regions full of life I had heard of but never seen; that then I desired more of practical experience than I possessed; more of intercourse with my kind . . . it is in vain to say human beings ought to be satisfied with tranquility: they must have action; and they will make it if they cannot find it. Millions are condemned to a stiller doom than mine, and millions are in silent revolt against their lot. . . . Women are supposed to be very calm generally: but women feel just as men feel; they need exercise for their faculties and a field for their efforts. (140–41)

Beginning with Virginia Woolf, feminists have turned to this speech to analyze Jane's revolt against "stagnation," and her plea for a wider life than "making puddings and knitting stockings . . . playing on the piano and embroidering bags" (141). "What are they blaming Charlotte Brontë for?" Woolf asks.[29] For seeking, in Jane's own words, to "do more or learn more than custom has pronounced necessary for their sex" (141).

This passage is often read as unprecedented in Jane's story, a sudden eruption of a dissatisfaction for which neither the reader nor Jane has been been particularly well prepared. But it is anything but anomalous. The outburst is impelled by the same imperatives which have motivated her since childhood. The "restlessness" which "agitated [her] to pain sometimes" is, as the grievances which bracket this speech make clear, her unsatisfied desire for a "fit audience," her need for a place within "the joyous conversational murmur." In the preceding chapter, Jane has been complaining of people who cannot sustain a conversation or tell a story, "people who seem to have no notion of sketching a character, or observing and describing salient points, either in persons or things" (136). She returns to this earlier complaint immediately after presenting her "manifesto," noting that "I made some attempts to draw . . . [Grace Poole] into conversation, but she seemed a person of few words: a monosyllabic reply usually cut short every effort of that sort" (142). Sophie, she adds, "was not of a descriptive or narrative turn [either], and generally gave such vapid and confused answers as were calculated rather to check than encourage inquiry" (142).

Jane's bold statement that "anybody may blame me who likes" is not simply an assertion of moral autonomy. It is a plea for an interlocutor and, as such, it parallels her own (and Brontë's) act of writing: gesturing to a future listener who, it is hoped, might be able to hear. By beginning defensively, Jane suggests that she would prefer an argument to continued "isolation." This is not, like James's Mrs. Farrinder, a preference for argument over conversation. But it is a preference for contact over loneliness. Far from unprecedented, this speech is part and parcel of Jane's ongoing willingness, as described to Helen Burns, to suffer virtually anything to "gain some real affection."

If, however, this "manifesto" is Jane's call, from whom, if anyone, does Jane's response come? Two candidates immediately present themselves. As ofen occurs when she is "thus alone," Jane's speech is answered by Bertha's "eccentric murmurs," which fascinate her but which she cannot meaningfully decipher.

And Rochester appears, only a page or so after Jane's speech, heralded by "a rude noise" and "a positive tramp, tramp" (143). There is much to suggest that he and not Bertha with her wild, childlike muttering is the answer to Jane's call for "intercourse with my kind." His arrival brings a "rill from the outer world flowing through" the house (150). He predicts that Jane will be "natural" with him and remarks that he finds it "impossible" to be conventional with her (170). Their earliest conversations establish a link between discourse and desire as Rochester reflects on the pleasure (his pleasure at least) of good talk: "'I ought to be at liberty to attend to my own pleasure. Miss Eyre, draw your chair . . . a little farther forward'" (161).

Rochester and Jane's romance is, in many ways, the chronicle of a seductive discourse, beginning with their first real conversation in which Rochester teases Jane about being a fairy and Jane pretends to take him seriously, "speaking as seriously as he had done" (154). Jane sums up the erotic quality of their teasing, poetic, mock-combative repartee when she states, "I knew the pleasure of vexing and soothing him by turns; it was one I chiefly delighted in . . . on the extreme brink I liked well to try my skill" (187). Indeed, Rochester and Jane are so bound up in seductive discourse, in the seductiveness *of* discourse, that it is hardly hyperbolic for Rochester to proclaim, as he does toward the end of the novel, that everything that matters to him in the world is "concentrated in my Jane's tongue to my ear" (464).

This expression positions Rochester as listener and Jane as narrator. While it is true that the ending of the novel seems to wrest narrative control away from him and hand it to her by ensuring that he "cannot read or write much" anymore (476),[30] Jane is usually positioned inside the story she tells *not* as narrator (and thus "a heroine of fulfillment") but as Rochester's narratee.

Although Jane *seeks* fulfillment through conversation with Rochester, what she finds is considerably more complicated and constrained. Feminist paradigms for reading this novel have, in the main, presumed that Jane's desires as a speaker are fulfilled with Rochester and that her (and Brontë's) desires as a writer are fulfilled with us. In what follows I am going to question both premises. While Brontë does indeed create a narrator who delights in narrative and, as almost every reader of *Jane Eyre* observes, offers extraordinary narrative delights, that narrator's struggle is not wholly successful.

"The Eagerness of a Listener"

Rochester poses as a gypsy to tell his guests their own stories. When Jane appears before him, the last of the women in the house to do so, she warns the "old Crone" that she has no "faith." Distinguishing herself from gossip-loving women with the caustic comment that "the eagerness of a listener quickens the tongue of a narrator" (228), she suggests her own indifference to having her fortune told.[31] Rochester, nonetheless, is quick to tell her that she is "cold" because "alone," "sick, because the best of feelings, the highest and sweetest given to man," is kept from her, and "silly, because, suffer as you may, you will not beckon it to approach, nor will you stir one step to meet it where it waits for you" (226).

This is hardly the first time that Jane has been in the uncomfortable position of listening to others narrate her story. Rochester frequently tells Jane her own story, depicting himself as a "master-wave" who will preserve her from being "dashed to atoms on crag points" (173) or depicting Jane as a "curious sort of bird . . . a vivid resolute captive" needing to be set free (170). As Mary Poovey observes, "Rochester's most serious transgression has been to usurp Jane's control over what is, after all, primarily her story."[32]

Rosemarie Bodenheimer has noted that "much of the drama in the Gateshead section of the novel is created through the tension between Jane's—and our—listening in outraged silence to the versions of her offered by members of the Reed household, and Jane's explosive outbreaks into speech."[33] But instances of such usurpation are legion, and they are by no means perpetrated only in that section or only by Rochester. Jane overhears her own family "narrative" as told by Mrs. Abbot to Bessie (58). She is the subject of an hour-long "homily" by Bessie proving "beyond a doubt that I was the most wicked and abandoned child ever reared under a roof" (60). Rosamond Oliver wants to rewrite Jane's life story—which she has not heard—as a "delightful romance" (394). The inkeeper near Thornfield insists, over Jane's protestations, on telling her a story of "a young lady, a governess at the Hall, that Mr. Rochester fell in [love with]," (451). And St. John Rivers, who speaks of his "impatience to hear the sequel of [Jane's] tale," decides that it is better to tell it himself: "on reflection, I find the matter will be better managed by my assuming the narrator's part, and converting you into a listener" (405).

Jane sets out to *find* an ideal listener, but she seems forced to settle, instead, for *being* one, being, as Rochester remarks a number of times, an "eager" listener:

> "Know that in the course of your life you will often find yourself elected the involuntary confidante of your acquaintances' secrets: people will instinctively find out, as I have done, that it is not your forte to tell of yourself, but to listen while others talk of themselves; they will feel, too, that you listen with no malevolent scorn of their indiscretion, but with a kind of innate sympathy, not the less comforting and encouraging because it is very unobtrusive in its manifestations." (167)

When he "tramps" into the novel, Rochester seems positioned to provide Jane with the opportunity to be a voluntary narrator rather than an involuntary confidante. Instead, however, he takes his "own pleasure" in discourse with Jane, making her, once again, the involuntary, eager, sympathetic, and comforting listener she has so often been before. "I, indeed, talked comparatively little, but I heard him talk with relish," Jane says (177), in a statement that might well sum up both the imbalances of their conversational exchange and the gender expectations that feminist sociolinguists have shown to be traditionally imposed upon women as men's conversational partners.

Jane maintains that she listens to Rochester with "relish," and that she had "a keen delight" in hearing his ideas and stories (176). But his talking is described as *his* cure and *his* redemption. Jane's listening is the agent of *his* pleasure and *his* refreshment: "'The more you and I converse,'" he maintains, "'the better; for while I cannot blight you, you may refresh me'" (175). Rochester's disposition to confess his life to Jane demonstrates Michel Foucault's insight that a sense of redemption and therapeutic cure accrue to confession: "spoken in time, to the proper party, and by the person who was both the bearer of it and the one responsible for it, the truth healed."[34] Rochester's restorative "right to get pleasure out of life," to "get sweet, fresh pleasure . . . as sweet and fresh as the wild honey the bee gathers on the moor" (167) drives the discursive dynamics between himself and Jane.

He tells her his life story twice, both times in an effort to redeem and heal himself. First, telling her the story of his affair with Céline Varens, he argues that keeping Adele, "that French floweret," was his way of "expiating numerous sins, great or small, by one good work" (171). Second, telling her the story of his marriage to Bertha Mason, he attempts to convince Jane that "'it would not be wicked to love me'" (343). "'Can you listen to me?'" he begins (332), then launches an exposition on why he is "'not married'" but "'free to love and be loved'" (331, 337). Explaining how he was tricked into marrying Bertha Mason, he describes how her growing madness soon ensured that "'kindly conversation could not be sustained between'" them (332). This gives him the "right," he argues, "to deliver" himself from the "hell[ish]" "pit" of his life, a "right," in short, to marital "pleasure."

In spite of the many differences between Rochester and Jane, the "hell[ish] pit" of his life resonates with hers. Jane, of course, has not married a sensual West Indian woman for her money, found their sensibilities incompatible, declared her insane, and locked her up in an attic. But Rochester's life, like Jane's, is hellish because it lacks "kindly conversation." When he asks Jane, "'can you listen to me?'"—having already established Jane's skill as a consummate listener, "'made to be the recipient of secrets'" (174)—this is no idle question. It is his hope of "pleasure" and of cure. His desire, in turn, is rooted in her willingness to play the "eager listener."

Rochester's narrative, however, fails to convince Jane of his "right to pleasure." She does not forget the basic inequalities of class and gender that divide them. She is convinced, rightly, the novel suggests, that if she were to "become the successor of these poor girls [his three former mistresses], he would one day regard me with the same feeling which now in his mind desecrated their memory" (339). Under conditions of inequality, Rochester has no more "right" to the conversational pleasure he desires than Jane has reason to expect a self-affirming dialogue where equality is not the rule.

While Rochester tells his story without the success he seeks, Jane never does tell her story in its entirety, except to "the Reader." In the final scene of the novel, which reconciles the lovers after Bertha's death and provides for their symbolic parity through Rochester's injuries and Jane's inheritance, Jane withholds her own story. "I listened to Mr. Rochester's narrative but made no disclosure in return," she states (472).

This is startling. Jane is still a listener, even when it seems no longer necessary, even when she has seemingly unlimited access to narrative control, even when she has a more than willing audience for her story. Brontë might easily have written: "Reader, ascertaining that my tale would no longer be insupportable to Mr. Rochester's weakened nerves, I poured out my story to him." But she didn't. "The act of witholding," as Bodenheimer puts it, is "curiously stressed at the end of the novel. . . . [Brontë] makes a special point of telling us that Jane withholds."[35] Jane, neither then nor later, indulges in the redemptive performance of self-disclosure. Why *doesn't* Jane tell Rochester her story? Why does she only tell it to her unknown "Reader" instead?

The novel offers us a fascinating and complex puzzle. We have a character who tells a story about struggling to use her voice. But the voice in which she tells that tale, as I will argue later, seems to bear no traces of that struggle. On the contrary, it addresses its unknown, heterogeneous public with remarkable grace, self-confidence, and strength. It is a supremely seductive voice. Jane's decision not to tell her story to Rochester has to do with her own complex, perhaps even contradictory criteria for what constitutes an ideal listener. On the one hand, Jane desires a listener/lover unlike herself. On the other hand, she seems able to speak only to a listener/lover with whom she can identify. This pull-and-tug—Jane's embodiment of the dialectic of identification and desire I discussed at the end of Chapter One—takes shape in a longing for "kinship" that ultimately applies to both.

"To Pine After Kindred"

Jane's longing for "kinship" is a complex one. It speaks to a number of different—and not necessarily reconcilable—desires and it has important political corrollaries. Recently, a number of feminist critics have drawn attention away from Jane's voice as a paradigm of resistance to focus on Brontë's deployment of national, colonial, imperial, and race narratives in constructing Bertha as Jane's "other." A politics of sameness, they argue, underlies this novel's seemingly egalitarian message. Questions of justice and rights, even implicitly of humanity, are germane only to those already like us, a likeness which can be read in both racial and national terms. Gayatri Spivak, in the most frequently cited of these recent essays, reads *Jane Eyre* as a central text in the construction of British national identity through the (fictively) necessary sacrifice of Bertha Mason, "an allegory of the general epistemic violence of imperialism, the construction of a self-immolating colonial subject for the glorification of the social mission of the colonizer."[36] Susan Meyer, similarly, reads *Jane Eyre* as questioning but ultimately reaffirming imperialist ideology through the construction—and ultimate destruction—of Bertha, whose race Meyer reads as ambiguously coded.[37]

What I want to suggest is that "coercive construction of likeness"[38] applies not only to the novel's politics of nation and race. It saturates Brontë's politics of gender, determines the possibilities for an erotics of talk, and, perhaps paradoxically, serves to enable a critique of the ideology of love and romance launched from well inside the boundaries *of* that very ideology. For Jane to be fulfilled through discourse—becoming as much a narrator as she has been a listener and affirming through that reflexivity what Giddens calls a degree of "ontological security"[39]—would not only codify romantic ideology and its convention of happy endings, but also complicate the very terms by which romance performs its cultural work of shoring up heterosexuality and an oppressive social order.

First, as I have already noted, the novel's erotics of talk decrees Jane's shift from *being* an ideal listener to *having* one, a shift which entails parity between narrator and narratee. But this equality does not mean a mere parity of power, or money, or class privilege. If such redistribution were enough to resolve Jane's dissatisfactions, Rochester's symbolic cripplings would be unnecessary; Jane's newfound family connections and inheritance would have sufficed to recalibrate their status. Prerequisite to Jane's romantic fulfillment is sameness, or as Jane puts it, "likeness" as well.

Second, the logic of a heterosexual romantic resolution of contradictions and differences would seem to be at odds with a desire for "likeness" and sameness.[40] Jane certainly represents it as such in a debate with St. John Rivers over various routes to "domestic happiness" (413). "Marry! I don't want to marry, and never shall marry," Jane asserts. Instead, "kindred . . . the craving I have for fraternal and sisterly love" (413) emerges as central to Jane's discourse of desire. "I do not want a stranger," Jane declares, "unsympathizing, alien, different from me; I want my kindred: those with whom I have full fellow-feeling" (413).

But marriage per se is not represented as inimical to this "intercourse with my kind." Far from representing the converse of such kinship, her love for Rochester appears to Jane as its very embodiment, reinforcing the democratizing impulses of intimacy:

> . . . "he is not of their kind. I believe he is of mine—I am sure he is—I feel akin to him—I understand the language of his countenance and movements: though rank and wealth sever us widely, I have something in my brain and heart, in my blood and nerves that assimilates me mentally to him . . . while I breathe and think, I must love him." (204)

Because Rochester "felt at times as if he were my relation rather than my master," Jane maintains, "I ceased to pine after kindred" (177).

Similarly, Rochester's language of love is peppered with assertions of kinship and likeness. "'Are you anything akin to me, do you think, Jane?'" he asks, just before proposing. "'My equal is here, and my likeness. Jane, will you marry me?'" (282). Rochester's language of love carries Jane's discourse of equality and kinship one step further. Making explicit what is only implicit in why Jane "must" love Rochester, Rochester recasts love of the other as self-love and sexuality as an erotics of likeness, a love of the same, in Irigaray's term, a "ho(m)mo-sexuality".[41] "'You—you strange, you almost earthly thing!—I love you as my own flesh'" (283), he proclaims.

In one sense, of course, this language of kinship is neither peculiar nor unique. Such an ethos and eros of "merger" merely articulates romance conventions adapted from religion and common to romance mythology. An idealist tradition of romantic love, as Irving Singer has shown, represents romance as the remedy for a permanent state of human loneliness by positing that

> the lovers are one and in some sense always have been. Throughout all possible separations, and despite the blind interference of external forces, they are really indissoluble. . . . In finding the beloved, each lover discovers the hidden reality which is himself [*sic*]. In this sense, the lovers have always been united, despite their physical separation, for they have always shared the same self-definition.[42]

The demand that Rochester be "like" Jane is embodied most forcefully (and violently) in the poetically just final accident that blinds and maims him, injuries which virtually all critics writing on the novel have agreed are feminizing wounds.[43] This feminization of Rochester challenges (or

compensates for) the differences of power and authority inscribed into gender inequality and, more important, suggests that a viable "ethical framework
for a democratic personal order" must include not just gender parity but
gender symmetry. For Rochester to be a good mate—and a potential listener—within the logic of this novel, he must be, in effect, a good sister, not
"unsympathetic and alien." By rewriting romance codes rather than aban-
doning the schema of romance altogether, Brontë is able to uphold romance
ideology in the face of the manifest inequalities of Victorian gender arrangements, to provide a happy ending for her romantic heroine even as she "writes
beyond" the formula of romantic resolution.[44] Rochester's transformation
into a good sister is what in Chapter One I called a heterocritical use of
romance conventions: critical of them, but critical from a vantage point located
firmly within heterosexual ideology and even within romantic idealism itself.
Romance is salvaged by being rerouted through a complex dynamic of voice
and conversation, one that ultimately, I want to show, is deeply invested in
romantic idealism. *Jane Eyre* offers a strong dose of poetic justice, in other
words, but the stress may be as much on "poetic" as it is on "justice." However much *Jane Eyre* offers the formulaic happy ending, a critique of romance
ideology also underlies the novel's particular economy of rewards.

   Nowhere is Brontë's hetero*critical* romance ideology more apparent
than in the demand that her romantic heroine be a subject and not merely
an object of male desire, that her subjectivity be constituted and not merely
constrained. The question is whether or not Jane's romance with Rochester plays into those ideals or cuts against them.

   It is hard to overstate the consensus of critical opinion which takes for
granted, following Jane's own descriptions of "pleasure," "perfect concord,"
and "reward" (476, 470), that Rochester embodies Jane's "true source of
earthly happiness."[45] In fact, however, Jane's most compelling description
of ideal human interaction and satisfaction of her desires for contact is offered
not in terms of Rochester, but, rather remarkably, in terms of her exchanges
with Diana and Mary Rivers, exchanges that recall Jane's friendship with
Helen Burns and with Miss Temple. Diana and Mary fulfill "the craving I
have for fraternal and sisterly love," she declares (413). They provide the
"delicious pleasure" (413) of "genial affections," "mutual happiness,"
"intimacy," the "full satisfaction" of "mutual affection—of the strongest
kind" (411, 377).

   In one of the most telling passages of the novel, Jane describes the
"unusual pleasure" (379) she secures from being able to "converse" with
Diana and Mary:

> There was a reviving pleasure in this intercourse, of a kind now tasted by me
> *for the first time*, the pleasure arising from perfect congeniality of tastes, sen-
> timents, and principles. . . . thought fitted thought: opinion met opinion: we
> coincided, in short, perfectly. (376–77, emphasis mine)

   That she experiences the curative, redemptive powers of talk only with
Diana and Mary is an interesting twist in a love story where seductive talk

unites the lovers. For Jane to find this pleasure not with her lover but with her symbolic sisters instead seems to question or complicate the (hetero) sexual contract underlying romantic fiction.[46]

When Jane leaves Diana and Mary, then, to answer Rochester's "telepathic" call, is she merely capitulating to the "sororophobic"[47] terms of the heterosexual romantic contract? Is Brontë's chief impulse, as Terry Eagleton maintains, "to negotiate passionate self-fulfillment on terms which preserve the social and moral conventions intact"?[48] Although Jane discovers "intellectual reciprocity" with Diana and Mary as opposed to "the authoritarian context of the master-student relationship she had with Rochester,"[49] is Brontë's vision, finally, as Elaine Showalter has maintained, a "world without female solidarity, where women in fact police each other on behalf of patriarchal tyranny"?[50] In making Helen (by death), Miss Temple (by marriage), and finally Diana and Mary (by convention) impossible objects of Jane's desire, does Brontë accept that feminization, as Luce Irigaray puts it, requires sororal repudiation?

> What exhilarating pleasure it is to be partnered with someone like oneself, with a sister, in everyday terms. . . . What need, attraction, passion, one feels for someone, for some woman, like oneself. . . . But the need, the charm felt for one's like will be repressed, denied, turned into their opposites in what is labeled "normal femininity."[51]

Does Jane, as Jean Wyatt has maintained, give up "the community at Moor House, which includes everything but romance, to return to Rochester and the fulfillments of passionate love,"[52] just as she had earlier elided the possibility of kinship with Bertha? Does she need to trade off identification against desire?

If we read Jane's return to Rochester as surpassing the "exhilarating pleasure" of kinship and mutual exchange she experienced with Diana and Mary, then, I believe, we would have to conclude that Brontë does harness romantic idealism to the task of enforcing "compulsory heterosexuality."[53] We know that Jane and Rochester talk "all day long," that Rochester "cannot read or write much" and that Jane describes feeling "a pleasure in my services, most full, most exquisite" (476). This would seem to suggest that if talking to Diana and Mary is a pleasure Jane experienced "for the first time," it is one which ultimately—if not to mention "all day long"—properly pertains to life with Rochester.

But the meaning of this is complicated by what Brontë does to problematize Rochester's gender identity. If "romance," as Cora Kaplan argues, "tends to represent sexual difference as natural and fixed,"[54] Brontë undermines this fixity by transgendering Rochester: both in the final scene of the novel and in his pose as a gypsy fortune teller. What does it mean that the lovers establish an "ethical framework for a democratic social order" through their talk only once Rochester is wounded and symbolically transformed? The central ambiguity by which Rochester becomes Jane's ideal listener/lover by virtue of both his difference—sexual and class—and the likeness to Jane he increasingly attains is crucial to the novel's working out of a romantic solution that is also a critique of romance.

To make matters even more complicated, Jane still holds back, even after Rochester's symbolic transformations. Jane refuses to position Rochester as her ideal interlocutor: "I listened to Mr. Rochester's narrative, but made no disclosure in return." While Bodenheimer claims that in marrying Rochester Jane "has acquired an endless supply of audience,"[55] and while Rochester seems certainly apt if not truly ideal at this point, Jane has apparently yet to achieve that completely "fit" listener she longs for.[56] How can we explain, in this most paradigmatic of romantic stories, the apparent failure of Jane's overwhelming desire? And why, having suggested that failure, does the novel seem at such pains to mask it by assuring us that Rochester and Jane do talk all day long?

To make sense of this logic, we must set aside the requirement that Jane be a (or our) "heroine of fulfillment." Insofar as her refusal to tell Rochester her story tempers the bliss of their reconciliation, Brontë is able to suggest that patriarchal, Victorian, British culture—like the racist, patriarchal culture of the antebellum South portrayed by Jacobs—*cannot* provide complete fulfillment or satisfaction for a woman such as Jane. Although Jane's ostensible reason for withholding part of her narrative is a wish to spare Rochester "unnecessary pain" (465) from things "too awful and inexplicable to be communicated or discussed" (472), ending the novel with Jane's story still untold (to Rochester) and, importantly, still unsolicited *by* him in any very insistent way, subtly resists the compensatory, apologetic machinery of romantic idealism.

The tension between a realized politics of voice and a utopian erotics of talk is grounded in two competing—even contradictory—paradigms of identity and desire. Insofar as they prove irreconcilable, the hope of meeting the double imperatives of voice to which Jane is impelled must, necessarily, be qualified.

On the one hand, Jane is able to demonstrate the efficacy of speaking up and talking back—"speak I must"—because she never loses faith in the transformational potential of human beings, in the ability of people to be changed by one another's point of view, in the usefulness of trying to show the "wicked people" why they should not "have it all their own way," because she never loses faith in rhetoric, we might say. Rochester's partial transformation from being a domineering, overpowering, possessive, and preemptory "master" to a "dependent," "powerless," "repentant," and tearful "Edward" is testimony to this potential for personal change, as is Miss Temple's changed opinion of Jane and Mrs. Reed's contrition at keeping Jane ignorant of her own family ties and inheritance. Behind this faith, and animating the actions Jane takes on its behalf, is a hypothesis that identity is mutable, constructed, and, potentially at least, fluid and transformable.

On the other hand, Jane's overwhelming need for "kindred," her inability to satisfy her craving for affection and talk with anyone other than a (symbolic) sister, suggests an essential—rather than a transformational or constructionist—model of identity.[57] If a politics of voice—"the trope par excellence of power," the challenge to "woman's place" and her "fate within the symbolic order"—can be exercised, given a certain personal boldness, regardless of one's relative disadvantages and lack of social power, an erotics of talk seems to require a different set of rules. Rochester, who partly satisfies both imperatives, was always "akin" to Jane. His injuries corporealize what was an essential (if provisional) sameness all along. Brontë, it seems to me, is staging her own ambivalence about the possibilities—and the outcomes—of speaking across difference, an ambivalence which, at some register, must register with us as well.

Feelings of true kinship cannot easily be acquired, as Jane has learned from St. John Rivers's inability to impede the encroachment of "little chilling differences" after Jane is first nominally and then actually "acknowledged his kinswoman," his inability to meet Jane's request for "more affection than the sort of general philanthropy you extend to mere strangers" (437). The difference between St. John and Rochester—a difference which makes the thought of sex with St. John repulsive and conversation with him an infinite regress of misunderstanding, "offence," and failure (438), with "no yearning after reconciliation" (436)—is the fact of difference itself. Jane can argue with St. John, but their fundamental—essential—differences of character and view will never, it is implied, allow for harmony or love. Jane can take "a pleasure in [her] service [to Rochester], most full, most exquisite" (476), but cannot "love [her] servitude" to St. John Rivers (423), because to wait on Rochester is, also in the strong sense, to serve her own self. He is different, in other words, but not too much so. As much as Jane may desire recognition that can cut across difference, Brontë is unsure, I'd suggest, of its potential.

This makes the story Jane withholds from Rochester all the more ironic. That story—"too awful and inexplicable to be communicated or discussed" (472), the story of their mystical, other-worldly exchange—is a story about utopian conversational exchange. It is the story of speaking to and hearing one another, in spite of differences not only in age, class, gender, and station, but in geography, betrayal, and deceit as well. It is not just her own story that Jane refuses to disclose to Rochester, but an image of conversational "bliss" that can transcend any boundary—psychological, social, or material, the very image which shapes the narrative desire of the novel.

We recognize this narrative desire because Jane does not, as she claims, keep "these things" to herself only to "ponder them in [her] heart" (472). Jane narrates "these things" for the reader, making clear, as she does so, that these are "things" no one else has been deemed fit to hear.

"Jane's Tongue to My Ear"

Are we to understand, then, that we—as readers—are the fit audience for whom Jane, and perhaps Brontë by implication, has longed? Are we to understand, then, that we are somehow more "akin" to Jane than anyone else? Precisely this assumption, I propose, has led not only to this novel's place of privilege in the feminist canon—Brontë's politics of voice alone could explain this—but to the particular romance which feminist criticism has long entertained with this text, what Adrienne Rich has described as its "special force and survival value" for women readers, the "sense that it contains," Rich wrote, reflecting on decades of rereading the novel, "some nourishment I needed then and still need."[58] This assumption has been made, as I want to suggest in this closing section, in spite of the fact that Brontë genders "the Reader" as male, positions this reader as a "judge" by representing Jane's discourse with this reader as a story wrenched from her not by affection or intimacy, but in consequence of some moral or personal censure. Something about the quality of Jane's voice provides generations of readers with a pleasure often experienced—akin to Rochester's own—as curative, redemptive, exhilarating, erotic, and essential.

The novel is not only about the political imperatives and erotic pleasures of talk, it also provides an erotically charged, politically resonant experience of talk which seems to offer many feminist readers just the pleasures of conversation Jane has sought.

Numerous readers describe the pleasure of reading *Jane Eyre* in nostalgic terms which directly evoke what many of us may remember as "girl talk": an erotically charged, intimate conversation that imbricated romance, sexuality, and sisterhood, that oscillated between gossip, social critique, and self-reflection, that provided so many occasions for affirmation, recognition, and social critique.[59] Harriet Martineau, for example, speaks for many generations of readers when she describes feeling "convinced that [*Jane Eyre*] was by some friend of my own, who had portions of my childhood experience in his or her mind."[60] In the words of Raymond Williams (not the most likely observer of this phenomenon, perhaps),

> the connecting power of Charlotte Brontë's fiction is in just this first-person capacity to compose an intimate relationship with the reader. . . . What matters throughout is this private confidence, this mode of confession: the account given as if in a private letter, in private talk . . . the awareness of the friend, the close one, the unknown but in this way intimate reader . . . that very particular personal voice—the direct "Reader, I married him"—is, with a necessary kind of intensity, making the direct invitation.[61]

Susan Lanser echoes this description when she writes that the novel positions its narratee as a "confidant":

> the addresses to the reader are a way of recapturing in a public fiction the immediacy of epistolary fiction. . . . Nowhere in previous literature have I found a *personal* voice so insistently, even compulsively, in contact with a public narratee. . . . The search for contact implied in these addresses certainly corresponds to the behavior of Jane as character, for voice is to her as much the trope of intimacy as of power.[62]

Good "girl talk" always worked by stirring up an array of issues. It provided opportunities for identification and self-differentiation. It was both familiar and exquisite. Desire was always on the table. *Jane Eyre*, like all good girl talk, covers a wide range of issues: psychological self-division (figured in the doubling of Jane and Bertha), ambivalence about passion and sexuality, anger over the supression of female desire and ambition, the difficulties of self-assertion (the autobiographical project itself). Like good girl talk, *Jane Eyre* also explores a range of potentially appealing—if not necessarily consistent—solutions and sources of satisfaction: reconstituted family, communal identity, changes in class and financial status, martyrdom, sexual liberation, adventure, social service, career (educational or artistic, of course), chastity, marriage, domesticity, and motherhood.

No wonder that feminist criticism has had such a romance with *Jane Eyre*. No wonder that a woman reader would report that in "rereading *Jane Eyre* I am led inevitably to feminist issues,"[63] that "women writers from Elizabeth Barrett Browning and Harriet Martineau to Doris Lessing and Adrienne Rich have named the novel as a primary authorizing source."[64] That, as Jean Wyatt reports, "students in Women in Literature classes, as well as female colleagues a generation older, respond to *Jane Eyre* passionately, feel it has something important to say about their own lives."[65] That novelist Jane Lazarre would describe rereading the novel as "part of [her] own healing process" when, after completing three earlier novels, she suffered a crisis of self-esteem about herself as a "chronic bad girl by social definition" that left her unable to write.[66] What Spivak refers to as the "cult" status of this novel and Rich as its "special force and survival value" is this ability to draw the reader into a rebellious voice that is passionate, affirming, exhilarating, and erotic. The question I want to take up here, in conclusion, is whether or not the text does, in fact, invest its reader with the erotic energies with which a generation of feminist readers, at least, has invested it.

Brontë's strategy of casting the novel as an autobiography cuts two ways. By making Jane an autobiographer, a writer who speaks to a public, Brontë can figure Jane gaining the chance to talk effectively, to give an account of herself over which she has both formal and substantial control, and to establish an intimate and familiar dialogue with a "sympathetic" listener. One could, however, as easily argue the opposite. In presenting Jane's story as a fictional autobiography that reveals all to the reader but—fully at least— to no one else, Brontë demonstrates the limits of Jane's potential to give such an account and to establish such a dialogue, the difficulty, even the futility, of her finding a "fit" listener. Brontë's use of autobiography, I am suggesting, serves less to suggest the forms of social recognition and fulfillment to which Jane might lay claim than to suggest the forms of social recognition and fulfillment which she is denied. The conceit of fictional autobiography, in this context, suggests that Jane tells her story not, as Elaine Showalter and others would have it, because she is a heroine of "fulfillment," but rather because she is still looking for a "fit listener," still longing for an ideal or at least apt interlocutor. Writing, in this sense, is directly homologous to Jane's "Anybody may blame me who likes" speech: a call for a response, a gesture, an invitation, one that cannot know what will follow, that cannot be guaranteed of its outcomes.

At times, certainly, the reader does seem to be positioned as that ideal confidante of what Williams describes as a "secret" discourse: "there are *secrets*, to put it at its plainest, that you and Charlotte Brontë are meant to share, as if you were on your own; tones which are not so easily accessible if other people are listening."[67] But what does being Jane's confidante mean? Might this position carry connotations other than the trusting, intimate, reciprocal familiarity embodied in "girl talk"?

Foucault's work on the genre of confession is suggestive here. The act of confiding, Foucault writes, is not only therapeutic. It is always, in part, an act of submission to authority, of compliance with the injunction "to tell" which can be demanded of the (relatively) disempowered on the part of the (relatively) empowered.[68] Confession is "a ritual that unfolds within a power relationship. . . . One does not confess without the presence (or virtual presence) of a partner who is not simply the interlocutor but the authority who requires the confession, prescribes and appreciates it, and intervenes in order to judge, punish, forgive, console, and reconcile."[69] Telling one's story *performs* the power of its listener. It is "an obligatory act of speech" that occurs under "imperious compulsion":

> one confesses—or is forced to confess. When it is not spontaneous or dictated by some internal imperative, the confession is wrung from a person by violence or threat; it is driven from its hiding place in the soul, or extracted from the body. Since the Middle Ages, torture has accompanied it like a shadow, and supported it when it could go no further: the dark twins.[70]

Foucault does not attempt to account for the very considerable differences between different narrative conditions that might occur contemporaneously. On his account, coercion is inscribed, more or less equally, into any moment of self-disclosure. Foucault interprets confession as a "technology of the self" which (mis)represents self-disclosure as freedom—the freedom to tell one's own story, for example—when it is in fact part of a regime of discipline and subjectification—the compulsion to submit one's story and hence one's "self" to the authorities for examination and interpretation. Foucault suggests that it is the recipient of a confession and not its author whom storytelling empowers: "the agency of domination [within the relations of confession] does not reside in the one who speaks (for it is he [*sic*] who is constrained), but in the one who listens and says nothing; not in the one who knows and answers, but in the one who questions and is not supposed to know."[71] The ideal of a self-affirming dialogue (of an affirmed "self" at all!), on this account, could never be other than a utopian reaching after discursive conditions that cannot exist. Such a utopian erotics would operate, in fact, as the inducement that goads us, tricks us even, into giving up our stories and empowering their listeners.

This explanation of confession as a form of coercion is compelling, but it cannot account for the *need* for a listener that Goffman, for example, describes. It cannot account for a model of dialogism such as the "unusual pleasure" Jane describes experiencing with Diana and Mary Rivers. It takes no account of a phenomenon such as "girl talk." We need to tease out from Foucault a more nuanced sense of the *particular* conditions of social power and regulation that differentiate and demarcate different moments of narrative exchange.

Throughout the nineteenth century, Foucault argues, the violence by which confession might be wrung was most routinely practiced against anyone seen as illegitimate or in any way "unnatural": "it was time for all these figures . . . to step forward and speak, to make the difficult confession of what they were."[72]

Jane, as the novel opens, has been charged with just such an "unnaturalness"—with being unsociable and unchildlike, unable to speak "pleasantly," neither "attractive" nor "sprightly." She is banished from society until such time as she might acquire, pace Mrs. Reed, "something lighter, franker, more natural, as it were" (39) in her manner. In explaining her determination not to marry St. John, Jane describes her resolve, quite rightly, as a life-or-death issue. "'If I were to marry you, you would kill me. You are killing me now'" (438). Jane's ability to figure the reality of his refusal (or inability) to recognize Jane's being horrifies St. John. She transgresses the borders of the unspeakable. The power of her language strikes St. John—who has striven to set himself up as Jane's language teacher—as evidence of her unnaturalness, just as Jane's earlier acts of naming had struck Mrs Reed. "'*I should kill you—I am killing you?* Your words are such as ought not to be used: *violent, unfeminine, untrue.* They betray an unfortunate state of mind: they merit reproof: they would seem inexcusable, but that it is the duty of man to forgive his fellow even until seventy-and-seven times'" (438).

Telling her story takes up the challenge of this charge, of proving that she is not unnatural, either in her attitudes toward justice and the rights of propertyless, orphaned women, or in her desire for "intimacy" and "'real affection,'" or in her use of language. But neither Mrs. Reed nor St. John, of course, is the recipient of this rebuttal. In fact, Jane explicitly refuses to reveal herself to either, to allow either to coerce her confession. She tells it to her "reader" instead. Does Jane's "Dear Reader" really compel or coerce her story, as Foucault might suggest? Is Jane's telling wrung by "violence"? What other imperatives—both psychological and social—impel its narration?

Jane Eyre is particularly inscribed with "power dynamics," but those dynamics point in multiple directions. For one thing, they are tied, as Lanser and Williams suggest, to effects of genre. Typically, Lanser writes, female governess novels "construct their narratees as judges to be pleased, appeased, or instructed." The heroine may even address herself juridically, creating a tension between older and younger versions of herself in which "the older 'I' is constructed as authoritative judge."[73] Williams reads Brontë as "very obviously at the head" of what he argues is an entire generic tradition of juridical, attestory narration—"the fiction of special pleading":

I mean that fiction in which the only major emotion, and then the relation with the reader, is that exact stress, that first-person stress: "circumstanced like me." The stress is this really: the world will judge me in certain ways if it sees what I do, but if it knows how I felt it would see me quite differently.[74]

On either account, Jane reserves a kind of power by remaining a listener in her everyday existence, even by effecting Rochester's cure rather than her own. Witholding her own story is as performative as confessing it would be, a way of both marking (so as to make visible) and resisting (without seeming to do so or seeming even to have reason to do so) Rochester's power to compel Jane's voice and coerce her behavior:

> "It would please me now to draw you out—to learn more of you—therefore speak" [Rochester commands].
>
> Instead of speaking, I smiled: and not a very complacent or submissive smile either.
>
> "Speak," he urged.
>
> "What about, sir?"
>
> "Whatever you like. I leave both the choice of subject and the manner of treating it entirely to yourself."
>
> *Accordingly I sat and said nothing*: "If he expects me to talk for the sake of talking and showing off, he will find he has addressed himself to the wrong person," I thought (164, emphasis mine).

Jane's refusal to tell her story to Rochester is a way of resisting his power, a way of refusing to "plead." By the same token, her telling it to the reader is more than, but not unrelated to, a form of submission to power. Alternatively, is it a sign that Jane and her reader are equal enough, perhaps even "kindred" enough, for power and judgment to no longer be at issue?

The fantasy of an ideal listener, as I have been suggesting, articulates social as well as personal desire. As Michael Holquist puts it:

> Poets who feel misunderstood in their lifetimes, martyrs for lost political causes, quite ordinary people caught in lives of quiet desperation—all have been correct to hope that outside of the tyranny of the present there is a possible addressee who will understand them. This version of the significant other, this "super-addressee," is conceived in different ways at different times and by different persons: as God, as the future triumph of the state, as a future reader.[75]

Whose fantasy makes us—the novel's readers—the bearers of such poetic justice? Does Brontë in fact project such a heroic image of the reader of Jane's writing or does she, as I think is the case, leave that question much more open-ended, sending the novel out, like Jane's speech from the ramparts, into a world in which intersubjective exchange may prove *either* nourishing or constraining—or, worse yet, altogether absent?

The text activates that very question by addressing a multiplicity of different readers—male and female, sympathetic and judgmental, competent and relatively inept. Although Jane's only gender-specific reference to the reader marks him as a man,[76] readers almost universally (and for generally good reasons) "think of the fictionalized reader . . . as female."[77] It is not just in terms of gender that Jane's implied reader may prove somewhat slippery but also in terms of competence. Sometimes her reader is addressed as knowing and understanding:[78] the reader who "knows" that Jane cannot help loving Rochester and cannot possibly love St. John Rivers (315). But there is also the reader who thinks Jane might forget Rochester "amidst these changes of place and fortune" (242) or thinks Jane "so worthless as to have grown tired of [Helen's] pure society," a reader who must be reassured that Jane would "never [have] tired of Helen Burns" (109) just as she could never have feared Rochester "in his blind ferocity" (456). When Jane begins her feminist manifesto with the words "Anybody may blame me who likes," she signals her awareness that "the reader shall judge" both her story and her life. These rhetorical gestures are devices, of course, conventions for letting Jane convey information or create impressions. But they also signal a broad awareness that one is *not* always addressing a fit listener, that the dialogic character of all discourse does not mean that each utterance hits its mark. On the contrary, it means that there is always a "loophole"[79] through which our intentions may fall—or slip back in. It is, as Holquist remarks, "a stern philosophy."[80]

Brenda Silver has argued that multiple narratees serve to juxtapose conventional judgments to more understanding, collaborative, sympathetic ones, to juxtapose an (implicitly male) reader who acts "as judge and jury" to "another (implicitly female) reader, a nonjudgmental reader" who acts as an "accomplice" and in whom "[Jane] can confide." That confidential reader, Silver maintains, "gradually dominates both readers and informs the text." Thus, Silver argues, Brontë "creates an audience who learns to read her narrative for what it is—the nontraditional story of a woman's life and a text in which she is not an invisible outsider but the informing presence."[81] She "creates an interlocutor capable of understanding,"[82] according to Silver, rather than solicits one or creates the space for one, as I would put it. On Silver's account, this transformation operates to instruct us in how to provide the narrator with "the power to grow and to speak, and with it the power to endure."[83]

Silver's idea is appealing (and echoes in many ways Stepto's argument, the appeal of which I've already discussed) particularly to that strand of feminist criticism which sees its work as the creation of an "intimate conversation" between the woman writer and the feminist critic.[84] It casts the novel as a kind of consciousness-raising session, a lesson in how the successful telling of women's stories can empower both tellers and hearers, how narrative exchange can provide both social identities and social change. Placing the reader, however, in the position of ideal listener, as the text's "super-addressee" in a "dialectics of desire" where the text proves, as Barthes describes it, "that it desires me,"[85] postulates the successful realization of the very erotics of talk that the novel's double-edged ending so purposefully calls into question, the differentiation of different potential listeners which is the text's hard-won message. It affirms that we—whoever we are—

can crack the text's code, that the novel needs us, depends upon us in fact, if its narrative pleasure is to be realized at all.

This raises some difficult questions, however. First, given a juxtaposition of various narratees, what is the agency of their transformation from limited to ideal? Is the text itself, as Jauss suggests, sufficient to work such transformations? Is talking to Rochester "all day long" part of this project? Or is such talking evidence that the project has been successfully completed? Second, does assuming that the text "desires me" re-perform the essentialism against which this novel strains by assuming that because we can identify with Jane we must be the listener/lover she desires?

Recuperative criticism has both challenged and reaffirmed the notion that the text is the historical medium of its own social transformations. Recognizing that the text may not be able to "create an interlocutor capable of understanding" or transform all of its uncomprehending or coercive readers into reciprocal, noncoercive, erotic partners, the recuperative critic offers to act as a collaborator and accomplice. But such intervention can also turn back on itself, coming full circle, as it were, by assuming that what we need to bring those changes about is to make ourself "kin" to the textual subject we rescue, a symbolic sister, in this case, to Jane.

Finally, such intervention may be freighted with its own romance ideology, with assumptions that the text's resolution, its romance with us, must provide compensations for whatever social failures and inadequacies it has exposed. For *Jane Eyre* to be a paradigm of "fulfillment," I have suggested, requires a crucial displacement. Our successful response to Jane's story must displace Rochester's failure to receive it and, in doing so, explain why *we* can hear it when he cannot. *We* must provide the sisterhood and sympathy that Rochester failed to produce. What I have tried to suggest is why it is worthwhile to resist this pull, how we might recuperate the text without resubjecting it to romance paradigms, including our own.

Jane is never unsure of what she wants or why she wants it. Her desires—for intimacy, recognition, sisterhood, a change in her gender and class position and in the meanings attached to such categories—resonate with every important theme in the history of feminist struggle. Our romance with this text, in that sense, is hardly unfounded. But if Jane knows just what she wants, the novel—quite rationally in my view—does not know how to give it to her. Even as it creates a paradigm of transcendence and romance, *Jane Eyre* also resists the unproblematic articulation of easy or utopian solutions. It remains unsure about how hierarchical Victorian conventions of gender, class, sexuality, and status might be overturned, ambivalent about the limits of both constructionism and essentialism, uneasy about the promises of romance and idealism, torn between identification and desire. These cautions, I believe, are worth taking to heart. If "politics," as John Brenkman has argued, "has the task of discovering the subversive work of desire,"[86] this means unfulfilled desires, such as those I have tried to uncover in *Jane Eyre*, at least as much—or more—as those desires we might celebrate as both fulfilled and, for us, fulfilling.

4

"That Oldest Human Longing": The Erotics of Talk in *Their Eyes Were Watching God*

"Mah tongue is in mah friend's mouf"

—Zora Neale Hurston,
Their Eyes Were Watching God[1]

"That Oldest Human Longing"

Reduced to its basic narrative components, Zora Neale Hurston's *Their Eyes Were Watching God* is the story of a young woman in search of an orgasm. From the moment Janie is "summoned to behold a revelation" (24) and witnesses the "panting," "frothing," "ecstatic," "creaming" fulfillment of a blossoming pear tree, her quest is set; she wants, as she puts it, "tuh utilize mahself all over" (169). The novel was written in a cultural context of multiple sanctions against any representation of black female sexuality.[2] Nonetheless, Hurston's description of Janie's "revelation" is one of the sexiest passages in American literature:

> It was a spring afternoon in West Florida. Janie had spent most of the day under a blossoming pear tree in the back-yard . . . she was stretched on her back beneath the pear tree soaking in the alto chant of the visiting bees, the gold of the sun and the panting breath of the breeze when the inaudible voice of it all came to her. She saw a dust-bearing bee sink into the sanctum of a bloom; the thousand sister-calyxes arch to meet the love embrace and the ecstatic shiver of the tree from root to tiniest branch creaming in every blossom and frothing with delight. . . . Janie felt a pain remorseless sweet that left her limp and languid. (23–24)[3]

But Janie's chances of fulfillment seem very attenuated. As her grandmother describes it, all Janie can expect is to tote "de load" and bear "de
burden":

> "Honey, de white man is de ruler of everything as fur as Ah been able tuh
> find out. Maybe it's some place way off in de ocean where de black man is in
> power, but we don't know nothin' but what we see. So de white man throw
> down de load and tell de nigger man tuh pick it up. He pick it up because he
> have to, but he don't tote it. He hand it to his womenfolks. De nigger woman
> is de mule uh de world so fur as ah can see." (29)

Not surprisingly, Janie does not see herself as the possible agent of the
ecstasy she has witnessed, but rather as a fairy tale or modern romance
heroine, "looking, waiting, breathing short with impatience" (25) for her
prince—or in this case her bee—to come. The first thing Janie sees when
she looks up from the pear tree is a man walking into her front yard:
"through pollinated air she saw a glorious being coming up the road. In
her former blindness she had known him as shiftless Johnny Taylor, tall and
lean. That was before the golden dust of pollen had beglamored his rags
and her eyes"(25). Janie's "conscious life" begins when she witnesses the
pear-tree's "snowy virginity of bloom," and then lets Johnny Taylor "kiss
her over the gatepost" (23).

But Janie mistakes the nature of the "revelation" she has been "summoned
to behold." Mistakenly concluding, after watching the pear tree's "creaming"
and "frothing" that "this was a marriage!" (24), Janie lets her grandmother
push her into marrying Logan Killicks, a man whose head is "long one way"
and "flat on the sides" and "whose toe nails look lak mule foots" (42), but
who happens to possess sixty acres, a mule, and an organ (musical). When she
finds it impossible to desire Killicks, Janie learns that "marriage did not make
love" (44). "'Ah wants to want him sometimes,'" she tells Nanny. "'Ah don't
want him to do all de wantin'. . . . Ah wants things sweet wid mah marriage
lak when you sit under a pear tree and think'" (41, 43).

But Janie decides to try again, this time marrying Jody Starks, who "did
not represent sun-up and pollen and blooming trees, but he spoke for the
far horizon" (50). Jody turns out to be a petit bourgeois entrepreneur who
wants nothing more than to buy himself a town and be a "'big voice,'" a
man whose signature is the expletive "'I God'" and whose speech is a long-
winded, self-important monologue. Jody takes her to Eatonville, where Janie
discovers that she "loved the conversation." But "Joe had forbidden her to
indulge" (85). Instead, he wants to make Janie an object of admiration,
like his store, his money, and his "gloaty, sparkly white" house (75). Janie
comes to realize that Jody, like Killicks, is incapable of being the "bee" she
was searching for. Consequently, "the bed was no longer a daisy-field for
her and Joe to play in. It was a place where she went and laid down when
she was sleepy and tired" (111).

When Jody dies, Janie tries one more time, marrying Vergible "Tea
Cake" Woods, a gambler who plays guitar, is twelve years younger than

she is, "looked like the love thoughts of women" (161), and takes her to "the muck," an Everglades community of migrant workers. This marriage is more successful, if short-lived, because Janie now has a "love game" (171), in which she can be a desiring subject rather than merely an object of desire. Tea Cake, Janie decides, "could be a bee to a blossom—a pear tree blossom in the spring" (161).

Their marriage ends in tragedy, however. Trying to save Janie from a mad dog, Tea Cake is bitten and contracts rabies. He becomes sicker and sicker, finally falling into a state of jealous dementia in which he pulls a gun on Janie. She is forced to shoot and kill him in self-defense. Tea Cake dies in Janie's arms, "his teeth in the flesh of her forearm" (273). Tried for his murder and acquitted, Janie returns to Eatonville where it is now "time to hear things and talk" (1).

As the novel opens she has just settled down on her porch, back home, to tell her story to her best friend Pheoby Watson.[4] This conversation with Pheoby is the frame that opens and closes the novel. The scene between them is one of the novel's most lyrical: as "the vari-colored cloud dust that the sun had stirred up in the sky was setting by slow degrees," Janie speaks "in soft, easy phrases" (15). When she pauses in her tale, "Pheoby's hungry listening helped Janie to tell her story" (23). And as Janie talks, the "fresh young darkness" around them "put on flesh and blackness" (23, 18). At the novel's close the two friends, sated by their long talking, sit "close" together in a "finished silence" in which Pheoby feels she has "'growed ten feet higher from jus' listenin' tuh'" Janie (18, 285, 284). They "hear the wind picking at the pine trees," sweeping "out all the fetid feeling of absence and nothingness" (285); "the place tasted fresh again" (285) and Janie, finally, feels at "peace" (286).

The meaning of Janie's pear tree "revelation," it turns out, is not marriage or a husband or sex, but talk itself, the experience of conversation, the act of storytelling and self-narration. Like Jane in *Jane Eyre*, Janie wants to narrate her own story, exercise her voice, and participate in what Jane calls the "joyous conversational murmur." It is only in telling her story to Pheoby that Janie is finally able to satisfy "that oldest human longing—self revelation" (18). Only in telling her story to Pheoby does she fulfill her quest for the satisfaction she beheld under the pear tree.[5] Telling her story to Pheoby is the erotic fulfillment Janie misunderstands as "marriage" (the plot of romance) and in this sense Pheoby, whose "hungry listening helps Janie to tell her story," is the "bee" to Janie's "blossom."[6]

The framing conversation between Janie and Pheoby has generally been understood as a mechanism for getting Janie's life story told. But I want to suggest that we look at this structure the other way around. Rather than seeing the frame as (merely) a convenient, technical device for getting a life story across, a way of creating an occasion for its telling, we might see Janie's life story as the medium of her conversation with Pheoby, a performative utterance that provides substance for the all-important act of telling or "self revelation."

"Hungry Listening"

Why does Hurston begin her novel with a woman awakening to her sexuality—an extremely bold move in a context where black woman's sexuality had been, as Gloria Naylor puts it, "deadened to the point of invisibility"[7] by white racist stereotypes of licentiousness and promiscuity as well as by black admonitions to counter such stereotypes with counter-images of asexual purity—and then rewrite desire itself as the desire to tell one's story? Why does she foreground female sexuality only to represent "the oldest human longing" as the longing to talk? Is the figuration of Pheoby as Janie's "bee" a lesbian alternative to romantic ideology and heterosexual narrative teleology or simply a sororal, asexual bond? Is Hurston participating in the long history of silencing black women's sexuality by displacing it onto safer, more legitimate, less controversial pleasures? Or is she eroticizing narration and conversation?

As I mentioned in the Introduction, some critics might respond that narrative is always already eroticized, that it has the form of sexual desire. In Robert Scholes's formulation this took the form of male orgasm: "tumescence and detumescence," "tension and resolution," "intensification to the point of climax and consummation."[8]

A less reductive answer could be sought in the dialogic theories of the linguists, narrative theorists, and philosophers I've mentioned who postulate that "self revelation" is constitutive of both personal subjectivity and social identity. For Mikhail Bakhtin, for example, the constitution of point of view is a complex process of being in relation: "the ideological becoming of a human being, in this view, is the process of selectively assimilating the words of others."[9] This means that all utterance, for Bakhtin, is directed toward a listener. "This orientation toward the listener is usually considered the basic constitutive feature of rhetorical discourse. . . . Every word is directed toward an *answer* and cannot escape the profound influence of the answering word that it anticipates. . . . All rhetorical forms. . . are oriented toward the listener and his answer,"[10] Bakhtin argues.

This orientation toward the listener also characterizes what narrative theorists often describe as the "motor" or motivating force of storytelling, the drive, as Peter Brooks puts it, "to be heard, recognized, understood,"[11] to meet, in Charles Taylor's terms, the "vital human need" for recognition.[12] When Hurston rewrites sexual desire as a longing to talk, she seems to value narrative accordingly: as a means of recognition and identity formation. My reading of the novel, however, comes to rather different conclusions.

Most critics argue that *Their Eyes Were Watching God* is about Janie's acquisition of voice and that her story goes from silence to speech, demonstrating how one woman's narrative can generate recognition and how the process of its telling constitutes her subjectivity.[13] Houston A. Baker, Jr., for example, argues that through the "capitalistic enabling conditions" of coming into possession of Starks's "petit bourgeois enterprises," Janie acquires her "blues" voice.[14] Henry Louis Gates, Jr., describes the novel as the story of "the quest of a silent black woman . . . to find a voice" and concludes that "Janie gains her voice and becomes a speaking subject inside her husband's store" when she begins to see things in terms of insides and outsides.[15] Similarly, Barbara Johnson has argued that "Janie's acquisition of the power of voice . . . grows not out of her identity but out of her division into inside and outside."[16] Taking this thesis about the literal and the figurative one step further, Karla Holloway argues that "Janie gains her voice from the available voice of the text and subsequently learns to share it with the narrator."[17] And Susan Lanser maintains that "Hurston's novel is indeed a record of Janie Crawford's struggle to find voice and through voice an identity . . . [;] only after the character Janie has 'found' her voice and spoken publicly in her own defense does the retrospective narration begin."[18] Against the grain of these readings, I hope to demonstrate that although Hurston devoted much of her life as a writer and anthropologist to documenting African American discursive, dialogic, and narrative forms of cultural expression,[19] her conception of narrative's social and psychological status is considerably more skeptical than such celebrations of her "voice" would grant.

For one thing, Janie never needs to *acquire* a voice through narrative or dialogic exchanges; she has one all along. In the words of her community she is a "born orator" (92). She is, for example, an able preacher, sermonizing movingly over her husband's liberation of Matt Bonner's old yellow mule, and putting, the townspeople say, "'jus' de right words tuh our thoughts'" (92). She is also adept at using words as a "weapon" when she wants to. Indeed, when she tells Jody that "'when you pull down yo' britches, you look lak de change uh life" (122–23), her words prove lethal, a public humiliation directly linked to Jody's subsequent death. In fact, the number of times that Janie is violently silenced by others—when Nanny, for example, slaps "the girl's face violently, and forced her head back so that their eyes met in struggle" because Janie argues with her about marrying Logan Killicks (29); or when Logan warns her not to "change too many words" with him or he'd "take holt uh dat axe and come in dere and kill" her because she argues with him about moving a pile of manure (53); or when Jody "struck Janie with all his might and drove her from the store" because she argued with him about his treatment of her (124); or when Tea Cake "stunned the argument with half a word" when Janie disagreed with him about what they should do in the face of the coming flood (237)— all testify to the power, both potential and real, of her voice. Telling her story to Pheoby does not develop or enable Janie's voice; it is only the final instance of verbal skills Janie displays throughout the novel. Hurston, in short, does not represent narrative as constitutive of social or personal identity. And for her, its salutary psychosocial outcome is always contingent and circumscribed, never guaranteed.

While contingency may seem implicit in the very idea that the narrative or dialogic encounter serves a *need*, it is often taken for granted, as I argued in the discussion of Harriet Jacobs, that the interactive reading or listening process itself transforms its readers or listeners, that narrative has the means, as Hans Robert Jauss put it, "to create an interlocutor capable of understanding."[20] Ross Chambers, for example, building on Brooks's idea that narrative must "captivate" a listener, argues that "seduction" is the chief mechanism of all narrative and is a *particularly* strong feature of all literature written from the margins of social power and literary authority. "Seduction," Chambers argues, is practiced by the "situationally condemned" narrator who has to "earn the authority to narrate in the very act of storytelling." Seduction wins narrative authority "from a situation from which power is itself absent."[21]

While I would agree that some narrators operate at a disadvantage to their own implied readers, "seduction" and "captivation" seem discouragingly gender- and race-blind tropes for the narrators' strategic response *to* that dilemma. Rather than seek to seduce or captivate possible listeners, feminist and African American fiction often seeks to dramatize its *lack* of listeners, the impossibility of finding competent—let alone ideal—interlocutors and therefore the impossibility of satisfying a "longing" for talk. When Janie pines for a "kissing bee" what she is really longing for is that elusive but necessary listener:

> She was seeking confirmation of the voice and vision, and everywhere she found and acknowledged answers. A personal answer for all other creations except herself. She felt an answer seeking her, but where? When? How? . . . She had glossy leaves and bursting buds and she wanted to struggle with life but it seemed to elude her. Where were the singing bees for her? Nothing on the place nor in her grandma's house answered her. (25)

The provision of Janie's ideal listener in Pheoby's "hungry listening," the description of Janie and Pheoby as "kissin'-friends" (19) does more than simply substitute a lesbian erotic for the heterosexual formula of narrative erotics—"tumescence and detumescence"—which many consider basic to all narrative.

The framing conversation represents unfulfilled as well as fulfilled desire by drawing attention to the circumstances under which Janie tells her story and by inscribing the novel's various historical and implied readers into its form, foregrounding how an ideal listener (Pheoby) responds to the story in contrast to how other readers do so. Pheoby's ideal listening frees Janie from either the juridical/attestory narrative position typical of slave narrators like Harriet Jacobs who must try to win the approval of hostile, usually uncomprehending listeners or the seductive narrative position typical of white women's romances which seek to captivate their listener even as the heroine is captivating her mate. But at the same time, because Pheoby arrives only after Janie's nearly twenty-five-year wait for a "hungry" listener, Hurston suggests that narrative may not necessarily always captivate or seduce, that its transformational and therapeutic properties may be contingent on whomever it addresses, that finding an ideal listener, in short, should never be taken for granted. The framing conversation is part of a larger narrative structure which includes not only Pheoby and the towns-people as potential audiences but also Tea Cake and the multiple audiences at Janie's trial, a structure fashioned to dramatize the disjunction between implied and ideal readers and, as I will argue, to inflect that disjunction with an aura of virtual inevitability, suggesting that finding a listener as ideal as Pheoby is a rare satisfaction indeed.

"Why Don't They Come Kiss and Be Kissed?"

Janie's refusal of either attestory or seductive, either persuasive or pleasure-oriented public narration is evident, from the first, in her refusal to tell her story to one of her own key potential audiences: the townspeople who are crowded eagerly on their porches, sitting in "judgment" like "lords of sounds and lesser things," passing "nations through their mouths," hop-ing to hear what happened to Janie since she left town with Tea Cake. The townspeople, or as Janie calls them, "'Mouth-Almighty,'" use their mouths as weapons to chew up, "gnaw on" (17), and "swallow with relish" (10) all the unkind thoughts they can. As Pheoby leaves "Mouth-Almighty" to welcome Janie home and bring her some dinner, she feels them "pelting her back with unasked questions. They hoped the answers were cruel and strange" (14). "'Ah don't mean to bother wid tellin' 'em nothin,'" Janie declares to Pheoby, "'tain't worth de trouble'" (17). She reiterates this important resolve to keep her story to herself again midway through the novel she declares "'Ah ain't puttin' it in de street, Ah'm tellin' *you*'" (172), and again when she finishes telling her story to Pheoby. While she feels some sympathy, she says, for how "'parched up [they are] from not knowin' things'" (285), she warns Pheoby not to waste her breath on people whose conversation is all one-sided, people who are, literally, all talk: "'dem meatskins is *got* tuh rattle tuh make out they's alive," she says to Pheoby, "'let 'em consolate theyselves wid talk'" (285).

Janie's response to the way "Mouth-Almighty" "made burning state-ments with questions and killing tools out of laughs" (10) is to ask Pheoby "'if they wants to see and know why they don't come kiss and be kissed? Ah could then sit down and tell 'em things'" (18). This kiss metaphor is one of the novel's central tropes. It not only makes talk and sex coterminous, but at the same time encodes the practices of discursive reciprocity which define what we might call the ethos of this novel's erotics of talk: an insistence on sympathy and equality between the listener and speaker and, concomitantly, a refusal to use discourse as a weapon or social wedge.[22]

In a stunning reversal of standard narrative practice, Hurston resituates the question of narrative reliability in terms of the reader rather than the narrator and makes fidelity to her own discursive ethos an implicit prin-ciple of readerly competence. The trope of the kiss is also part of a broader narrative collapse of sex and talk. When Nanny, half-asleep, intuits Janie's first kiss, for example, what she imagines is an improper conversation:

> In the last stages of Nanny's sleep she dreamed of voices. Voices far-off but persistent, and gradually coming nearer. Janie's voice. Janie talking in whispery snatches with a male voice she couldn't quite place. That brought her wide awake. She bolted upright and peered out of her window and saw Johnny Taylor lacerating her Janie with a kiss. (25–26)

And desire first comes to Janie as a voice. At first it is an "*inaudible* voice," but it becomes one Janie can hear.[23]

Hurston relies on the trope of the kiss particularly strongly in the beginning of the novel to mark out the social and discursive situations within which Janie must operate. When Janie complains to Nanny about her marriage to Logan Killicks, Nanny worries that Logan is beating her: "'Lawd, Ah know dat grass-gut, liver-lipted nigger ain't done took and beat mah baby already! Ah'll take a stick and salivate 'im!'" (40). "'No'm,'" Janie answers, "'he ain't even talked 'bout hittin' me. He says he never mean to lay de weight uh his hand on me in malice. He chops all de wood he think Ah wants and den he totes it inside de kitchin for me. Keeps both water buckets full'" (40). Nanny's response to what might seem like reassuring information is more worry, this time that Janie is being spoiled. Nanny articulates her anxiety through the metaphor of the kiss or, better, the difference between different kinds of kisses: "'Humph!'" Nanny says, "'don't 'spect all dat tuh keep up. He ain't kissin' yo' mouf when he carry on over yuh lak dat. He's kissin' yo' foot and 'tain't in uh man tuh kiss foot long. Mouf kissin' is on uh equal and dat's natural but when dey got to bow down tuh love, dey soon straightens up'" (40–41).

Pheoby and Janie are "'kissin'-friends'" (19). And it is in the opening stages of Janie telling Pheoby her story that this important trope is first worked out. The darkness surrounding the porch is "kissing," the bees are "kissing bees," and Janie expresses her trust in Pheoby's ability to speak for her by declaring that "'mah tongue is in mah friend's mouf'" (17). This figuration goes beyond "female bonding"[24] to suggest not only the intimate familiarity of their friendship and its erotic tracings, but also both the intimacy and eros necessary for a successful discursive "self revelation." It is hard to imagine a more apt expression for an eroticized image of competent listening and satisfying talk.

Because the townspeople don't understand "mouf kissin" and don't know enough to "kiss and be kissed," they cannot possibly be competent listeners for Janie. The ethos of reciprocity and equality Hurston expresses in the trope of "mouf kissin" helps explain why if the oldest human longing is self-revelation we have a story about a character distinguished by her *lack* of listeners and her *refusal* to tell her own story. Whereas Pheoby's "hungry listening" helps Janie to tell her story and earns Pheoby the right to hear it, this novel sees something shameful, like being caught talking to yourself, Goffman might say, about telling your story to hostile or incompetent audiences. Jacobs, similarly, rebels against attestory speech, but she neither eroticizes talk nor speechifies sex. Brontë, who does eroticize talk, is more willing, I think, to risk the consequences of "self talk." The wariness about being caught in "self talk," on Jacobs's and Hurston's parts, has to do, I suspect, with the extreme vulnerability of a speaking position inflected not only by gender and class, as is Jane's, but by race as well.

The figure of Annie Tyler haunts this novel—although she is a relatively minor character—because she represents the sexual and verbal humiliation Janie manages to escape. Having left town a widow (like Janie) and gone off (like Janie) with a much younger man, Annie Tyler returns a ruined woman:

> Hair all gray and black and bluish and reddish in streaks. All the capers that cheap dye could cut was showing in her hair. Those slippers bent and griped just like her work-worn feet. The corset gone and the shaking old woman hanging all over herself. Everything that you could see was hanging. Her chin hung from her ears and rippled down her neck like drapes. Her hanging bosom and stomach and buttocks and legs that draped down to her ankles. She groaned but never giggled.
>
> *She was broken and her pride was gone, so she told those who asked what had happened.* . . . They put her to bed and sent for her married daughter from up around Ocala to come see about her. The daughter came as soon as she could and took Annie Tyler away to die in peace. (178–79, emphasis mine)

Telling her story is the sine qua non of her shame and collapse. Rather than constitute subjectivity, in other words, self-revelation may destroy it and even lead to death. Staging one's private misery in public, in contrast to Jane Eyre's desire to tell "anyone who asks me" her story, is represented here as self-debasement and self-destruction. The fact that Annie Tyler never actually appears in the novel but is merely described in the third person only renders her discursive self-erasure more complete. No longer having a voice of her own, she is nothing but a tale told by others. Janie and Pheoby both recognize Janie's vulnerability to Annie Tyler's fate. "'Ah sho would hate tuh see her come up lak Mis' Tyler,'" Pheoby declares. "'Janie, you be keerful 'bout dis sellin' out and goin' off wid strange men. Look what happened tuh Annie Tyler. . . . It's somethin' tuh think about'" (172).

Hurston privileges dialogue and storytelling at the same time as she represents, and applauds, Janie's *refusal* to speak. She valorizes and eroticizes self-narration at the same time as she underscores what may be the impossibility of its fulfillment (given how rarely—if ever—listeners as ideal as Pheoby are available). To understand the seeming paradoxes of this erotics of talk we need to situate it within the representational cultural politics to which it responded and in which it sought to intervene.

"Colored Women Sittin' on High"

Although *Their Eyes Were Watching God* has always been taken as ahistorical and set in a vague and undetermined/undeterminable past,[25] the conversation between Janie and Pheoby takes place at a very precise historical moment: the opening years of the Harlem Renaissance. Surprisingly, no critic has ever dated the novel's story, even though the clues to its historical moment are not particularly obscure.[26] On the contrary, they are ones which Hurston should have safely been able to predict her readers would notice.

In the second chapter, Nanny, who grew up under slavery, relates her own family history to Janie and describes how her master left to join the Civil War when Leafy (Janie's mother) was just a week old. He departs just after Sherman's troops have invaded Atlanta: 1864. Seventeen years later, Leafy is raped and, still seventeen, gives birth to Janie: 1881 or 1882. Since Janie is sixteen when Nanny tells her story, it is 1897 or 1898 when Janie's "conscious life" begins. She is forty when she returns home: 1921 or 1922, the *anni mirabilis* of the Harlem Renaissance (as well as of modernism), the two years which saw the founding of Marcus Garvey's African Orthodox Church, the opening of the first all-black play, "Shuffle Along," the establishment of the Pan-African Congress, the approval by the House of Representatives of the nation's first anti-lynching legislation, and the publication of *Harlem Shadows, The Book of American Negro Poetry, Bronze*, and Carter Woodson's *The Negro in Our History*, only one year before the publication of *Cane* and *The Philosophy and Opinions of Marcus Garvey* and three years before the publication of *The New Negro*, and *Color*, among other significant works.

While the rural setting of the novel makes its relationship to the central literary and political preoccupations of the Harlem Renaissance seem oblique or tangential, its treatment of desire and voice responds to that movement's most central debates. The boldness with which Hurston represents female desire was transgressive in a context in which black publication guidelines warned that nothing liable to add fuel to racist stereotypes of wanton licentiousness and primitivism would be printed: "nothing that casts the least reflection on contemporary moral or sexual standards will be allowed. Keep away from the erotic! Contributions must be clean and wholesome."[27] While a number of Harlem Renaissance male writers and artists—Claude McKay, Jean Toomer, Langston Hughes, Bruce Nugent, Wallace Thurman, and Aaron Douglas, for example—did explore questions of sexuality, admonitions against its representation were much more rigorously applied to the work of black women. "Racist sexual ideologies," Hazel Carby writes, "proclaimed the black woman to be a rampant sexual being, and in response black women writers either focused on defending their morality or displaced sexuality onto another terrain."[28] By insisting on Janie's right to erotic pleasure, Hurston takes on this complex politics of sexuality.

She is even more critical, however, of the Harlem Renaissance's politics of voice, the idea that literature and the arts offered African Americans their best means of advancement and social protest, the recognition, as one *Negro World* article put it in 1921, that "the history and literature of any race are the credentials on which that race is admitted to the family of civilized men and are the indications of its future possibilities."[29] *The Book of American Negro Poetry*, published one year later, began with James Weldon Johnson's declaration that "the final measure of the greatness of all peoples is the amount and standard of the literature and art they have produced. The world does not know that a people is great until that people produces great literature and art. No people that has produced great literature and art has ever been looked upon by the world as distinctly inferior."[30]

Much of the coherence of the Harlem Renaissance as a literary-political movement was due to such shared assumptions about the role of black arts. In 1926, for example, when W.E.B. Du Bois addressed the NAACP on the "Criteria of Negro Art" he began by remarking that "a group of radicals trying to bring new things into the world, a fighting organization which has come up out of the blood and dust of battle, struggling for the right of black men to be ordinary human beings" did not "turn aside" from its mission "to talk about Art." On the contrary, he argued, "talk about art" was not a turning aside from battle, but a better way to fight.[31] "After trying religion, education, politics, industrial, ethical, economic, [and] sociological approaches," James Weldon Johnson wrote, "through his artistic efforts the Negro is smashing [the race barriers] faster than he has ever done through any other method."[32]

To suggest, in this context, that "'talkin' don't amount tuh uh hill uh beans when you can't do nothin' else'" (285), that narrative and self-revelation "'tain't worth de trouble,'" was to subvert the entire representational agenda behind the cultural politics of African American activism from the early 1920s through the 1930s and beyond. While this view of art as a political weapon was most powerfully articulated in the postwar rhetoric of the Harlem Renaissance, its roots go much farther back, originating in pre-emancipation debates over literacy and in the post-enlightenment emphasis on writing as the "sign of [human] reason," as Gates puts it.[33] "If blacks could write and publish imaginative literature, then they could, in effect, take a few 'giant steps' up the chain of being in an evil game of 'Mother, May I?'"[34] Hurston's challenge to the value and status of self-revelation as a means of social transformation was tantamount to heresy. It strikes directly at the two available political models of African American resistance.

Influential works like W.E.B. Du Bois's "Returning Soldiers," with its call to "return fighting," and Claude McKay's "If We Must Die," with its admonition that even if black men are "pressed to the wall" and "far outnumbered" they should die "fighting back," helped construct what I would call the contestational aesthetic of the Harlem Renaissance, an art and rhetoric based not only on the belief that letters and literacy would serve—as they indisputably did—as effective tools of social liberation, but also on themes, images, metaphors, and discourses drawn directly from combat and warfare and dependent upon a grounding in normative masculinity, often specifically drawn from the riveting martial imagery of the returning, triumphant, black 369th Regiment.

This rhetoric, while clearly empowering in many ways, put radical black women in a very difficult position. On the one hand, they were often accused by their contemporaries of holding back black militancy through their "genteel" or feminine commitment to respectability, manners, and propriety. Langston Hughes, for example, in "The Negro Artist and the Racial Mountain," one of the period's most influential essays on art and politics, makes a brilliant and compelling case for aesthetic self-determination. "We younger Negro artists," Hughes writes,

> who create now intend to express our individual dark-skinned selves without fear or shame. If white people are pleased we are glad. If they are not, it doesn't matter. We know we are beautiful. And ugly too. The tom-tom cries and the tom-tom laughs.
>   If colored people are pleased, we are glad. If they are not, their displeasure doesn't matter either. We build our temples for tomorrow, strong as we know how, and we stand on top of the mountain, free within ourselves.[35]

But when Hughes goes on to imagine the impediments to this agenda, it is the figure of a woman, specifically a "Philadelphia Clubwoman" whose girlish fears and lack of masculine courage stand in the way of its realization. "'Oh, be respectable, write about nice people, show how good we are,'" she whines to Hughes's imaginary black male artist.[36] By the same token, should a black woman desire to show her radical credentials in print, to indicate her own refusal to be bamboozled by white values and standards, the "martial and manly" rhetoric of fighting back would hardly have stood her in good stead.[37] Her role was seen to be—and criticized for being—conciliatory, not contestatory.

This is not to say of course that there isn't a vital, militant black feminism going back through the 1800s. Hurston is not only aware of this vibrant tradition, her characterization of Nanny parodies it nearly as derisively (if for different reasons) as did some of her male colleagues. As Janie's erotics of talk stages a rejection of the contestational aesthetic of Harlem Renaissance artists, writers, and intellectuals, her rejection of Nanny's politics also repudiates available models of black feminist resistance which developed or depended upon a contestational discursive aesthetic, implicitly and paradoxically implicating an entire black feminist tradition characterized by organizations like the National Association of Colored Women and the Black Women's Club Movement in the anti-female and anti-erotic strains she discerns in Harlem Renaissance political discourse.

Although Nanny advises Janie to marry a man she does not love, to face the fact that, as a black woman, she is the "mule of the world," and to "leave things de way dey is"—"Youse young yet. No tellin' whut mout happen befo' you die. Wait awhile, baby. Yo' mind will change'" (43)—she is not simply an accommodationist or a conservative. In fact, more than anything else, she wants to be an activist and spokeswoman for the rights of black women. "'Ah wanted to preach a great sermon about colored women sittin' on high,'" she tells Janie, "'but they wasn't no pulpit for me.

. . . Ah said Ah'd save de text for you. Ah been waitin' a long time, Janie, but nothin' Ah been through ain't too much if you just take a stand on high ground lak Ah dreamed'" (31–32). Some critics have suggested that Nanny's "stand on high ground" is an essentially materialistic notion, tied more to parlors and pianos than pulpits and politics. But it is no mistake that Hurston has Nanny's rhetoric resonate so strongly with Hughes's fiery and militant call to self-determination, to "stand on top of the mountain, free within ourselves." Nanny's position, however unrealizable, is a feminist alternative to the male radicalism of African American cultural politics of the 1920s.

Nanny's history as a black slave woman gives her a particular purchase on sexual abuse and romantic ideology, issues central to the black feminism she would have "preached" had there been a pulpit for her. Nanny was raped by her white slave master, and Leafy, Janie's mother, was raped by a black schoolteacher.[38] Given this history, Nanny, not surprisingly, fears for Janie's safety and longs to see her married to someone who can secure her a "stand on high ground" (32) and protect her from "de menfolks white or black . . . makin' a spit cup outa" her (37). Nanny's view of marriage is practical and unsentimental: a man with "a house bought and paid for and sixty acres uh land" (41) is better than one with nothing. Her view of love is a straightforward, witty, and tough-minded repudiation of heterosexual romantic ideology. Love, she argues, is a myth, a form of social control, a tool of the patriarchy to trick women into compliance with their own subordination: "'*Dat's de very prong all us black women gits hung on. Dis love!* Dat's just whut's got us uh pullin' and uh haulin' and sweatin' and doin' from can't see in de mornin' till can't see at night'" (41, emphasis mine). While slavery, not love, has turned Nanny into a "cracked plate" (37), an "old tree that had been torn away by storm" (26), romance is implicated in the structures of oppression that ensure that "'de white man is de ruler of everything [and] . . . de nigger woman is de mule uh de world" (29).[39] So Nanny tries to raise Janie to be a feminist activist like Harriet Tubman, Sojourner Truth, Anna Julia Cooper, Mary McLeod Bethune, or Ida B. Wells-Barnett, a woman who can "preach" in public about the rights and dreams of black women. But Janie rejects this idea, just as much as she does the contestational aesthetic of the Harlem Renaissance. She repudiates her grandmother's life and values and looks back only in resentment, refusing even to visit her grandmother's grave: "she hated her grandmother and had hidden it from herself all these years under a cloak of pity" (137–38).

Janie's politics of voice can seem downright reactionary. Whereas both Nanny and the community view voice as a mode of negotiating into and within the public sphere, Janie's view of voice seems private and personal, even privatistic. Throughout the novel she consistently chooses not to fight back with her voice. In general, "Janie took the easy way away from a fuss. She didn't change her mind but she agreed with her mouth" (99). When Janie witnesses the townsmen cruelly taunting the yellow mule with whom she had often identified, for example, she "wanted to fight about it. . . . A little war of defense for helpless things was going on inside her . . . [but] 'Ah hates disagreement and confusion, so Ah better not talk. It makes it hard tuh git along'" (90). Hurston also relates that "the years took all the fight out of Janie's face, no matter what Jody did, she said nothing" (118). Janie chooses not to fight back with her voice because in her view "it didn't do her any good" (111).

Hurston could not have been unaware that this skeptical representation of the politics of voice was controversial. In a passage from *Mules and Men*, her earlier anthropological collection, Hurston describes such self-censorship as a racial strategy, one which she clearly endorses as a form of self-protection:

> . . . The Negro, in spite of his open-faced laughter, his seeming acquiescence, is particularly evasive. You see we are a polite people and we do not say to our questioner, "Get out of here!" We smile and tell him or her something that satisfies the white person because, knowing so little about us, he doesn't know what he is missing. The Indian resists curiosity by a stony silence. The Negro offers a feather bed resistance. That is, we let the probe enter, but it never comes out. It gets smothered under a lot of laughter and pleasantries.
>
> The theory behind our tactics: "The white man is always trying to know into somebody else's business. All right, I'll set something outside the door of my mind for him to play with and handle. He can read my writing but he sho' can't read my mind. I'll put this play toy in his hand, and he will seize it and go away. Then I'll say my say and sing my song."[40]

Race turns out to be a trope for gender here, since it is gender that gives real meaning to Hurston's disturbing rape metaphor of a "probe" which is allowed to "enter" but "never comes out." This speaker, having gotten rid of an inept, hostile audience in the person of a white, male "questioner," will now "say my say and sing my song." But to whom? Some critics would argue that she can now turn to "say" and "sing" to the (implicitly) black community who (implicitly) observes the speaker's strategy and whose collective voice she has ostensibly taken over in her adoption of the pronoun "we." What I want to stress, however, is first, the way in which this passage renders public speech as meaningless foolishness and, second, the relatively inconsequential role it assigns to *any* listener, whether black or white, male or female, "us" or them. The speaker of this passage, like Janie, needs a competent listener to hear—but not constitute—her song; her song exists independently of either the misrecognitions or recognitions of its possible listeners. This speaker, moreover, is not in the least anxious to avoid the appearance of "self talk." On the contrary, she welcomes it.

Does Janie, then, simply embody an apolitical, individualistic aesthetic? Many of Hurston's critics have suggested as much, from Richard Wright's claim that "her novel carries no theme, no message, no thought"[41] to Hazel Carby's assessment of Hurston's as a "limited vision, a vision which in its romantic evocation of the rural and the folk avoids some of the most crucial and urgent issues of cultural struggle."[42] But I think Hurston was challenging, not simply ignoring, the idea of politics to which such assessments appeal. For her, in Marcuse's words, "the fight for Eros is the *political* fight."[43] Janie rejects her grandmother (and, implicitly, the cultural politics of many of her contemporaries) because Nanny gives up on female desire. Nanny, as Janie describes it, had taken the horizon—or desire itself—and "pinched it in to such as little bit of a thing that she could tie it about her grand-daughter's neck tight enough to choke her" (138). Such erotic erasure has no place in Janie's political economy. Nor, more paradoxically, does self-revelation to hostile or antagonistic audiences. But even this position is not the disengagement and resignation it seems. Susan Lanser identifies what she calls "self-silencing" as a "willful [albeit often staged] refusal to narrate" that refuses the compromises embedded in narrative conventions, protects narrators or characters from "direct contact with an unfriendly or uncomprehending readership" and indicts the audience to which the narrator will not speak as unreliable, unworthy, or otherwise inadequate.[44] Building on Lanser's description of the subversive imperatives of "self-silencing," I want to argue that Janie's various refusals of public voice, self-revelation, and fighting back do constitute an important, if historically idiosyncratic, form of political protest.

"The Understandin' to Go 'Long Wid It"

Let us turn to the one other instance in the novel where Janie does indulge, as she did in her conversation with Pheoby, in "self revelation" and attempt to tell her story to others. Juxtaposing these two scenes helps explain why Hurston seems at once to privilege narration and doubt its social or personal value. Rather than affirm storytelling as a means of improving social conditions, the trial scene destabilizes narrative's privileged status as a personal or social "talking cure" by first elevating its importance and then, ironically, undercutting its effectiveness. Janie must here tell her story to save her life, but she knows that her storytelling may beget misrecognition and alienation. Just as much as the framing conversation between Janie and Pheoby, the trial scene serves as a microcosm for the novel as a whole, an allegory of the dilemma Janie faces in seeking the audience with whom she might satisfy her longing for self-revelation.[45]

Janie finds herself in a southern courtroom, on trial for Tea Cake's murder and facing two hostile audiences. The black community is there, "with their tongues cocked and loaded. . . . They were all against her, she could see. So many were there against her that a slap from each one of them would have beat her to death. She felt them pelting her with dirty thoughts" (275). The white community is also there with its all-male jury—"twelve strange men who didn't know a thing about people like Tea Cake and her were going to sit on the thing" (274)—and its female observers who are not authorized to pass judgment, impose sentence, or dispense sympathy: "it would be nice if she could make *them* know how it was instead of those menfolks" (275).

Janie is silent throughout most of the trial, merely looking on as a series of white men tell her story for her. First, "the sheriff took the stand and told how Janie had come to his house with the doctor and how he found things when he drove out to hers. . . . Then they called Dr. Simmons and he told about Tea Cake's sickness and how dangerous it was. . . . then the strange white man that was going to talk for her got up there" (276–77). By the time Janie herself is called to the stand her testimony has already been undercut.

Janie is trapped. And she knows it. She has no alternative but to testify to these "twelve strange men": "They all leaned over to listen while she talked. First thing she had to remember was she was not at home. . . . She had to go way back to let them know how she and Tea Cake had been with one another so they could see she could never shoot Tea Cake out of malice. . . . She didn't plead to anybody. She just sat there and told and when she was through she hushed" (278).[46]

In this representation of Janie's trial, Hurston enacts the social history of African American voice. Janie is silent, like African Americans denied the right to testify, vote, or learn to read and write. And Janie also speaks, taking on the role of post-Reconstruction blacks who agitated and argued on their own behalf. Why, then, is Janie's testimony rendered only in the narrator's summary and not directly, in the first person, in her own dramatic voice?[47] Hurston is having it both ways here. By having Janie deliver her testimony in court, she acknowledges the relatively recent historical amelioration of the most overt and brutalizing forms of enforced African American silence. But by also opting not to render Janie's voice directly at this most crucial of narrative moments—Janie's very life and freedom are, after all, on the line here— Hurston is suggesting that black female voices are still constrained, although perhaps now in more covert, complex, and less absolute ways.

The largest problem Janie faces is that whatever she says to the jury, she knows they lack the necessary "understandin' to go 'long wid it" (19) and that without that understanding, "self revelation" just "'tain't worth de trouble'" and wouldn't, as she considered earlier, "do her any good." Since she and the jury lack shared values, she can only attempt to open their horizons through narrative, approximating experience with story. But this dialogic back and forth cannot function in what is, for Janie, a closed circle— without common experiences her audience/jury cannot understand her story; her story is the only tool she has to provide a sense of commonality. Narrative, in this situation, can neither close the gap between worlds nor break the closed circle of necessity/inadequacy in which it circulates.

While the jury does acquit Janie, it is entirely unclear whether her story has been decisive in that outcome. After she finishes testifying, there is no response from anyone in the courtroom: "She had been through for some time before the judge and the lawyer and the rest seemed to know it. But she sat on in that trial chair until the lawyer told her she could come down," (278). Either the courtroom has been moved to silence by Janie's story, or they have been paying no attention to her at all, having already made up their minds based on the testimony of the string of white men who precede—and authorize—Janie's speech.

Is Janie's paradoxical double bind intrinsic to all narrating situations or, rather, is the dubious heuristic value of her testimony a factor of its reception context? Immediately following the courtroom scene, Hurston returns us to the framing conversation between Janie and Pheoby in order to juxtapose their nonjuridical dialogue to the juridical one we have just witnessed and to contrast the strong effect Janie's story has had on Pheoby to the dubious effect it had in court. But the topic, at this point, of Janie and Pheoby's conversation is, appropriately enough, the singular importance *and* the dubious value of talk.

> "Lawd!" Pheoby breathed out heavily, "Ah ain't satisfied wid mahself no mo'. Ah means tuh make Sam take me fishin' wid him after this. Nobody better not criticize yuh in mah hearin'."
>
> "Now, Pheoby, don't feel too mean wid de rest of 'em 'cause dey's parched up from not knowin' things. Dem meatskins is *got* tuh rattle tuh make out they's alive. Let 'em consolate theyselves wid talk. 'Course, talkin' don't amount tuh uh hill uh beans when yuh can't do nothin' else. And listenin' tuh dat kind uh talk is jus' lak openin' yo' mouth and lettin' de moon shine down yo' throat. It's uh known fact, Pheoby, you got tuh *go* there tuh *know* there. Yo' papa and yo' mama and nobody else can't tell yuh and show yuh. Two things everybody got tuh do fuh theyselves. They got tuh go tuh God, and they got tuh find out about livin' fuh theyselves." (284–85)

You can't, Janie concludes, approximate experience with story. Janie does not respond to Pheoby's "hungry listening" by reaffirming the positive effects of storytelling. On the contrary, in spite of how the story has affected Pheoby's growth, self-esteem, feelings of worth, Janie reiterates the message of her courtroom scene: that narrative is mostly a waste of breath, that there is no real relation between storytelling and experience, that narrative cannot substitute for experience and perhaps doesn't even count *as* experience, since you have to "*go* there tuh *know* there."

But shouldn't we read this statement ironically? Janie's staged self-silencing, after all, occurs within a text which *does* tell her story, which is not silent, which in fact delivers Janie's self-revelation to a larger reading public. Doesn't this publicity affirm the very value of narrative that Janie seems to want to shut down? Is Hurston representing the efficacy of narration or, ultimately, its uselessness? The likelihood or the unlikelihood of black female satisfaction through "self revelation"?

Robert Stepto argues that frame structures demonstrate the reading models which readers are meant to adapt, and that, as such, they interpolate their readers into the text:

> Framed tales by their nature invent storylisteners within their narratives and storyreaders, through their acts of reading, may be transformed into story-listeners. In tale after tale, considerable artistic energy is brought to the task of persuading the reader to constitute himself as a listener, the key issue affecting that activity being whether the reader is to pursue such self-transformations in accord with or at variance with the model of the listener found within the narrative itself. (312)

Ideal listeners such as Pheoby, then, are there as heuristic models for the reader; they teach us what we need to learn and how we ought to read. This account not only assumes the constitutive dynamics of storytelling; it has its own erotic appeal. If the activity of reading can make us better listeners (even if we begin badly), then we, like Pheoby, can come "kiss and be kissed." We, like Pheoby, will have Janie's tongue in our mouth. Talk will be more than simply an empty longing. It will amount to more than "uh hill uh beans."

But are we, as Stepto's model suggests, really meant to identify with Pheoby? Is any (or every) reader capable of being the ideal listener for whom this text has been waiting, the "bee" to this textual "blossom"? Or are we, instead, like Janie's various courtroom audiences, either inaccessible, incompetent, or somehow antagonistic? Are we meant to discover that we are probably as unteachable as they? These are difficult questions. Hurston structures an ambiguity into the novel's relation to its reader by deliberately juxtaposing audiences and portraying the only ideal audience as a virtual mirror of Janie herself. The framing device Hurston uses gives the entire novel the quality of, as Lorranie Bethel puts it, an "overheard conversation."[48] While we can hear Janie's story, in other words, we do so in the form of a reminder that *we* are *not* its ideal audience, that it is not addressed to us, that we are not having a conversation with Janie and that we, unlike Pheoby (and apparently regardless of whoever "we" in fact happen to be) do not have our tongue in either Janie's or Hurston's mouth.

"With Their Tongues Cocked and Loaded"

"Women writers," Tania Modleski writes, "have always had their own way of 'evening things up'" through a "hidden, but ubiquitous plot of revenge that . . . protest[s] against the authority of fathers and husbands."[49] Revenge may include hurting the heroine to induce the hero's remorse and self-blame, mutilating the hero, as in *Jane Eyre*, or, ultimately, killing him. The satisfaction of romance, Modleski maintains, comes chiefly through its "revenge fantasy," a form of poetic justice.[50]

Both of Janie's first two husbands are punished for being bad listeners, as well as for being unable to arouse or sustain Janie's desire. Janie's "revenge" on Logan Killicks is relatively mild; she simply walks away from him, after letting him know that "'you ain't done me no favor by marryin' me'" (53).[51] Jody, who "never was the flesh and blood figure of her dreams[,] just something she had grabbed up to drape her dreams over" (112) receives harsher treatment for making her tie up her hair so none of the other men can appreciate it, making her work in the store, beating her, and isolating her from the town's verbal play and "lying" sessions. But Jody's greatest crime is in becoming deaf to Janie and refusing to listen to her. This, Janie tells him, is why he has "got" to die: "'now you got tuh die tuh find out dat you got tuh pacify somebody besides yo'self if you wants any love and any sympathy in dis world. You ain't tried tuh pacify *nobody* but yo'self. Too busy listening tuh yo' own big voice'" (133).

The novel's revenge on Nanny is more problematic since she does not seem to refuse to listen in quite the same way. She seems to merit more sympathy than she receives. Her own dreams and desires, after all, have never been fulfilled. And those dreams were selfless ones, centering around the needs of Janie and other black women. While surprisingly harsh, Janie's repudiation of Nanny is consistent with the novel's erotics of talk. Nothing, apparently, forgives the repression of desire; its expression forgives much else.

The novel's dramatic and vivid revenge on Tea Cake, the very embodiment of the "love thoughts of women," has baffled many readers. Initially, Tea Cake encourages both talk and play. Janie and Tea Cake "run" their "conversation from grass roots tuh pine trees" (160); they talk about everything from checkers to passenger trains, from Janie's good looks to Tea Cake's past loves. Tea Cake teaches Janie to play checkers and Janie "found herself glowing inside. Somebody wanted her to play. Somebody thought it was natural for her to play" (146).

But Hurston's description of their romance is double-edged. Within the positive and sometimes even idyllic depictions of Janie and Tea Cake's love affair there is also something suffocating, almost sinister: "Janie awoke next morning by feeling Tea Cake *almost kissing her breath away*. Holding her and caressing her *as if he feared she might escape* his grasp" (162); "Janie looked down on him and felt a *self-crushing love*" (192); "He seemed to be *crushing* scent out of the world with his footsteps. *Crushing* aromatic herbs with every step he took" (161, all emphasis mine). While the life Tea Cake and Janie share on the muck is often glorious, it is not shared equally:

> *Tea Cake's house* was a magnet, the unauthorized center of the "job." The way he would sit in the doorway and play his guitar made people stop and listen and maybe disappoint the jook for the night. He was always laughing and full of fun too. He kept everybody laughing in the bean field.
>
> Janie stayed home and boiled big pots of black-eyed peas and rice. Sometimes baked big pans of navy beans with plenty of sugar and hunks of bacon laying on top. That was something Tea Cake loved. (197, emphasis mine)

Increasingly, Tea Cake attempts to speak for Janie, to *tell* her what her own desires are. But Janie's tongue isn't in Tea Cake's mouth. When he speaks Janie's desires for her, he often gets them wrong. After their first night together, for example, Janie wants to get up and fix breakfast, but Tea Cake "wouldn't let her get him any breakfast at all. He wanted her to get her rest. He made her stay where she was. In her heart she wanted to get his breakfast for him. But she stayed in bed long after he was gone" (163).

Tea Cake worsens. He beats Janie without reason. And his inability— or refusal—to listen makes him dangerous. When the Seminole Indians correctly read the natural signs of an impending flood, Tea Cake discounts them—and Janie. "'Indians don't know much uh nothin', tuh tell de truth,'" he declares (231). Once they are already trapped by flood waters, Janie cautions against leaving the house, but Tea Cake "stunned the argument with half a word" (237) and consequently they venture out into the flood which is ultimately responsible for Tea Cake's rabies and subsequent death.

At the emotional register, Tea Cake's death is of course a tragedy. But within the narrative logic of this novel, Tea Cake's death also liberates Janie to continue her quest and, ultimately, to satisfy her "oldest human long-ing—self revelation" with someone who *can* listen. As yet another in a long succession of failed listeners, his death is part of what we might call this poetic novel's erotic justice.

In representing Janie's desperate—and largely unfulfilled—need for a listener, Hurston dramatizes the impossibility of the social situation she depicts, resisting what Fredric Jameson has described as literature's ideo-logical task: "inventing imaginary or formal 'solutions' to unresolvable social contradictions."[52] Whereas Houston Baker would chide critics for failing "to provide the kind of comprehensive hearing offered by Pheoby,"[53] I am suggesting that Hurston very deliberately figures Pheoby's "comprehen-sive listening" as a hard act to follow. The presence of multiple—and mostly failed—listeners in the novel reminds us that there are also multiple narratees, implied readers, and historical readers. And there is no reason to assume, out of hand, that all of these are either successful or ideal. Any given reader may as easily resemble "Mouth-Almighty" as Pheoby.

This is of course not to say that there aren't now and haven't been read-ers very much like Pheoby. But remembering that Hurston allegorizes such a reader as not only black, female, from the same background as Janie and with similar experiences, but also as operating from a position of sympathy (Pheoby's "hungry listening"), sensuality and erotic openness to Janie ("'mah tongue is in mah friend's mouf'"), generosity and nurturance (Pheoby's "mulatto rice"), protectiveness ("'nobody better not criticize yuh in mah hearing'"), and, finally, discursive passivity (the willingness to remain a listener, not to demand an exchange of places, not to insist on telling her own story as well), we must conclude that her depiction is an exaggerated idealization, just as all objects of romantic desire and fantasy are exagger-ated and idealized. But it is also, like most, an idealization with political bite, coming as it does from a black woman writer who we know had such good reasons to distrust her own reception and to doubt the motives of her audience(s), as much when they chose to celebrate her as when they chose to vilify her.

To say that Hurston's allegory of intersubjective understanding (as I read the framing conversation) has political bite is not to say that it is politically unambiguous. On the contrary. Eroticizing Janie and Pheoby's dialogue seems to affirm storytelling, narration, and communication in just the way we might expect from an anthropologist and writer who devoted so much of her life to documenting African American discursive, dialogic, and storytelling practices. But at the same time, Hurston's construction of ideal listening as virtual mirroring seems essentialistic, seems to suggest that she either could not imagine communicability across differences or that she could not imagine (or locate) the nurturant, sympathetic community in which such communication might be possible, conclusions which resonate with her eventual withdrawal from her own community and, finally, from publicity and writing itself—her apparent decision to live out her life in near isolation and cultural exile.[54] The frame, then, not only gives shape to aesthetic and political questions of rhetoric and reception which we can now recognize as reflecting back on the aesthetic and political debates of the Harlem Renaissance, it also embodies a paradoxical political position generally associated with the reclusive, diffident, self-isolating Hurston of the fifties, not the exuberant cultural radical of the twenties or thirties.

On Hurston's account, the necessary condition for an ideal speech situation is not merely, as Habermas might have it, adherence to a coherent and fair set of procedural norms. Instead, I believe, she seeks a homogeneity sufficiently strong that such procedural norms, in fact, would probably not be needed. Janie's ideal listener is not someone who masters discursive fairness or learns the skills necessary to recognize the concrete particularity of someone who is different. Pheoby is so like Janie that, as Molly Hite points out, they are practically "interchangeable."[55] Pheoby's ideal listening is a reversal of the narrative strategies Jacobs deploys. Where Jacobs seeks to make her reader feel comfortable and competent, Hurston provides an ideal listener meant, I propose, to discomfort most of us.

This is not a very inviting stance for a writer to take, perhaps. But Hurston, I am arguing, is not the optimistic, celebratory writer she has so often been taken to be. Whereas Richard Wright and Hazel Carby, among others, fault Hurston for clinging to and sentimentalizing the folk community, I am suggesting that she is sentimental about no communities, no heterogeneous public spheres. Unlike Brontë's Jane, she is unconvinced that she can either transcend or substantially alter the cultural conversation. Hence, she elects, when possible, not to "play" the "talking game" she documents. Nor does this strike me as a terribly unreasonable position for a black woman writer at odds with a mainstream white culture which loved her for the wrong reasons and an oppositional black one which often did not love her at all. Given her perspective as a double outsider, it might be that Hurston was not so much advocating essentialism as trying to indicate the absence of any community—heterogenous or homogeneous—in which she felt she (or a woman like Janie) could exercise her voice in quite the way she wanted to, without capitulating either to requests from black contemporaries for representations of upper-middle-class urban black life or from white patrons for primitivistic, simplistic, and sensationalizing stereotypes. Perhaps if Hurston herself had been able to find the listener she allegorizes in Pheoby, if she believed that she had found that listener through her writing, she would not have withdrawn as she did.

It may be in consideration of the possible homology between the implied reader and these disappointing communities, these versions of

"Mouth-Almighty," that Janie's repudiation of both the Eatonville and "muck" (or Everglades) communities has been hard for critics to accept, just as Rochester's limitations as Jane's interlocutor have been hard to accept. If Janie will not speak to them, then is Hurston also rejecting us, keeping us at bay as Janie distances herself from "Mouth-Almighty"? This homology is potentially very unsettling; it reverses the conventional problem of narrative authority by asking whether the reader is authorized and competent to *listen*, instead of whether the narrator is authorized to speak. The question of narratee authority is potentially so troubling because it raises a further question: if we *don't* have the "understandin' to go long wid" the story we are reading, if we, like the community, can't tell a "mink skin" from a "coon hide" (19), then where would we get that authority? Can we, to reverse Ross Chambers's problematic formulation that narrators "earn the authority to narrate in the very act of storytelling,"[56] earn the authority to *hear* in the very act of storylistening?

The answer would be "yes" if we could convince ourselves that Janie and her community are reconciled and that, if only symbolically, she does "reveal" herself to them. And critics again and again try to return Janie to her community. "Janie's voice," Nellie McKay argues, "emerges from the community she helps to form and . . . [which] also forms her."[57] Janie has "come home" to tell her story, Priscilla Wald writes.[58] Janie "learns to be one of the people," claims Elizabeth Meese.[59] Both Robert Hemenway and Barbara Christian describe Janie's psychological maturation in terms of her reintegration into communal life. "Janie's 'blossoming,'" writes Hemenway, "refers personally to her discovery of self and ultimately to her meaningful participation in black tradition."[60] According to Christian, "Janie Stark is not an individual in a vacuum. She is an intrinsic part of a community, and she brings her life and its richness, joys, and sorrows back to it."[61] Baker, who initially argues against "romantic readings of *Their Eyes Were Watching God*," also writes that Janie "returns to the communal landscape . . . as a storyteller and blues singer par excellence . . . returns to sing to an exclusively black audience."[62] Even Mary Helen Washington, who argues, as I noted earlier, that Janie is "outside of the folk community," sees a potential for Janie's reintegration into her community by virtue of her very rejection of it: "Janie has, of course," Washington argues, "reformed her community by her resistance to its values."[63]

This "of course" is precisely what Hurston puts in question in *Their Eyes Were Watching God* through the text's admonition *not* to assume that verbal resistance leads ineluctably to the reformation or transformation it seeks. The reconciliation of Janie and her community on the part of contemporary critics responds, I think, to our own longing and nostalgia for forms of communal life, for the relations of intersubjective, discursive exchange that seem to be waning conditions of modernity. As critic Jean E. Kennard would have it, texts should "satisfy us" and "comfort us by providing that sense of community we read for in the first place."[64] Such imaginary reconciliation asks that the novel reflect back the image of ourselves we would most like to see. Northrop Frye, in *The Anatomy of Criticism*, argues that "framing" is a way to give the most anxious romance a happy ending. "A characteristic feature of this phase" of resolution, Frye writes,

> is the tale in quotation marks, where we have an opening setting with a small group of congenial people and then the real story told by one of the members. . . . The history is conceived not only as a progression but as a cycle of which the audience is the end, and, as the last page indicates, the beginning as well. . . . The effect of such devices is to present the story through a relaxed and contemplative haze as something that entertains us without, so to speak, confronting us, as direct tragedy confronts us. . . . The romance . . . is physically associated with comfortable beds or chairs around fireplaces or warm and cozy spots generally.[65]

When critics imagine that Janie "acquires" a voice or that she speaks to or for her community, they reinterpret the novel's frame device as affirming narrative rather than calling its efficacy into question on behalf of women who face the kinds of social conditions Janie faces. Reintegrating Janie into her community transforms the novel into a "cuddle fiction," as Frye calls it. Such a reading resolves not Hurston's dilemmas or her narrator's, but our own; it rewards us (with comfort and a premodern pastoral world) regardless of the kinds of listeners we, in fact, may be.

But reading *Their Eyes Were Watching God* as a story of communal reintegration and reconciliation mediated through the positivity of love and voice occludes the ways in which Hurston's revision of the romance narrative (denying Janie her conventional lover-hero and granting her a heroine-listener instead) works to *deepen* rather than to reduce the contradictions cutting across it.

There is a laudable political agenda behind romanticizing readings—a desire to see narrative, dialogue, and conversation not only as forms of personal and social recognition but also as means of social transformation, a way of righting the conditions which make Janie's choices so limited and her satisfaction so elusive, a way of administering poetic justice. Insofar as we want to believe, along with critics like Bernard Bell and Elizabeth Meese, that "Hurston empowers Janie Crawford to liberate herself and her friend Pheoby through storytelling,"[66] that "Hurston presents a forceful resistance to black women's oppression . . . a map of a woman's personal resistance to patriarchy,"[67] we need to be, ourselves, proof of Hurston's transformational success. If the community—and by extension the reader—remains unchanged by her life and her story, after all, in what sense can Janie's resistance (or Hurston's) be called effective? The problem is that Janie's community *doesn't* change and that Janie (and perhaps Hurston) believes that hearing her story won't help.

Romanticization, in other words, blunts the force of Hurston's social indictment. She is willing to question narrative on behalf of black women who face the kinds of social conditions Janie does. By having Janie speak only to Pheoby—and only indirectly to us—Hurston braves a form of symbolic "self-talk" to articulate, as I discussed in the Introduction, the culture's failure to make good on its own promises (and premises) of intersubjectivity. Displays of "self-talk," as we know, can be painful to watch. But if Hurston's structures of implied address are meant to dramatize just such a discursive scenario, to indicate a *refusal* to enter the cultural conversation on its own terms, then it is important not to supply the missing discursive community, the missing ideal listener, that gives the story its punch.

I have put this in moral terms, but the problem, I recognize, is substantially methodological. How, in recuperating this novel, can we avoid assuming that we are already its reconstituted, transformed, ideal reader— even as we effectively read and analyze its longing for just such a reception? How can we avoid romanticizing away its narrative skepticism and distrust of discourse in the name of our own emancipatory project and in implicit historicization of our own recuperation of that very message? In contrast to John Callahan's claim that "Hurston invites her readers to respond as listeners and participants in the storytelling,"[68] I'd suggest that only by including oneself in Hurston's blanket indictment, assuming that one is, for whatever reason, a different reader than Hurston's idealized, eroticized, and romanticized projection, can one learn to listen, to listen differently, and to help, thereby, create the very conditions under which black female longing for narration and self-revelation might, someday, be satisfied.

5

"Somebody I Can Talk To": Teaching Feminism Through *The Color Purple*

"us talk and talk . . ."

—Alice Walker,
The Color Purple[1]

"She Tell Lies"

In *The Color Purple*, Alice Walker gives us a heroine, like the others I've discussed, whose being in some way hinges on her ability to narrate her life story and to find an audience fit to hear and understand it. Where the other texts I've discussed use tropes of discursive and social exchange to critique the liberal premise that anyone can participate as an equal in the cultural conversation, Walker gives us a heroine whose story works transformative magic, putting all of its listeners—including the reader—on the same footing and thereby representing exchange as just the equalizing and fair social machinery it represents itself to be.

If *Their Eyes Were Watching God* can only imagine a satisfying discursive exchange within a dyadic, female, identificatory, homogeneous, and private public sphere (the back porch), Alice Walker's *The Color Purple* is prepared to celebrate the utopian possibilities of discourse, community, and social exchange without the reserve and distrust exhibited by the other texts I've discussed. Those texts distrust the transformational effects of narratives written from the social margins to be read by those in positions of relatively greater power even as they attempt to generate just such effects. *The Color Purple*, by contrast, suggests that there is no need for skepticism or withdrawal, since simply through the intersubjective exchange created when we speak to one another it is in our power to create a perfect (or nearly perfect) world which realizes the values of intimacy we prize in the private sphere. This perfect world is, ultimately, in fact, the private sphere writ large.

In Walker's hands, the trope of an erotics of talk becomes the model for the way things finally are in Celie's transfigured, ideal, familiar, feminist world.

What are we to make of this? In a sense, Walker offers just the happy ending which feminist criticism has sought to read into many fables of women's talk: making the mad narrator of "The Yellow Wallpaper" or the women readers of "The Blank Page" and "A Jury of Her Peers" heroic rescuers in an enterprise of recuperative reading, imagining successful contracts for Linda Brent, projecting ourselves as the ideal listener/lover Jane and Janie long for. In Michael Awkward's words, The Color Purple's story is "the achievement of (comm)unity."[2] Here at last the imperatives of a politics of voice and an erotics of talk are no longer at odds. By speaking out, Celie transfigures her world. In her new community, anyone can talk, everyone listens; talk is, indeed, the "language game" of justice in which, as Lyotard puts it, "one speaks as a listener."[3]

Given its instructive, inspiring story of an oppressed, abused, isolated woman who learns to fight back, speak for herself, defend other women, "git man off her eyeball" (204), and make her way in a racist, patriarchal world that would deny her subjectivity, agency, and pleasure, it is hardly surprising that Walker's The Color Purple "took the feminist world by storm."[4] Or that it has been taken up as a "feminist fable."[5] Or that Celie has become a "role model for contemporary feminists,"[6] "an example of woman's oppression and liberation,"[7] a symbolic "'Everywoman'" in both her reduction to object and her struggles to become a speaking subject.[8]

Although The Color Purple has occasioned heated debates over black cultural representation and white patronage, a debate that is sometimes reminiscent of the fiery polemics of the twenties,[9] Jacqueline Bobo, in her interviews with African American women about their responses to the novel, reported "overwhelmingly positive reactions."[10] Even Trudier Harris, who joined a number of black male critics in faulting the novel for a "reaffirmation of many old stereotypes" and for giving "validity to all the white racist's notions of pathology in black communities,"[11] celebrates Walker's depiction of "a woman who struggles through adversity to assert herself against almost impossible odds."[12]

Whereas many black feminist critics stress the racial specificity of Walker's portrayal, reading the novel as an allegory of "the process and problematics of writing for the black woman,"[13] white feminist critics have often universalized the novel as a "paradigm of change,"[14] rejoicing in how "Celie wrests language from those who would persecute and silence her."[15] A novel like The Color Purple, Alison Light writes, "can be popular with a whole range of women readers, cutting across the specificity of its black history, in its concern with family, emotionality, sexual relations, and fantasy life."[16]

There are good reasons for this novel's privileged status as a pedagogical and political model. Celie ruptures the patriarchal injunction to silence— "'You better not never tell nobody but God. It'd kill your mammy'" (1).

And she keeps faith with her own perception, in spite of the way others try to invalidate it: "'She tell lies,'" "Pa" tells Mr.____ as he hands her over to him (9), just as Jane is branded a "liar" when she is passed between Mrs. Reed and Mr. Brocklehurst.[17] Celie refuses to accept that her own view is a "lie."

Alice Walker is a writer working within the recuperative, archeological tradition of feminist criticism; she has dedicated herself to uncovering the voices of women she calls "Crazy Saints . . . our mothers and grandmothers . . . who died with their real gifts stifled within them."[18] "I'm always trying to give voice to specific people," Walker writes.[19] *The Color Purple* was written, Walker remarked in a *Newsweek* interview, so that "people can hear Celie's voice."[20] Walker wants us to understand such recuperation as an act of self-preservation. "The life we save," she asserts, "is our own."[21] Without freeing earlier artists "from their neglect and the oppression of silence forced upon them because they were black and they were women," the contemporary African American woman writer, Walker believes, will be condemned to similar silence and neglect.[22] "We are a people. A people do not throw their geniuses away. And if they are thrown away, it is our duty as artists and as witnesses for the future to collect them again for the sake of our children, and, if necessary, bone by bone."[23]

The fictional act of recovering Celie's narrative grounds *The Color Purple* in the politics of voice and recuperation I have discussed earlier. Celie, as Linda Abbandonato writes, is "an 'invisible woman' . . . traditionally silenced and effaced in fiction; and by centering on her, Walker replots the heroine's text."[24] Walker, Linda Kauffman writes, "views history from the bottom up and reconstructs it to reflect the voices of the oppressed, the disenfranchised, the silenced."[25] Celie herself models this archeological enterprise by recuperating Nettie's buried voice; with Shug's help she saves Nettie's story, shares it, puts it in order.[26]

Also clearly grounded in the topos of an erotics of talk, the novel has Celie long for an ideal listener, someone who will listen to her story, sympathize with it, understand it (and her), and respond accordingly.[27] Walker makes explicit what *Jane Eyre* and *Their Eyes Were Watching God* imply: Celie's ideal listener—a woman—is also her ideal lover, and vice versa. Shug and Celie, as Henry Louis Gates, Jr., puts it, are "literal 'kissin-friends.'"[28]

In fact, *The Color Purple* "signifies" upon Hurston's novel by rejecting its ethics of disengagement, even as it builds on its aesthetic of reciprocity by providing Celie with a nearly endless supply of desirable, conversational partners. Contesting one's community, Walker implies, can transform it. Even Mr.____in the end becomes "somebody I can talk to," Celie says. This transformation, and the theory of narrative exchange it articulates, will be the focus of much of what follows.

Exchange is at the heart of our self-understandings as autonomous *and* social beings, as Seyla Benhabib has argued. The normative ideals of bourgeois society—the right of all to freedom, equality, property—are expressed in social relations of exchange between citizens, who are equal in their

abstract right to voluntarily dispose of what belongs to them. "Social relations of exchange in the marketplace actualize the norms of equality, freedom, and property."[29]

On the face of it, Celie's exclusion from language—"you better not
never tell"—holds this normative self-understanding up to the scrutiny of
actual social relations, calling into question the very ideal of exchange as
an equalizing norm. "When the *norms* of bourgeois society are compared
with the *actuality* of the social relations in which they are embodied, the
discrepancy between ideal and actuality becomes apparent."[30] The dimension of the novel which makes this discrepancy apparent is its rehearsal of
failed exchanges: between Celie and various members of her community,
between Nettie and Celie, between Nettie (and company) and the Africans,
between Africans and European imperialists, between southern American
blacks and whites, between men and women. These failed exchanges suggest not only that ideals and actualities do not mesh, but more important
that the ideals represented by social exchange are, in fact, effaced by the
practice of exchange itself. In short, under conditions of radical inequality,
exchange relations benefit the advantaged. Exchange, by itself, is not a
medium for redistributing social and symbolic resources but, Walker suggests, for recirculating them back to their original proprietors. The novel's
most interesting moments of social critique, in my view, are all refracted
through such failed exchanges, failed communications. It is when, suddenly,
such failures as Mr._____'s inability to listen become successes that I would
question the way exchange is operating in this novel and, in turn, the sort
of model *The Color Purple* offers for either liberation or, read allegorically,
criticism.

"You Got to Fight"

It would be hard to disagree with Gates's assessment that *The Color Purple* is
an exemplary text of "voice."[31] It does not merely represent a new version of
Hurston's Janie on a quest for voice. It also polemicizes *against* black female
texts like *Incidents in the Life of a Slave Girl* and *Their Eyes Were Watching
God* which express ambivalence about the effectivity—and desirability—of
discursive contestation.[32] It seems to suggest that however delegitimated one's
discursive position may be, self-isolation is not a viable, moral position. It
both valorizes "voice" in the sentimentalizing terms I have criticized and
seems, until the end, to question that very sentimentalization.

Walker, in fact, does not really represent Celie as "finding" a voice. Even
in her most oppressed state, she is able to express herself by writing. It is
the process of developing that voice, orienting it toward her different audiences, that is really at stake. Above all, Celie needs to learn to use her voice
to resist oppression. She must be convinced that resistance and contestation are not incompatible with fulfillment and satisfaction. Making this
convincing, as we shall see, proves a very difficult task.

Numerous times, other women tell Celie that she must learn to fight back. "You got to fight. You got to fight," Nettie tells Celie when she sees how Mr. _____'s children ride roughshod over her (18). "You've got to fight," Nettie writes (131). "I don't know how to fight. All I know how to do is stay alive," Celie replies (18). Having internalized the patriarchal warning that the wages of rebellion are death, Celie believes that resistance and survival are necessarily at odds.[33] "It's like seeing you buried," Nettie writes, hoping to free Celie's voice (18).

Celie's next letter reopens the same debate. "You got to fight them, Celie, she [Mr. _____'s sister, Kate] say. I can't do it for you. You got to fight them for yourself" (22). "I don't say nothing," Celie says, "I think about Nettie, dead. She fight, she run away. What good it do? I don't fight, I stay where I'm told. But I'm alive" (22). Celie, it is important to note, is not entirely misguided. Resistance and rebellion *are* costly. And just as Nettie's resistance has caused her absence, so Kate is kicked out of Mr. _____'s house and hence out of Celie's life for trying to speak on Celie's behalf and protest her mistreatment by Mr. _____ and his sons.

But Celie also misreads this lesson. Her inability to associate fighting *with* survival is, it is implied, tied to her mistaken faith in authoritative narratives, her failure as an "overreader," to return to the problematic explored in Chapter One. As Mr. _____ drags Nettie away, Celie enjoins her to "write" (just as Nettie has been enjoining Celie to "fight"). "Nothing but death can keep me from it," Nettie promises. Never again hearing from Nettie, Celie presumes that she is dead. Celie does not know how to "overread": filling in gaps, reading between the lines, learning to hear the "voice" of silence, madness, babbling, muttering, or screaming—women's "self-talk." Before Celie can learn to "fight," she must identify her models and resources by learning—like Walker "reading" the hundred-year-old quilt of an anonymous black woman in Alabama,[34] like the protagonist of "The Yellow Wallpaper" reading the "sub-pattern" of "bars" and "the woman behind it . . . as plain as can be,"[35] like the "old and young nuns, with the Mother Abbess herself'" reading the "blank page" of the anonymous, missing princess,[36] like Mrs. Peters and Mrs. Hale, reading the uneven stitches of Mrs. Foster's quilt block,[37] or like Nettie trying to get Corrine to read Celie's story in a quilt (193)—to recognize the alternative texts that code and preserve women's stories of resistance. Only after Celie has discovered Nettie's hidden letters and learned, therefore, that there *are* hidden, unofficial, even silent stories to be recuperated from behind the official—and false—narratives that obscure them does she begin to "fight back" with her own self-narrations.

Walker makes *The Color Purple*'s project a panegyric to the therapeutic and transformational potential of telling counternarratives: the unofficial histories of the private or intimate sphere over and against official histories of the public sphere.[38] It is "a historical novel" that "starts not with the taking of lands, or the births, battles, and deaths of Great Men, but with one woman asking another for her underwear."[39] In place of the so-called "antinarrativism" often assumed to be the inevitable outcome of poststructural skepticism about "historical unities, subjects and totalizations,"[40] Walker champions what one critic has recently called the "tactical value of narrative" in the "struggle against dominant culture," its ability to represent what Toni Morrison calls "discredited" and Michel Foucault "unauthorized" forms of knowledge.[41]

In this context, Steven Spielberg and screenwriter Menno Meyjes were right to make cinematic hay out of what are relatively brief mentions of literacy and education in the novel. Through a dramatic tracing-paper flutter of hand-lettered signifieds—"apples," "iron," "kettle," "eggs," "shelf," "honey," "jar," "window," "hair," "arm," "sleeve," "stocking," and, of course, "sky" (which Celie finds on the floor long after Nettie is gone)—the film depicts the importance of narrative mastery.[42] Insofar as a coherent sense of self depends upon becoming the "author of a coherent life-story,"[43] Celie's very being depends upon her access to narrative and her ability to construct a counternarrative that (re)tells the story of her own life over and against the disembodied patriarchal injunction to self-silencing which speaks first in the novel and the misrepresentations—"she tell lies"—that those in power promote.

Celie's pointed inability to do this opens the novel, much as negation and dissatisfaction open *Jane Eyre* and *Their Eyes Were Watching God*. Self-description becomes self-erasure in her aborted effort to proclaim herself a good girl. "I~~am~~" (1). "Not only am I not a good girl, but I am not." "I do not exist." "I am no one." By coaching her to "fight," other women prompt Celie to develop narratives that can assert both her "goodness" and her being, a provocation Celie finally answers when she articulates the exploitation at the heart of family romance:[44] "You was all rotten children, I say. You made my life a hell on earth. And your daddy here ain't dead horse's shit" (207). Her tongue-lashing ends with the crucial replacement of "I'm here" (214) for her earlier self-erasure "I~~am~~."

Telling a counternarrative, it would seem, heals Celie's fragmented self and enables her coherent self-assertion. This power of renaming is repeated several times. Sexual desire seems foreclosed for Celie, who experiences sex as pure objectification and humiliation: "he get up on you, heist your nightgown round your waist, plunge in. . . . Never ast me how I feel, nothing. Just do his business, get off, go to sleep." But by renaming Celie "still a virgin" (81), Shug unsutures sexuality and abuse. She calls it not it, we might say, echoing the pun exchanged by Mrs. Hale and Mrs. Peters in "A Jury of Her Peers." Shug uncovers Celie's buried desire as Celie is later to uncover Nettie's buried voice, designating her as alive not dead, present not absent. It is a short step from here to uncovering a buried voice by renaming it. "Squeak, Mary Agnes, what difference do it make?" Harpo asks. "It make a lot, say Squeak. When I was Mary Agnes I could sing in public" (210).

This privileging of counternarratives shapes the novel's form. Interweaving the historical narratives of Africa and Georgia is a way of countering the official, racist, pathologizing representations of slavery and black southern life with an unofficial and variegated history of poor, rural, post-Reconstruction small-town life, an unofficial history of African American resistance and entrepreneurship, as well as with the often repressed story of black African participation in the slave trade. A web of contestations emerges. *American blacks versus Africans*: "No one else in this village wants to hear about slavery. They acknowledge no responsibility whatsoever" (171); "the Africans don't even *see* us. They don't even recognize us as the brothers and sisters they sold" (243). *European and American imperialism versus black African culture*: "the things they have brought back! . . . jewels, furniture, fur carpets, swords, clothing, even *tombs*" (145). *Black African men versus black African women*: "the Olinka don't believe in educating girls" (162). *The European rubber industry versus African roofleaf. Black versus white missionaries* (who show no real interest in Africans). *Straight white male Englishmen versus an (implicitly) lesbian white Englishwoman writer*: "she wanted to write books. Her family was against it. They hoped she'd marry. Me *marry!* she hooted" (235). *The North* (where Nettie travels prior to leaving for Africa) *versus the South*. This web of contestations, formally at least, suggests a heterogeneous speech community and the importance of speaking across it. It suggests the importance of contestation and argument.

The question of what counts not merely as true but also *as* narration takes shape in myriad jokes over mainstream white *history* ("I learned all about Columbus in first grade, but look like he the first thing I forgot" (10)); *journalism* ("The news always sound crazy. People fussing and fighting and pointing fingers at other people, and never even looking for no peace. People insane, say Shug. Crazy as betsy bugs" (217)); and *national identity* ("white people busy celebrating they independence from England July 4th, say Harpo, so . . . us can spend the day celebrating each other" (294)).

The question of what counts is also particularly sharp when Celie learns her own buried family history: her successful father was lynched for his store and her grieving mother was driven insane and taken advantage of by a "stranger." While these parents are buried in unmarked graves and Celie has no record of their lives, the record of "Pa's" (that is, the stranger's) life both mirrors and mocks hegemonic modes of memorialization. As Celie enters the graveyard where "Pa" is buried she sees "something like a short skyscraper . . . sure enough it's got Alphonso's name on it. Got a lot of other stuff on it too. Member of this and that. Leading businessman and farmer. Upright husband and father. Kind to the poor and helpless" (252).[45] The counternarratives that connect Columbus to cucumbers and newspapers to science fiction, that render national celebrations ludicrous and reduce the memory of Alphonse to a lying concrete phallus, are given both a therapeutic and a revolutionary force. They can heal communities and contest hegemony. Or so the novel *seems* to insist.

"I Was Dying to Tell"

As much as Celie must learn to "fight back," winning battles isn't really what Celie's war is all about. For Celie to become a "dignified" subject and enter into the public sphere as an agent to be reckoned with, she must not only find her voice, she must exercise it with someone besides herself, must avoid seeming to engage in what Goffman calls "self talk" or "muttering."[46] As Molly Hite writes, "the drama of Celie's epistolary self-creation revolves around the discovery of a female audience that finally fulfills the ideal of co-respondence. . . . The process of finding her speaking voice is a process of finding her audience."[47]

Unlike Hurston's Janie, for Celie, finding a listener and finding her voice are inextricably related, just as believing one has an ideal and sympathetic listener may give one the courage to fight back against others. Only when her sister-in-law Kate tells her, "'You deserve more than this,'" does she begin to consider, "Maybe so. I think" (22). Becoming Nettie's ideal listener and saving her letters from oblivion teaches Celie about how good listeners help others to survive, how social and personal identities are constructed by our relations with others and their recognitions of us. When Celie finally does talk back to Mr._____, saying "I'm pore, I'm black, I may be ugly and can't cook . . . but I'm here," her "voice" speaks to "everything listening" (214). Without "everything listening," everything's "hungry listening," we might say, her response would not have been possible. Without a sympathetic audience, such as Shug, Celie might never have been able to go from her first self-effacing statement "~~I am~~" to her later declaration, "I'm here" (214).

But there is also a tension between these two imperatives. "Finding a voice" means one thing, for example, when the audience to be addressed is a group of hostile "others": the courthouse Janie faces, Minnie Foster will face, or Linda Brent might have faced had she either been caught or had tried to press her legal "rights" to her children. It means another thing altogether when the audience to be addressed is Pheoby, Shug Avery, Mrs. Peters and Mrs. Hale, the woman in the wallpaper, or Diana and Mary Rivers.

Earlier I suggested that Walker's "signifies" on Hurston's text by imagining a much wider and much more successful field of discursive contestation for Celie. Celie does "fight"—even with God ("us fight" (204))—in ways that Janie resists. *The Color Purple* could, in fact, be read as re-staging Hurston's courtroom scene in *Their Eyes Were Watching God*, a revision in which the "accused" defends herself, in her own voice, in front of all of her different constituencies. Walker not only "signifies" on Hurston's politics of voice, suggesting that Janie—and perhaps Hurston as well—"got to fight." She also sends Celie out on Janie's quest for a "bee for her blossom," a search for the "creaming," "frothing," delight of "self revelation."

Nettie's letters to Celie and Celie's letters to God dramatize their unmet needs for the conditions enabling such "creaming" and "frothing." "I remember one time you said your life made you feel so ashamed you couldn't even talk about it to God, you had to write it, bad as you thought your writing was. Well, now I know what you meant," Nettie writes from Africa, where she suffers from having "hardly anybody to talk to, just in friendship" (170). Nettie, like Celie before she meets Shug, like Jane in *Jane Eyre*, like Janie before Pheoby, is "dying to tell" her story (198) but has no one to tell it to.

The epistolary form is particularly well suited for dramatizing this. While epistolary narratives may well embody a "desire for exchange,"[48] Linda Kauffman points out that they are more likely to depict that desire as a thwarted one: "letters are repeatedly lost, withheld, seized, misdirected, or misplaced. . . . An addressee who is absent, silent, or incapable of replying is one of the distinguishing characteristics of epistolarity." Failed exchange, Kauffman argues, is "endemic" to the form.[49]

Many critics have argued that Nettie's letters are digressive and boring compared with Celie's.[50] But they play a vital role in developing the novel's initial skepticism about the utopian possibilities of discursive and social exchange. Nettie's letters dramatize the problematic of failed exchange.

Nettie writes often about communicative and intersubjective failure, describing the "indifference," for example, with which the Africans greet the black missionaries who've come to "help" them. "Sometimes I feel our position is like that of flies on an elephant's hide," she confides to Celie (242). "They never even listen to how we've suffered. And if they listen they say stupid things" (243). She describes the men's indifference to women: "there is a way that the men speak to women that reminds me too much of Pa. *They listen just long enough to issue instructions*," Nettie writes (168, emphasis mine). She describes Corrine's indifference to the truth about who Adam and Olivia's mother is: "Oh Celie, unbelief is a terrible thing" (191).

It is not only in personal relations that Nettie witnesses failed exchange. The social relations she takes note of all have to do with failures of exchange as well. The chief of the Olinka, for example, engages in what Nettie describes as a "pathetic exchange." He tries to explain to the white governor of the English rubber company that their road and rubber trees are wiping out their livelihood. But the Olinka not only lose their village, they end up paying rent to farm there and taxes to use their own water.

Nettie not only describes failed exchanges, she also fantasizes about exchange. "I imagine that you really do get my letters and that you are writing me back: Dear Nettie, this is what life is like for me" (161), she writes.

There is a lesson for Celie in all of these failed exchanges between people of different social status and power. These failures lead those on the losing end of bad transactions to call for revolt. They imply that Celie ought to do so as well. As a consequence of their chief's "pathetic exchange" with the white men, the Olinka conclude that it's a waste of breath to argue with men who can't—or won't—listen. "We will fight the white man," they declare (176). Samuel, a voice of rationality and caution, finally comes to the same conclusion: "He said the only thing for us to do if we wanted to remain in Africa, was join the Mbeles [the resistance fighters] and encourage all the Olinka to do the same" (238).

Celie, like Nettie, lacks an appropriate audience. Her letters parallel Nettie's by documenting failed exchanges, chiefly in the private, domestic sphere. God, Celie decides, is just like the other men she has known. "The God I been praying and writing to is a man," she says, "and act just like all the other mens I know. Trifling, forgitful, and lowdown. *If he ever listened to poor colored women the world would be a different place, I can tell you. . . . just sit up there glorying in being deef*" (199–200, emphasis mine). Shug points out to Celie that there is no point in being angry at God for not listening, because there was no point ever expecting that he could. "You mad cause he don't seem to listen to your prayers. Humph! Do the mayor listen to anything colored say? Ask Sofia" (202). "I don't have to ast Sofia. I know white people never listen to colored, period. If they do, they only listen long enough to be able to tell you what to do," Celie replies (202).

Celie not only lacks a listener, she is, like the Olinka, on the losing end of discursive, economic, and social systems of exchange.[51] Speaking across differences of gender and race proves as vexed for her as it is for them: "I don't have nothing to offer and I feels poor" (15). In the white man's store, which has replaced the store of Celie's lynched father, Corrine is made to buy 40 cents' worth of thread in "bout the right color" that she does not want (15). This scene, omitted entirely in the movie, portrays the women's inability to participate as equals in a system of exchange based on prerogatives of status and race from which they are, by definition, excluded. As simple an act as buying fabric and thread becomes humiliating.

Celie's first positive exchange with another woman immediately follows this scene and in a sense compensates for it. Celie sees Corrine at a loss for a safe place to wait for her husband's return and realizes that she *does* have something to offer: a seat in her wagon. In return, Corrine thanks her for her "'*Horse*pitality'" "'I git it and laugh,'" Celie says, "it feel like to split my face" (16).

Celie is not the only character to experience difficult or imbalanced exchanges. We see this again and again with the black women in the novel. Addie Beasley, for example, the schoolteacher, tries to argue "Pa" out of his decision to take the girls out of school, but when he brings Celie out and parades her pregnancy, Addie Beasley "stop talking and go" (11). A similar failed exchange occurs when Mr. ____'s sisters, Carrie and Kate, argue over his first wife, Annie Julia. Kate tries to defend her, pointing out that Mr. ____ "just brought her here, dropped her . . . nobody to talk to, nobody to visit" (21). But Carrie remains unmoved. When Kate argues with

Mr. _____ she is thrown out of the house. When Sofia fights with Harpo, they separate. She is subsequently jailed for "sassing" the mayor and his wife.

The failed exchanges I am rehearsing here are part of the novel's formal as well as thematic structure. Although Walker interweaves the narratives of Africa and Georgia by paralleling certain of Nettie and Celie's experiences—falling in love, growing up, raising other people's children, and so on—the two narrative strains nonetheless operate at a considerable distance from one another. They are never, in short, *about* each other. Although they are implicitly joined by a history of slavery and by a problematic of failed exchanges, nothing that happens in Milledgeville, Georgia, is shown to bear on Africa, and nothing that happens in Africa is shown to bear on Georgia. There is no trace of a pan-Africanist sensibility among Harpo and his juke joint friends, for example. None of the forms of vernacular expression which are prized in the novel is tied back to the African cultures in which it may have originated. These stories never really speak *to* each other. It is as if they never quite learn one another's tongue.

But this paradigm of failed exchange does not apply across the board. Walker attributes it most often to the public, heterogeneous sphere. In the world of romance and female friendship (which for Walker are on the "lesbian continuum" Adrienne Rich has described),[52] exchange is a far less problematic, far more pleasurable proposition. As the story develops, characters increasingly find ideal interlocutors with whom they can "change words" as an erotics of talk.

The relationship between Celie and Shug, for example, turns around talk. At Christmas, for example, Celie relates that "me and Shug cook, talk, clean the house, talk, fix up the tree, talk, wake up in the morning, talk" (114). "I talk so much my voice start to go" (123). "Shug talk and talk" (126). The romance between Samuel and Nettie also turns on talk. Samuel satisfies Nettie's need for a listener: "[He] asked me to tell him about you," Nettie writes, "and the words poured out like water. I was dying to tell someone about us" (198). Their courtship, like Jane and Rochester's or Janie and Tea Cake's, is a "simple conversation" (239). Tashi and Adam also court through seductive talk, a bantering reminiscent, in fact, of Rochester and Jane. "I wish you could have seen [Adam and Tashi] as they staggered into the compound," Nettie writes to Celie, "filthy as hogs, hair as wild as could be. Sleepy. Exhausted. Smelly. God knows. But *still arguing*" (285, emphasis mine).

How is this discursive pleasure and free exchange related to the need to "fight back" in the public sphere? Does the one develop from the other? Do they flow in both directions? What allows for shifts between them?

Walker's economy is in fact a one-way street. Whereas Walker's private sphere of intimate, reciprocal values can ultimately transform the public sphere of debate and contestation, there is no exchange of discursive form in the other direction. On the contrary. The erotics of talk that shapes the novel's romances, including the "romance" between Celie and Nettie, does not grow out of situations where characters have learned to use their voices to "fight back." In each of these instances, an erotics of talk is made possible only once the speakers turn their backs (give up, in effect) on arguing with their oppressors and begin to speak to one another instead. Turning away from Mr. _____ allows Celie both to "change words" with Shug and to foster an alternative economy. Similarly, Samuel and Nettie are able to realize their conversational romance only after they first give up on fighting the Europeans and prepare to leave Africa altogether. Tashi and Adam emerge from the forest as sweethearts precisely at the moment that Adam takes Tashi away from the fighting Mbeles.

What are we to make of these apparent renunciations of rebellion in a novel which, as I have argued, seems to take issue with Hurston's *Their Eyes Were Watching God* precisely for Janie's refusal to "fight back" with her voice? Is Walker, like Hurston, endorsing a strategy of "feather bed resistance"? Is she suggesting, as Janie does, that "fighting back" against oppression just "'tain't worth de trouble'"?

No character in *The Color Purple* is more known for her rebellious, contestatory voice and for "fighting back" than Sofia. Sofia even walks like a soldier. "Look like the army change direction, and she heading off to catch up" (33). Sofia's willingness to fight is her signature trait. She simply cannot resist contestation, whether it is telling Mr. _____ that she's not in trouble, "big though" (32), or whether it is telling the mayor's wife "Hell no" she didn't want to be her maid, a rebuff that takes twelve years off Sofia's life and reminds us of the costs of resistance. What is it, exactly, that drives Sofia to fight? Is it, like Mrs. Farrinder, the love of conflict for its own sake? What is she fighting? Sofia is fighting conflict itself: "All my life I had to fight. I had to fight my daddy. I had to fight my brothers. I had to fight my cousins and my uncles. A girl child ain't safe in a family of men. But I never thought I'd have to fight in my own house," she says sadly (42).

Sofia separates a politics of voice and an erotics of talk. She articulates the strand of the narrative logic that I have been tracing in descriptions of failed exchange. This strand of the narrative demonstrates that those at the bottom of the social order cannot transfigure the world simply by speaking their minds or, even more benignly, by telling their stories and sharing their painful experiences. All the more surprising, then, that what happens in the conclusion is exactly the reverse. The utopian conclusion of the novel argues that those whose lives are "oppressed almost beyond recognition"[53] can transfigure the world purely through the power of their voices, even when they have ceased to engage their oppressors at all.

The Color Purple has often been celebrated precisely for the force of its narrative dialectic of psychological cure and social transformation. Among feminists it is often venerated, as in Christine Froula's treatment of the novel, as a "radical cure of the hysterical cultural text that entangles both women and men," celebrated for its representation of a "hero . . . who recreates the universe by telling her story to the world."[54]

The Color Purple is a disarmingly complex novel, a novel in many ways at war with its own narrative logic. On the one hand, Walker creates an almost formulaic and sentimentalizing construction of the rebellious and curative voice of the disempowered. Yet, until the conclusion, *The Color Purple* not only deploys its own ambivalence about narrative's healing and transformational power, it affords us a "cautionary tale" about what happens when we assume that Celie's rebellious voice has the power to "liberate speaker and auditor alike."[55] For much of the novel, Walker works, I want to continue to demonstrate, with a productive tension between a politics of voice and an erotics of talk, with the necessary back and forth between them. Her conclusion, however, collapses the very tension that has given the novel its energy.

"Somebody I Can Talk To"

Although it takes both Jane and Janie nearly their whole lives to find one ideal listener, Celie seems to spend her life in constant conversation. Nearly everyone becomes her "co-respondent," as we see in the utopic family reunion that closes both the novel and the film. Many critics have remarked that Mr. _____'s transformation strains readerly credulity,[56] but it is not only Mr. _____ who is magically transformed. Transformation is the rule of a world in which anyone may become "somebody I can talk to."[57]

Spielberg, Molly Hite notes, played on this transformational emphasis by making Mr. _____'s "change of heart the turning-point of the action"[58] and adding what Hite rightly calls a "textually gratuitous daddy" for Shug. Shug's filmic daddy will not speak or listen to her. But eventually he is converted, like Mr. _____, into someone she can talk to and take comfort in. Spielberg gets the narrative logic right: anyone can be transformed into an ideal listener. (Counter)narratives create the transformations they desire.

Stepto argues that African American writers, motivated by their distrust of literate culture and mainstream audiences, attempt to create that sense of direct and immediate exchange which, according to Benjamin, is lost to modernity. African American storytelling, Stepto argues, attempts to recreate telling and hearing as a social transaction, to constitute the reader as "a hearer, with all that that implies in terms of . . . the *responsibilities* of listenership." This is a matter of active transformation and change. Responsible hearers engage in what I have described as acts of collaboration which answer the "prompting" of the text.[59]

Mr. _____'s "collaboration" is particularly notable. "When you talk to him now he really listen," Celie writes (267). He attempts to "do right" by Celie by locating Nettie, Samuel, Adam, Olivia, and Tashi and securing their return to America. Not only can Mr. _____ now understand how Celie feels and thinks, not only does he become her audience for transmitting the tales of Africa she has learned from Nettie, but he even enters into Celie's alternative economy by becoming a maker of shirts to go with her "folkspants" and by joining the "ethic of care" that predominates in Celie's female community.[60] Sewing while he listens, Mr. _____ pauses to "look at the different color thread us got" (280), differentiating himself from the men in the store who force Corrine to buy thread in "bout" the right color, as if such "trifles," as the men in "A Jury of Her Peers" might say, don't matter. In his sewing, Mr. _____ demonstrates his ability to listen to people's needs: "Got to have pockets, he say. Got to have loose sleeves. And definitely you not spose to wear it with no tie. Folks wearing ties look like they being lynch" (290). Mr. _____ learns to identify with others.

This is not the only male transformation in the novel. Harpo, who originally wanted to beat Sofia into submission, becomes the primary caretaker of their (or rather Sofia's) daughter Henrietta. In place of criticizing Sofia, he offers verbal and practical support: "I loves every judgment you ever made," he tells her (289). Like Mr. _____, Harpo participates in an alternative economy: promoting the vernacular culture of African American music through his juke joint "way back" in the woods (73).

It is not only black men who can change and be good friends to black women, Walker implies. White women can learn to hear also, *if* they are "told off." When Eleanor Jane reappears at the end of the novel she is all talk, in the worst sense. She pesters Sofia to say that Reynolds Stanley Earl, her son, is "sweet," "the smartest baby you ever saw," "*innocent*," "cute," and that Sofia "just love him" (271). "You know how some whitefolks is," Celie adds in her letter to Nettie, "they gon harass a blessing from you if it kill" (270). But Sofia, clearly fed up with being "harass[ed]" to say what she doesn't believe, finally lets Eleanor Jane have it:

> No ma'am, say Sofia. I do not love Reynolds Stanley Earl. Now. That's what you been trying to find out ever since he was born. And now you know. . . . [He] head straight for Sofia's stack of ironed clothes and pull it down on his head. . . . He can't even walk and already he in my house messing it up. Did I ast him to come? Do I care whether he sweet or not? Will it make any difference in the way he grow up to treat me what I think? . . . I don't feel nothing about him at all. I don't love him, I don't hate him. I just wish he couldn't run loose all the time messing up folks stuff.
>
> I just don't understand, say Miss Eleanor Jane. All the other colored women I know love children. The way you feel is something unnatural.
>
> I love children, say Sofia. But all the colored women that say they love yours is lying. They don't love Reynolds Stanley any more than I do. But if you so badly raise as to ast 'em, what you expect them to say? Some colored people so scared of whitefolks they claim to love the cotton gin. . . . I got my own troubles and when Reynolds Stanley grow up, he's gon be one of them. (272–73)

We know that Eleanor Jane is transformed when, a few pages later, we learn that she has gone to her mother to ask why Sofia "come to work for them" in the first place (288). Because she really listens to the answer, Eleanor Jane turns her back on the white world and comes to work for Sofia, disproving Celie's earlier hypothesis that "white people never listen to colored, period. If they do, they only listen long enough to be able to tell you what to do" (202). Like Mr. _____ and Harpo, Eleanor Jane has learned to identify with black women.

Transforming Mr. _____, Harpo, and Eleanor Jane into good listeners allows Walker a double articulation. First, that "the reader" is a fiction. There is no neutral audience. Instead, multiple factors, such as race and gender, condition how different readers will respond to different narratives and inflect whether or not they will be likely to understand them. Second, by transforming all these bad listeners into good ones, Walker suggests, as I have stated, that everyone can become "somebody I can talk to."

Well, perhaps not everyone. It is one thing, after all, to convert black men and white women and another thing altogether to convert white men. Or is it? "Colored don't count to those people," as Celie well knows (287). And the world white men create just seems silly and bizarre to black folk. When it isn't gendered, racial foolishness—"white women . . . laughing, holding they beads out on one finger, dancing on top of motorcars. Jumping into fountains" (54)—it's gendered, racial violence: a white sheriff who rapes Squeak, a white mayor who beats and imprisons Sofia, a white man's war that nearly kills Nettie, Samuel, Adam, Olivia, and Tashi.

Even white men, however, end up transformed by *The Color Purple*'s vision. Many critics argue that Celie throws over her "big and old and tall and graybearded and white" God (201) and replaces him with a sense of spirit, commonality, and moral goodness.[61] But the change in Celie's God is exactly like the other transformations I've discussed. Celie tells God off for lynching her parents, giving her a rapist for a stepfather, making her life, as she says, "a hell on earth" (207): "you must be sleep," she tells him (183). Celie asserts that the world would be different if God listened to poor colored women. And within a very few pages the world *is* a very different place for Celie. "I am so happy," she tells Nettie. "I got love, I got work, I got money, friends and time" (222). God is now listening, as becomes clear in Celie's last letter. She includes God once again in her address, verifying that he too, at last, has become somebody Celie "can talk to." "*Dear God*. Dear stars, dear trees, dear sky, dear peoples. Dear everything. *Dear God*" (292).

So what is wrong with this? Why shouldn't Walker give us a vision in which even the worst, most recalcitrant antagonist is converted and transformed by the power of a poor black woman's voice? Who is to say that she's wrong?

The Color Purple is built on a fundamental contradiction. The very logic of discursive transformation which the conclusion affirms has been undermined and exposed as illusory—or, at best, contingent—throughout the story. Only by effacing difference altogether and creating as her utopia a homogeneous world where everyone speaks the same language, where everyone, symbolically speaking, has their tongue in everyone else's mouth, can Walker reconcile this contradiction. When critics celebrate the novel's affirmation of "voice," taking for granted that it establishes a "collaborative" dialogue with us, they only obscure this contradiction between its two competing logics.

"We Get Real *Quiet and Listen*"

Not all listeners are the same; a novel has to register that difference and devise a strategy of response. According to Goffman, there are three potential sorts of listeners: those who *over*hear, those who are "ratified participants but are not specifically addressed by the speaker," and those who are "ratified participants who *are* addressed."[62] Only Nettie and God are ever officially "ratified" as the designated recipients of Celie's story. Although they are addressed directly, Celie never really expects a response from either of them, although she *desires* a response from both. Shug, on the other hand, is not addressed directly, but she is very much a "ratified" participant, and a response is certainly expected and desired of her, as it is of participants such as Sofia and Squeak, who are never even addressed. Harpo and Mr. ____, on the other hand, are never addressed directly, no response is expected of them, but they are ratified participants nonetheless. Deborah McDowell has argued that Celie's audience (and Walker's) is clearly intended to be other African American women and that everyone else is in the unratified position Goffman describes as "overhearing," a position, McDowell argues, reinforced by "the act of reading letters that are written and intended for other eyes."[63] *The Color Purple* is thus a paradigmatic text of "private narrative fiction," addressing itself to "a private readership, or one within that cultural matrix. . . . The qualitative differences between the letters to God and those to Nettie imply a causal connection between a receptive audience (imaged as one with 'kinship' ties to the writer) and the emergence of a forceful, authoritative, and self-validating narrative voice."[64]

McDowell raises an intriguing question. Is Walker structuring a gap between some readers and the more "ratified" listeners so as to make a point about who is or is not able to engender the "voice" of this text? And if so, are critics, like Froula, who take for granted their own "ratified" positions, simply missing the point of what, for McDowell, is a conception of gender particularized by both gender and race? McDowell, I believe, would suggest that they are. But this is a generous reading of the novel's logic. Walker's arrangement of listeners, addressed and ratified, fictive and real, ultimately has the effect of making everyone into "ratified participants who *are* addressed, that is, oriented to by the speaker in a manner to suggest that his [*sic*] words are particularly for them, and that some answer is therefore anticipated from them."[65] By transforming all listeners, ratified and non-ratified, receptive and nonreceptive, into allegories of an intersubjective, discursive ideal, Walker dehistoricizes and departicularizes what sets different social groups apart. Even the particularity of black women is distilled down to an Archimedean magic: the most oppressed black woman has the power (and perhaps the responsibility?) to revolutionize everyone else.

McDowell also suggests that Walker represents a receptive audience as one with "'kinship' ties to the writer." It is the meaning of that symbolic kinship that needs to be taken into account. Where Brontë and Hurston both contrast the difficulty of converting adversaries with the pleasure of conversing with friends, Walker tries to reconcile the two by making all adversaries over *into* friends. *The Color Purple* attempts to dissolve the tension between a contestatory discursive ethos and an erotic discursive aesthetic through the same strategy Brontë and Hurston use to heighten it.

A complex logic of sameness undergirds the novel's resolution of its contradictory attitudes toward both narrative exchange and "kinship." As Keith Byerman puts it, the novel resolves its tensions "by making all males female (or at least androgynous), all destroyers creators, and all difference sameness."[66] It reduces sexuality and desire to familial affection and identification, thus erasing the relationship between the public and private spheres that much of the narrative has been at such pains to create.

Mr. _____ does not merely become a good listener. He becomes someone increasingly *like* Celie herself: a good housekeeper, a designer of folk-shirts, a nurturing member of a principally female and decidedly domestic world. *The Color Purple* expands the discursive horizons of *Their Eyes Were Watching God*, in other words, not by making it possible for Janie to talk to "Mouth-Almighty" but by converting "Mouth-Almighty" into a sea of Pheobys. The political implications of this "signifying" revision are complex. Reconciling Celie to her community as Hurston will not do for Janie or Brontë for Jane (who lives in the very private sphere of Ferndean, tucked back in the woods, away from everyone and everything else) works not finally by making the public sphere accountable to the practices and values of the private sphere, but by making the public sphere an image of that most private sphere of all: the family. The world transformed is nothing more than a romantic image of an extended family. The public sphere against which the values of this novel have strained and contested simply and suddenly evaporates.

Here too Spielberg and Meyjes alter the novel in a way that goes to the heart of its narrative logic. In the novel, the song that Shug sings for Celie, called simply "Celie's song," has no lyrics. "It all about some no count man doing her wrong again," Celie remarks (77). But in the film version, "Miss Celie's Blues" is given the following lyrics:

> Sister, you been on my mind
> *Oh Sister, we're two of a kind*
> Oh Sister, I'm keeping my eye on you.
> I bet you think I don't know nothing
> but singing the blues,
> Oh sister,
> have I got news for you
> I'm something,
> I hope you think you're something too. (emphasis mine).

This song fits a scenario in which sisterhood, as a metaphor for both safety and similarity, comes increasingly to dominate and shape all other forms of social relation, at the expense of *both* difference and eros. Shug and Celie "sleep like sisters" (152) more than they sleep like lovers. This logic of "sisterhood" or kinship solves the novel's narrative problems, particularly the tension around talk's uses and its limits.

The problem with making everyone a symbolic sister is that it begs the very question it seeks to address. When Brontë and Hurston tie the possibilities of discursive effectivity and pleasure to a (perhaps essentialistic) notion of kinship, their position is that difference is not easily breached. But when Walker uses kinship as the key to transforming bad listeners into good ones, she suggests not that we can speak across differences but more precisely that talk (alone) can meld difference into sameness. Bad listeners cannot "hear" because they are too different. But if only sameness or "kinship" can transform them, then difference remains at best problematic and at worse unbridgeable. Where Walker gives us a story that is sensitive to difference, the underlying structure of that story remains wedded to a normative investment in identicality and sameness.

If all bad listeners can be converted into "kin" simply by being "told off," what a wonderfully changed world results simply from exchanging our stories and talking to each other. This is purely poetic justice. It is utopianism with a vengeance. Or rather, it is utopianism without vengeance, without its admission that it presents its idylls *because* they are unrealizable, without its acknowledgment that to do so is both to step outside of and to peer critically into the world and conventions of realism. As Benhabib puts it in her important discussion of utopianism, the critical force of the utopian is its ability to "project beyond the limits of the present,"[67] not to apologize for the present by making it out to be much more pleasant than it is. It would be unfair to say that Walker simply affirms the social world. But her conclusion, having built all its premises around opposition to the social world, suddenly forgets about the social world altogether.

Although Walker provides compelling representations of failed exchanges and suggests the larger political issues they entail, she ultimately vitiates her own critique by exempting storytelling, narrative, and talk, treating them as capable of transcending the social relations from which they emerge, by attempting to explain how everyone can change. Transforming everyone in the novel into an ideal listener makes this novel, to borrow a phrase of Walker's, a "cautionary tale."[68]

The transformed world which closes this novel is a premodern and sentimentalizing answer to the problematic of exchange relations the novel itself addresses, often quite compellingly. It is utopian in that it is a world in which there is nothing left to protest or "fight." But it is also a world in which difference, desire, and, ultimately, exchange itself, have been effaced. Walker's utopia is static. Her homogeneous, ideal community is sterile— and strikingly un-erotic. By providing aesthetic solutions to the very problems that the other texts I've discussed portray as aesthetically irresolvable, Walker undermines her own aesthetic and political project.

Mr. _____'s transformation into a competent, perhaps even ideal, interlocutor is evidence of what one critic has appropriately labeled the novel's "passionate hopefulness."[69] This is the same passionate hopefulness that we have seen in feminist readings of "The Blank Page," "A Jury of Her Peers," "The Yellow Wallpaper," *Incidents in the Life of a Slave Girl, Jane Eyre*, and *Their Eyes Were Watching God*, particularly regarding the possibilities for "dialogue" between the feminist critic and her texts and the possibilities for a woman's tongue being both political weapon and source of pleasure. In its working out of this double—and sometimes contrary—desire, *The Color Purple* is a particularly apt text with which to conclude this study of feminist criticism's political investment in recovering women's voices and in the difficult and not always progressive pleasures such recovery may provide. If I am right that feminist criticism has often asked that its classic texts hold up a positive and affirming mirror of its own critical enterprise, Walker's *The Color Purple* reflects just such acts of mirroring. Self-consciously recuperative, rebellious, and transformative, it fulfills those desires for recognition and reciprocity often experienced as foreclosed by racist, patriarchal, capitalist society. Walker's dramatization of failed communication turns out to be just a foil for her ultimate romance with communication. Or to put it another way, all of her insights into social wrongs are righted by her romance with transformation itself.

In faulting Walker for appealing to nostalgic forms of community and for failing, in a sense, to be utopian *enough*, I recognize the peculiarity of suggesting that *The Color Purple*—of all books—fails its own utopian project. What could be more utopian, after all, than a novel which transforms an impoverished, abused woman of color into a successful, proper-tied entrepreneur, delighting in her own sexuality, enmeshed in a supportive, loving, multigenerational community of men and women, connected to a nurturing, extended, even transnational family, a story which either buries her abusers or transforms them into pleasant, helpful, supportive, conversational friends?

A useful vocabulary for assessing Walker's utopianism is provided by the distinction Benhabib makes between two visions which she differentiates as the "politics of fulfillment" and the "politics of transfiguration."[70] A "politics of fulfillment" asks bourgeois civil society to make good on its own promises. It corresponds to a politics of voice in that it can be grasped, as Paul Gilroy has observed, "through what is said, shouted, screamed, or sung."[71] Benhabib's "politics of transfiguration," on the other hand, corresponds to an erotics of talk. It represents those forms of friendship, intimacy, and recognition that appear unrealizable under the conditions and apparent trajectory of modern bourgeois civil society. Through it emerge, in Benhabib's words, "qualitatively new needs, social relations, and modes of association."[72] Despite the apparent tension between these two conceptions, as Benhabib shows, no truly useful social vision—literary or critical—can fail to do justice to them both. We must maintain this tension if we are to "understand the dreams of the present [by] also showing that these dreams cannot become a reality in the present."[73] Maintaining this tension may mean leaving certain things unexplained and unresolved, refusing to close gaps that cannot be healed textually.

For Mr. _____ and the other bad listeners to be converted into "somebody I can talk to," the transformational effect of counternarratives has to be presupposed as an intrinsic feature of discursive exchange. But to suggest that ideal understanding or perfect exchange may always already be immanent in the communicative act is a form of wish fulfillment. A world of perfect, immanent understanding and homogeneous sisterhood, moreover, means that even exchange itself is no longer necessary. Why communicate experiences, after all, that everyone else has already had, that everyone else already understands just as we would like them to? Walker's ideal world is both private and miniaturized. Her utopian resolution simply could not obtain in a variegated, complex, larger society—the very society that this utopian resolution at some level must seek to address.

If we imagine ourselves, as empathetic "sisters," to participate only in a text's erotics of talk, to "fulfill" the text rather than being "told off" and truly transfigured by it, then to whom is its contestatory, transfiguring, and oppositional message addressed? Is "the subversive voice we find representative of the age," one that does not criticize us but merely lets us participate in criticizing others? And who and where are they? Doesn't keeping faith with the project of enabling the self-articulations of concrete others demand that we avoid assuming that our position as somebody the text can talk to, somebody who fulfills *its* erotics of talk, can simply be taken for granted?

The Color Purple, unlike the other texts I have looked at, invites us to take that for granted. Instead of reminding us that we are likely to be neither Nettie or Shug, that we may be only eavesdropping (not "ratified"), it reassures us that everyone ("dear everything") is welcome. This alone, perhaps, may not account for the novel's enormous popularity and for the fact that it has so often been used as an exemplary model of feminism. But I am suggesting that our most successful counternarratives, those we read and those we write ourselves, will energize us toward the transfigurations and transformations yet to come, not merely reassure us about the fulfillments we have already enjoyed.

The family picnic at the close of the novel resonates with all of my earliest memories of consciousness-raising: a familiar, familial space, cleared—putatively at least—of uncomfortable difference and contestation. A "safe" space to eat (although not barbecue, usually), trade our stories, heal the wounds of a culture that told us we had no one to talk to, that accused us of "muttering" when we did—at last—find our voices. I miss the safety of that space. And when I read *The Color Purple* I am grateful to Walker for recreating it for me. But I am also on my guard against such seductive—

and sexy—pleasures. It is not only, as Helena Michie has argued, that the discourse of the family and of sisterhood has too often collapsed into a "therapeutic idiom . . . as if all female difference is something that needs to be gotten over, grown out of,"[74] it is also that I have learned, even as I continue to seek its comforts, that feminism's "family home"—the space of safety, homogeneity, familiarity, and sameness, a community intent on identification and self-affirmation to the exclusion of difference, desire, and critique—can also be, in Adrienne Rich's words, a "dangerous place."[75]

Conclusion: Auditions

On my desk is an anthology of "voices from the next feminist generation." Its title is "Listen Up."[1] "Listen Up" is a wonderfully contradictory phrase. It can be said in anger, as a frustrated challenge to an obnoxious, overbearing opponent. It can be said in authority, as one would address an unruly group of children lined up for a field trip. It can be said familiarly, as one would intimate to a good friend that the "good stuff," the "real story" is about to begin. In this case, the title points in three directions at once: to a mainstream culture that doesn't listen, but should; to a generation of feminists who haven't been listening, but better (the tone suggests) start now; to other feminists (including the same generation of non-listeners?) to whom the "new voices" can dictate and who *can* be presumed to understand. Like this title, the metaphorics of an erotics of talk (in women's writing *and* in feminist paradigms) also points many ways at once.

Throughout this study I have been distinguishing dialogues that aim to contest and persuade from those that incline toward pleasurable recognition and a sense of familiar place. Such distinctions matter.

First, they are tied to extraordinary innovations in narrative form. A range of creative narrative strategies—how readers are addressed and represented, the forms of dialogue a narrative can construct and project, its provision or withholding of resolutions and happy endings—develop out of detailed and painstaking efforts to juxtapose desirable and appealing forms of social discourse to those which seem oppressive, constraining, or even just plain dull and, equally important, to dramatize and emphasize such juxtapositions.

All writers will not be equally attentive to these differences, of course, just as all people will not prove good conversationalists, or even able to distinguish a good chat from a dreadful monologue. An attention to the vagaries of social discourse will be particularly acute for writers who experience a relative absence of other forms social of recognition and belonging—access to high-status roles in the public sphere that provide cultural capital, access to resources of power and privilege, for example—as is the case in the black and white women's literature I have examined here.

Second, the distinctions we draw between our different forms of talk are tied to the crucial political and personal decisions we make every day: whether to get in on what I have been calling the cultural conversation or try to opt out of it, whether to stage a confrontation or look for compensations elsewhere. The process of choosing our battles is always one of gauging where we can make a difference and what our chances for justice—or pleasure—are likely to be, of deciding, in short, where it is and isn't worthwhile to put our energies.

So these are important distinctions. But they are also not absolute.

Perhaps the most important lesson offered by the classic texts I've studied here is the impossibility of choosing between getting in on the cultural conversation and getting out of it, the impossibility of finally choosing between the contestatory imperatives of a politics of voice and the utopian satisfactions of an erotics of talk. Every attempt to address an ideal listener will be, in part, a persuasive or seductive performance, an audition, a try-out that hopes for audience appreciation it cannot take for granted. And every rhetorical intervention, every confrontation or contest, will be, in part, an effort to create an ideal listener, to reach that perfect understanding that keeps receding on the horizon. Every attempt to opt out of the cultural conversation is a commentary that pulls us back into it, just as our participation in the cultural conversation may impel us away from it, toward imagined alternatives.

A contestatory politics of voice and a utopian erotics of talk are at odds but inseparable. We cannot, ultimately, choose to practice one rather than the other. Instead, these are dialectically linked discursive structures, whose contrary pull and tug engenders each other—and ourselves.

Feminist criticism has provided us with cautionary tales about the necessary and dialectical tension between different forms of talk and the structures of social relation they allegorize. But as I have argued, it has not always absorbed the contradictory lessons of its own most cherished texts. In particular, feminist criticism, I have been suggesting, has not always attended sufficiently to the performative dimensions of women's writing, African American women's writing especially.

The Color Purple does present an image of women's dialogue as a safe haven and conversation as that form of talk in which one can feel "in place among persons," "living together" with intimacy," and feeling "at home" (see epigraph, p. 2). A presupposition of sisterhood underlies *The Color Purple*'s strangely de-eroticized finale and nostalgic privileging of community. As one feminist critic writes, the book's pleasures are "identification, affirmation, celebration."[2] It invites "fantastic collaboration": "with Celie, we undergo a metamorphosis. . . . We actually begin to *think* as Miss Celie— like Shug, we have her song scratched out of our heads—because by participating in her linguistic process, we collaborate in her struggle to construct a self."[3]

But many of the other texts now classic to feminist critics signal their wariness about being able to speak, contract, or dialogue with others on an equal basis, about whether or not their "voices" will make a difference, about the conditions under which they can "create an interlocutor capable of understanding." This distrust need not manifest itself in silence or complete disengagement. No act of publication, after all, is finally an act of silence. It may manifest itself, as I have shown, in any number of complicated strategies for representing the gap between ideal and less than ideal interlocutors and for indicting a society that supplies so little of the one and so much of the other.

Aside from *The Color Purple,* many of feminism's classic texts posit the difficulties of sisterhood and female community, difficulties caused as much by conflicts between women as by patriarchy's investment in keeping women apart. In "The Yellow Wallpaper" the heroine goes crazy for lack of someone to understand and sympathize with her. But the sisterhood she concocts is both demented and suffocating. "A Jury of Her Peers" indicts women for failing to look after one another—the real "crime" of which Mrs. Hale and Mrs. Peters are guilty. It suggests that we (more on this vexed pronoun later) fail to do so not only because "the law" compels our allegiance, but also because we are lazy or scared, because it is easier not to make an effort, because it is hard to keep each other in mind. There is also a failure of sisterhood in "The Blank Page," one with a particularly contemporary bite. The story's cultural critics who revere a woman's text lionize and celebrate her as a symbol, but they also fail to intervene into her life or change the conditions against which she strained. The critical performance practiced by the nuns' gallery with its blank sheet goes hand in hand with, indeed is even enabled by, their very complicity in the patriarchal system their exhibition exposes. And Harriet Jacobs's narrative offers an even stronger representation of the limits of feminist community. Dependent as she might be on the help of benevolent white "sisters," Linda Brent never loses sight of how she is different than them or hopes for more than the most local sorts of relief.

These feminist classics offer a double—and perhaps doubly discouraging—message. On the one hand, they suggest that sisterhood is as often vexed as it is utopic, a disturbing thought for a movement traditionally founded on female solidarity. And on the other hand, they construct a powerful version of poetic justice, all the while insisting that justice cannot be merely poetic. They present powerful textual dialogues and a compelling, seductive textual erotics, all the while insisting on the limitations of such symbolic responses to social problems, also a disturbing—even awkward—message for a movement that has found (and founded) so much of its political energy in the power of textual representation. As a metaphorics and a symbolic narrative structure, an erotics of talk replaces inadequate conversational/social partners with better ones. Such poetic justice may be satisfying. It may even gratify our desire for revenge. But revenge is not justice. And symbolic revenge is not revenge.

I have been critical here of celebratory readings of the "voice" of "subversion" which often take for granted identifications and linguistic effects that in fact cannot be presupposed. And throughout this study I have been suggesting that we need a more nuanced theory of "voice" and a more cautionary account of "subversion" than the traditional politics of "voice" which privileges, in bell hooks's phrase, the act of "talking back":

> moving from silence into speech is for the oppressed, the colonized, the exploited, and those who stand and struggle side by side a gesture of defiance that heals, that makes new life and new growth possible. It is that act of speech, of "talking back," that is no mere gesture of empty words, that is the expression of our movement from object to subject—the liberated voice.[4]

How could anyone but concur? That "the oppressed, the colonized, the exploited" need to find their voices is a sine qua non of any liberatory politics. The real question is how to imagine such movement and how to achieve it. We need to consider the conditions of its success. We need to take account of how vectors of power such as race, class, and sexuality inflect that possibility of success, without assuming that models of discursivity can be divided up neatly into racial, economic, or sexual categories.

On the one hand, an erotics of talk seems to cut across race, nation, and historical period. Both black and white narrators yearn, as we have seen, for ideal listeners and the recognition they seem to promise. But race, class, and sexuality shape the tropes whose social meanings and concomitant narrative forms I have traced. They do so in complicated ways. Skepticism about discursive engagement and transformation seems strongest in the black women's texts I have studied here. There is good reason—good social and historical reason—for such doubt. Yet it would nonetheless be wrong to infer that these tropes are either black or white. Just as black women's writing uses an erotics of talk, so white women's writing uses a discourse of distrust and tries, in different ways, to hold back from entering the cultural conversation. The tropes of a discourse of distrust and an erotics of talk, in other words, are coded and particularized by vectors such as gender, race, historical location, and sexual identification; but they do not line up neatly. They resist categorizations. Black writers like hooks and Walker may seem most sanguine about "talking back," while white writers like Glaspell and Gilman may express grave doubts.

The feminist canon is filled with contradictions: narrators lamenting an absence of fit listeners as they praise the reader's ideality; characters validating sisterhood as they marry their romantic male heroes; talk appearing as both a form of social oppression and a means of social equality. This may not seem very conclusive. But it prompts me to restate one of the presuppositions that has grounded my project from the onset: namely, that politics and desire impinge on one another in complex and unpredictable ways. Knowing what to expect does not make us stop desiring something different. On the contrary, the worse our expectations, the stronger, it would seem, are our countervailing desires.

So it should be surprising neither that an erotics of talk points many ways at once nor that feminist criticism has advanced cautionary narratives without always absorbing their contradictory lessons. Feminist criticism is anything but a seamless enterprise. And although restorations of women's "voice" that celebrate universalizing myths of subversion and sorority may oversentimentalize textual dialogics and, at the same time, underread textual erotics, such tendencies to sentimentalize or de-eroticize are not uniformly characteristic of all feminist criticism at all times. Feminism itself is a contradictory business.

As a figurative trope for intersubjectivity which mediates between the demands of the textual on the one hand and the limits of the social on the other, an erotics of talk works by contradictions. This is its strength. It highlights—or performs—the disjunction between the implicit promises of narrative exchange and the actual social, discursive, and material conditions faced by women writers, the conditions within which any exchange must actually take place.

I have shown how feminist criticism has sometimes (and somewhat paradoxically) resisted the contradictory messages offered by its most cherished texts, with critics often endeavoring, to one degree or another, to imagine that a feminist reading—in and of itself—might suffice to redress the balance between narrative promise and social limitation. But for two reasons this resistance is really not surprising. First, the very disjunctions and social failures an erotics of talk can represent have been rendered visible *because* of feminist criticism's exposures of women writers' longings for positive reception on the one hand and the social and political histories of their actual receptions on the other. In this sense, a feminist reading may not be sufficient to ameliorate the disparities the metaphor of an erotics of talk reveals, but such a reading is prerequisite to any hope of future amelioration. Second, feminism itself is beset, sometimes overwhelmed, by contradictions. There does not seem to be a coherent feminist movement in this country. Many are calling into question the identity of feminism itself. Feminists frequently find themselves at odds, neither speaking the same language nor anticipating the same goals. Even the title "Listen Up" seems frustrated that feminists have not been listening to each other and at the same time hopeful that such listening is not—yet—out of the question.

Animating my project from the outset has been a deep commitment to the future of feminism and the possibilities for meaningful feminist engagement. I believe that productive feminist conversation also works by contradiction and that women's writing—our recuperated and cherished classics—still has something to teach feminist critics about how to make such contradiction work.

What I have argued for throughout this study is a critical practice alert to the structuring contradictions that inform women's writing. In concluding, I want to turn to the structuring contradictions that currently inform contemporary feminism itself—particularly the tension between feminism's traditional commitment to women and poststructural challenges to the possibility of such collective self-identification—and to ask if the feminist tradition can be moved forward by its own contradictions just as women's writing, as I have tried to demonstrate, uses forceful contradictions to project itself into the future and imagine possible resolutions.

There has long been considerable feminist debate over whether (and how) women can appropriate "the master's tools"[5] for liberatory ends, since language is not simply a means for achieving social change but is already part of the problem women face. Virtually no feminist, no matter how strong her advocacy of "talking back," would venture the claim that talk is either all that we have or all that we need. Hélène Cixous, for example, famously argued that "woman must write herself," must "bring women to writing" because "a feminine text cannot fail to be more than subversive," that woman's voice is "volcanic" and "brings about an upheaval" of "the imperatives handed down by an economy that works against us and off our backs."[6] But she also writes, "I don't think that the revolution is going to happen through language either."[7] Even hooks, who has continually advocated "talking back" and "coming to voice," also admits that talking back, by itself, is not enough: "Our speech . . . was often the soliloquy, the talking into thin air, the talking to ears that do not hear you—the talk that is simply not listened to."[8] Insofar as it is really persuasion that is at issue, the efficacy of any discursive intervention is always an audition: a question of being heard, a need to try out and perform for an audience who may or many not be appreciative. As an enterprise, feminist criticism, in other words, cannot offer simple answers to the questions I have posed, any more than can those texts to which it has looked and on which it has relied.

At best, it would seem, feminist criticism and its classic literary canon offer a divided, even contradictory, answer to the questions with which I began: whether talk can help reframe culture; whether we can theorize a form of cultural conversation that will provide the basis for a more just and equal society; whether feminism's ethical imperative can survive, let alone thrive, in an ungrounded, destabilized, de-identified moral/discursive universe.

But this apparent inconclusiveness is not an impasse. And these contradictions do not spell chaos. On the contrary. As far as I am concerned, the strength of feminism is as much in its contrary responses to such questions as it is in any hope of consensus. It is feminism's very contentiousness that I am seeking to preserve—and that I have always found so sexy.

The perception that feminism is in crisis is widespread. One hears it internally, as feminists lament fragmentation and splitting, representing

feminist discussion as a disordered cacophony, devoting public presenta-
tions to finger-pointing and blaming disrespectful younger feminists, or
unyielding women of color, or trouble-making lesbians, or unsophisticated
foremothers.[9] And one hears it externally, when feminism's purported or
predicted demise titillates the press and the pundits, when rabid anti-
feminists like Camille Paglia are touted both as feminism's just deserts and
as its next wave. This morbid glee is merely another sorry example of mainstream recalcitrance to meaningful change, as self-explanatory as it is self-
propelling. Within feminism, however, this language of crisis bears closer
examination and deserves an explanation. I think this perception emanates
from two sources.

First, there is a sense that the very basis of feminism, its appeal to justice for and on behalf of women, is no longer viable. Linda Alcoff argues
that there is an "identity crisis in feminist theory" caused by the fact that
"for many contemporary feminist theorists, the concept of woman is a problem. . . . Our very self-definition is grounded in a concept that we
must deconstruct and de-essentialize in all of its aspects."[10] Alcoff, like many
others, wonders if this categorical dilemma "threatens to wipe out feminism itself." She asks, How can we possibly "ground a feminist politics that
deconstructs the female subject?"[11] Feminist politics, Judith Butler writes,
seems to have "lost the categorical basis of its own normative claims. What
constitutes the 'who,' the subject for whom feminism seeks emancipation?
If there is no subject, who is left to emancipate?"[12]

Given this "crisis in the concept of 'woman,'"[13] speaking for, as, with,
or on behalf of women becomes a dance on hot coals. Even writers long
associated with the project of speaking for silenced and marginalized women
—what I have called feminism's ethic of accountability—have begun to
express a critical uneasiness about making generalizations, appealing to
women as a collectivity, trying to make connections outside their own identity or affinity groups. "I wrote a sentence just now and x'd it out," Adrienne
Rich writes.

> In it I said that women have always understood the struggle against free-float-
> ing abstraction even when they were intimidated by abstract ideas. I don't
> want to write that kind of sentence now, the sentence that begins, "Women
> have always." . . . If we have learned anything in these years of late twentieth-
> century feminism, it's that that "always" blots out what we really need to know:
> when, where and under what circumstances has the statement been true?[14]

Rich is advocating a nuanced, particularized, and localized conception of
"women," not the erasure of such referencing gestures.

But for other feminist thinkers, the impossibility of that "always" makes
"woman" nothing but a "regulatory fiction," as Butler puts it, one that fixes
identity within the hegemonic ground of normative heterosexuality and the
identicality (or bipolarity) it demands. Political appeals to "women," Butler has argued, tend to shore up, not subvert, domination.[15] Hence, she
suggests that we eschew the category of "women" altogether as imposing

"political closure on the kinds of experience articulable as part of a feminist discourse."[16] This call to forgo "women" as feminism's categorical base is often predicated on an even broader mandate to drop any form of collective self-address, any attempt to speak for, as, or with a collective voice. "The 'us' who gets joined through such a narration is a construction built upon the denial of a decidedly more complex cultural identity—or non-identity, as the case may be," Butler argues.[17] The "term 'feminism,'" Peggy Kamuf writes, is a "closed system [and we should] . . . drop the name *as a form of self-address.* . . [as a] way of *affirming* the future of, yes, feminism."[18]

Second, there is a widespread impression that a proliferation of different feminisms threatens to destroy the feminist project. Rosalind Delmar, for example, writes that "the different meanings of feminism . . . have manifested themselves as a sort of sclerosis of the movement, segments of which have become separated from and hardened against each other. . . . There are radical feminists, socialist feminists, marxist feminists, lesbian separatists, women of color, and so on."[19] "Painful fragmentation among feminists," Donna Haraway agrees, constitutes "the sources of a crisis in political identity."[20]

This lament over "crisis" deplores the disorderly shape of feminist conversations and debates with mainstream culture. But such a lament is self-contradictory; it produces the very phenomenon it claims to deplore and becomes a self-fulfilling prophecy.

In fact, a proliferation of differences has always been one of feminism's most salient features. Feminist historiographers have shown that conflict *between* women has been one of the signal characteristics of American feminism throughout the nineteenth and twentieth centuries. Such conflict has engendered and sustained feminist thought. Nor should we find this surprising. "There is an element of . . . predictability in any fragmentation that follows a united front of women," Nancy Cott proposes, "for as much as women have common cause in gender issues, they are differentiated by political and cultural and sexual loyalties, and by racial, class and ethnic identities, which inform their experience of gender itself."[21]

If conflict and difference have so consistently characterized feminism, why is a language of crisis so prevalent? Why, both politically and interpretively, does there seem to be such resistance to conflict and contradiction?

Something more than historical forgetfulness is at stake in the current perception of crisis. Beneath the descriptions of a hopelessly fragmented feminism flows a current of nostalgia for an imagined utopian moment of sisterhood and mutual recognition. For conflict-free consolidations of women. For seamlessness.

This language of crisis can be found in a surprising range of feminist writings, from those of poststructuralists to those of radical feminists, but it has not, in the main, been a characteristic discourse of women of color and lesbians. Those feminists did not experience the cultural conversation as familiar and safe, as a place they could feel "at home." This itself should give us pause. At the heart of nostalgia, as we know, is resistance to change.

At the heart of this feminist nostalgia is there resistance to the kinds of challenges posed by women of color and lesbians who found feminism's putative sisterhood a cultural conversation that did not include them and whose rules and norms did not provide a base for adequate intervention?[22]

Just as our interpretive goal need not be the symbolic provision of all that a text identifies as lacking, so the problem that feminism now faces, in my view, is not a need to resolve its cacophony and disorder into some safer, less chaotic form of talk. The cacophony some see as a crisis should be embraced as an opportunity. Whenever feminism hasn't seemed cacophonous, it merely meant that we had been failing to listen to dissenting voices, failing, as Lyotard puts it, "to speak as a listener." The challenge is not to quiet the roaring, but to channel it, a challenge not to be taken lightly.

Clearly, feminism as a genteel and ordered conversation has little appeal for me. And fortunately for me, such an ideal can never be realized. But neither do I suggest that we stop trying to speak with, as, for, or on behalf of "women" because we can't agree on what the term means or because it has so many possible meanings or because there is the danger that those meanings may "fix" or constrict.

We are, of course, engaged in fierce debates over who "we" are, what "feminism" is, what it means to be a "woman," what the status of "women" as a category is. That's exactly the point. Such contention is crucial to sorting out our various possibilities. To eschew that process, for whatever reason, is the one threat that truly would menace feminism's future. I am uncomfortable with any formulation that treats feminist contention as a problem to be solved. Any attempt to forestall and repress debate, no matter what its motives, is a step in the wrong direction. How can a commitment to difference, to disrupting fixed identities and norms, not go hand in hand with a commitment to debate, even fiery, unpredictable, uncontrollable, sometimes uncomfortable debate? The alternative to continuing to listen to each other, engage with each other, fight with each other over categories like "feminism" and "woman" would be a return to assumptions of identicality and putative sameness: as Benhabib warns, "without engagement, confrontation, dialogue and even a 'struggle for recognition' in the Hegelian sense, we tend to constitute the otherness of the other by projection and fantasy or ignore it in indifference."[23]

Bracket for a moment the fact that it is impossible to avoid rhetorical appeals to "we" or to "us." It is simply not the case that every such address, every representational gesture, every appeal on behalf of "women," every demand in the name of feminism will lead to Butler's dreaded "limitation, prohibition, regulation, control."[24] As part of our ongoing political process such gestures of self-referencing can be as generative as they can be restrictive. Which is to say that they need not presume illusory identities, reify gender, nor practice an exclusionary and self-policing politics. On the contrary, the more self-consciously we engage in such gestures and the contestation they inevitably engender, the more we *enable* the very destabilizations of gender and identity that theorists like Butler and Kamuf advance.

In arguing that we must resist any effort to produce the subject "women" or to speak on such a subject's behalf, Butler, among others, maintains that new configurations of politics and identity become articulable only once "identities were no longer fixed . . . and politics no longer understood as a set of practices derived from the alleged interests that belong to a set of ready-made subjects." When such premises no longer stand in the way, Butler writes, "a new configuration of politics would surely emerge from the ruins of the old."[25] Butler is exactly right that destabilizations allow for new configurations, but she misses the political implications of that point. New configurations will "emerge from the ruins of the old" if and only if we engage in that process of disputing and contesting false premises, if we try them out, if we audition them, as it were, to see what works and what doesn't. Ironically, the dilemma that Butler's logic seeks to avoid is precisely the condition of a heterogenous, contentious, and partial public, one that entails conflict, contestation, debate, disagreement, experimentation, and projection, including—perhaps especially—conflict over the most basic premises and categories of our thinking.[26] It is gestural self-designations such as "we" that cannot help but "open up other configurations." Isn't that exactly what "we" want?

Rather than avoid the feminist "we," then, I am suggesting that we use it, but that we do so as a *proleptic* term, one which points not to an essential reality that preexists or transcends its evocation, but to solidarities which it tries, at the moment of its speaking, to instantiate. "We" *is* a performative. We can use it provocatively—expecting, even hoping, that those we seek to include may shoot back with a differently configured "we" of their own. (Auditions. Tryouts.)

And my point is not simply to up the ante on free-wheeling contestation. It is not enough to simply throw all voices into a big discursive pot and see, in effect, whose "we" is finally stronger. We need a mechanism not only for staging exchanges with one another, but also for generating the social-discursive conditions through which those exchanges might be meaningful and productive. Without that effort, as Hurston warns us, our heteroglossic, contestatory conversation may not "amount tuh uh hill uh beans." "Consensual discourse requires not only the right and wherewithal to speak, but in addition, the possibility that speech will be listened to and heard in the fullest sense possible."[27]

Feminism needs, in short, a new communicative ethics. Which does not dismiss our psycho-social needs for recognition. Which does not curtail or forestall debate. Which does not assume that we have essential, immutable, and unconstructed—let alone similar—selves which we need to reveal. Which neither assumes that our conditions for being heard already exist nor takes for granted that the mere exercise of our voices will create them.

Where could such a communicative ethics come from? I want to suggest two—surprising, perhaps—possible sources. One is consciousness-raising. The other is performativity. Consciousness-raising and performativity are the two most developed attempts, in the history of contemporary feminism and gender studies, to articulate a theory of cultural conversation that would also be a blueprint for practice. Each has its strengths and weaknesses.

It is probably the case that no social practice has ever gone so far in attempting to articulate not just a theory of communicative ethics but also to develop its necessary protocols and a working program for its realization as feminist consciousness-raising of the sixties and seventies.[28] It is easy to deride consciousness-raising for self-indulgence, assumptions of female sameness, a failure to address sufficiently the effects of race, class, and sexuality, a kind of generalized and operative naivete. But it is also hard to overstate the positive, political impact of women's groups gathered to talk. Anita Shreve estimates that in 1973 alone at least 100,000 women belonged to consciousness-raising groups and that even those who didn't belong were benefiting from the ground-breaking challenges to gender roles and social expectations issuing forth from private living rooms and going on to ground an increasingly powerful national movement.

Consciousness-raising represented both a politics of voice and an erotics of talk. It took for granted that the exercise of women's voices would have a profound impact on the cultural conversation. As it did. And it consciously sought to provide a context of safety, intimacy, and social-discursive pleasure for women. As it also did. What those who were in consciousness-raising groups remember most vividly is the profound sense of recognition women experienced in talking to one another: a sudden shock of discovering that you were not, in fact, crazy, that other women could affirm and indeed had even experienced what you were describing and what you had always feared was "just me." Consciousness-raising often turned what had felt like a lifetime of "self-talking" into a vibrant and challenging conversation premised on protocols such as honesty, respect, and mutual support.

Consciousness-raising, in spite of popular misconceptions, was not all talk. Consciousness-raising groups presupposed that for a woman to get in on the cultural conversation certain material conditions had to be met. Group members did everything from provide child-care services to help each other get jobs or get out of stifling relationships in the belief that life changes had to precede, not just result from, women's ability to speak freely. This lesson went to the heart of a rapidly developing materialist feminism.

Consciousness-raising also provided a framework for juxtaposing different forms of cultural discourse and reexamining their claims for validity and legitimation, an enterprise at the heart of deconstruction and post-structuralism. Consciousness-raising was often mocked and derided as "girl talk" and consciousness-raising sessions were characterized as "hen parties."[29] While this was painful for many of the participating women, it served to dramatize the extent to which talking to other women could not free women from being seen as "self talkers" and the extent to which female conversation was seen as a cultural threat. Such derision, inadvertently, helped reinforce the growing suspicion that feminist dialogue could be a form of power.

The process of consciousness-raising, even with its rigid and often constraining rules on interruption and remaining nonjudgmental, was what Shreve accurately describes as a form of "basic training."[30] By insisting upon the articulation of concrete needs and desires, consciousness-raising could offer a model of the public sphere, specifically, a heterogeneous public in which people might speak from particular, concrete wishes: a challenge to the liberal ideal of impartiality which posits a "unified and universal moral point of view," an alternative to "the logic of identity [which] denies or represses difference."[31] Consciousness-raising, in short, could be an exercise in participatory democracy, a "training" reinforced in leadership-building practices such as rotating chairwomen and avoidance of designated spokeswomen. The success of such "basic training" became visible throughout the seventies as women increasingly entered political organizations and women's political organizations became increasingly sophisticated and well run.[32]

I stress that consciousness-raising *could* be a training ground for participatory democracy because, ultimately, it was neither as challenging nor as provocative as it might have been. Consciousness-raising often failed to reach a truly heterogeneous group of women or even to appreciate the heterogeneity of its own potential practitioners. Many women left consciousness-raising groups disappointed at not being heard and fed up with the subtle pressures to conform to particular viewpoints or to avoid taboo subjects, especially about race and class, about feelings of hostility toward other women and feelings of desire for them.[33] Moreover, the assumption, as Kathie Sarachild, one of the architects of consciousness-raising, put it, that "most women were like ourselves—not different,"[34] and the protocols which demanded that women "never challenge anyone else's experience," never interrupt, never contradict one another, ultimately proved debilitating.[35] Shreve maintains that "this prohibition against criticizing or praising another's testimony was probably a pivotal element in the success of CR. Women who had never before had an opportunity to talk about themselves without being dismissed or interrupted by their husbands, boyfriends, or parents could now risk expressing themselves."[36] While this may have been true in the very early stages, such prohibitions, I suspect, also proved self-destructive. Without some license for challenge, disagreement, and question, how could participants hope to transform one another, to recreate understandings, to challenge and provoke new forms of consciousness itself?

I am positing that consciousness-raising did not fail, in other words, because its practitioners failed to listen to one another sympathetically or supportively. In fact, mandating recognition and mutual support apparently proved unworkable. The posture of empathy, in which we imagine ourselves to be already identified with the speaker or, in the case of literature, imagine ourselves to be just the listener the text can speak to and desires, can silence the very voices we might seek to enable. A mandate to recognize and support one another will produce illusory recognitions that cannot help but disappoint. It will not generate "concrete others" about and from whom we need to learn, but "generalized others" we can imagine we already understand. As Benhabib writes: "the ability to take the standpoint of the other into account is not empathy although it is related to it."[37] What Habermas calls an "ideal speech situation" cannot be created, as I have argued, simply by providing mechanisms that ensure equal access. But neither can it be created by mandating conditions of support, empathy, and respect that have not, as yet, been earned and tested in a dialogic process— an audition—which acknowledges the possibility of failure and the necessity of change.

Consciousness-raising sometimes seems like a lumbering dinosaur, waddling off to be replaced by sleeker, more elegant, less sentimental paradigms, ones that don't rely on identification and essentialism, that recognize the mutability and contingency of identity, that better understand the built-in difficulties of audition and recognition. Consciousness-raising seems particularly sentimental and nostalgic when held up against those paradigms now dominant in the academy—like performativity—which seem not to need the ideals of comfort and "home" that were such a part of the feminist seventies.[38]

But feminism cannot be periodized quite so neatly.[39] In spite of its theoretical sophistication, elegance, and insights, performativity is prey to some of the same problems which plagued consciousness-raising. Like consciousness-raising it helps illuminate what a feminist communicative ethics might look like. But also like consciousness-raising it fails to explain how we might achieve one.

It is entirely logical that a paradigm of performativity would have replaced one of consciousness. Subtending consciousness-raising was an understanding of gender as a set of roles and a dominant ideology, a consciousness which needed to be contested and reformed. Within the academy, at least, that conception has been supplanted by a complex understanding of gender as an effect of discourse in its constitution of subjectivity, not merely as expectation or ideology. Feminists talk about gender now in principally linguistic terms.[40]

Performativity explains how discourse creates social "footing" by naturalizing conventions and norms through a repetition that makes them appear merely "given" or true. According to Eve Kosofsky Sedgwick, who along with Judith Butler is responsible for making performativity a kind of recent cause célèbre, "discussions of linguistic performativity have become a place to reflect on ways in which language really can be said to produce effects: effects of identity, enforcement, seduction, challenge. They also deal with how powerfully language positions."[41]

Because I have been arguing that feminist criticism has not always attended sufficiently to the performative dimensions of women's writing, and because I have argued that writers like Jacobs, Brontë, and Hurston use performative narrative strategies both to participate in the cultural conversation and to dramatize their alienation and disengagement from it, I want to take up the question of whether performativity, as it is currently theorized, can make good on its own implicit promise: a way of getting in on the cultural conversation without *endorsing* its ground rules or conventions. A theory of the performative, I'd maintain, can help us do this, can help us break the double bind of a writer, like those I've studied above, facing uncomprehending or hostile audiences with only the tools of language to win them over and transform them. But a theory of the performative can help to do this only if we read performativity against the grain of some of its more prominent articulations, drawing different conclusions about the possibilities for collective action and reconnecting performative strategies to the domain of normative debates.

A "performative," as Butler defines it, "is that discursive practice that enacts or produces that which it names"; it is the reiterative means by which "a phenomenon is named into being," a "citation."[42] What lends a performative its authority—and performatives are first and foremost modes of cultural, social, and linguistic authority—is precisely this "citationality," this ability to refer back to or even rest upon an already constructed chain of significations and norms. Discourse, Butler writes, gains "the authority to bring about what it names through citing the linguistic conventions of authority."[43]

This insight into how language positions, or "foots," us through "citationality" has been particularly important for queer studies, gender studies, and feminism.[44] Gender, Butler explains, is the result of repetitive signifying practices which work to naturalize a set of normative ideals. Gender *constitutes* the identities it purports to merely name through chains of repetitive significations.[45]

If gender is constituted through "citationality" or through marshaling a chain of already constituted meanings, conventions, and signifying practices, it follows that resignification might disrupt and even subvert those citations and the cultural norms they rely on. On Butler's account, performativity "has contemporary political promise" because its "citational politics" allow for exposure and, hence, reconfigurations of the signifying practices from which our norms and conventions are derived.[46] Subversive citationality can reveal and delegitimate the self-authorizations upon which citationality itself is based. In other words, performatives expose and dramatize the structural ground of our cultural conversation and the fissures that cut through it.

As a descriptive, the theory of performativity offers many rich insights: that speech is a ritualized act; that it is built on reiteration, resignification, and citationality; that it marshals identification in the process of resignification; that identification both brings identity into being and calls it into question; that the success of a speech act is always provisional or contingent on those identifications; that the identifications thus marshaled are neither willful nor volitional; that our social identities are constituted through such ritual acts. But rich and provocative as these insights are, nothing programmatic automatically or obviously follows from them. Whereas advocates of a Rortian or Habermasian model of productive "cacophony" or "ideal speech" often slide from the diagnostic to the programmatic, without sufficiently accounting for how we get from here to there, advocates of performativity as subversive political practice, especially as *sufficient* political practice, often slide from theorizing a cultural mechanism to political conclusions that may or may not follow from such description: from defining to arguing by definition. Jane Gallop, for example, celebrates "impersonation" as theory and pedagogic program.[47] "Practices of parody," Butler writes, "can serve to reengage and reconsolidate the very distinction between a privileged and naturalized gender configuration and one that appears as derived, phantasmatic, and mimetic." But can't parody also work to *recon*solidate the very citations we want to disrupt? And doesn't such success or failure hinge, in large part, on how the audience responds, on what it does and doesn't grasp? "It is only *within* the practices of repetitive signifying that a subversion of identity becomes possible," Butler maintains.[48] I am prepared, even happy, to grant that. But is it *always* within such practices that such subversion occurs?

One of the difficulties in Butler's explanation of performativity is that she uses it to mean two things at once. On the one hand, it defines the process by which "the materiality of sex is constructed through a ritualized repetition of norms." This process, Butler writes, is "one domain in which power acts *as* discourse," and, hence, "performatives are forms of authoritative speech." On the other hand, "performativity" also describes the process through which such ritualization is contested and challenged, the process of "resignification" by which such discursive positioning might be reexamined and rearranged. "Performance is thus a kind of talking back."[49] Describing performativity as both a regime of discursive power *and* the means of its subversion begs the questions at hand. Without a means of distinguishing these two senses of performativity, there would seem to be no cause to celebrate, any more than we might celebrate any cultural/linguistic diagnosis.

Accepting the descriptive, even diagnostic, value of performative theory, as a number of feminist thinkers point out, does not necessarily mean accepting the sometimes sweeping political claims being advanced in its name. Butler's explanation of performativity, Linda Nicholson writes, "provides no means to distinguish or explain those instances of performativity which generate new kinds of significations from those which are merely repetitions of previous performative acts."[50] "Since Butler's term [resignification] carries no implication of validity or warrant its positive connotations are puzzling," Nancy Fraser points out. "Why is resignification good? Can't there be bad (oppressive, reactionary) resignifications?"[51] "What keeps Butler's purposeful redeployment from being, yet again, redeployed, with perhaps drastically different purposes?" Lynne Huffer asks. "Nothing, we all admit, since iterability as repetition is precisely the point. Which is precisely why performativity alone is inadequate as political theory."[52]

What I have tried to show in my analysis of the performative dimensions of women's writing is how unpredictable the outcome of any particular performative may be. Janie's courtroom testimony, to return to one of the most extraordinary performatives we have seen, is left deliberately ambiguous. It may have moved its audience, even transformed them from dismissive racists into listeners who understand the devastating effects of their own ignorance and the power and beauty of Janie's black, female voice. Or it may have left them unmoved, failing to reach their assumptions that black women have nothing to say and aren't worth listening to. And it is unclear, in Hurston's novel, what would guarantee the effectiveness of Janie's performative: Her own verbal skills? A change in her audience (remember the white women she wishes to speak to instead)? The passage of sufficient historical time? The intervention of more perceptive intermediaries? Her performative, as I have shown, is both brilliant and complex. It exposes a history of gender and race assumptions. It restages a tradition of black female "footing." But it cannot guarantee its own subversivity. That is always a relational problem, dependent on the limits and understandings of the audience at issue.

To be fair, Butler declares her project to be an interrogation of "what constitutes a subversive repetition"[53] rather than a presumption of subversivity. But the thrust of language such as "citational politics" and the "contemporary political promise" she sees in parody reveal a marked tendency to celebrate performativity in itself as a strategy of subversion and disruption. Fraser is right to point out that "resignification" is not merely a descriptive term for Butler; it "carries a strong, if implicit, positive charge."

There is a circularity here which threatens to undermine what may be the richest insight performative theory has to offer: its insight into persuasion itself, into what it takes for a speech to have a transformative rather than merely reiterative effect.

"If a performative provisionally succeeds," Butler writes, "(and I will suggest that 'success' is always and only provisional), then it is not because an intention successfully governs the action of speech, but only because that action echoes prior actions, and *accumulates the force of authority through the repetition or citation of a prior and authoritative set of practices*."[54] What this success boils down to, in short, is whether or not a performative is able to create a sense of community between the speaker and audience, to "interpellate" the audience into the conventions the performance cites such that those assumptions seem merely reasonable and true. This transformation is mediated by witnesses, whether present or only implied, who observe the performance and constitute its meanings. Any performative, then, is always a mechanism of consensus-building and, hence, of social consolidation. Performatives invoke—and create—a presumption of consensus between the speaker and her listener. If that consensus can be successfully marshaled, the performative succeeds. If not, it fails. A subversive performative, in theory, would marshall a new consensus, a differently oriented community of witnesses.[55] Put most idealistically, it would create a new critical community. In the case of Janie's trial, to return to my earlier example, her performance of social exclusion would change the jury such that inclusion and participation become meaningful possibilities. It might bring more women into the room, feminize the "twelve white men" she's stuck with, make her black audience more sensitive to gender, or all of the above.

While this insight into the persuasive community-building function of successful performatives is made possible by theories of performativity, ironically, it is at the same time strikingly absent from celebrations of performativity as a new modality of social critique and political action. If performatives cannot be worked volitionally to marshal new communities and create a new consensus, then there is no reason to celebrate them. And if they *can* be worked volitionally then we need to address such difficult questions as why certain acts work for some communities and not others, whether parody is always an effective performative, what makes some kinds of parody more successful than others, and so on. In other words, the value of a performative, of performativity, like the value of participation in any particular cultural conversation, can neither be fully theorized in the abstract nor reliably predicted in advance. This is what it means to operate in relational territory. A theory of the subversiveness of performativity per se is no more useful than a theory of the subversivity of "voice." The proof of whether it's been, as Janie might put it, "worth the trouble," is still in the pudding.

Consciousness-raising's history proves my point. I would argue that consciousness-raising's repetition of the categories "woman" and "women" was as performative as it was essentialistic, a citational or resignifying practice aimed at rearticulating gender norms. It was the operative communicative norms, I'd maintain—agree, don't interrupt, empathize, identify— which kept such citations from having subversive effects. As Iris Marion Young puts it, "to promote a politics of inclusion . . . participatory democrats must stand forth with their differences acknowledged and respected, *though perhaps not always understood by others.*"[56] That room for misunderstanding and difference, the space for contestation and transformation that misunderstanding opens up, cannot be merely endorsed in theory. Procedural norms must guarantee it.

Neither a sentimental commitment to an erotics of talk nor a poststructuralist distrust of the so-called "violence" of truth claims should be used to justify curtailment of debate. Every truth claim, every representational gesture, every identity category is tied to power, is a bid for power that may become coercive, even violent. But if such bids for power are both inevitable and unavoidable, as I maintain they are, what we need are procedures for letting them conflict with one another in productive ways. Conflict over our most basic self-understandings and identities is not the problem. On the contrary. "It is precisely when assent cannot be elicited through argument that the use of force becomes a temptation."[57] Truth claims will be *more*, not less coercive the more we restrict vigorous argument and debate. Whether we do so in the name of cozy, familiar dialogue or in an effort to avoid totalizing gestures of power and violence, the result will be the same.

Communicative norms, in other words, may impinge on the potential subversivity of performativity's potential for creating a new community or citing alternative conventions. But operating without such communicative norms is hardly an alternative. Without an elaboration of the communicative norms which might explain, let alone work to increase, the circumstances under which performatives might succeed in creating a consensus or forging a new community, performativity has no particular or predictable value as political practice. And there's the rub, the reason we need a new pronominal politics and cannot abandon the vexed effort of collective self-identification and self-understanding. Communicative norms, prerequisite to the social changes necessary to facilitate exchange, cannot be theorized from the pure perspective of the "I." It makes sense to articulate and argue over communicative norms only if we can do so from a perspective that is relational, interactive, intersubjective, if we do so from the space of what I would call a collective imaginary, an imagination of collectivity which knows that collectivity *is imagined* and that proceeds nonetheless precisely on that basis.

It's not surprising, I'd suggest, that performative theory has shied away from the discussion of communicative norms and what an ethical dialogic practice might look like. It's embarrassing these days to talk about our conversational and intersubjective ideals, to express desires for recognition (which we know is always illusory and deferred), to describe what might be our ideal listener (since we know there is no such person and that there can never be one). No one wants to sound sappy or sentimental. But this fear of utopian figurations, just like a fear of vigorous debate and contestation, may be little more, finally, than a bad effect of a particular academic climate and institutional/professional ethos. We shouldn't give in to it. In fact, we should contest it. As I have already suggested, if a politics of voice and an erotics of talk are at odds, they are also two sides of a necessary tension and dialectic. There cannot be a language of justice that is merely comfortable and cozy. But neither can there be a language of justice, a productive and progressive cultural conversation, which fails to factor in our desires, whatever difficult, even embarrassing shape they may take.

Where consciousness-raising suffered, ultimately, from the *one-sidedness* of its own communicative norms, from its mandate to create only an erotics of talk at the expense of the contestation that might realize such utopian "ideal speech situations," performativity, recast as a theory of cultural conversation, is hampered by a complete *absence* of communicative norms, an unwillingness to venture any hypotheses about the kinds of commitments we need to make if an "ideal speech situation" would be realized, even momentarily.

A new communicative ethics would need to acknowledge the likelihood, even the desirability, of contestation and failure. But it would also need to acknowledge desire. Our desire to be understood. Our desire to be recognized. Our desire to be part of supportive communities and sisterhoods that might feel both productive and safe. And if we are to provide more than merely performative or poetic justice we need clearer blueprints for meaningful social action, as well as rich insights into questions of meaning itself.

Imagine, for a moment, a performative practice of consciousness-raising, one that might salvage its commitment to listening to each other and learning from each other but without presuming identicality, without treating propositions as essential "truths," but instead as auditions, tryouts: a discursive practice which could speak to and as women, but which would do so proleptically and playfully, expanding who we think we are even as we address one another "in error." Imagine the communicative ethics of consciousness-raising without its politics of identification. Imagine the insights of performativity backed up and supported by a progressive set of normative ideals.

Just another erotics of talk? Another utopic fantasy of an impossible "ideal speech situation"? I don't think so. A new communicative ethics cannot, as I have argued, be laid out in manifestos or programs. Yet we can still imagine what it might look like and what its effects might be. In terms of feminist criticism, it would allow us to search out the subversive voices of women's texts without at the same time insisting that those texts validate us, love us, seek us out as their ideal listener/lovers. In terms of feminist politics, it would allow us to act on behalf of "women" even as we recognize that the category "women" is only an audition, a performance, a speech act that hopes to persuade and move its audience. Imagine that we could learn to enjoy conflict and struggle in the same way—for the same reasons—that we have enjoyed sisterhood, solidarity, and support. Imagine that it became hard to tell them apart.

Imagine a performative consciousness-raising session, a group of women, say in their late twenties or early thirties, sitting in a circle, sharing their stories, trying to learn from each other. Imagine that they are skeptical about their own project, that they don't want consciousness-raising to be an attempt "to *fix* identification," that they don't "accept the idea of a *fixed* self" but hope, nevertheless, for "a *liberated* self." Imagine that they come to the session with their stories already textualized, already written out. Imagine that one is "full of references. It's written in French. Another is written in, well, baby talk. The last one, though, is very clean, totally error-free." Imagine that they question the space between identification and desire. That they conjure up the figure of a woman, say Victoria, of Victoria's

Secret perhaps, and they ask themselves: "did I want to buy her? Be her? Do her?" Imagine that they are serious about becoming better listeners and learning from each other. But imagine that they are silly also, that they pretend, just for the fun of it, "that we do have selves and that they can be liberated like beautiful banners unfurling in the wind." Imagine that they begin with the proposition that "the Woman category is contingent upon oppositions" and so they go around the room, sharing oppositions, "figuring out how to be a woman."

The above quotes are all from a performance by the V-Girls of a consciousness-raising session. Their performance is a parodic resignification. But it is a parody built on real nostalgia, real desire for those seemingly lost moments, "the glory days of early seventies feminism," when women talked to each other and when doing so seemed politically and personally worthwhile. It is a parody built on a set of communicative norms that continue to privilege honesty, debate, exchange, and narrative.

Imagine, remarks a V-Girl, midway through her parodic performance, imagine "that consciousness-raising could lead us back to a more meaningful feminist politics."[58]

It couldn't, of course.

But then again . . .

Notes

Introduction: In Search of an Ideal Listener

1. Erving Goffman, *Frame Analysis: An Essay on the Organization of Experience* (New York: Harper & Row, 1974), 499.

2. Susan Faludi, *Backlash: The Undeclared War Against American Women* (New York: Crown, 1991), 6. Faludi is summarizing Shere Hite's *Women and Love: A Cultural Revolution in Progress* (New York: Knopf, 1987).

3. Marcelle Clements, rev. of "Madison County," *Ms.*, 7, no. 2 (Sept./Oct. 1995): 88.

4. Henry James, *The Bostonians* (Harmondsworth, Middlesex, England: Penguin, 1985), 71.

5. Ibid., 71.

6. Ernest Hemingway, *In Our Time* (New York: Scribner's, 1925), 72.

On modernism as a gendered battle over language, see Sandra M. Gilbert and Susan Gubar's three-volume study, *No Man's Land: The Place of the Woman Writer in the Twentieth Century* (New Haven: Yale Univ. Press, 1988, 1989, 1994), esp. vol. I: "The War of the Words."

7. See epigraph above.

Erving Goffman, who has written extensively about the social meanings of our different "forms of talk," suggests that whereas an argument plays out and plays upon the social status and power of its participants, it is in our ideas of conversation that we invest our ideals of equality and reciprocity. Conversation's economy of exchange is regulated, Goffman argues, by utopian (even nostalgic), laws:

[Conversation is] the talk occurring when a small number of participants come together and settle into what they perceive to be a few moments cut off from

165

(or carried on to the side of) instrumental tasks; a period of idling felt to be an end in itself, during which everyone is accorded the right to talk as well as to listen and without reference to a fixed schedule; everyone is accorded the status of someone whose overall evaluation of the subject matter at hand—whose editorial comments, as it were—is to be encouraged and treated with respect.

Erving Goffman, *Forms of Talk* (Philadelphia: Univ. of Pennsylvania Press, 1981), 14 n.8.

If "language reflects . . . [an] individual's place in society," as Peter Burke suggests, then we display our social place, what Goffman calls our "footing," not only through such localized signals as interruption, address, bullying, hedging, qualification, apology, silence, disclosure, pitch, tag questions, commands, joking, hesitation, dismissal, and self-deprecation, but also through the larger genres of discursive exchange in which we engage, in which we tend to find ourselves, which we encourage or invite, discourage or avoid. Peter Burke, *The Art of Conversation* (Cornell Univ. Press, 1993), 23.

8. Gloria Naylor, *Mama Day* (New York: Ticknor & Fields, 1988). Future references are to this edition and will be cited parenthetically.

9. Walter Benjamin, "The Storyteller," in *Illuminations*, ed. Hannah Arendt (New York: Schocken Books, 1969), 83.

10. Charles Taylor, *Multiculturalism and "The Politics of Recognition"* (Princeton: Princeton Univ. Press, 1992), 36–37.

11. Taylor, *Multiculturalism*, 35.

12. See epigraph, p. 2.

13. "Footing" is Erving Goffman's term for the social positioning that is both expressed and constructed discursively. See his *Frame Analysis: An Essay on the Organization of Experience* (New York: Harper & Row, 1974) and *Forms of Talk* (Philadelphia: Univ. of Pennsylvania Press, 1981).

14. With a few exceptions, these debates have not been taken up by feminist literary criticism. But as I hope to show, the questions raised in these debates over how to theorize cultural conversation are not only germane to textual interpretation, they go to the heart of the feminist critical enterprise, particularly insofar as the feminist critic (like the reader of African American, gay, lesbian, or "minority" texts) so often finds herself in the position of speaking for—even imaginatively as—someone who has been silenced or marginalized, whose speech has been rendered mute or meaningless.

15. Richard Rorty, *Philosophy and the Mirror of Nature* (Princeton: Princeton Univ. Press, 1979), 389, 157, 378.

16. Nancy Hartsock, "Rethinking Modernism: Minority vs. Majority Theories," *Cultural Critique* 7 (Fall 1987): 200–201, 199.

17. While the literature on how language use is inflected by gender is too vast for a comprehensive listing, the following texts provide a useful overview of the field: Nancy M. Henley, *Body Politics: Power, Sex, and Nonverbal Communication* (Englewood Cliffs: Prentice-Hall, 1977), 67–82; Robin Lakoff, *Language and Woman's Place* (New York: Harper and Row, 1975); Dale Spender, *Man Made Language* (London: Routledge and Kegan Paul, 1980); Nancy Henley and Barrie Thorne, "Womanspeak and Manspeak: Sex Differences and Sexism in Communication, Verbal and Nonverbal," in *Beyond Sex Roles*, ed. Alice Sargent (St. Paul, Minn.: West Publishing, 1976); Nancy M. Henley and Barrie Thorne, *Language*

and Sex: Difference and Dominance (Rowley, Mass.: Newbury House, 1975);
Nancy M. Henley and Barrie Thorne, *She Said/He Said: An Annotated Bibliography of Language, Speech, and Nonverbal Communication* (Pittsburgh: Know,
1975); Nancy Henley, Chris Kramarae, and Barrie Thorne, *Language, Gender and
Society* (Rowley, Mass.: Newbury House, 1988); Sally McConnell-Ginet, Ruth
Borker, and Nelly Furman, eds., *Women and Language in Literature and Society*
(New York: Praeger, 1980), xi; Deborah Tannen, *Talking Voices: Repetition,
Dialogue, and Imagery in Conversational Discourse* (Cambridge: Cambridge
Univ. Press, 1989); Tannen, *Conversational Style: Analyzing Talk among Friends*
(Norwood, N.J.: Ablex, 1984); Tannen, ed., *Gender and Conversational Interaction* (New York: Oxford Univ. Press, 1993); Tannen, *That's Not What I Meant!
How Conversational Style Makes or Breaks Relationships* (New York: Ballantine,
1986); Tannen, *You Just Don't Understand: Women and Men in Conversation*
(New York: Ballantine, 1990).

Some recent research has begun to challenge long-standing findings that men
talk more than women, that they interrupt women more than women interrupt
men, and, in general, that men exercise strategies of control and dominance in
mixed-sex conversational settings. See, for example, Deborah James and Sandra
Clarke, "Women, Men, and Interruptions: A Critical Review," and Deborah James
and Janice Drakich, "Understanding Gender Differences in Amount of Talk: A
Critical Review of Research," both in *Gender and Conversational Interaction*,
231–80 and 281–312. In place of potentially essentializing categories such as
gender, race, and age, researchers are increasingly beginning to work in terms of
varied forms of differential status and power.

18. Hartsock, "Rethinking Modernism," 199. To be fair, one would have
to concede that Rorty's privileging of cacophony, disorder, and "abnormal discourse" is an attempt to turn the tables of what has passed for normal (i.e., normalizing) discourse.

19. Jürgen Habermas, *The Theory of Communicative Action*, Vol. I: *Reason
and the Rationalization of Society*; Vol. II: *Lifeworld and System: A Critique of
Functionalist Reason*, trans. Thomas McCarthy (Boston: Beacon Press, 1981,
1987).

20. Peter Dews, *Logics of Disintegration: Post-Structuralist Thought and the
Claims of Critical Theory* (London: Verso, 1987), 221.

21. John Brenkman, *Culture and Domination* (Ithaca: Cornell Univ. Press,
1987), 49–50.

22. Jürgen Habermas, *Der Philosphische Diskurs der Moderne* (Frankfurt,
1985), 378, as cited by Dews, *Logics of Disintegration*, 221, emphasis in original.

23. Throughout this study I will be sometimes using "we" and "us" in a
deliberatively provocative, proleptic sense. For a discussion of the non-essentialistic
possibilities of this pronominal politics, see the Conclusion.

24. Iris Marion Young, *Justice and the Politics of Difference* (Princeton:
Princeton Univ. Press, 1990), 34, emphasis mine.

For additional feminist critiques of Habermas, see also Iris Marion Young,
Throwing like a Girl and Other Essays in Feminist Philosophy and Social Theory
(Bloomington: Indiana Univ. Press, 1990); Johanna Meehan, ed., *Feminists Read
Habermas: Gendering the Subject of Discourse* (New York: Routledge, 1995); and
Rita Felski, *Beyond Feminist Aesthetics: Feminist Literature and Social Change*
(Cambridge: Harvard Univ. Press, 1989).

For a particularly useful collection of debates on communicative ethics, although not necessarily from a feminist perspective, see Seyla Benhabib and Fred Dallmayr, eds., *The Communicative Ethics Controversy* (Cambridge: MIT Press, 1990).

25. Fraser writes:

It does indeed seem doubtful that the project of reaching agreement with a criminal, of positing her or him as an autonomous subject of conversation, could ever in fact be anything other than manipulation and control of linguistic behavior, given that *ex hypothesi* it is to be carried out in the quintessentially non-"ideal speech situation" of involuntary incarceration. The same may also hold for women in the bourgeois patriarchal family, students in institutions of compulsory education, patients in mental asylums, soldiers in the military—indeed, for all situations where the power that structures discourse is hierarchical and asymmetrical and where some persons are prevented from pressing their claims either by overt or covert force or by such structural features as the lack of an appropriate vocabulary for interpreting their needs.

But the fact that the humanist ideal of autonomous subjectivity is unrealizable, even co-optable, in such "disciplinary" contexts need not be seen as an argument against that ideal. It may be seen, rather, as an argument against hierarchical, asymmetrical power. One need not conclude, with Foucault, that humanist ideals must be rejected on strategic grounds. One may conclude instead, with Habermas, that it is a precondition for the realization of those ideals that the "power" that structures discourse be symmetrical, nonhierarchical, and hence reciprocal.

"Michel Foucault: A 'Young Conservative?,'" in Fraser, *Unruly Practices: Power, Discourse, and Gender in Contemporary Social Theory* (Minneapolis: Univ. of Minnesota Press, 1989), 46–47.

26. Nancy Fraser, "What's Critical about Critical Theory? The Case of Habermas and Gender," in ibid., 126; 120; 128.

27. M. M. Bakhtin, *The Dialogic Imagination*, ed. Michael Holquist, trans. Caryl Emerson and Michael Holquist (Austin: Univ. of Texas, 1981); Mikhail Bakhtin, *Problems of Dostoevksy's Poetics*, ed. and trans. Caryl Emerson (Minneapolis: Univ. of Minnesota Press, 1984); M. M. Bakhtin, *Speech Genres and Other Late Essays*, ed. Caryl Emerson and Michael Holquist, trans. Vern W. McGee (Austin: Univ. of Texas Press, 1986); Mikhail Bakhtin, *Rabelias and His World*, trans. Hélène Iswolsky (Cambridge: MIT Press, 1968); M. M. Bakhtin and P. N. Medvedev, *The Formal Method in Literary Scholarship: A Critical Introduction to Sociological Poetics*, trans. Albert J. Wehrle (Baltimore: Johns Hopkins Univ. Press, 1991).

There have been numerous appropriations of Bakhtinian dialogics by feminist criticism. See, for example, Dale M. Bauer, *Feminist Dialogics: A Theory of Failed Community* (Albany: State Univ. of New York Press, 1988); Mae Gwendolyn Henderson, "Speaking in Tongues: Dialogics, Dialectics and the Black Women Writer's Literary Tradition," in *Changing Our Own Words: Essays on Criticism, Theory and Writing by Black Women*, ed. Cheryl A. Wall (New Brunswick: Rutgers Univ. Press, 1989), 16–37; Laurie A. Finke, *Feminist Theory, Women's Writing* (Ithaca: Cornell Univ. Press, 1992); Anne Herrmann, *The Dialogic and Difference: "An/Other Woman" in Virginia Woolf and Christa Woolf* (New York: Columbia Univ. Press, 1989); and the essays collected in *Feminism, Bakhtin, and the Dialogic*, ed. Dale M. Bauer and S. Jaret McKinstry (Albany: State Univ. of New York

Press, 1991), and *A Dialogue of Voices: Feminist Literary Theory and Bakhtin*, ed. Karen Horne and Helen Wussow (Minneapolis: Univ. of Minnesota Press, 1994).

28. Hans Robert Jauss, *Toward an Aesthetic of Reception*, trans. Timothy Bahti (Minneapolis: Univ. of Minnesota Press, 1982), 21. See also Hans Robert Jauss, *Question and Answer: Forms of Dialogic Understanding*, ed. and trans. Michael Hays (Minneapolis: Univ. of Minnesota Press, 1989), especially "Dialogic Understanding in Literary Communication," 207–18.

29. Hans-Georg Gadamer, *Truth and Method* (New York: Crossroads 1982), 341.

30. Ross Chambers, *Story and Situation: Narrative Seduction and the Power of Fiction* (Minneapolis: Univ. of Minnesota Press, 1984), 214; Ross Chambers, *Room for Maneuver: Reading (the) Oppositional (in) Narrative*, 11.

31. Jonathan Culler, *Structuralist Poetics: Structuralism, Linguistics, and the Study of Literature* (Ithaca: Cornell Univ. Press, 1975).

32. Gadamer, *Truth and Method*, 341.

33. Peter Brooks, *Reading for the Plot: Design and Intention in Narrative* (New York: Vintage, 1985), 53.

34. Patrocinio P. Schweickart, "Reading Ourselves: Toward a Feminist Theory of Reading," in *Gender and Reading*, ed. Elizabeth Flynn and Patrocinio P. Schweickart (Baltimore: Johns Hopkins Univ. Press, 1986), 31–62.

35. Judith Kegan Gardiner, "Empathic Ways of Reading: Narcissism, Cultural Politics, and Russ's *Female Man*," ms. See also *Rhys, Stead, Lessing, and the Politics of Empathy* (Bloomington: Indiana Univ. Press, 1988). Gardiner provides one of the most systematic and provocative attempts to defend an "empathic" or "dialogic" model of feminist reading.

36. See note 14 above and note 37 below.

37. Susan Sniader Lanser, *Fictions of Authority: Women Writers and Narrative Voice* (Ithaca: Cornell Univ. Press, 1992), 3. Lanser, one of the few critics to attempt a systematic description of this ubiquitous term, has also written about "voice" from a more strictly narratological perspective in *The Narrative Act: Point of View in Prose Fiction* (Princeton: Princeton Univ. Press, 1981), see esp. chap. 3, "From Person to Persona: The Textual Voice," 108–48. As Lanser points out, "other silenced communities—peoples of color, peoples struggling against colonial rule, gay men and lesbians—have also written and spoken about the urgency of 'coming to voice.'"

Many efforts to decode the overtly heterosexual plots of Western literature and uncover their covert stories of homosocial, homosexual, lesbian, or gay desire have also turned on efforts to find the text's "voice": a "subtext that explores female desire while the main text does not," for example, or the voice of gay Harlem in the twenties, or an "unnamed presence in the literary text." See, for example, Marilyn R. Farwell, "Heterosexual Plots and Lesbian Subtexts: Toward a Theory of Lesbian Narrative Space," in *Lesbian Texts and Contexts: Radical Revisions*, ed. Karla Jay and Joanne Glasgow (New York: New York Univ. Press, 1990), 102; Eric Garber, "A Spectacle in Color: The Lesbian and Gay Subculture of Jazz Age Harlem," in *Hidden from History: Reclaiming the Lesbian and Gay Past*, ed. Martin Duberman, Martha Vicinus, and George Chauncey, Jr. (New York: Meridian, 1990), 318–31; and Gloria T. Hull, "'Lines She Did Not Dare': Angelina Weld Grimké, Harlem Renaissance Poet," in *The Lesbian and Gay Studies Reader*, ed. Henry Abelove, Michèle Aina Barele, and David M. Halperin (New York: Routledge, 1993), 453–66; Sharon O'Brien, "'The Thing Not Named': Willa

Cather as a Lesbian Writer," *Signs* 9, no. 4 (Summer 1984); 576–99, reprinted in *The Lesbian Issue: Essays from Signs*, ed. Estelle B. Freedman, Barbara C. Gelpi, Susan L. Johnson, and Kathleen M. Weston (Chicago: Univ. of Chicago Press, 1985), 67–90.

In African American studies, a politics of voice has also been privileged. Because "black people had to represent themselves as 'speaking subjects' before they could even begin to destroy their status as objects," the "search for a voice," Henry Louis Gates, Jr., argues, has been central to black letters. "For just over two hundred years, the concern to depict the quest of the black speaking subject to find his or her voice has been a repeated topos of the black tradition, and perhaps has been its most central trope." Henry Louis Gates, Jr., *The Signifying Monkey: A Theory of African-American Literary Criticism* (New York: Oxford Univ. Press, 1988), 129, 239. On the African American quest for freedom as a quest for freedom *and literacy*, see also Robert B. Stepto, *From Behind the Veil: A Study of Afro-American Narrative* (Urbana: Univ. of Illinois Press, 1979).

38. For a useful history of consciousness-raising, see Anita Shreve, *Women Together, Women Alone: The Legacy of the Consciousness-Raising Movement* (New York: Viking, 1989). A number of early consciousness-raising documents are contained in the aptly titled anthology *Voices from Women's Liberation*, ed. Leslie B. Tanner (New York: New American Library, 1970).

39. See Adrienne Rich, *The Dream of a Common Language: Poems 1974–1977* (New York: W. W. Norton, 1978) and *Poems: Selected and New, 1950–1974* (New York: W. W. Norton, 1975).

40. Written July 7, 1969, reprinted in *Voices from Women's Liberation*, 109–111.

41. Roland Barthes, *The Pleasure of the Text*, trans. Richard Miller (New York: Hill and Wang, 1975), 6, emphasis in original.

42. Goffman, *Forms of Talk*, 109.

43. Ibid., 87.

44. See Patricia Meyer Spacks, *Gossip* (New York: Alfred A. Knopf, 1985).

45. Françoise Lionnet writes that the speaker "who feels that s/he is preaching to those who don't want to (can't) hear" may give up, find alternative means of speaking, or resort to violence and "confrontational tactics." See *Autobiographical Voices: Race, Gender, Self-Portraiture* (Ithaca: Cornell Univ. Press, 1989), 163.

46. Goffman, *Forms of Talk*, 85.

47. Luce Irigaray, "Commodities among Themselves," *This Sex Which Is Not One*, trans. Catherine Porter (Ithaca: Cornell Univ. Press, 1985), 196.

48. Young, *Justice and the Politics of Difference*, 5–6.

49. Ibid., 6.

50. Nancy Armstrong and Leonard Tennenhouse, *The Ideology of Conduct: Essays on Literature and the History of Sexuality* (New York: Methuen, 1986), 2.

51. The *locus classicus* for expanded feminist understandings of the erotic as a form of social and personal "power" is Audre Lorde's "Uses of the Erotic: The Erotic as Power," in *Sister Outsider* (Freedom, Calif.: Crossing Press, 1984), 53–59. The passages cited above are from p. 55.

"The erotic," Lorde writes, "is a measure of the beginnings of our sense of self and the chaos of our strongest feelings. It is an internal sense of satisfaction to which, once we have experienced it, we know we can aspire. For having experienced the fullness of this depth of feeling and recognizing its power, in honor and self-respect we can require no less of ourselves" (54).

Lorde's discussion of the erotic works against a whole history of the sexual objectification of women of color. Her insistence on an erotic/sexual framework for black feminist politics, for any meaningful feminist politics at all, needs to be understood, in part, in that context. My own thinking about utopian language structures in women's writing, including feminism, is deeply indebted to Lorde's determination to think through the possibilities of devalued—even taboo—topics and discourses.

52. "One possible interpretation of communicative ethics," Iris Marion Young writes, "is that normative claims are the outcome of the expression of needs, feelings, and desires which individuals claim to have met and recognized by others under conditions where all have an equal voice in the expression of their needs and desires. This interpretation thus tends to collapse the distinction between public reason and a private realm of desire, need, and feeling." *Justice and the Politics of Difference*, 118.

53. On Giddens's account, the interrelationship between the private and public spheres is dynamic and dialectical. "A symmetry exists between the democratising of personal life and democratic possibilities in the global political order at the most extensive level," he writes. "Democratisation in the public domain, not only at the level of the nation-state, supplies essential conditions for the democratising of personal relationships. But the reverse applies also. The advancement of self-autonomy in the context of pure relationships [defined by reciprocity and equality] is rich with implications for democratic practice in the larger community."

Anthony Giddens, *The Transformation of Intimacy: Sexuality, Love & Eroticism in Modern Societies* (Stanford: Stanford Univ. Press, 1992), 188, 194, 195.

54. Goffman opposes his understanding of eros to Freud's. But Freud's discussion of eros as a drive need not be seen as incompatible with Giddens's emphasis on the communicative. On Freud's use of Eros, see the following essays, all reprinted in *The Standard Edition of the Complete Psychological Works of Sigmund Freud*, trans. James Strachey (London: Hogarth Press, 1961): "The Interpretation of Dreams," vols. IV and V; "Beyond the Pleasure Principle," vol. XVIII, pp. 7–64; "The Ego and the Id," vol. XIX, pp. 3–66, esp. "The Two Classes of Instincts," pp. 40–47; "An Outline of Psychoanalysis," vol. XXIII, pp. 144–207.

55. Catherine Belsey suggests that because "women were the first writers and readers of the novel in the eighteenth century[,] women were permitted to be experts on desire." "Desire," she writes, "imagines a utopian world, envisaging a transformation and transfiguration of the quotidian which throws into relief the drabness we too easily take for granted." *Desire: Love Stories in Western Culture* (Oxford: Blackwell, 1994), 4, 7.

56. Brooks, *Reading for the Plot*, 61, 48, 53–54, emphasis mine.

57. Robert Scholes, *Fabulation and Metafiction* (Urbana: Univ. of Illinois Press, 1979), 26. It is not only in narrative theory, of course, that such masculinist models obtain. On Freud's "notorious" description of the "one libido," for example, and its relations to narrative, see Belsey, *Desire*, 46.

58. Teresa de Lauretis, "Desire in Narrative," in *Alice Doesn't: Feminism, Semiotics, Cinema* (Bloomington: Indiana Univ. Press, 1984), 105–6, as cited by Jay Clayton, *The Pleasures of Babel: Contemporary American Literature and Theory*

(New York: Oxford Univ. Press, 1993), 78. See especially his "Theories of Desire," 61–89.

59. Judith Roof, *A Lure of Knowledge: Lesbian Sexuality and Theory* (New York: Columbia Univ. Press, 1991), 118.

60. Rachel Blau DuPlessis, *Writing beyond the Ending: Narrative Strategies of Twentieth-Century Women Writers* (Bloomington: Indiana Univ. Press, 1985), 149.

61. Luce Irigaray, "When Our Lips Speak Together," in *This Sex Which Is Not One*, 205–18; Hélène Cixous, "The Laugh of the Medusa," in *New French Feminisms: An Anthology*, ed. Elaine Marks and Isabelle de Courtivron (New York: Schocken, 1981), 245–64.

62. The founding argument of what remains a widely held position can be found in Domna C. Stanton's "Language and Revolution: The Franco-American Dis-Connection," in *The Future of Difference*, ed. Hester Eisenstein and Alice Jardine (New Brunswick: Rutgers Univ. Press, 1980), 73–87. Not all feminist critics, by any means, have accepted this divide. Patricia Yaeger, for example, argues that "linguisticality" is a "touchstone" of both the French and the American traditions. See *Honey-Mad Women: Emancipatory Strategies in Women's Writing* (New York: Columbia Univ. Press, 1988).

63. "You can't get de best of no woman in de talkin' game," Hurston writes, "her tongue is all de weapon a woman got." *Mules and Men* (Bloomington: Indiana Univ. Press, 1978).

64. "Stipulate": (1) to specify as a condition of agreement; require by contract; (2) to guarantee in an agreement; (3) to make an express demand or provision in an agreement; (4) to form an agreement (*The American Heritage Dictionary*).

What are stipulated are facts; stipulation generally occurs in an adversarial, legal, or juridical context.

Chapter 1.
Reading Feminist Readings: The Silent Heroine

1. See Gayle Rubin, "The Traffic in Women: Notes on the 'Political Economy' of Sex," in *Toward an Anthropology of Women*, ed. Rayna R. Reiter (New York: Monthly Review Press, 1975), 157–210.

2. Jane Marcus makes a similar point in "Daughters of Anger/Material Girls: Con/Textualizing Feminist Criticism," *Women's Studies* 15 (1988): 281–308.

3. Tillie Olsen, *Silences* (New York: Delacorte Press, 1978).

4. Virginia Woolf, *A Room of One's Own* (New York: Harcourt, Brace and World, 1978), 18. All future references are to this edition and will be cited parenthetically.

5. Olsen, *Silences*, 44. And only a few years later Olsen was to record her satisfaction that this call was being answered: "five years later (1976), it is unmistakable that out of the sense of wrong has come substantial yields for literature: its enlargement and vivification through reclamation of obscured writers and intensified rereading of classic ones; an enhancement and deepening of literary scholarship, criticism, and theory" (181).

6. See her poem "Diving into the Wreck" for a working out not only of the need for recuperation and recovery, but also of the difficulties and dangers of a recuperative enterprise in which saving one's self cannot be divorced from saving and being dependent upon others, living and dead, historical and material, male

and female. In Adrienne Rich, *Diving into the Wreck: Poems, 1971–1972* (New York: W. W. Norton, 1973).

7. Rich, "When We Dead Awaken: Writing as Re-Vision," *College English* 34:1 (Oct. 1972), reprinted in *On Lies, Secrets, and Silence: Selected Prose, 1966–1978* (New York: W. W. Norton, 1979), 35.

8. Patricia Spacks's *The Female Imagination*, Elaine Showalter's *A Literature of Their Own* and "Feminist Criticism in the Wilderness," Ellen Moers's *Literary Women*, Barbara Smith's "Toward a Black Feminist Criticism," Judith Fetterley's *The Resisting Reader*, Sandra Gilbert and Susan Gubar's *The Madwoman in the Attic* and *Shakespeare's Sisters*, Annette Kolodny's "A Map for Rereading; Or, Gender and the Interpretation of Literary Texts" and "Dancing Through the Minefield," Deborah E. McDowell's "New Directions for Black Feminist Criticism," Rachel Blau DuPlessis's "For the Etruscans," Bonnie Zimmerman's "What Has Never Been: An Overview of Lesbian Feminist Criticism," Nancy K. Miller's "Emphasis Added: Plots and Plausibilities in Women's Fiction," and Alicia Ostriker's "The Thieves of Language: Women Poets and Revisionist Mythmaking," to name a few.

9. Susan Gubar, for example, concludes her classic essay on "The Blank Page" by talking about her "own sense of excitement at engaging in such a task," and it is with almost religious reverence that she speaks of "how attentive and patient we must be before the blank page to perceive genuinely new and sustaining scripts." "'The Blank Page' and the Issues of Female Creativity," in *Writing and Sexual Difference*, ed. Elizabeth Abel (Chicago: Univ. of Chicago Press, 1982), 93.

Elaine Hedges writes that "as Rich said in 1971, and as we believed, "'hearing our wordless or negated experiences affirmed' in literature could have visible effects on women's lives." "'Out at Last'? 'The Yellow Wallpaper' after Two Decades of Feminist Criticism," in *The Captive Imagination: A Casebook on the Yellow Wallpaper*, ed. Catherine Golden (New York: Feminist Press, 1992), 328.

10. Rich, "When We Dead Awaken," 49.

11. Patrocinio Schweickart, "Reading Ourselves: Toward a Feminist Theory of Reading," in *Gender and Reading: Essays on Readers, Texts, Contexts*, ed. Elizabeth A. Flynn and Patrocinio P. Schweickart (Baltimore: Johns Hopkins Univ. Press, 1986), 51.

12. The phrase "regulatory fiction" is Judith Butler's. "Gender Trouble, Feminist Theory, and Psychoanalytic Discourse," in *Feminism/Postmodernism*, ed. Linda J. Nicholson (New York: Routledge, 1990), 3. See also Linda Alcoff, Jane Flax, Diana Fuss, Sandra Harding, Julia Kristeva, Denise Riley, and Monique Wittig. On the "identity crisis" in feminist theory, see also my "The Language of Crisis in Feminist Theory," in *"Turning the Century": New Directions in Feminist Criticism*, ed. Glynis Carr (Lewisburg: Bucknell Review Press, 1992).

13. Hedges, "'Out at Last.'"

14. Ann Rosalind Jones, "Imaginary Gardens with Real Frogs in Them: Feminist Euphoria and the Franco-American Divide, 1976–88," in Gayle Greene and Coppélia Kahn, eds., *Changing Subjects: The Making of Feminist Literary Criticism* (London: Routledge, 1992), 69.

15. Anita Shreve, *Women Together, Women Alone: The Legacy of the Consciousness-Raising Movement* (New York: Viking, 1989), 243–44.

16. Jones, "Imaginary Gardens," 68.

17. Shreve, *Women Together*, 30.

18. Alice Walker, "In Search of Our Mothers' Gardens," *Ms.* May 1974,

reprinted in *In Search of Our Mothers' Gardens* (New York: Harcourt, Brace, Jovanovich, 1983), 232–33.

19. Ibid., 239.

20. Sally Munt, ed., *New Lesbian Criticism: Literary and Cultural Readings* (New York: Columbia Univ. Press, 1992), xiii.

21. Helena Michie, *Sororophobia* (New York: Oxford Univ. Press, 1992).

22. Susan Gubar, "Sapphistries," in *The Lesbian Issue: Essays from Signs*, ed. Estelle B. Freedman, Barbara C. Gelpi, Susan L. Johnson, Kathleen M. Weston (Chicago: Univ. of Chicago Press, 1985), 91–110.

23. Walter Benjamin, "Theses on the Philosophy of History," in *Illumina-tions*, trans. Harry Zohn (New York: Schocken, 1969), 256.

For a particularly illuminating discussion of this thesis, see John Brenkman, *Culture and Domination* (Ithaca: Cornell Univ. Press, 1987), 3–5.

24. Taylor, *Multiculturalism*, 34.

25. Sandra M. Gilbert and Susan Gubar, *The Madwoman in the Attic: The Woman Writer and the Nineteenth-Century Literary Imagination* (New Haven: Yale Univ. Press, 1979), 48.

26. Ibid., 51, 48.

27. Ibid., 49.

28. For comprehensive explanations of identity as a discursive and inter-subjective construction, see Charles Taylor, *Sources of the Self: The Making of the Modern Identity* (Cambridge: Harvard Univ. Press, 1989); Anthony Giddens, *Modernity and Self-Identity: Self and Society in the Later Modern Age* (Stanford: Stanford Univ. Press, 1991); Seyla Benhabib, *Situating the Self: Gender, Commu-nity and Postmodernism in Contemporary Ethics* (New York: Routledge, 1992); and Diana Fuss, *Identification Papers* (New York: Routledge, 1995).

29. Elaine Showalter, *Sister's Choice: Tradition and Change in American Women's Writing* (New York: Oxford Univ. Press, 1991), 174.

30. Christine Froula, "The Daughter's Seduction: Sexual Violence and Lit-erary History," *Signs* 11:4 (Summer 1986): 622. All future references are to this edition and will be cited parenthetically.

31. On the racial politics of Froula's essay, see also Ann Ardis, "The White Daughter's Seduction: Christine Froula's Family Romance of Canon-Formation," unpublished ms.

32. Deborah E. McDowell, "The Changing Same: Generational Connections and Black Women Novelists," *New Literary History* 18 (1987): 281–30, reprinted in *Reading Black, Reading Feminist*, ed. Henry Louis Gates, Jr. (New York: Meridian, 1990), 93.

33. Ibid., 104.

34. Ibid., 107.

35. Ibid., 95.

36. Janice Haney-Peritz, "Monumental Feminism and Literature's Ances-tral House: Another Look at 'The Yellow Wallpaper,'" *Women's Studies* 12:2 (1986): 113–28, reprinted in Golden, ed., *The Captive Imagination*, 270.

37. Jane Marcus, "Alibis and Legends: The Ethics of Elsewhereness, Gen-der and Estrangement," in *Women's Writing in Exile*, ed. Mary Lynn Broe and Angela Ingram (Chapel Hill: Univ. of North Carolina Press, 1989), 273.

38. Kolodny, "Map," 149.

39. See particularly Toril Moi's critical, and I think inaccurate, assessment

of Gilbert and Gubar in *Sexual/Textual Politics: Feminist Literary Theory* (New York: Methuen, 1985).

40. Gilbert and Gubar, *Madwoman*, 51.

41. Haney-Peritz, "Monumental Feminism," 269.

42. Susan S. Lanser, "Feminist Criticism, 'The Yellow Wallpaper,' and the Politics of Color in America," *Feminist Studies* 15:3 (Fall 1989): 419–20.

Not everyone, of course, would concede that this is an automatically or necessarily bankrupt operation. Carolyn Heilbrun, for example, writes that "in deconstructing literature and life, we ourselves becomes novelists, making fictions out of the texts, and lives, other women have left us." This is, she writes, "one of the most appealing characteristics of feminist criticism." "Critical Response II: A Response to *Writing and Sexual Difference*," in Abel, ed., *Writing and Sexual Difference*, 291.

43. Nancy K. Miller, "Arachnologies: The Woman, the Text, and the Critic," in *Subject to Change: Reading Feminist Writing* (New York: Columbia Univ. Press, 1988), 87, 83.

44. Isak Dinesen, "The Blank Page," in *The Last Tales* (New York: Vintage, 1957), reprinted in *The Norton Anthology of Literature by Women*, ed. Sandra M. Gilbert and Susan Gubar (New York: W. W. Norton, 1985), 1419. All future references are to this edition and will be cited parenthetically.

45. Lanser, "Feminist Criticism," 415.

46. Gilbert and Gubar, *Madwoman*.

47. Elaine R. Hedges, "Small Things Reconsidered: Susan Glaspell's 'A Jury of Her Peers,'" *Women's Studies* 12 (1986): 89–90.

48. Showalter, *Literature*, 146.

49. Judith Fetterley, "Reading about Reading: 'A Jury of Her Peers,' 'The Murders in the Rue Morgue,' and 'The Yellow Wallpaper,'" in Flynn and Schweickart, eds., *Gender and Reading*, 154.

50. Catherine Golden, "One Hundred Years of Reading 'The Yellow Wallpaper,'" in *The Captive Imagination*, 9. There is a particularly rich tradition of criticism on "The Yellow Wallpaper." Much of it has been recently collected, along with interesting background materials, in *The Captive Imagination*.

51. Charlotte Perkins Gilman, "The Yellow Wallpaper," *New England Magazine* (May 1892), reprinted in ibid., 24. All future references are to this edition and will be cited parenthetically.

52. "The narrator," Annette Kolodny notes, "progressively gives up the attempt to *record* her reality and instead begins to *read* it" (156). Or, as Paula Treichler puts it, "the more the wallpaper comes alive, the less inclined is the narrator to write in her journal—'dead paper.'" "Escaping the Sentence: Diagnosis and Discourse in 'The Yellow Wallpaper,'" in *Feminist Issues in Literary Scholarship*, ed. Shari Benstock (Bloomington: Indiana Univ. Press, 1987), reprinted in Golden, ed., *The Captive Imagination*, 194.

"Blocked from expressing herself *on* paper," Judith Fetterley observes, "she seeks to express herself *through* paper. Literally, she converts the wall*paper* into her text. . . . Indeed, one might argue that the narrator over-interprets the wallpaper, the one stimulus in her immediate environment, as a reaction against this sensory deprivation."

She "engages," Susan Lanser writes, "in a form of feminist interpretation when she tries to read the paper on her wall" (1989, p. 418).

Somewhat less sympathetically, Mary Jacobus has argued that the narrator's "is a case of hysterical (over)reading." "An Unnecessary Maze of Sign Reading," in *Reading Women: Essays in Feminist Criticism* (New York: Columbia Univ. Press), reprinted in Golden, ed., *The Captive Imagination*, 279.

53. Hedges, "Afterword" to "The Yellow Wallpaper" (New York: Feminist Press, 1973), reprinted in Golden, ed., *The Captive Imagination*, 131.

54. Ibid.

55. Haney-Peritz, "Monumental Feminism," 268.

56. Hedges, "'Out at Last,'" 326.

57. Hedges, "Afterword," 132.

58. Catherine Golden, "The Writing of 'The Yellow Wallpaper': A Double Palimpsest," in *The Captive Imagination*, 302.

59. Susan Glaspell, "A Jury of Her Peers," *Everyweek* (March 5, 1917), reprinted in *Images of Women in Literature*, ed. Mary Anne Ferguson (Boston: Houghton Mifflin, 1973). All future references are to this edition and will be cited parenthetically.

60. Gubar, "'The Blank Page,'" 89.

61. Gubar, "Sapphistries," 95.

62. On feminist "collaboration" between the woman writer and reader as an erotically charged, homoerotic "seduction," see Jane Marcus's extremely provocative essay, "Sapphistry: Narration as Lesbian Seduction in *A Room of One's Own*," in *Virginia Woolf and the Languages of Patriarchy* (Bloomington: Indiana Univ. Press, 1987). See also Jane Marus, *Art & Anger: Reading Like a Woman*, (Columbus: Ohio State Univ. Press, 1988), esp. "Still Practice, A/Wrested Alphabet: Toward a Feminist Aesthetic." While I disagree with Marcus's suggestion that the "erotic" pleasures of "female reading" are necessarily "expressive of the desire to merge with the mother." ("Still Practice," 237), I am indebted to her brilliant discussion of an "erotics of reading."

63. Gubar, "Sapphistries," 95. It is surprising, given the intriguing rhetorics of normativity at play in all three of these texts, that lesbian readings have not, to my knowledge, previously been suggested. Even as we guard against anachronistic attributions, it is hard not to mark the ways these stories incorporate words like "gay" and "queer" in the service of defining and marking out the normative. The third sentence of "The Yellow Wallpaper," for example, reads: "still I will proudly declare that there is something queer about it" (924). And "A Jury of Her Peers" repeats the word "queer" no less than nine times. Minnie Foster looks "queer"; holding Minnie's quilt block makes Mrs. Hale "feel queer" as the other woman seems to move into her and speak through her; and Mrs. Peters, as she comes to sympathize more and more with Minnie Foster, begins speaking in a "queer" voice. Dinesen's startling description (which in 1957 carried the same homosexual connotations it does now) in "The Blank Page" of the women's procession and pilgrimage to the portrait gallery as "both sacred and secretly gay" (1421) seems pointedly double-voiced. Indeed, without the double meaning of "gay," this sentence is virtually meaningless, since this pilgrimage is anything but celebratory. It is a somber, self-reflective, often mournful journey for the women who undertake it.

By 1917 when "A Jury of Her Peers" was published, "queer" was already in common, if not widespread, usage as a term for homosexual men. "Gay" acquired its double meaning in America at least as early as the 1920s where it appears, along with "queer," in such novels as *The Scarlet Pansy*. On the use of the term "queer" before the 1920s, see George Chauncey's brilliant essay, "Christian Brotherhood or Sexual Perversion? Homosexual Identities and the Construction of Sexual Boundaries in the World War I Era." I am grateful to Nina Miller, Gary Schmidgall, Joseph Wittreich, and Michael Warner for their generous help in my (unsuccessful) attempt to fix the exact dates when these terms first came into common American usage. As far as I have been able to determine, this important genealogical work still remains to be done.

64. On compulsory heterosexuality, see Rich, "Compulsory Heterosexuality and Lesbian Existence," *Signs* 5:4 (1980): 631–60. The phrase "heteronormativity" is Michael Warner's.

65. See Hannah Arendt, *The Human Condition* (Chicago: Univ. of Chicago Press, 1958), 50 & ff.

66. Judith Mayne, "A Parallax View of Lesbian Authorship," in *Inside/Out: Lesbian Theories, Gay Theories*, ed. Diana Fuss (New York: Routledge, 1991), 181.

67. Teresa de Lauretis, "Film and the Visible," in *How Do I Look?: Queer Film and Video*, ed. Bad Object-Choices (Seattle: Bay Press, 1991), 257–58.

68. de Lauretis, "Film and the Visible," 260, emphasis mine.

69. Jane Gallop's discussion of the dialectic of identification and desire is particularly provocative for matters of reading and critical interpretation. See *The Daughter's Seduction: Feminism and Psychoanalysis* (Ithaca: Cornell Univ. Press, 1982).

70. Diana Fuss, "Fashion and the Homospectatorial Look," *Critical Inquiry* 18 (Summer 1992): 737. See also Diana Fuss, *Identification Papers* (New York: Routledge, 1995). Fuss argues that there is a "fundamental indissociability of identification and desire"; "as hard as Freud labors to keep desire and identification from infecting one another, the signs of their fluid exchanges surface everywhere to challenge and to weaken the *cordon sanitaire* erected between them" (12, 45–46).

"It is important to consider that identification and desire can coexist," Judith Butler writes, "and that their formulation in terms of mutually exclusive oppositions serves a heterosexual matrix." "Imitation and Gender Insubordination," in Fuss, ed., *Inside/Out*, 13–31.

Ruth Leys also develops a very provocative account of the imbrication of identification and desire. They are not only interconnected, she argues, but it is actually mimesis itself which precedes desire: "a violent act of cultural repression is required to force desire away from its natural origins in a mimetically induced homosexual desire . . . sexual identity is a consequence or effect of mimetic identification and not, as Freud will argue, the other way around." "The Real Miss Beauchamp: Gender and the Subject of Imitation," in *Feminists Theorize the Political*, ed. Judith Butler and Joan W. Scott (New York: Routledge, 1992), 167–214.

71. Judith Kegan Gardiner, *Rhys, Stead, Lessing, and the Politics of Empathy* (Bloomington: Indiana Univ. Press, 1988), 167.

72. On identifications as "erotic, intellectual, and emotional," as "sites of erotic investiture continually open to the sway of fantasy, [such that] the meaning of a particular identification critically exceeds the limits of its social, historical, and political determinations," see Fuss, *Identification Papers*, 2, 8.

73. Elaine Hedges, "'Out at Last,'" 324.

74. Woolf, *Room of One's Own*, 118.

Chapter 2.
Recuperating Agents: *Incidents in the Life of a Slave Girl*

1. Harriet A. Jacobs, *Incidents in the Life of a Slave Girl, Written by Herself,* ed. Jean Fagan Yellin (Cambridge: Harvard Univ. Press, 1987). All future references to the text, or to Yellin's introduction to it, are to this edition and will be cited parenthetically.

2. Sondra R. Herman, "Loving Courtship or the Marriage Market? The Ideal and its Critics, 1871–1911," *American Quarterly* 25, no. 2 (May 1973): 235–52. This repudiation of the marriage ideal, in the context of a narrative about slavery, freedom, and agency, is a particularly bold move on Jacobs's part. Marriage, as Eugene Genovese points out, was the centerpiece of slaveholders' defense of slavery. The patriarchal family, many slaveholders held, was "the institution on which all government and, in fact, all civilization rest[ed]," and slavery was not merely analogous to the patriarchal family, but was an important embodiment of its principle of the natural rule of subordinates by a benevolent and proper superior. See Eugene D. Genovese, *The World the Slaveholders Made* (New York: Vintage, 1971), 195–97 & ff.

3. See also Carla Peterson, "Capitalism, Black (Under)development, and the Production of the African-American Novel in the 1850's," *American Literary History* 4, no. 4 (Winter 1992): 559–83. Peterson, whose article appeared after this chapter was written, discusses the difficulties faced by black Americans who sought to transform themselves from property into possessive individuals. On the status of black Americans as objects of property rather than possessors of it, the lingering implications and consequences of this history, and the "deadening power" of contracts see Patricia J. Williams, "On Being the Object of Property," *Signs* 14, no. 1 (1988): 5–24. While Williams's description of contracts in some ways runs counter to my own, my reading of Brent's vision of freedom is nevertheless indebted to Williams's provocative self-recuperation.

4. Carole Pateman provides an excellent discussion of this political-philosophical premise. See *The Sexual Contract* (Stanford: Stanford Univ. Press, 1988) and *The Disorder of Women: Democracy, Feminism and Political Theory* (Stanford: Stanford Univ. Press, 1989). Future references are to *The Sexual Contract* and will be cited parenthetically.

5. The historical relationship between slavery and contract is an extremely complicated one (and might well be the topic of a different essay on Brent's relation to contract). Throughout debates over American slavery both defenders and critics found ample ground for their positions in theories of contract. On the one hand, as Pateman has demonstrated, "the natural freedom and equality of men can be used to denounce the immorality, violence, and injustice of slavery, an argument used extensively by abolitionists" (60). But at the same time, contract legitimates itself partly through its own expansiveness. True contractarian freedom, in this view, means the freedom to exchange *anything*, including one's freedom: "men as 'individuals' may legitimately contract out their own services, the property they own in their own persons . . . [a man] may decide that his interests are best met by contracting out his services for life in return for the protection (subsistence) that such a contract affords. . . . Civil slavery becomes nothing more than one example of legitimate contract" (60, 67).

This does not mean that defenders of slavery were necessarily extreme contractarians. On the contrary, as Eugene Genovese has shown, George Fitzhugh's influential defense of slavery as a paternalistic social and economic system in opposition to capitalism rested upon a profoundly anti-contractarian view. Fitzhugh, Genovese writes, "denounced Locke's theory of social contract and argued that man was naturally a slave of society and had no rights to surrender to it. 'Man is born a member of society and does not form society.'" Eugene D. Genovese, *The World the Slaveholders Made* (New York: Vintage, 1969).

6. For a different reading of Jacobs's relation to the liberal, domestic ideologies inscribed in the female spheres of home, family, motherhood, and marriage, see Claudia Tate, *Domestic Allegories of Political Desire: The Black Heroine's Text at the Turn of the Century* (New York: Oxford Univ. Press, 1992).

7. Seyla Benhabib, *Situating the Self: Gender, Community, and Postmodernism in Contemporary Ethics* (New York: Routledge, 1992), 24.

8. See also Dana Nelson, *The Word in Black and White: Reading "Race" in American Literature, 1638–1867* (New York: Oxford Univ. Press, 1992), 140–41. Nelson, whose book appeared after this chapter was completed, argues that *Incidents* "critiques and redefines the 'sympathetic' framework for understanding that featured prominently in both domestic and abolitionist texts of the period."

9. John Blassingame, *The Slave Community* (New York: Oxford Univ. Press, 1972), 233–34, as quoted by Jean Fagan Yellin, "Written by Herself: Harriet Jacobs' Slave Narrative," *American Literature* 53, no. 3 (Nov. 1981): 480 n. 2.

10. See Yellin, "Written by Herself," 479–86.

11. Henry Louis Gates, Jr., *The Signifying Monkey: A Theory of African-American Literary Criticism* (New York: Oxford Univ. Press, 1988), 131; *Figures in Black: Words, Signs, and the Racial Self* (New York: Oxford Univ. Press, 1987), 104. On literacy, voice, and the "quest for freedom and literacy" as the "pre-generic myth of Afro-America," see also Robert B. Stepto, *From Behind the Veil: A Study of Afro-American Narrative* (Urbana: Univ. of Illinois Press, 1979).

12. James Olney, "'I Was Born': Slave Narratives, Their Status as Autobiography and as Literature," in *The Slave's Narrative*, ed. Charles T. Davis and Henry Louis Gates, Jr. (New York: Oxford Univ. Press, 1985). On the disavowal of fictionality, see also William L. Andrews, *To Tell a Free Story: Toward a Poetics of Afro-American Autobiography, 1760–1865* (Urbana: Univ. of Illinois Press, 1986). On the "authenticating machinery" of slave narratives, see also Houston A. Baker, Jr., "Autobiographical Acts and the Voice of the Southern Slave," in Davis and Gates, eds., *The Slave's Narrative*, and Robert B. Stepto, *From Behind the Veil*.

13. One interesting passage in Brent's narrative details her efforts to teach a fellow slave to read (72–73). In an ironic twist on white antebellum anxieties, Brent intimates that literacy will not endanger *or* empower slaves, but will merely make them better Christians, even less threatening than their illiterate brethren. I am grateful to Houston Baker for bringing this passage to my attention.

14. Minrose C. Gwin, "Green-Eyed Monsters of the Slavocracy: Jealous Mistresses in Two Slave Narratives," in *Conjuring: Black Women Writers and Literary Tradition*, ed. Marjorie Pryse and Hortense J. Spillers (Bloomington: Indiana Univ. Press, 1985), 39–52.

15. Valerie Smith, *Self Discovery and Authority in Afro-American Narrative* (Cambridge: Harvard Univ. Press, 1987), 28.

16. Yellin, "Introduction" to Jacobs, *Incidents in the Life of a Slave Girl*, xxix.

17. Herbert Marcuse, "The Affirmative Character of Culture," in *Negations*, trans. Jeremy J. Shapiro (Boston: Beacon, 1968).

18. Ibid.

19. Ross Chambers, *Story and Situation: Narrative Seduction and the Power*

of Fiction (Minneapolis: Univ. of Minnesota Press, 1984) and *Room for Maneuver: Reading (the) Oppositional (in) Narrative* (Chicago: Univ. of Chicago Press, 1991). Future references, unless otherwise indicated, are to *Story and Situation* and will be cited parenthetically.

20. That Jacobs chooses letters is particularly interesting, given their privileged status as private, female communication, "'one of the few compensations for women's lack of participation in the public sphere. Letter writing allowed a woman to create a network of relations maintained primarily on paper and to construct a subjectivity tailored to the expectations of the addressee.'" Lyn Lloyd Irvine, *Ten Letter Writers* (London: Hogarth Press, 1932), 27, as quoted by Anne Hermann, *The Dialogic and Difference: "An/Other" Woman in Virginia Woolf and Christa Wolf* (New York: Columbia Univ. Press, 1989), 37.

21. Andrews, *To Tell a Free Story*, 252.

22. Smith, *Self Discovery and Authority*, 29.

23. Houston A. Baker Jr., *Blues, Ideology, and Afro-American Literature: A Vernacular Theory* (Chicago: Univ. of Chicago Press, 1984), 53. Future references will be cited parenthetically.

24. Andrews, *To Tell a Free Story*, 259.

25. See Elaine Showalter, "Literary Criticism," Review Essay, *Signs* 1 (Winter 1975): 435–60.

26. Anthony Giddens, *The Constitution of Society: Outline of a Theory of Structuration* (Berkeley: Univ. of California Press, 1984), 3.

27. Ibid., 6.

28. I thank Louise Yelin for this formulation. Jane Marcus also argues that the feminist critic may be complicit in the very silence she recuperates and seeks to redress. See her "Still Practice, A/Wrested Alphabet: Toward a Feminist Aesthetic," in *Art & Anger: Reading like a Woman* (Columbus: Ohio State Univ. Press, 1988), 216–17.

29. Northrop Frye, *Anatomy of Criticism: Four Essays* (New York: Atheneum, 1968), 76.

30. Stanley Fish, *Is There a Text in This Class? The Authority of Interpretive Communities* (Cambridge: Harvard Univ. Press, 1980).

31. Raymond Williams, *Keywords: A Vocabulary of Culture and Society* (New York: Oxford Univ. Press, 1983), 80.

32. See, for example, Steven Mailloux, *Interpretive Conventions: The Reader in the Study of American Fiction* (Ithaca: Cornell Univ. Press, 1982), and Peter J. Rabinowtiz, *Before Reading: Narrative Conventions and the Politics of Interpretation* (Ithaca: Cornell Univ. Press, 1987).

33. Jonathan Culler, *Structuralist Poetics: Structuralism, Linguistics, and the Study of Literature* (Ithaca: Cornell Univ. Press, 1975), 193, 214. Future references will be cited parenthetically. For particularly useful discussions of contract in literature, see Nancy Armstrong, *Desire and Domestic Fiction: A Political History of the Novel* (New York: Oxford Univ. Press, 1987), and Tony Tanner, *Adultery in the Novel: Contract and Transgression* (Baltimore: Johns Hopkins Univ. Press, 1979).

34. Smith, *Self Discovery and Authority*, 2, 30.

35. Ibid., 42.

36. Yellin, "Introduction," xxiv; "Text and Contexts of Harriet Jacobs' *Incidents in the Life of a Slave Girl, Written by Herself*," in Davis and Gates, eds., *The Slave's Narrative*, 277.

37. Carby, *Reconstructing Womanhood*, 47, 49, 53.

38. Carla Peterson and Claudia Tate also argue that Brent willingly engages in acts of self-commodification. See Peterson, "Capitalism," 571, and Tate, *Domestic Allegories*, 30.

39. Claudia Tate, however, argues that *Incidents* represents marriage as "an ideal, though unrealizable, sign of liberation." *Domestic Allegories*, 32.

40. See also Houston A. Baker, Jr., *Workings of the Spirit: The Poetics of Afro-American Women's Writing* (Chicago: Univ. of Chicago Press, 1991). In his more recent discussion of *Incidents in the Life of a Slave Girl*, Baker considers how scenes of silencing in Brent's tale work to gender her narrative position, particularly in her treatment of her own "historicized body" as a "willed object of exchange" (20–21).

41. Robert B. Stepto, "Distrust of the Reader in Afro-American Narratives," in *Reconstructing American Literary History*, ed. Sacvan Bercovitch (Cambridge: Harvard Univ. Press, 1986), 305, 309, 301.

42. Ibid., 309.

43. Ibid., 306, 309.

44. Elizabeth Fox-Genovese, "To Write My Self: The Autobiographies of Afro-American Women," in *Feminist Issues in Literary Scholarship*, ed. Shari Benstock (Bloomington: Indiana Univ. Press, 1987), 169, 166–69.

45. Stepto, "Distrust of the Reader," 309–10.

46. Ibid., 315.

47. For a contrary reading of Brent's addresses to her reader, see Beth Maclay Doriani, "Black Womanhood in Nineteenth-Century America: Subversion and Self-Construction in Two Women's Autobiographies," *American Quarterly* 43, no. 2 (June 1991): 199–222.

48. On silence as a "resting point," see also Françoise Lionnet, *Autobiographical Voices: Race, Gender, Self-Portraiture* (Ithaca: Cornell Univ. Press, 1989), 20.

49. William L. Andrews, "Dialogue in Antebellum Afro-American Autobiography," in *Studies in Autobiography*, ed. James Olney (New York: Oxford Univ. Press, 1988), 91.

50. Ibid., 93.

51. Ibid., 93–95.

52. In fact, the progressive appeal of contracts may make them particularly effective tools of control and coercion because they speak to something so deep in us. Contracts, for example, turn out to be "the most useful and powerful clinical tools at the disposal of the therapist to set effective limits on what is otherwise out-of-control behavior" on the part of patients with multiple personality disorders. Contracts exert sufficient pull that all of the multiples—or alters—of a multiple personality disorder can usually be counted on to honor a contract, regardless of whether or not they were "present" for its negotiation, informed of its goals, or consented to its implementation. Frank W. Putnam, M.D., *Diagnosis and Treatment of Multiple Personality Disorder* (New York: Guilford Press, 1989), 144–151. See also *Multiple Personality Disorder from the Inside Out*, ed. Barry M. Cohen, Esther Giller, and Lynn W. (Baltimore: Sidran Press, 1991), 60–62. I am grateful to Cathy Caruth for bringing these materials to my attention.

Chapter 3. Girl Talk: *Jane Eyre*

1. Charlotte Brontë, *Jane Eyre* (Harmondsworth, Middlesex, England: Penguin, 1986), 476. All future citations to the novel are to this edition and will be cited parenthetically.

2. Gayatri Chakravorty Spivak, "Three Women's Texts and a Critique of Imperialism," *Critical Inquiry* 12 (Autumn 1985): 244.

3. One vivid example of this privilege can be gleaned from a recent anthology of feminist criticism, an over 1000-page collection entitled *Feminisms*, edited by Diane Price Herndl and Robyn Warhol (New Brunswick: Rutgers Univ. Press, 1991). Their expanded table of contents orients the reader to feminist positions on important contemporary questions with such headings as "body," "class," "desire," "discourse," "history," "imperialism," "lesbian writers," "madness," "psychoanalysis," "sexuality," and others. Among these, only one text—*Jane Eyre*—rates its own listing as a crucial feminist topic.

Jane Eyre, like the feminist classics I have been discussing in Chapters One and Two, has been the object of extensive feminist recuperative/archeological work: "the significance of Brontë's use of structure, language, and female symbolism has been misread and under-rated by male-oriented twentieth-century criticism, and is only now beginning to be fully understood and appreciated," writes Elaine Showalter. The bulk of this recuperative work has concentrated on the novel's description of women's social conditions, female psychology, and women's relation to writing, storytelling, and voice. See, for example, Virginia Woolf, "*Jane Eyre* and *Wuthering Heights*," in *The Common Reader* (New York: Harcourt, Brace, Jovanovich, 1925): Patricia Meyer Spacks, *The Female Imagination* (New York: Avon, 1972); Adrienne Rich, "The Temptations of a Motherless Woman"; Ruth Bernard Yeazell, "More True than Real: Jane Eyre's 'Mysterious Summons,'" *Nineteenth-Century Fiction* 29 (1974):127–43; Maurianne Adams, "*Jane Eyre*: Woman's Estate," in *The Authority of Experience*, ed. Arlyn Diamond and Lee R. Edwards (Amherst: Univ. of Massachusetts Press, 1975), 137–59; Ellen Moers, *Literary Women* (New York: Doubleday, 1976); Elaine Showalter, *A Literature of Their Own: British Women Novelists from Brontë to Lessing* (Princeton: Princeton Univ. Press, 1977); Sandra M. Gilbert and Susan Gubar, "A Dialogue of Self and Soul: Plain Jane's Progress," in *The Madwoman in the Attic: The Woman Writer and Nineteenth-Century Literary Imagination* (New Haven: Yale Univ. Press, 1979); Rosemarie Bodenheimer, "Jane Eyre in Search of Her Story," *Papers on Language and Literature* 16, no. 3 (Summer 1980): 387–402; Margaret Homans, *Bearing the Word: Language and Female Experience in Nineteenth-Century Women's Writing* (Chicago: Univ. of Chicago Press, 1986); Nancy Armstrong, *Desire and Domestic Fiction: A Political History of the Novel* (New York: Oxford Univ. Press, 1987); Mary Poovey, "The Anathematized Race: The Governess and *Jane Eyre*," in *Uneven Developments: The Ideological Work of Gender in Mid-Victorian England* (Chicago: Univ. of Chicago Press, 1988); Susan Sniader Lanser, "*Jane Eyre*'s Legacy: The Powers and Dangers of Singularity," in *Fictions of Authority: Women Writers and Narrative Voice* (Ithaca: Cornell Univ. Press, 1992), 176–93.

Interestingly, even feminist critics who seek to decenter *Jane Eyre*'s privileged position in the feminist canon, to critique its racial and national politics, nonetheless continue to treat *Jane Eyre* as a paradigmatic text. See, for example, Jean Rhys, *Wide Sargasso Sea* (Harmondsworth, Middlesex, London: Penguin, 1960), and, most recently, Spivak, "Three Women's Texts and a Critique of Imperialism"; Susan Meyer, "Colonialism and the Figurative Strategy of *Jane Eyre*," *Victorian Studies* 33 (Winter 1990): 247–68;" Deirdre David, "The Governess of Empire: Jane Eyre Takes Care of India and Jamaica," in *Rule Britannia: Women, Empire, and Victorian Writing* (Ithaca: Cornell Univ. Press, 1995); and Suvendrini Perera,

Reaches of Empire: The English Novel from Edgeworth to Dickens (New York: Columbia Univ. Press, 1991).

4. Cora Kaplan, *Sea Changes: Culture and Feminism* (London: Verson, 1986), 173.

5. Poovey, *Uneven Developments*, 139. See also Homans, *Bearing the Word*, and Joan D. Peters, "Finding a Voice: Towards A Woman's Discourse of Dialogue in the Narration of *Jane Eyre*," *Studies in the Novel* 23, (Summer 1991): no. 2 217–36.

6. Gilbert and Gubar, *Madwoman*, 339.

If Gilbert and Gubar are right that Jane posits herself as an "Everywoman," this act itself may be a form of subversion insofar as "the very authority of masculine autobiography derives from the assumption held by both author and reader that the life being written/read is an exemplary [i.e. white, male, bourgeois] one." See Bella Brodzki and Celeste Schenck, eds., "Introduction" to *Life/Lines: Theorizing Women's Autobiography* (Ithaca: Cornell Univ. Press, 1988), 2–3.

7. Lanser, *Fictions of Authority*, 177, 183.

8. Carol T. Christ, "Imaginative Constraint, Feminine Duty, and the Form of Charlotte Brontë's Fiction," *Women's Studies* 6, no. 3 (1979): 287–96, reprinted in Barbara Timm Gates, ed., *Critical Essays on Charlotte Brontë*, (Boston: G. K. Hall, 1990), 67.

9. Homans, *Bearing the Word*, 86.

10. Charles Taylor, *Multiculturalism and "The Politics of Recognition"* (Princeton: Princeton Univ. Press, 1992), 32.

11. Ibid., 34.

12. Mikhail Bakhtin, *Problems of Dostoevsky's Poetics*, ed. and trans. Caryl Emerson (Minneapolis: Univ. of Minnesota Press, 1984), 183.

13. Hans-Georg Gadamer, *Truth and Method* (New York: Crossroads, 1982), 330. See also Vincent Crapanzano, "On Dialogue," *The Interpretation of Dialogue*, ed. Tullio Maranhão (Chicago: Univ. of Chicago Press, 1990), 269–91.

14. Radway, *Reading the Romance: Women, Patriarchy, and Popular Culture* (Chapel Hill: Univ. of North Carolina Press, 1984), 151.

15. Anthony Giddens, *The Transformation of Intimacy: Sexuality, Love & Eroticism in Modern Societies* (Stanford: Stanford Univ. Press, 1992), 184–85.

16. See also Rita Felski, *Beyond Feminist Aesthetics: Feminist Literature and Social Change* (Cambridge, Mass.: Harvard Univ. Press, 1989).

17. Kathleen Tillotson, *Novels of the 1840's* (New York: Oxford, 1967), 8.

18. Giddens, *Transformation of Intimacy*. On intimacy as a social form which articulates political desires—desires for a polity that may not exist—see also John Brenkman, "Aesthetics of Male Fantasy," in *Culture and Domination* (Ithaca: Cornell Univ. Press, 1987); Niklas Luhmann, *Love as Passion: The Codification of Intimacy* (Cambridge, Mass.: Harvard Univ. Press, 1986); and Richard Sennett, *The Fall of Public Man: On the Social Psychology of Capitalism* (New York: Vintage, 1974).

Vanishing forms of "symbolic-affective" ties in the public sphere, Brenkman writes, are "recreated in the form of the so-called intimate sphere of bourgeois life. The intimate sphere is inadequately understood as an 'inner realm.' Grounded in heterosexual love, marriage, and the family, 'intimacy' is the historical product of the evolution of society. . . . Being in love inherits the symbolic-affective ties of the vanishing society and reinscribes them on the scene of intimacy as history erases them from the social world as a whole. . . . The symbolic residue of the social relations uprooted in the development of capitalism survives in the structures of feeling and forms of interaction that organize the private individual's 'inner life'" (203–4, 206).

19. On reading, for Brontë and for an emerging nineteenth-century middle-class readership, as "an index of one's personality," see Mark M. Henelly, Jr., "*Jane Eyre's* Reading Lesson," *ELH* 54, no. 4 (Winter 1984): 693–717.

On Jane as a reader and on Jane's reading, see also Carla L. Peterson, *The Determined Reader: Gender and Culture in the Novel from Napoleon to Victoria* (New Brunswick, N.J.: Rutgers Univ. Press, 1986), esp. 82–112. Peterson's discussion of nineteenth-century reading is particularly illuminating as well; see also pp. 10–27.

20. On Jane's attempt to generate a story from this tablet as an "emblem" of her difficulties as an autobiographer, see Linda H. Peterson, *Victorian Autobiography: The Tradition in Self-Interpretation* (New Haven: Yale Univ. Press, 1986). Peterson views Jane's "experiment in the autobiographical mode" (132) as an exercise in self-interpretation, "the need to interpret her life for herself" (135), and places that imperative in the context of spiritual autobiography.

21. See also Yeazell, "More True than Real," on the psychic logic of this telepathic exchange. Yaezell reads this passage, as I do, as "the crucial stroke in the novel's psychological design." My emphasis, however, is not on the psychology of dependence and independence embodied by this exchange, but on its creation of an ideal of intimacy that can function, covertly, as a critique of the very public sphere which it may seem to celebrate and endorse.

22. Giddens, *Transformation of Intimacy*, 188.

23. Brenda R. Silver, "The Reflecting Reader in *Villette*," in *The Voyage In: Fictions of Female Development*, ed. Elizabeth Abel, Marianne Hirsch, and Elizabeth Langland (Hanover: Univ. Press of New England, 1983), 102.

24. Showalter, *A Literature of Their Own*, 112.

25. These two opposing positions correspond to many schematizations of the "divide" between American and French, or poststructuralist feminist theory. While I am dubious about other deployments of this so-called "divide," I would concur that feminist theorizing of the past fifteen years evinces two radically different attitudes toward the limits of language and narrative, attitudes that tend to follow, roughly, along the two sides of this imaginary border.

26. One could argue, as Anthony Giddens does, for example, that self-representation and subjectivity—as relational, discursive practices—are always juridical constructs. But this would not answer the question of how such social pressures are differently—and historically—inscribed in a variety of literary forms.

27. *Jane Eyre*, as far as I know, has never been considered in relation to American slave narratives. One of the consequences of the novel's recuperation as a feminist model of resistance and self-realization has been a tendency, in fact, to decontextualize it from literary and social history so as to emphasize its universality. Recent criticism of the novel, hence, has often turned precisely on the importance of such recontextualization. Susan Lanser and Mary Poovey, for example, read *Jane Eyre* in the context of governess novels like Mary Brunton's *Discipline* (1815), Mary Martha Sherwood's *Caroline Mordant* (1835), and Anne Brontë's *Agnes Grey* (1847). Raymond Williams reads *Jane Eyre* in the context of steam printing, British serial publication, and the expansion of a mass reading public. Gayatri Spivak, Susan Meyer, and Deirdre David all read the novel in the context of individualism and British imperialism.

I do not mean to suggest that Brontë may have been influenced by slave narratives, although this is not impossible. Far more likely, however, as a reference point for her strategies of authentication, is the long, independent tradition of prefaces in English fiction such as *The History of Mary Prince* or the works of Richardson. One advantage, however, of reconfigured disciplines such as women's studies and cultural studies is the license they provide to cross national, racial, historical, and generic boundaries in seeking to understand how different writers respond to similar situations.

28. Bodenheimer, "Jane Eyre in Search of Her Story," 389.

29. Virginia Woolf, *A Room of One's Own* (New York: Harcourt, Brace, Jovanovich, 1929), 71.

30. "At the end of the novel," Bodenheimer writes, "Rochester's blindness leaves Jane in sole command of the narrative field; she becomes the single source of evidence, the voice which tells what her audience cannot see, and the arbiter of what is and is not to be told" (393). "Jane Eyre in Search of Her Story." See also Peterson, *Determined Reader,* 107–8, on Jane's ability to become a writer as a consequence of Rochester's maiming.

31. One could read this scene as ironic, insofar as gossip, as Patricia Meyer Spacks has shown, is a form of intersubjective exchange very like what Jane seems to strive for. "Gossip," Spacks writes, "provides a resource for the subordinated (anyone can *talk*; with a trusted listener, anyone can say anything), a crucial means of self-expression, a crucial form of solidarity." *Gossip* (New York: Knopf, 1985), 5.

32. Poovey, *Uneven Developments.*

33. Bodenheimer, "Jane Eyre in Search of Her Story," 389.

34. Michel Foucault, *The History of Sexuality,* vol. I: *An Introduction* (New York: Vintage, 1980), 67.

35. Bodenheimer, "Jane Eyre in Search of Her Story," 394.

36. Spivak, "Three Women's Texts and a Critique of Imperialism," 251.

37. Susan Meyer, "Colonialism and the Figurative Strategy of *Jane Eyre.*" See also Deirdre David, "Governess of Empire."

38. Poovey, *Uneven Developments,* 108–9.

39. Anthony Giddens, *Modernity and Self-Identity: Self and Society in the Late Modern Age* (Stanford: Stanford Univ. Press, 1991), 36.

40. For arguments that Brontë's metaphorics of kinship is merely a means of desexualizing their romance so as to recast it along safer, more familial, more "Victorian" lines, see Maurianne Adams, "*Jane Eyre:* Women's Estate," Helene Moglen, "*Jane Eyre:* The Creation of a Feminist Myth," in *Charlotte Brontë: The Self Conceived* (New York: Norton, 1976), and George Steiner, "Eros and Idiom," in *On Difficulty and Other Essays* (New York: Oxford Univ. Press, 1978).

Janice Radway's reading of romance is that the conventional happy ending of romance, epitomized by Rochester and Jane's reconciliation, is always a disguised family romance and that the genre is always a displacement of the longing to return to the security of the pre-oedipal world, to the "original, blissful symbiotic union between mother and child that is the goal of all romances despite their apparent preoccupation with heterosexual love and marriage." While I do not find this mother-daughter plot sufficient or compelling, I would agree with Radway that this formulaic ending needs to be put in symbolic, allegorical terms, including the terms of "kinship," broadly conceived. *Reading the Romantic Heroine: Women, Patriarchy, and Popular Literature* (Chapel Hill: Univ. of North Carolina Press, 1984), 156. See also Laurie Langbauer, *Women and Romance: The Consolations of Gender in the English Novel* (Ithaca: Cornell Univ. Press, 1990).

41. Luce Irigaray, *This Sex Which Is Not One*, trans. Catherine Porter (Ithaca: Cornell Univ. Press, 1985), 171.

Lacan writes: "'It's one's own ego that one loves in love, one's own ego made real on the imaginary level.'" Jacques Lacan, *Seminaire I* (Paris: Seuil, 1975), as cited by Michael Warner, "Homo-Narcissism; or, Heterosexuality," in *Engendering Men: The Question of Male Feminist Criticism*, ed. Joseph A. Boone and Michael Cadden (New York: Routledge, 1990), 190. While a reading of heterosexuality as an economy of likeness or kinship is implicit in much of Lacan's discussion of the dialectic of identification and desire, this suggestion remains only implicit in Lacan, who, like Freud, remains wedded to a concept of normative heterosexuality.

42. Irving Singer, *The Nature of Love*, vol. II: *Courtly and Romantic* (Chicago: Univ. of Chicago Press, 1984), 5–6.

43. See, for example, Richard Chase, Terry Eagleton, Helene Moglen, Adrienne Rich, George Steiner, and Elaine Showalter, among others.

Harold Bloom takes the anomalous, almost inexplicable position that "we are [not] to apply the Freudian reduction that Rochester has been somehow castrated, even symbolically . . . but certainly he has been rendered dependent upon Jane, and he has been tamed into domestic virtue and pious sentiment. . . . The charmingly wicked and Byronic Rochester . . . is given a lot more punishment than he deserves." "Introduction" to *The Brontës: Modern Critical Views* (New York: Chelsea House, 1987), 3–4.

On the symbolism of gendering wounds in another context, see Coppélia Kahn, "Antony's Wounds, in *Warriors, Wounds and Women: The Sexual Politics of Shakespeare's Roman Works*" (New York: Routledge, forthcoming, 1996).

44. Rachel Blau Du Plessis, *Writing Beyond the Ending: Narrative Strategies of Twentieth-Century Women Writers* (Bloomington: Indiana Univ. Press, 1985).

45. Joseph Allen Boone, *Tradition Counter Tradition: Love and the Form of Fiction* (Chicago: Univ. of Chicago Press, 1987), 9.

46. See Nancy Armstrong, *Desire and Domestic Fiction: A Political History of the Novel* (New York: Oxford Univ. Press, 1987).

47. Helena Michie, *Sororophobia: Differences among Women in Literature and Culture* (New York: Oxford Univ. Press, 1992).

48. Terry Eagleton, "Jane Eyre's Power Struggles," in *Myths of Power: A Marxist Study of the Brontës* (Totowa, N.J.: Barnes and Noble, 1975), reprinted in *Jane Eyre: A Norton Critical Edition*, 2nd ed., ed. Richard J. Dunn (New York: W. W. Norton, 1987), 491–96.

49. Helene Moglen, "Creation of a Feminist Myth," 134.

50. Showalter, *A Literature of Their Own*, 107.

51. Luce Irigaray, *Speculum of the Other Woman*, trans. Gillian C. Gill (Ithaca: Cornell Univ. Press, 1985), 103–4.

Helena Michie notes that Irigaray's description of same-sex desire rests on identification and sameness, on desire between women as a form of autoeroticism. "Marks of difference disappear," Michie writes, "as 'same' and 'like' get absorbed into the text and into the undifferentiating and capacious trope of sisterhood." *Sororophobia*, 177. One could certainly argue, however, that the rhetorical strategies of Irigaray's writing self-consciously and self-reflexively draw attention to this very problem.

52. Jean Wyatt, "A Patriarch of One's Own: *Jane Eyre* and Romantic Love," *Tulsa Studies in Women's Literature* 4 (1985): 209. See also Adams, "*Jane Eyre*: Woman's Estate," 193–94.

53. Adrienne Rich, "Compulsory Heterosexuality and Lesbian Existence," in *Blood, Bread, and Poetry: Selected Prose, 1979–1985* (New York: W. W. Norton, 1986).

54. Cora Kaplan, *Sea Changes*, 148.

55. Bodenheimer, "Jane Eyre in Search of Her Story," 394.

56. For very different readings of Jane's remarkable decision not to tell Rochester that she has heard him, see also C. Armour Craig, "The Unpoetic Compromise: On the Relation Between Private Vision and Social Order in Nineteenth-Century English Fiction," in *Society and Self in the Novel*, ed. Mark Schorer (New York: Columbia Univ. Press, 1956), and Joan D. Peters, "Finding a Voice." Peters argues that in spite of Jane's refusal, there is an evolution "towards communication" and not "towards narrative concealment" (231).

57. For an argument that questions the opposition between essentialism and constructionism, see Diana Fuss, *Essentially Speaking: Feminism, Nature, and Difference* (New York: Routledge, 1989).

58. Rich, *Blood, Bread, and Poetry*, 89.

59. See, for example, Adams, "*Jane Eyre*: Woman's Estate"; Lanser, *Fictions of Authority*, 186; Wyatt, "A Patriarch of One's Own," 199–216.

The narrative voice of *Jane Eyre*, Lanser observes, is so unprecedented and "singular" that it has sometimes "been perceived as almost tyrannical in its power to impose a stance." Indeed, Harold Bloom, altogether missing the narrative's search for intimacy and contact, reports feeling "battered" by Jane's voice: "'Reader!' Jane keeps crying out, and then she exuberantly *cudgels* that reader into the way things are, as far as she is concerned. Is that *battered* reader a man or a woman?" Bloom anxiously inquires. "Introduction" to *The Brontës*, 4, emphasis mine.

Joan Peters argues that this "genuine, mutually-controlled interplay of feelings and ideas between novel and reader" (219) does not develop until the last third of the novel, where, Peters contends, Jane develops "a voice capable of dialogical confrontations with other narrative voices" (220).

On "girl talk" as a specific, and gendered, form of cultural expression, see also Penelope Eckert, "Cooperative Competition in Adolescent 'Girl Talk,'" in *Gender and Conversational Interaction*, ed. Deborah Tannen (New York: Oxford Univ. Press, 1993), and Spacks, *Gossip*.

60. As quoted by Moers, *Literary Women*, 99, and Wyatt, "A Patriarch of One's Own," 199.

61. Raymond Williams, *The English Novel: From Dickens to Lawrence* (London: Chatto & Windus, 1970); Raymond Williams, "Forms of English Fiction in 1848," in *Writing in Society* (London: Verso, n.d.), 156.

On confession as an "exemplary model of consciousness-raising," see Rita Felski, *Beyond Feminist Aesthetics: Feminist Literature and Social Change* (Cambridge, Mass.: Harvard Univ. Press, 1989). Confession, Felski argues, makes particular claims to intimacy, to being "an intimate communication addressed to them [the readers or audience] personally by an author" (98). Felski writes:

> . . . the feminist confession simultaneously encodes an audience. It self-consciously addresses a community of female readers rather than an undiffer-

entiated general public. This sense of communality is accentuated through a tone of intimacy, shared allusions, and unexplained references with which the reader is assumed to be familiar. The implied reader of the feminist confession is the sympathetic female confidante . . . the importance of the reader's role is directly related to the belief that she will understand and share the author's position . . . [feminist confession attempts] to evoke the illusion of face-to-face intimacy. (99–100)

62. Lanser, *Fictions of Authority*, 186.

63. Adams, "Jane Eyre: Woman's Estate," 183.

64. Lanser, *Fictions of Authority*, 188.

65. Wyatt, "A Patriarch of One's Own," 199.

66. Jane Lazarre, "'Charlotte's Web': Rereading *Jane Eyre* over Time," in *Between Women*, ed. Carol Ascher (Boston: Beacon Press, 1984), 226, 223. "Now I am writing a new novel about a rebel-girl," Lazarre reports, "a born survivor who must choose the proper medium for the expression of her powers. Her name of course is Charlotte."

67. Williams, *Writing in Society*, 156.

68. On confession as an "antimodel for the specular relationship necessary to produce meaning between the implied author and implied reader," see also Françoise Lionnet, *Autobiographical Voices: Race, Gender, Self-Portraiture* (Ithaca: Cornell Univ. Press, 1989), 174–89.

69. Foucault, *History of Sexuality*, 61–62.

70. Ibid., 59.

71. Ibid., 62.

72. Ibid., 62, 39.

73. Lanser, *Fictions of Authority*, 178, 179.

74. Raymond Williams, "Charlotte and Emily Brontë," in *The English Novel*, reprinted in Bloom, ed., *The Brontës*.

75. Michael Holquist, *Dialogism: Bakhtin and His World* (London: Routledge, 1990), 38.

76. To form an accurate impression of Miss Temple, she remarks, "let the reader add to complete the picture, refined features; a complexion, if pale clear; and a stately air and carriage, and *he* will have, at least as clearly as words can give it, a correct idea of the exterior of Miss Temple" (80, emphasis mine).

77. Silver, "The Reflecting Reader in *Villette*."
Silver puts Brontë's gender attributions in Foucauldian terms, as an index of where the social power to compel and judge stories is located. Brontë "may deliberately be positing a male audience to emphasize that the power to pass both literary and moral judgments on her story belonged, in the public sphere, predominantly to men," she writes.

78. "I had not intended to love him; *the reader knows* I had wrought hard to extirpate from my soul the germs of love there dectected" (204); "Now I never had, *as the reader knows*, either given any formal promise or entered into any engagement; and this language was all much too hard and much too despotic for the occasion" (439); "the church, *as the reader knows*, was but just beyond the gates; the footman soon returned" (315).

79. Bakhtin, *Problems of Dostoevsky's Poetics*.

80. Holquist, *Dialogism*, 39.

81. Silver, "The Reflecting Reader."

82. Hans Robert Jauss, *Toward an Aesthetic of Reception*, trans. Timothy Bahti (Minneapolis: Univ. of Minnesota Press, 1982), 21.

83. Silver, "The Reflecting Reader."

84. Patrocinio P. Schweickart, "Reading Ourselves: Toward a Feminist Theory of Reading," in *Gender and Reading*, ed. Elizabeth Flynn and Patrocinio P. Schweickart (Baltimore: Johns Hopkins Univ. Press, 1986), 31–62.

85. Roland Barthes, *The Pleasure of the Text*, trans. Richard Miller (New York: Hilland Wang, 1975), 6.

86. Brenkman, *Culture and Domination*, 196.

Chapter 4.
"That Oldest Human Longing": *Their Eyes Were Watching God*

1. Zora Neale Hurston, *Their Eyes Were Watching God* (Urbana: Univ.of Illinois Press, 1978), 17. Future references are to this edition and will be cited parenthetically.

2. See Mary Dearborn, *Pocahontas's Daughters: Gender and Ethnicity in American Culture* (New York: Oxford Univ. Press, 1986); Gloria T. Hull, *Color, Sex, and Poetry: Three Women Writers of the Harlem Renaissance* (Bloomington: Indiana Univ. Press, 1987); Deborah E. McDowell, "Introduction" to Nella Larsen, *Quicksand* and *Passing* (New Brunswick: Rutgers Univ. Press, 1986), xii; Hazel Carby, *Reconstructing Womanhood: The Emergence of the Afro-American Woman Novelist* (New York: Oxford Univ. Press, 1987), 176. During the period in which Hurston is writing, black women, Hull writes, had to be "especially careful to counter negative stereotypes of themselves as low and sluttish" (12). This caution, Deborah McDowell explains, has a long history:

> During slavery the white slave master constructed an image of black female sexuality which shifted responsibility for his own sexual passions onto his female slaves. They, not he, had wanton, insatiable desires that he was powerless to resist. The image did not end with emancipation. . . . Given this context, it is not surprising that a pattern of reticence about black female sexuality dominated novels by black women in the nineteenth and early twentieth centuries. They responded to the myth of black women's sexual licentiousness by insisting fiercely on her chastity.

3. For an entirely different reading of this passage, see Houston A. Baker, Jr.'s argument that the novel is really about economics, not sexuality or desire at all: "the pear tree metaphor is a deceptively prominent construction in *Their Eyes Were Watching God*; it leads away from the more significant economic dimensions of the novel." *Blues, Ideology and Afro-American Literature: A Vernacular Theory* (Chicago: Univ. of Chicago Press, 1984), 57.

4. Hurston's spelling of Pheoby's name is inconsistent. I am adopting her more frequent spelling rather than the more common "Phoebe."

5. Janie's gradual improvement in choice of lovers is measured, however, by their successively improved conversation. Whereas Johnny Taylor, Janie's first kiss, doesn't speak, and Logan Killicks soon "stopped speaking in rhymes to her" (45), the first sign of love between Janie and Jody is a conversation: "they sat under the tree and talked" (49). Tea Cake is distinguished by his witty banter and his encouragement that Janie talk and laugh. As she later tells Pheoby, "'he done taught me de maiden language all over'" (173).

6. "The relation of female narrator to female audience," Molly Hite also argues, "is highly sexual, suggesting . . . that the narratorial couple composed of Janie and Phoeby has displaced the heterosexual couple as the desired union that motivates and finally terminates the action." "Romance, Marginality, Matrilineage: Alice Walker's *The Color Purple* and Zora Neale Hurston's *Their Eyes Were Watching God*," *Novel* 22:3 (Spring, 1989): 269.

7. Gloria Naylor, "Love and Sex in the Afro-American Novel," *Yale Review* 78, no. 1 (Autumn 1988), 22.

8. Robert Scholes, *Fabulation and Metafiction* (Urbana: Univ. of Illinois Press, 1979), 26. See Introduction, pp. 16–17.

9. M. M. Bakhtin, "Discourse in the Novel," in *The Dialogic Imagination*, ed. Michael Holquist (Austin: Univ. of Texas Press, 1981), 341.

10. Ibid., 280. See also Hans Robert Jauss, *Question and Answer: Forms of Dialogic Understanding*, ed. and trans. Michael Hays (Minneapolis: Univ. of Minnesota Press, 1989).

11. Peter Brooks, *Reading for the Plot: Design and Intention in Narrative* (New York: Vintage, 1985), 53–54.

12. Charles Taylor, "The Politics of Recognition," Working Papers and Proceedings of the Center for Psychosocial Studies (Chicago: Center for Psychosocial Studies, 1992), 1–2.

Following this argument, one would expect that misrecognized and demeaned social groups—blacks, women, Asians, Latinos, lesbians and gays, and so on—would be particularly invested in narrative as a means of reconstructing damaged identities. And indeed, critics of African American, Asian American, Latin American, gay, and women's writing increasingly advance this argument, sometimes by focusing on the development of specific cultural forms, such as African American call-and-response or women's consciousness-raising, sometimes in broader claims for the therapeutic and revolutionary potential of narrative and other means of self-revelation.

See, for example, Joanne Frye, *Living Stories, Telling Lives: Women and the Novel in Contemporary Experience* (Ann Arbor: Univ. of Michigan Press, 1986); and Jay Clayton, "The Narrative Turn in Recent Minority Fiction," *American Literary History* 2, no. 3 (Fall 1990): 375–93. Houst A. Baker Jr., drawing on the work of Michael Awkward, puts this tendency in historical context by reading the need "for a participatory expressive return to wholeness or, in Awkward's term, '(comm)unity'" as a response, in part, to being the "split subject of slavery's 'othering.'" *Workings of the Spirit: The Poetics of Afro-American Women's Writing* (Chicago: Univ. of Chicago Press, 1992), 63.

Bruce Robbins has recently argued that there is a basic "antinarrativism" in contemporary theory. "Within literary studies," Robbins writes, "narrative is everywhere spoken against, and precisely because it is taken to embody authority. . . . It is associated with the illegitimate authority of the foregone conclusion and of the pregiven telos, with social or psychological resolution, with an orderly conventionality imposed on the meaningless successiveness of historical reality, with the tyranny of single, authoritative meaning." While I agree with Robbins that we have, broadly speaking, a "professional preference for the indeterminacy of discourse over the authoritarianism of story," I would also maintain, as I suggested above, that when the speaker or narrator is seen as marginalized or disempowered—especially in feminist and African American criticism—there is more of a celebration of narrative than a tendency to be distrustful of its pretenses to power. See his "Death and Vocation: Narrativizing Narrative Theory," *PMLA* 107, no. 1 (Jan. 1992): 38–50.

13. See, however, Mary Helen Washington, "'I Love the Way Janie Crawford Left Her Husbands': Hurston's Emergent Female Hero," in *Invented Lives: Narratives of Black Women, 1860–1960* (New York: Doubleday, 1987), 237–54; Mary Helen Washington, "Foreword" to *Their Eyes Were Watching God* (New York: Harper and Row, 1990); and Michael Awkward, "'The inaudible voice of it all': Silence, Voice, and Action in *Their Eyes Were Watching God*," in *Inspiriting Influences: Tradition, Revision, and Afro-American Women's Novels* (New York: Columbia Univ. Press, 1989).

Washington argues, as I do, that the novel represents "a woman outside of the folk community" and her exclusion "from the power of oral speech." Awkward, like Washington, argues that Janie "refuses to become a public spokesperson" and that "by the time she has returned to Eatonville, she has learned that individual voice is either tyrannical or ineffectual." Where both Washington and Awkward, however, read the limits on Janie's voice principally in terms of her relation to her community and the possibility of agency, my reading of those limits moves in the direction of the novel's narrative and erotic logics.

Both Washington's and Awkward's readings of voice include important debates with other critics over the meaning of Hurston's rhetorical strategies for suggesting rather than directly rendering Janie's voice. See, especially, Henry Louis Gates, Jr., "Zora Neale Hurston and the Speakerly Text," in *The Signifying Monkey: A Theory of African-American Criticism* (New York: Oxford Univ. Press, 1988), and Robert Stepto, *From Behind the Veil: A Study of Afro-American Narrative* (Urbana: Univ. of Illinois Press, 1979), 164–67.

14. Baker, *Blues, Ideology, and Afro-American Culture*, 58–59.

15. Henry Louis Gates, Jr., *Signifying Monkey*, 169, 202.

16. Barbara Johnson, "Metaphor, Metonymy and Voice in *Their Eyes Were Watching God*," in *Black Literature and Literary Theory*, ed. Henry Louis Gates, Jr. (New York: Methuen, 1984), 212.

17. Karla F. C. Holloway, *The Character of the Word: The Texts of Zora Neale Hurston* (New York: Greenwood Press, 1987), 40.

18. Susan Lanser, *Fictions of Authority: Women Writers and Narrative Voice* (Ithaca: Cornell Univ. Press, 1992), 201–2.

19. See, especially, Hurston's "Characteristics of Negro Expression," in *Negro: An Anthology*, ed. Nancy Cunard (London: Negro Univ. Press, 1969); and *Mules and Men, Tell My Horse*, and *Mule Bone*, all recently reprinted by Harper & Row.

20. Hans Robert Jauss, *Toward an Aesthetic of Reception*, trans. Timothy Bahti (Minneapolis: Univ. of Minnesota Press, 1982), 21.

21. Ross Chambers, *Story and Situation: Narrative Seduction and the Power of Fiction* (Minneapolis: Univ. of Minnesota Press, 1984), 214.

22. "The kiss" has been brilliantly explored by Catherine Stimpson as a "staple of lesbian fiction," a particularly strong and resilient symbol because it can neither "wholly reveal" nor "wholly deny, lesbian eroticism." See her "Zero Degree Deviancy: The Lesbian Novel in English," in *Where the Meanings Are: Feminism and Cultural Spaces* (New York: Methuen, 1988), 99, 103.

While the friendship between Janie and Pheoby has received substantial critical attention, few critics have commented on Hurston's explicitly lesbian eroticizing of that friendship and of their storytelling exchange. See, however, Lorraine Bethel,

"'This Infinity of Conscious Pain': Zora Neale Hurston and the Black Female Literary Tradition," in *All the Women Are White, All the Blacks Are Men, But Some of Us Are Brave: Black Women's Studies*, ed. Gloria T. Hull, Patricia Bell Scott, and Barbara Smith (New York: Feminist Press), 187.

On this discursive ethos, see also John Callahan, *In the African-American Grain: The Pursuit of Voice in Twentieth-Century Black Fiction* (Urbana: Univ. of Illinois Press, 1984). Hurston, Callahan writes, "seeks to transcend the tradition of verbal combat . . . storytelling and narration lead to an intimate mutual response" (118). Where Callahan sees the novel as inscribing "call-and-response" between Janie and Hurston, I would argues that it also inscribes a pattern of anticipated (or feared) call-and-no-response between the text and its own reception. Callahan does not consider the eroticism of this ethos or the possibility that it constructs a subtle lesbian alternative to the more traditional heterosexual romance plot.

23. For a different analysis of the "inaudible voice" in this passage, see Awkward, "'The inaudible voice of it all.'"

24. Nellie McKay, "'Crayon Enlargements of Life': Zora Neale Hurston's *Their Eyes Were Watching God* as Autobiography," in *New Essays on Their Eyes Were Watching God*, ed. Michael Awkward (Cambridge, Eng.: Cambridge Univ. Press, 1990), 62.

25. It has long been a critical commonplace to view *Their Eyes Were Watching God* as ahistorical, as Hortense Spillers puts it, a "timeless current . . . [of] ahistorical, specifically rustic, image clusters." Or, as Hazel Carby puts it, a "limited vision, a vision which in its romantic evocation of the rural and the folk avoids some of the most crucial and urgent issues of cultural struggle." Susan Willis makes a more pointed accusation, citing Hurston with a "utopian betrayal of history's dialectic." Hortense J. Spillers, "A Hateful Passion, a Lost Love," in *Feminist Issues in Literary Scholarship*, ed. Shari Benstock (Bloomington: Indiana Univ. Press, 1987), 195; Carby, *Reconstructing Womanhood*, 175; Susan Willis, *Specifying: Black Women Writing the American Experience* (Madison: Univ. of Wisconsin Press, 1987), 48.

Wahneema Lubiano argues, as I do, that such a romanticizing reading "leaves out a necessary historicizing of Hurston and her deliberate interventionary project," a historicization she does not there attempt. See her "Constructing and Reconstructing Afro-American Texts: The Critic as Ambassador and Referee," *American Literary History* 1, no. 2 (Summer 1989): 433–47. See also Missy Dehn Kubitschek, "'Tuh de Horizon and Back': The Female Quest in *Their Eyes Were Watching God*," *Black American Literature Forum* 17, no. 3 (Fall 1983), reprinted in *Zora Neale Hurston's Their Eyes Were Watching God*, ed. Harold Bloom (New York: Chelsea, 1987).

One way romances can be seen, however, to resolve historical problems is by creating an ahistorical moment putatively free of them. "The romance," Northrop Frye argues,

> is the nearest of all literary forms to the wish-fulfillment dream, and for that reason it has socially a curiously paradoxical role. . . . The perennially child-like quality of romance is marked by its extraordinarily persistent nostalgia, its search for some kind of imaginative golden age in time or space. . . . The quest-romance is the search of the libido or desiring self for a fulfillment that will deliver it from the anxieties of reality but will still contain that reality.

The Anatomy of Criticism (New York: Atheneum, 1957), 186, 193.

26. John Callahan does mention, in passing, Janie's return to Eatonville as occurring in the 1920s. See *In the African-American Grain: The Pursuit of Voice in Twentieth-Century Black Fiction* (Urbana: Univ. of Illinois Press, 1988), 121, 129.

27. George Schuyler, "Instructions for Contributors," as cited by Henry Louis Gates, Jr., *The Signifying Monkey: A Theory of African-American Criticism* (New York: Oxford Univ. Press, 1988), 179.

28. Carby, *Reconstructing Womanhood*, 176. See, also, Ann Allen Shockley, *Afro-American Women Writers, 1746–1933* (New York: New American Library, 1988), 401–12.

29. William Ferris, "The Arts and Black Development," *Negro World*, April 30, 1921, as quoted in *Voices of a Black Nation: Political Journalism in the Harlem Renaissance*, ed. Theodore G. Vincent and Robert Chrisman (San Francisco: Ramparts Press, 1973), 327.

30. James Weldon Johnson, "Preface" to *The Book of American Negro Poetry* (New York: Harcourt, Brace, Jovanovich, 1922). Among a number of possible others, Jews would be one obvious exception to Johnson's point.

31. W. E. B. Du Bois, "Criteria of Negro Art," published text of address to the Chicago Conference of the National Association for the Advancement of Colored People, *The Crisis*, Oct. 1926, pp. 290–97. Taking this quote out of context and mis-assigning it to Du Bois himself, David Levering Lewis concludes that Du Bois was disappointed with the direction of Negro arts and that by midcentury, "the old warrior was not in the mood for art." *When Harlem Was in Vogue* (New York: Oxford Univ. Press, 1979), 177.

32. James Weldon Johnson, "Race Prejudice and the Negro Artist," *Harper's* 157 (Nov. 1928), quoted in Lewis, *When Harlem Was in Vogue*, 193.

33. Henry Louis Gates, Jr., *Figures in Black: Words, Signs and the "Racial" Self* (New York: Oxford Univ. Press, 1987), 6.

34. Henry Louis Gates, Jr., "Writing 'Race' and the Difference it Makes," *Critical Inquiry* 12, no. 1 (Autumn 1985): 8.

35. Langston Hughes, "The Negro Artist and the Racial Mountain," *The Nation* 122 (June 1926), reprinted in Nathan Irvin Huggins, *Voices from the Harlem Renaissance* (New York: Oxford Univ. Press, 1976), 305–9.

36. Hughes, "The Negro Artist and the Racial Mountain."

37. I am not suggesting that black women's resistance was, in any sense, less forceful, effective, or determined than that of black men, only that the prevailing political-aesthetic *rhetoric* did not lend itself to women's issues or their voices. On black women's political participation during this period, see Rosalyn Terborg-Penn, "Discontented Black Feminists: Prelude and Postscript to the Passage of the Nineteenth Amendment," in *Decades of Discontent: The Women's Movement, 1920–1940*, ed. Lois Scharf and Joan M. Jensen (Boston: Northeastern Univ. Press, 1983), 261–78; Paula Giddings, *When and Where I Enter: The Impact of Black Women on Race and Sex in America* (New York: Bantam, 1984); Nancy F. Cott, *The Grounding of Modern Feminism* (New Haven: Yale Univ. Press, 1987); Darlene Clark Hine, ed., *Black Women in United States History*, 4 vols. (New York: Carlson, 1990); Dorothy Salem, *To Better Our World: Black Women in Organized Reform, 1890–1920* (New York: Carlson, 1990); and Darlene Clark Hine, ed., *Black Women's History, Theory and Practice*, 2 vols. (New York: Carlson, 1990).

38. Few historical figures are more glorified in nineteenth- and early twentieth-century black American literature than the Reconstruction schoolteacher. In mak-

ing Janie's father not simply a rapist but a Reconstruction schoolteacher as well, Hurston seems to suggest that rape is a trans-historical fact of life, at least for black women. That he apparently tries later, unsuccessfully, to find Leafy and marry her may only deepen this scathing portrayal, given this novel's critique of the institution of marriage.

39. As Ann duCille has shown, there is a tradition of black women's novels of the 1930s and 40s (which Hurston may be drawing on) in which "marriage is no longer the relation of rescue and protection it was in the nineteenth century; holy wedlock is no longer a site of utopian partnernship, but a seat of emotional confinement, sexual commodification, and male domination, as well as infidelity, brutality, and betrayal" (112). "Part of what *Their Eyes* confronts," duCille writes, "is the consequences for women of buying the myth, of seeking personal fulfillment in a primal male partner and equating sexual pleasure with marriage" (117). DuCille argues, as I do, that "to interpret *Their Eyes* as a celebration of heterosexual love or as a privileging of female independence and homosocial sisterhood is, respectively, to under- or overread, if not completely misread, the novel" (120). See *The Coupling Convention: Sex, Text, and Tradition in Black Women's Fiction* (New York: Oxford Univ. Press, 1993).

40. Zora Neale Hurston, *Mules and Men* (Bloomington: Indiana Univ. Press, 1978), 4–5. For a different discussion of this passage, see Barbara Johnson, "Thresholds of Difference: Structures of Address in Zora Neale Hurston," *Critical Inquiry* 12, no. 1 (Autumn 1985): 280.

41. Richard Wright, "Between Laughter and Tears," review of *Their Eyes Were Watching God, New Masses*, Oct. 5, 1937, pp. 22–25.

42. Carby, *Reconstructing Womanhood*, 175.

43. Herbert Marcuse, *Eros and Civilization: A Philosophical Inquiry into Freud* (Boston: Beacon, 1955), xxv.

44. Lanser, *Fictions of Authority*, 201.

45. See also Rachel Blau DuPlessis, "Power, Judgment and Narrative in a Work of Zora Neale Hurston: Feminist Cultural Studies," in *New Essays on Their Eyes Were Watching God*, ed. Michael Awkward (Cambridge, Eng.: Cambridge Univ. Press, 1990), 95–123.

46. Janie's testimony has particularly strong symbolic resonance given, on the one hand, a history of legal prohibitions against black Americans testifying on their own behalf, and, on the other hand, a tradition of cultural practices, such as "call and response" and "testifying" grounded in the importance of individual and communal rites of testimony. To "testify," Geneva Smitherman explains:

> is to tell the truth through story . . . the content of testifying, then, is not plain and simple commentary, but a dramatic narration and a communal reenactment of one's feelings and experiences. Thus one's humanity is reaffirmed by the group and his or her sense of isolation diminished.

Testifying and "call and response" are performative rituals of recognition; they dramatize the constitutive force of a reception context and they enact the conferral and confirmation of both individual and collective identity. As Barbara Bowen puts it, "'call and response'" is the drama of finding authority through communal voice." Geneva Smitherman, *Talkin and Testifyin: The Language of Black America* (Boston: Houghton Mifflin, 1977), 150; Barbara Bowen, "Untroubled Voice: Call and Response in *Cane*," in *Black Literature and Literary Theory*, ed. Henry Louis Gates, Jr. (New York: Methuen, 1984), 195. See also Mae Gwendolyn Henderson,

"Speaking in Tongues: Dialogics, Dialectics, and the Black Woman Writer's Literary Tradition," in *Changing Our Own Words: Essays on Criticism, Theory, and Writing by Black Women* (New Brunswick: Rutgers Univ. Press, 1989), 21–22, 24.

47. As I indicated earlier (n. 13), this is a lively and important debate among Hurston scholars. While it is not practical for me to rehearse this debate here, the interested reader might see, among others: Washington; Awkward; Lanser; McKay; Callahan; Gates, "Zora Neale Hurston and the Speakerly Text"; Stepto, *From Behind the Veil*; and Bernard Bell, *The Afro-American Novel and Its Tradition* (Amherst: Univ. of Massachusetts Press, 1987).

48. Bethel, "This Infinity of Conscious Pain," 180.

49. Tania Modleski, *Loving with a Vengeance: Mass-Produced Fantasies for Women* (New York: Methuen, 1984), 16, 25.

50. Ibid., 45. Alice Walker argues that the "revenge fantasy" of the novel is specifically tied to Tea Cake's adoption of sexual submission and colorism. See her "If the Present Looks like the Past, What Does the Future Look Like?," in *In Search of Our Mother's Gardens* (New York: Harcourt, Brace, Jovanovich, 1983), 290–312, esp. 304–7. See also Mary Helen Washington, "'I Love the Way,'" and Susan Willis, *Specifying*, 51. Neither Modleski nor Walker question the limits of this poetic justice. But Hurston does, as do the other writers I've looked at for whom revenge is not the same thing as justice and symbolic revenge may not be revenge at all.

51. See also Washington, "'I Love the Way.'"

52. Fredric Jameson, *The Political Unconscious: Narrative as a Socially Symbolic Act* (Ithaca: Cornell Univ. Press, 1981), 79.

53. Baker, *Workings of the Spirit*, 64.

54. See Hemenway, *Zora Neale Hurston*.

55. Hite, "Romance," 269.

56. Chambers, *Story and Situation*, 214.

57. McKay, "'Crayon Enlargements,'" 56–7.

58. Priscilla Wald, "'Becoming Colored': The Self-Authorized Language of Difference in Zora Neale Hurston," *American Literary History* 2, no. 1 (Spring 1990): 95.

59. Elizabeth A. Meese, "Orality and Textuality in Zora Neale Hurston's *Their Eyes Were Watching God*," in *Crossing the Double Cross: The Practice of Feminist Criticism* (Chapel Hill: Univ. of North Carolina Press, 1986), 53.

60. Robert E. Hemenway, *Zora Neale Hurston: A Literary Biography* (Urbana: Univ. of Illinois Press, 1977).

61. Barbara Christian, *Black Women Novelists* (Westport: Greenwood Press, 1980), 57.

62. Houston A. Baker Jr., *Blues, Ideology and Afro-American Literature: A Vernacular Theory* (Chicago: Univ. of Chicago Press, 1984), 60, 59.
Kubitschek, who also wants to challenge "the common critical portrait of Zora Neale Hurston . . . [as] a romantic elitist," romanticizes community as well. "The novel," Kubitschek writes, "strongly implies communal enjoyment of, and benefit from, the quester's prize. . . . [Janie is] the successful quester returning with a boon for her community . . . an artist who enriches Eatonville by communicating her understanding. . . . [The] crucial frame story concerns her return to community and the resultant possibility for communal as well as personal growth." Kubitschek, "'Tuh De Horizon,'" 19–22.

63. Washington, "'I Love the Way,'" 250.

64. Jean E. Kennard, "Convention Coverage or How to Read Your Own Life," *New Literary History* 13, no. 1 (Autumn 1981): 86.

65. Frye, *Anatomy of Criticism*, 203, 202.

66. Bernard W. Bell, *The Afro-American Novel and Its Tradition* (Amherst: Univ. of Massachusetts Press, 1987), 25.

67. Meese, "Orality and Textuality."

68. Callahan, *In the African-American Grain*, 118.

Chapter 5.
"Somebody I Can Talk To": *The Color Purple*

1. Alice Walker, *The Color Purple* (New York: Simon & Schuster, 1982), 204. All future references are to this edition and will be cited parenthetically.

2. Michael Awkward, *Inspiriting Influences: Tradition, Revision, and Afro-American Women's Novels* (New York: Columbia Univ. Press, 1989).

3. Jean-François Lyotard, *Just Gaming* (Minneapolis: Univ. of Minnesota Press, 1985), 72.

4. Alison Light, "Fear of the Happy Ending: *The Color Purple*, Reading and Racism," in *Plotting Change: Contemporary Women's Fiction*, ed. Linda Anderson (London: Edward Arnold, 1990), 85.

5. Dinitia Smith, review of *The Color Purple*, *The Nation*, Sept. 4, 1982, reprinted in *Alice Walker: Critical Perspectives, Past and Present*, ed. Henry Louis Gates, Jr., and Kwame Anthony Appiah (New York: Amistad, 1993), 20.

6. Gina Michelle Collins, "*The Color Purple*: What Feminism Can Learn from a Southern Tradition," in *Southern Literature and Literary Theory*, ed. Jefferson Humphries (Athens: Univ. of Georgia, 1990), 75.

I want to mark this ascription as vexed, particularly given Walker's own differentiation of "womanist" perspectives from "feminist" ones and her care to mark the alienation and exclusion women of color have often felt from white, mainstream American feminism. Part of my interest in the feminist reception of Walker's novel inheres in the question of how such distinctions have been ignored and over-ridden (potentially even by Walker herself) in the process of making this novel a feminist "classic." On Walker's definition of "womanist," see *In Search of Our Mother's Gardens: Womanist Prose* (New York: Harcourt, Brace, Jovanovich, 1983).

7. Deborah E. McDowell, "'The Changing Same': Generational Connections and Black Women Novelists," *New Literary History* 18:2 (Winter 1987), reprinted in *Reading Black, Reading Feminist*, ed. Henry Louis Gates, Jr. (New York: Meridian, 1990), and *Alice Walker: Modern Critical Views*, ed. Harold Bloom (New York: Chelsea House, 1989), 190.

8. Linda Abbandonato, "Rewriting the Heroine's Story in *The Color Purple*," originally published as "A View from 'Elsewhere': Subversive Sexuality and the Rewriting of the Heroine's Story in *The Color Purple*," *PMLA* 106 (Oct. 1991), reprinted in Gates and Appiah, eds., *Alice Walker*, 302.

9. On the twenties, see in particular the symposium entitled "The Negro in Art: How Shall He Be Portrayed?" which ran for a number of months in *The Crisis* of 1926; Langston Hughes, "The Negro Artist and the Racial Mountain," *The Nation* 122 (June 1926); Alain Locke, "Art or Propaganda," reprinted in Nathan Huggins, *Voices from the Harlem Renaissance* (New York: Oxford Univ. Press, 1976), 305–9; W. E. B. Du Bois, "Criteria of Negro Art," in *W. E. B.*

Du Bois: Writings (New York: Library of America, 1986), 993–1002, first published in *The Crisis*, Oct. 1926, pp. 290–97; George Schuyler, "The Negro-Art Hokum," reprinted in Huggins, ed., *Voices,* and "Instructions for Contributors," as quoted by Henry Louis Gates, Jr., *The Signifying Monkey: A Theory of Afro-American Criticism* (New York: Oxford Univ. Press, 1988); William Ferris, "The Arts and Black Development," *Negro World,* April 30, 1921; James Weldon Johnson, "Race Prejudice and the Negro Artist," *Harper's* 157 (Nov. 1928); and Zora Neale Hurston, "Characteristics of Negro Expression," in *The Negro: An Anthology,* ed. Nancy Cunard (New York: Frederick Ungar, 1970), 24–31.

On the African American male reception of *The Color Purple,* see David Denby, "Purple People-Eater," *New York,* Jan. 13, 1986 (Denby calls the novel "a hate letter to Black men"); Gerald Early, "*The Color Purple* as Everybody's Protest Art," *Antioch Review* (Winter 1992) ("*The Color Purple,* by black feminist writer Alice Walker, is not a great novel," Early declares); Courtland Milloy, "A 'Purple' Rage Over a Rip-Off," *Washington Post,* Dec. 24, 1985; William H. Willimon, "Seeing Red over *The Color Purple,*" *Christian Century,* April 2, 1986; Manthia Diawara, "Black Spectatorship: Problems of Identification and Resistance," *Black American Cinema* (New York: Routledge, 1993); Philip M. Royster, "In Search of our Fathers' Arms: Alice Walker's Persona of the Alienated Darling," *Black American Literature Forum* 20:4 (1986): 347–70; and Marlianne Glicksman, "Lee Way" (interview with Spike Lee), *Film Comment,* Oct. 1986. The novel and film were also denounced by Louis Farrakhan, as Cheryl B. Butler reports in "The Color Purple Controversy: Black Woman Spectatorship," *Wide Angle* 13 (1991): 63–69. For other African American feminist overviews of this reception see Jacqueline Bobo, "Sifting Through the Controversy: Reading *The Color Purple,*" *Callaloo* 12, no. 2 (1989): 332–42; Jacqueline Bobo, "Black Women as Cultural Readers," *Female Spectators,* ed. Deidre Pribram (London: Verso, 1988); and Deborah E. McDowell, "Reading Family Matters," in *Changing Our Own Words: Essays on Criticism, Theory, and Writing by Black Women,* ed. Cheryl A. Wall (New Brunswick: Rutgers Univ. Press, 1989), 75–97.

For critiques of the novel or film's handling of racial stereotypes (Harpo's clowning, in particular), class, lesbianism, primitivism (particularly the film's cross-cutting of the scene of facial scarification, depicted as bloodthirsty and savage, with the scene of Celie raising a razor over Mr. _____'s head after she has learned of his hiding Nettie's letters), and history, see Barbara Christian, "De-Visioning Spielberg on Walker, *The Color Purple,* The Novel and the Film," unpublished ms.; Michelle Wallace, "Blues for Mr. Spielberg," *Village Voice,* March 18, 1986; Kenneth Turan, "Movies," *California Magazine,* Feb. 11, 1986; Barbara Smith, "'*Color Purple* Distorts Class, Lesbian Issues," *Guardian,* Feb. 19, 1986; Jacqueline Bobo, "Black Women as Cultural Readers"; John Peacock, "When Folk Goes Pop: Consuming *The Color Purple,*" *Film Literature Quarterly* 19, no. 3 (1991); Gerald Early, "Everybody's Protest Art"; and Vincent Canby, "From a Palette of Cliches Comes 'The Color Purple,'" *New York Times,* Jan. 5, 1986.

10. Bobo, "Black Women as Cultural Readers." Responses such as the following were typical, Bobo reports: "'The Lady was a strong lady, like I am. And she hung in there and she overcame.'"

11. Trudier Harris, "From Victimization to Free Enterprise: Alice Walker's *The Color Purple,*" *Black American Literature Forum* 14: 1 (1986): 1–17.

12. Trudier Harris, "On *The Color Purple,* Stereotypes, and Silence," *Black American Literature Forum* 18:4 (Winter 1984): 160.

13. McDowell, "'The Changing Same,'" in Harold Bloom, ed., *Alice Walker: Modern Critical News* (New York: Chelsea House, 1989), 143, emphasis mine.

14. Cora Kaplan, "Keeping the Color in *The Color Purple*," in *Sea Changes: Culture and Feminism* (London: Verso Press, 1986), 185.

15. Linda S. Kauffman, *Special Delivery: Epistolary Modes in Modern Fiction* (Chicago: Univ. of Chicago Press, 1992), 191.

16. Light, "Fear of the Happy Ending."

17. On such exchanges of women as a form of "narrative desire," what structures the movement of story and what structures a story seeks—or desires—to replicate, see especially Eve Kosofsky Sedgwick, *Between Men: English Literature and Male Homosocial Desire* (New York: Columbia, 1985); René Girard, *Deceit, Desire, and the Novel: Self and Other in Literary Structure*, trans. Yvonne Freccero (Baltimore: Johns Hopkins Univ. Press, 1972); Claude Lévi-Strauss, *The Elementary Structures of Kinship* (Boston: Beacon Press, 1969); and Gayle Rubin, "The Traffic in Women: Notes Toward a Political Economy of Sex," in *Toward an Anthropology of Women*, ed. Rayna Reiter (New York: Monthly Review Press, 1975).

18. Walker, "In Search of Our Mother's Gardens," in *In Search of Our Mother's Gardens.*

This point has also been made by James C. Hall, "Towards a Map of Mis(sed) Reading: The Presence of Absence in *The Color Purple*," *African-American Review* 26, no. 1 (Spring 1992), and Jacqueline Bobo, "Black Woman as Cultural Readers." Hall writes that *The Color Purple* is "a model for the reconstruction of a black feminist literary tradition" (89). Bobo notes that the novel was written during a black female "renaissance" concerned with (re)constructing "the personal lives and collective histories of Black women. The writers are reconstructing a heritage that has either been distorted or ignored" (104).

19. Alice Walker, "A Conversation with Sharon Wilson," *Kalliope* 6 (1984), reprinted in Gates and Appiah, eds., *Alice Walker.*

20. Alice Walker, as quoted by Mae G. Henderson, "*The Color Purple*: Revisions and Redefinitions," *Sage: A Scholarly Journal on Black Women* 2, no. 1 (Spring 1985).

Since childhood, Philip Royster writes, Walker "has seen herself as a writer who rescues." "In Search of Our Fathers' Arms," 348. Royster's essay, while perceptive in this instance, quickly becomes an ad hominem polemic against Alice Walker that quickly takes the inevitably self-revealing form of amateur psychoanalysis. Royster's argument is that Walker "has been inadequately prepared to be a rescuer of victims" because, unlike Gandhi, she does not know how to withstand suffering or how to practice self-denial and because she is too committed to being a dutiful daughter, not committed enough, in Royster's eyes, to be a "true" rebel (353).

21. Alice Walker, "Saving the Life That Is Your Own: The Importance of Models in the Artist's Life," in *In Search of Our Mother's Gardens*, 14.

22. Alice Walker, "A Talk: Convocation 1972," in ibid., 36.

23. Alice Walker, "Zora Neale Hurston: A Cautionary Tale and a Partisan View," in ibid., 92 (emphasis in original).

Marjorie Pryse, echoing Walker's call to recuperate the silenced voices of African American women, writes that "we" (by which she clearly means other feminists of color) must all take an oath "to continue the work of speaking with each others' tongues in our mouths, thereby illuminating women's lives." *Conjuring: Black Women, Fiction, and the Literary Tradition*, ed. Marjorie Pryse and Hortense Spillers (Bloomington: Indiana Univ. Press, 1985).

This "struggle to make articulate a heretofore repressed and silenced black female's story and voice," Michael Awkward writes, is "the dominant image in recent creative and critical writing of Afro-American women." *Inspiriting Influences,* 1.

24. Abbandonato, "Rewriting the Heroine's Story," 296.

25. Kauffman, *Special Delivery,* 203.

26. Steven Spielberg and screenwriter Menno Meyjes emphasize Celie's re-cuperation of Nettie's story by putting Nettie's letters not in Mr. ＿＿＿'s trunk, where they are hidden in the novel, but literally burying them under the floor boards beneath it.

27. Walker's penchant for discursive utopias appears often in her work. In-deed, in an interview discussion of a later novel, *The Temple of My Familiar,* Walker explained, as Deborah Tannen reports, "that a woman in the novel falls in love with a man because she sees in him '*a giant ear.*' Walker went on to remark that although people may think they are falling in love because of sexual attraction or some other force, '*really what we're looking for is someone to be able to hear us.*'" Deborah Tannen, *You Just Don't Understand: Women and Men in Conversation* (New York: Ballantine, 1990), 48, emphasis mine.

28. Henry Louis Gates, Jr., "Color Me Zora: Alice Walker's (Re)Writing of the Speakerly Text," in *Signifying Monkey,* 255.

29. Seyla Benhabib, *Critique, Norm, and Utopia: A Study of the Foundations of Critical Theory* (New York: Columbia Univ. Press, 1986), 107.

30. Ibid.

31. Gates, *Signifying Monkey,* 131. The novel, Gates argues, is a "literal rep-resentation of a protagonist creating her self by finding her voice, but finding her voice in the act of writing."

In African American history, the relationship between voice and subjectivity, Gates argues, is particularly vexed. European philosophers drew on the absence of a written, collective black voice "to deprive African slaves of their humanity" (104). *Figures in Black: Words, Signs, and the "Racial" Self* (New York: Oxford Univ. Press, 1987).

32. For other views of how Walker "signifies" upon earlier African Ameri-can women's texts, see Gates, "Color Me Zora"; Marjorie Pryse, "Zora Neale Hurston, Alice Walker, and the 'Ancient Power' of Black Women," in *Conjuring,* the essays collected in *Alice Walker and Zora Neale Hurston: The Common Bond,* ed. Lillie P. Howard (Westport: Greenwood Press, 1993); Diane Sadoff, "Black Matrilineage: The Case of Alice Walker and Zora Neale Hurston," *Signs* 11, no. 1 (1985); and Molly Hite, "Romance, Marginality, Matrilineage: Alice Walker's *The Color Purple* and Zora Neale Hurston's *Their Eyes Were Watching God,*" *Novel: A Forum on Fiction* 22:3 (Spring 1989). "If Hurston could have imagined a novel in which Janie had indeed gone home to look for her mother and 'maybe tend her grandmother's grave,' then she might have written Alice Walker's *The Color Purple,*" Pryse writes (15).

33. For an opposite reading, that Celie's "survival resides in her *failure* to *internalize* patriarchal structures," see Collins, "What Feminism Can Learn."

34. Alice Walker, "In Search of Our Mothers' Gardens," 239.

35. Charlotte Perkins Gilman, "The Yellow Wallpaper," in *The Captive Imagination: A Casebook on "The Yellow Wallpaper,"* ed. Catherine Golden (New York: Feminist Press, 1992).

36. Isak Dinesen, "The Blank Page," in *The Norton Anthology of Literature*

by Women, ed. Sandra M. Gilbert and Susan Gubar (New York: W. W. Norton, 1985).

37. Susan Glaspell, "A Jury of Her Peers," in *Images of Women in Literature*, ed. Mary Anne Ferguson (Boston: Houghton Mifflin, 1973).

38. For a critique of attempts to document, preserve, and recuperate the "experience" of marginalized or disempowered peoples which argues that such efforts "establish a realm of reality outside of discourse," see Joan W. Scott, "The Evidence of Experience," *The Lesbian and Gay Studies Reader*, ed. Henry Abelove, Michèle Aina Barale, David M. Halperin (New York: Routledge, 1993), 397–415.

39. Alice Walker, "Writing *The Color Purple*," in *In Search of Our Mothers' Gardens*, 356.

40. Bruce Robbins, "Death and Vocation: Narrativizing Narrative Theory," *PMLA*, no. 107 (Jan. 1992): 39. Narrative, Robbins writes, is " . . . a hyperstructured vehicle of dogmatic belief that desperately needs to be relativized. It is associated with the illegitimate authority of the foregone conclusion and of the pregiven telos, with social or psychological resolution, with an orderly conventionality imposed on the meaningless tyranny of single, authoritative meaning" (42).

41. Jay Clayton, *The Pleasures of Babel: Contemporary American Literature and Theory* (New York: Oxford Univ. Press, 1993), 94–95.

42. Literacy, as Linda Kauffman puts it, "is the only thing that keeps Celie from being 'buried' alive." Kauffman, *Special Delivery*, 192. But as she argues later, however, and as I would emphasize, literacy is not an unproblematic social good. "The acquisition of literacy, so important to Celie's individual liberation at home, is an important phase of cultural domination abroad" (201). "Nettie's formal education abroad bleaches the color and life out of the black folk English that characterizes Celie's."

43. Seyla Benhabib, *Situating the Self: Gender, Community, and Postmodernism in Contemporary Ethics* (New York: Routledge, 1992), 198.

44. See, especially, Sigmund Freud, "Family Romances," in *The Standard Edition of the Complete Psychological Works*, ed. James Strachey (London: Hogarth Press, 1959), IX: 237–41.

45. On monumentalization, see also John Brenkman, "Politics and Form in *The Song of Solomon*," *Social Text* 39 (Summer 1994): 57–82. "Morrison," Brenkman writes, "challenges the habit of thinking of cultural heritage exclusively as the monuments and masterworks—comparable to the reduction of history to great events and actors. Such a model is acutely inappropriate for the history of a people whose enslavement denied them literacy and whose oppression in the century since Emancipation denied them the material and institutional means of assembling a monumental culture."

46. Erving Goffman, *Forms of Talk* (Philadelphia: Univ. of Pennsylvania, 1981).

47. Molly Hite, "Romance, Marginality, Matrilineage," 269–70.

48. Janet Gurkin Altman, *Epistolarity* (Columbus: Ohio State Univ. Press, 1982), 89, as quoted by Michael Awkward, *Inspiriting Influences*, 145.

49. Kauffman, *Special Delivery*, 195, 166, 186.

50. "The sequence of letters from Nettie," Abbandonato writes, in what I think is something of an overstatement, "invariably disappoint readers." See "Rewriting the Heroine's Story," 299.

51. Michael Awkward has argued that "Celie's letters lack a desire for exchange" and that "Celie must develop . . . a more acute sense of audience," but

this fails to take account of what Celie's limited choices are or of how Walker dramatizes those limits by representing Celie in situations of failed exchange, failed communication, inept interlocutors. Awkward, *Inspiriting Influences*, 148–49.

52. See both "Compulsory Heterosexuality and Lesbian Existence," *Blood, Bread, and Poetry* (New York: W. W. Norton, 1986), 23–75, and "'It Is the Lesbian in Us,'" *On Lies, Secrets, and Silence* (W. W. Norton, 1979), 199–202.

53. This is Walker's description of the life of black women. See "Coretta King: Revisited," in *In Search of Our Mother's Gardens*, 149.

54. Christine Froula, "The Daughter's Seduction: Sexual Violence and Literary History," *Signs* 11, no. 4 (Summer 1986): 633, 644.

55. Cheryl A. Wall, "Introduction: Taking Positions and Changing Words," in *Changing Our Own Words*, 11. "Cautionary tale" is Walker's phrase.

56. Early, for example, writes that "the ending, which gives us the transformation of Mr. Albert, is not simply far-fetched, which would have been acceptable, but utterly impossible since nothing in his society as we are given to understand it would generate or support such a change." "Everybody's Protest Art," 404.

"The novel provides fairytale explanations of social relations," Lauren Berlant writes. "Race, Gender, and Nation in *The Color Purple*," *Critical Inquiry* 14 (Summer 1988), reprinted in Gates and Appiah, eds., *Alice Walker*, 232.

57. "Pa," of course, is killed rather than transformed. But bad as men are, "Pa" is so much worse than others that his fate seems to suggest how distantly the boundary of irredeemability is fixed. "Any man would have done what I done" Pa says. "Maybe not, say Shug."

58. Hite, "Romance, Marginality, Matrilineage," 265.

59. Stepto, "Distrust of the Reader," 306.

60. Sewing is a common feminist metaphor for female textuality and speech. For an argument about the limits of this metaphor, see my "The Language of Crisis in Feminist Theory," in *"Turning the Century": New Directions in Feminist Criticism*, ed. Glynis Carr (Lewisburg: Bucknell Review Press, 1992), 68–89.

On the "ethic of care" in feminist thinking, see *An Ethic of Care: Feminist and Interdisciplinary Perspectives*, ed. Mary Jeanne Larrabee (New York: Routledge, 1993).

61. See, for example, McDowell, "'The Changing Same,'" 143. McDowell argues that Celie exchanges an external God for one "inside herself."

62. Goffman, *Forms of Talk*, 9–10.

63. McDowell, "Changing Same," 151. For a similar argument, from the perspective of a white feminist critic, see Cora Kaplan, "Keeping the Color in *The Color Purple*." "If [black] writers spoke to both Black and white Americans their 'ideal' reader was always Black," Kaplan writes.

Gates, by contrast, suggests that all readers, regardless of race or gender, are meant to experience themselves as textual eavesdroppers. "Celie writes her text, and is a text, standing in discrete and episodic letters, which we, like voyeurs, hurriedly read before the addressees (God and Nettie) interrupt our stolen pleasures." "Color Me Zora," 246.

64. McDowell, "Changing Same," 137, 145.

65. Goffman, *Forms of Talk*, 9–10.

66. Keith Byerman, "Women's Blues: The Fictions of Toni Cade Bambara and Alice Walker," in *Fingering the Jagged Grain: Tradition and Form in Recent Black Fiction* (Atlanta: Univ. of Georgia Press, 1985) reprinted in Gates and Appiah, eds., *Alice Walker*, 66.

67. Seyla Benhabib, *Critique, Norm, and Utopia: A Study of the Foundations of Critical Theory* (New York: Columbia Univ. Press, 1986), 4.

68. Alice Walker, "Zora Neale Hurston: A Cautionary Tale and a Partisan View," in *In Search of Our Mothers' Gardens*, 90.

69. Light, "Fear of the Happy Ending," 87.

Ann duCille argues that "'Happy endings,' in which the female hero manages to outstride her male oppressors, resist the bonds of love, and escape the burdens of patriarchy, might make for powerful feminist manifestos, but they would represent ideological shifts inconsistent with the social conventions and material conditions out of which these texts were produced and which they necessarily inscribe." *The Coupling Convention: Sex, Text, and Tradition in Black Women's Fiction* (New York: Oxford Univ. Press, 1993).

70. Benhabib, *Critique, Norm, and Utopia*.

71. Paul Gilroy, *The Black Atlantic: Modernity and Double Consciousness* (Cambridge: Harvard Univ. Press, 1993), 37–38.

72. Benhabib, *Critique, Norm, and Utopia*, 13.

73. Ibid.

74. Helena Michie, *Sororophobia: Differences among Women in Literature and Culture* (New York: Oxford Univ. Press, 1992), 6.

75. See Adrienne Rich, *Your Native Land, Your Life* (New York: Norton, 1986).

Conclusion: Auditions

1. Barbara Findlen, ed., *Listen Up: Voices from the Next Feminist Generation* (Seattle: Seal Press, 1995).

2. Alison Light, "Fear of the Happy Ending: *The Color Purple,* Reading and Racism," in *Plotting Change: Contemporary Women's Fiction*, ed. Linda Anderson (London: Edward Arnold, 1990), 85.

3. Linda Abbandonato, "Rewriting the Heroine's Story in *The Color Purple*," originally published as "A View from 'Elsewhere': Subversive Sexuality and the Rewriting of the Heroine's Story in *The Color Purple*," *PMLA* 106 (Oct. 1991), reprinted in *Alice Walker: Critical Perspectives, Past and Present*, ed. Henry Louis Gates, Jr., and Kwame Anthony Appiah (New York: Amistad, 1993), 299.

4. bell hooks, *Talking Back: thinking feminist, thinking black* (Boston: South End Press, 1989), 9.

5. Audre Lorde, "The Master's Tools Will Never Dismantle the Master's House," in *Sister Outsider* (Freedom, Calif.: 1984), 110–13.

6. Hélène Cixous, "The Laugh of the Medusa," *Signs* (Summer 1976), reprinted in *New French Feminisms: An Anthology*, ed. Elaine Marks and Isabelle de Courtivron (New York: Schocken, 1981), 245–64.

7. Hélène Cixous and Catherine Clement, *The Newly Born Woman*, trans. Betsy Wing (Minneapolis: Univ. of Minnesota Press, 1986), 157. Of course, Cixous's noted disengagement from feminism itself raises its own thorny set of questions.

8. hooks, *Talking Back*, 6.

9. Generational finger-pointing seems to have caught on particularly strongly these days in some circles. At the 1994 Modern Language Association convention, for example, in a panel on the future of feminist criticism starring Barbara Christian, Jane Gallop, Florence Howe, Nancy K. Miller, and Elaine Showalter,

both Miller and Showalter sounded the theme of intellectual matricide to a sometimes bewildered audience, mostly of nonfeminists, numbering well into the
hundreds.

10. Linda Alcoff, "Cultural Feminism versus Poststructuralism: The Identity Crisis in Feminist Theory," *Signs* 13, no. 3 (Spring 1988): 405–6.

11. Ibid., 419.

12. Judith Butler, "Gender Trouble, Feminist Theory, and Psychoanalytic
Discourse," in *Feminism/Postmodernism*, ed. Linda J. Nicholson (New York:
Routledge, 1990), 327.

13. Rosalind Delmar, "What Is Feminism?," in *What Is Feminism? A Re-
Examination*, ed. Juliet Mitchell and Ann Oakley (New York: Pantheon, 1986).

14. Adrienne Rich, "Notes Towards a Politics of Location," in *Blood, Bread,
and Poetry: Selected Prose, 1979–1985* (New York: Norton, 1986), 214. For a more
extended discussion of Rich's shift away from speaking for the "other woman"
and toward poststructuralism, see my "The Poetics of Accountability: Adrienne
Rich's Politics of Location," paper delivered at the Modern Language Association conference, December 1989.

15. Judith Butler, *Gender Trouble: Feminism and the Subversion of Identity*
(New York: Routledge, 1990).

16. Ibid., 325.

17. Ibid., 339.

18. Peggy Kamuf, "Parisian Letters: Between Feminism and Deconstruction"
(exchange with Nancy K. Miller), in *Conflicts in Feminism*, ed. Marianne Hirsch
and Evelyn Fox Keller (New York: Routledge, 1990), 131–32.

19. Delmar, "What Is Feminism?."

20. Donna Haraway, "A Manifesto for Cyborgs," reprinted in Nicholson,
ed., *Feminism/Postmodernism*, 197.

21. Nancy Cott, "Feminist Theory and Feminist Movements: The Past Before Us," in Mitchell, ed., *What Is Feminism?*, 58.

22. Throughout the late seventies and early eighties, women of color insisted
that "the differences between us did not permit our speaking in one voice." Maria
C. Lugones and Elizabeth V. Spelman, "Have We Got a Theory for You! Femi-
nist Theory, Cultural Imperialism and the Demand for 'The Woman's Voice,'"
Women's Studies International Forum 6, no. 6 (1983): 573. Feminism's putative
universality but practical exclusivity prompted many women of color, such as Hazel
Carby, to ask white feminists, "What exactly do you mean when you say 'WE'?"
Hazel V. Carby, "White Woman Listen! Black Feminism and the Boundaries of
Sisterhood," in *The Empire Strikes Back: Race and Sexism in 70's Britain* (London: Hutchinson, 1982), 233. This insistence by women of color that "there is a
pretense to a homogeneity of experience covered by the word *sisterhood* that does
not in fact exist," and that "white women stand in a power relation as oppressors
of black women," shocked (and continues to shock) many white feminists. Audre
Lorde, "Age, Race, Class, and Sex: Women Redefining Difference," in *Sister
Outsider,* 116; Carby, "White Woman Listen!," 214. In the wake of such challenges, suddenly it seemed to many self-identified feminists that nothing in feminist theory, practice, or history was untainted by or invulnerable to the paralyzing
charge of racism, elitism, blindness, and exclusivity. Strengthened by the force of
these initial challenges, anger toward feminism seemed to come from everywhere
at once and many established feminists felt themselves to be under attack. Lesbians, older women, prostitutes, disabled women, "post"-feminists, pro-pornography

advocates, and others all took courage from women of color and declared their alienation from a feminism which, they argued, did not speak for them.

23. Seyla Benhabib, *Situating the Self: Gender, Community, and Postmodernism in Contemporary Ethics* (New York: Routledge, 1992), 168.

24. Butler, *Gender Trouble*, 2.

25. Ibid., 149.

26. Most recently, Butler has recanted or at least moderated the extremes of this position, suggesting that a nonfoundationalist use of the category need not be eschewed. She writes: "if feminism presupposes that 'women' designates an undesignatable field of differences, one that cannot be totalized or summarized by a descriptive identity category, then the very term becomes a site of permanent openness and resignifiability. I would argue that the rifts among women over the content of the term ought to be safeguarded and prized, indeed, that this constant rifting ought to be affirmed as the ungrounded ground of feminist theory." "Contingent Foundations: Feminism and the Question of 'Postmodernism,'" in *Feminist Contentions: A Philosophical Debate,* ed. Seyla Benhabib, Judith Butler, Drucilla Cornell, and Nancy Fraser (New York: Routledge, 1995), 50. And again: "I am permanently troubled by identity categories . . . and understand them, even promote them, as sites of necessary trouble." "Imitation and Gender Insubordination," in *Inside/Out: Lesbian Theories, Gay Theories,* ed. Diana Fuss (New York: Routledge, 1991), 14. But in affirming this rifting and promoting this trouble, Butler makes a case only for the "performative" use of these categories, a position with some of the same circular logic of her position on "women." In her most recent book, Butler again affirms that "it remains necessary to lay claim to 'women,' 'queer,' 'gay,' and 'lesbian'" and that "laying claim to such terms in reverse will be necessary to refute homophobic deployments of the terms in law." She goes on to argue that "the necessity to mobilize the necessary error of identity (Spivak's term) will always be in tension with the democratic contestation of the term which works against its deployments in racist and misogynist discursive regimes." *Bodies That Matter: On the Discursive Limits of "Sex"* (New York: Routledge, 1993), 229. Here, Butler reveals again her tendency to assume, mistakenly in my view, that any mobilization of constituencies will always operate as regulatory, illusory, and constraining. I take up some of the political consequences of this view below.

27. Johanna Meehan, "Introduction" to *Feminists Read Habermas: Gendering the Subject of Discourse,* ed. Johanna Meehan (New York: Routledge, 1995), 12.

28. I stress the uniqueness of consciousness-raising as a feminist development, but as we should also remember, consciousness-raising had its origins in practices used by Chinese and Latin American revolutionaries, as well as by black civil rights groups in the North American South.

29. See Anita Shreve, *Women Together, Women Alone: The Legacy of the Consciousness-Raising Movement* (New York: Viking), 10. Judith Hole and Ellen Levine suggest the extent to which escaping a charge of "self-talking" means engaging those with cultural authority when they point out that when women talk to one another it "is considered a hen *qua* therapy party." *Rebirth of Feminism* (New York: Quadrangle Books, 1971), 138.

30. Shreve, *Women Together,* 30.

31. On impartiality and the public sphere, see Iris Marion Young, *Justice and the Politics of Difference* (Princeton: Princeton Univ. Press, 1990), esp. "The Ideal of Impartiality and the Civic Public," 96–121. The passages cited above are, respectively, from pp. 10 and 98.

32. See Sara Evans, *Personal Politics: The Roots of Women's Liberation in the Civil Rights Movement and the New Left* (New York: Vintage, 1980), 137, 231, and ff.

33. On the breakup of consciousness-raising groups, see Evans, *Personal Politics*, Shreve, *Women Together*, and Alice Echols, *Daring to Be Bad*: Radical Femnism in America, 1967–1975 (Minneapolis: Univ. of Minnesota Press, 1989).

34. Kathie Sarachild and Patricia Mainardi, "*Ms.* Politics and Editing: An Interview," in *Feminist Revolution*, ed. Redstockings (New Paltz: Redstockings, 1975), 172, as cited by Echols, *Daring to Be Bad*, 10.

35. The early consciousness-raising manifestos and protocols are very explicit about discourse rules and procedures, about mandating that "we respond with recognition to someone's account." See, for example, Pamela Allen, *Free Space: A Perspective on the Small Group in Women's Liberation* (New York: Times Change Press, 1970). The above quote is from Allen's book, one of the earliest consciousness-raising handbooks (26). One finds these protocols repeated almost word for word elsewhere, in a number of handbooks and guides: "you are not to judge"; "Don't interrupt or talk to your neighbor while a sister is speaking"; and so on. I am grateful to Erin Cramer for directing my attention to these handbooks and for sharing with me her vast knowledge about consciousness-raising, as well as her personal library. I would also like to thank Andrea Fraser for her generous help in sharing those protocols used by the V-Girls.

36. Shreve, *Women Together*, 45.

37. Benhabib, *Situating the Self*, 168.

38. Performativity has been particularly influential in gay and gender studies, but the breadth of its influence goes well beyond those arenas and can be gauged not only in a spate of new books with titles such as *Performativity and Performance*, *Performing Feminisms*, *Acting Out: Feminist Performances*, and *Unmarked: The Politics of Performance* but also in the recent proliferation of MLA panels and papers using performance and performativity in their titles: "Performance and Praxis," "Performance I: History," "Text as Performance," "Robin Hood and Performance," "Performance II: Practicing Theory," "Performing Postcoloniality," for example (all from 1994), and others.

39. Even as early as 1968, there were splits between feminists committed to a politics of consciousness, or ideology, and those committed to performance and performative activism. On the history, for example, of WITCH—originally Women's International Terrorist Conspiracy from Hell—see Hole and Levine, *Rebirth of Feminism*, 126 and ff.

40. No wonder that, as Benhabib puts it, "the paradigm of language has replaced the paradigm of consciousness." *Situating the Self*, 208.

41. Eve Kosofsky Sedgwick, *Tendencies* (Durham, N.C.: Duke Univ. Press, 1993), 11. See also Sedgwick's *Epistemology of the Closet* (Berkeley: Univ. of California Press, 1990) and "Queer Performativity: Henry James's *The Art of the Novel*," *GLQ: A Journal of Lesbian and Gay Studies*. 1, no. 1 (1993): 1–16.

42. Butler, *Bodies That Matter*, 13.

43. Butler, "Burning Acts: Injurious Speech," in *Performativity and Performance*, ed. Andrew Parker and Eve Kosofsky Sedgwick (New York: Routledge, 1995), 205.

44. Whether performativity will also prove important to race studies is, as yet, an open question.

45. See *Gender Trouble*, 25 and passim.

46. Butler, *Bodies That Matter*, 21.

47. See Jane Gallop, "Im-Personation: A Reading in the Guise of an Intro-duction," in *Pedagogy: The Question of Impersonation*, (Bloomington: Indiana Univ. Press, 1995). I am grateful to Peggy Phelan, whose theories of performance have had an enormous influence on theories of the performative, for bringing this text to my attention.

48. Butler, *Gender Trouble*, 146, 145.

49. Butler, *Bodies that Matter*, x, 225, 132.

50. Linda Nicholson, "Introduction" to Benhabib et al., eds., *Feminist Contentions*, 11.

51. Nancy Fraser, "False Antitheses: A Response to Seyla Benhabib and Judith Butler," in ibid., 67–68.

52. Lynne Huffer, "Luce *et veritas*: Toward an Ethics of Performance," *Yale French Studies*, no. 87 (1995), special issue, "Another Look, Another Woman: Retranslations of French Feminism," p. 23 n. 11. Huffer provides an excellent over-view of performativity and a provocative challenge to its ethical self-understanding. I am grateful to her for our discussions of performativity and ethics.

53. Butler, "Imitation and Gender Insubordination," in Fuss, ed., *Inside/Out*, 27.

54. Butler, "Burning Acts," 205.

55. See Parker and Sedgwick, "Introduction" to *Performativity and Performance*, for a wonderfully succinct discussion of how this "presumption of con-sensus" works. I would like to thank Eve Sedgwick for very graciously and gener-ously making this text available to me in manuscript.

56. Young, *Justice and the Politics of Difference*, 119.

57. Peter Dews, *Logic of Disintegration: Post-Structuralist Thought and the Claims of Critical Theory* (London: Verso, 1987), 222.

58. The V-Girls, "Daughters of the Revolution," *October* 71 (Winter 1995): 121–40.

Bibliography

Abbandonato, Linda. "A View from 'Elsewhere': Subversive Sexuality and the Rewriting of the Heroine's Story in *The Color Purple*." *PMLA* 106 (5) (Oct. 1991): 1106–15. Reprinted as "Rewriting the Heroine's Story in *The Color Purple*." In *Alice Walker: Critical Perspectives*, ed. Gates and Appiah, pp. 296–308.

Abel, Elizabeth, ed. *Writing and Sexual Difference*. Chicago: Univ. of Chicago Press, 1982.

Abelove, Henry, Michèle Aina Barele, and David M. Halperin, eds. *The Lesbian and Gay Studies Reader*. New York: Routledge, 1993.

Adams, Maurianne. "*Jane Eyre*: Woman's Estate." In *The Authority of Experience*, ed. Diamond and Edwards, pp. 137–59.

Alcoff, Linda. "Cultural Feminism versus Poststructuralism: The Identity Crisis in Feminist Theory." *Signs* 13(3) (Spring 1988): 405–36.

Allen, Pamela. *Free Space: A Perspective on the Small Group in Women's Liberation*. New York: Times Change Press, 1970.

Andrews, William L. "Dialogue in Antebellum Afro-American Autobiography." In *Studies in Autobiography*. Ed. James Olney. New York: Oxford Univ. Press, 1988. Pp. 89–98.

———. *To Tell a Free Story: Toward a Poetics of Afro-American Autobiography, 1760–1865*. Urbana: Univ. of Illinois Press, 1986.

Ardis, Ann. "The White Daughter's Seduction: Christine Froula's Family Romance of Canon-Formation." Unpublished ms.

Arendt, Hannah, ed. *Illuminations*. New York: Schocken, 1969.

Armstrong, Nancy. *Desire and Domestic Fiction: A Political History of the Novel*. New York: Oxford Univ. Press, 1987.

Armstrong, Nancy, and Leonard Tennenhouse. *The Ideology of Conduct: Essays on Literature and the History of Sexuality.* New York: Methuen, 1986.

Austin, J. L. *How to Do Things with Words.* 2nd ed., ed. J. O. Urmson and Marina Sbisà. Cambridge: Harvard Univ. Press, 1975.

Awkward, Michael. *Inspiriting Influences: Tradition, Revision, and Afro-American Women's Novels.* New York: Columbia Univ. Press, 1989.

Baker, Houston A., Jr. "Autobiographical Acts and the Voice of the Southern Slave." In *The Slave's Narrative,* ed. Davis and Gates.

———. *Blues, Ideology and Afro-American Literature: A Vernacular Theory.* Chicago: Univ. of Chicago Press, 1984.

———. *Workings of the Spirit: The Poetics of Afro-American Women's Writing.* Chicago: Univ. of Chicago Press, 1992.

Bakhtin, Mikhail. *The Dialogic Imagination: Four Essays.* Ed. Michael Holquist. Trans. Caryl Emerson and Michael Holquist. Austin: Univ. of Texas Press, 1981.

———. *Problems in Dostoevsky's Poetics.* Ed. and trans. Caryl Emerson. Minneapolis: Univ. of Minnesota Press, 1984.

———. *Rabelais and His World.* Trans. Hélène Iswolsky. Cambridge: M.I.T. Press, 1968.

———. *Speech Genres and Other Late Essays.* Ed. Caryl Emerson and Michael Holquist. Trans. Vern W. McGee. Austin: Univ. of Texas Press, 1986.

Bakhtin, Mikhail, and P. N. Medvedev. *The Formal Method in Literary Scholarship: A Critical Introduction to Sociological Poetics.* Trans. Albert J. Wehrle. Baltimore: Johns Hopkins Univ. Press, 1991.

Barthes, Roland. *The Pleasure of the Text.* Trans. Richard Miller. New York: Hill and Wang, 1975.

Bauer, Dale M. *Feminist Dialogics: A Theory of Failed Community.* Albany: State Univ. of New York Press, 1988.

Bauer, Dale M., and S. Jaret McKinstry, eds. *Feminism, Bakhtin, and the Dialogic.* Albany: State Univ. of New York Press, 1991.

Bell, Bernard. *The Afro-American Novel and Its Tradition.* Amherst: Univ. of Massachusetts Press, 1987.

Belsey, Catherine. *Desire: Love Stories in Western Culture.* Oxford: Blackwell, 1994.

Benhabib, Seyla. *Critique, Norm, and Utopia: A Study of the Foundations of Critical Theory.* New York: Columbia Univ. Press, 1986.

———. *Situating the Self: Gender, Community, and Postmodernism in Contemporary Ethics.* New York: Routledge, 1992.

Benhabib, Seyla, Judith Butler, Drucilla Cornell, and Nancy Fraser, eds. *Feminist Contentions: A Philosophical Debate.* New York: Routledge, 1995.

Benhabib, Seyla, and Fred Dallmayr, eds. *The Communicative Ethics Controversy.* Cambridge: MIT Press, 1990.

Benjamin, Walter. "The Storyteller." in *Illuminations,* ed. Arendt, Pp. 83–109.

———. "Theses on the Philosophy of History." In *Illuminations,* ed. Arendt, pp. 253–64.

Benstock, Shari, ed. *Feminist Issues in Literary Scholarship.* Bloomington: Indiana Univ. Press, 1987.

Berlant, Lauren. "Race, Gender, and Nation in *The Color Purple.*" *Critical Inquiry* 14 (Summer 1988). Reprinted in *Alice Walker: Critical Perspectives,* ed. Gates and Appiah, pp. 211–38.

Bernheimer, Charles, ed. *In Dora's Case: Freud—Hysteria—Feminism*. New York: Columbia Univ. Press, 1985.

Bethel, Lorraine. "'This Infinity of Conscious Pain': Zora Neale Hurston and the Black Female Literary Tradition." In *All the Women Are White*, ed. Hull, Scott, and Smith.

Bloom, Harold, ed. *Alice Walker: Modern Critical Views*. New York: Chelsea House, 1989.

———. *The Anxiety of Influence: A Theory of Poetry*. New York: Oxford Univ. Press, 1973.

———, ed. *The Brontës: Modern Critical Views*. New York: Chelsea House, 1987.

Bobo, Jacqueline. "Black Women as Cultural Readers." In *Female Spectators*. Ed. Deidre Pribram. London: Verso, 1988. Pp. 90–109.

———. "Sifting Through the Controversy: Reading *The Color Purple*." *Callaloo* (12(2) (1989): 332–42.

Bodenheimer, Rosemarie. "Jane Eyre in Search of Her Story." *Papers on Language and Literature* 16 (3) (Summer 1980): 387–402.

Boone, Joseph Allen. *Tradition Counter Tradition: Love and the Form of Fiction*. Chicago: Univ. of Chicago Press, 1987.

Boone, Joseph Allen, and Michael Cadden, eds. *Engendering Men: The Question of Male Feminist Criticism*. New York: Routledge, 1990.

Booth, Wayne C. "Freedom of Interpretation: Bakhtin and the Challenge of Feminist Criticism." In *Bakhtin: Essays and Dialogues on His Work*. Ed. Gary Saul Morson. Chicago: Univ. of Chicago Press, 1981.

Bowen, Barbara. "Untroubled Voice: Call and Response in *Cane*." In *Black Literature*, ed. Gates, pp. 187–203.

Brenkman, John. *Culture and Domination*. Ithaca: Cornell Univ. Press, 1987.

———. "Politics and Form in *The Song of Solomon*." *Social Text*, 39 (Summer 1994): 57–82.

Brodzki, Bella and Celeste Schenck, eds. *Life/Lines: Theorizing Women's Autobiography*. Ithaca: Cornell Univ. Press, 1988.

Broe, Mary Lynn and Angela Ingram. *Women's Writing in Exile*. Chapel Hill: Univ. of North Carolina Press, 1989.

Brontë, Charlotte. *Jane Eyre*. Harmondsworth, Middlesex, England: Penguin, 1986.

Brooks, Peter. *Reading for the Plot: Design and Intention in Narrative*. New York: Vintage, 1985.

Burke, Peter. *The Art of Conversation*. Ithaca: Cornell Univ. Press, 1993.

Butler, Cheryl B. "The Color Purple Controversy: Black Woman Spectatorship." *Wide Angle* 13(3, 4) (July-Oct. 1991): 63–69.

Butler, Judith. *Bodies That Matter: On the Discursive Limits of "Sex."* New York: Routledge, 1993.

———. "Burning Acts: Injurious Speech." In *Performativity and Performance*, ed. Parker and Sedgwick, pp. 197–227.

———. "Contingent Foundations: Feminist and the Question of 'Postmodernism.'" In *Feminist Contentions*, ed. Benhabib et al., pp. 35–57.

———. *Gender Trouble: Feminism and the Subversion of Identity*. New York: Routledge, 1991.

———. "Gender Trouble, Feminist Theory, and Psychoanalytic Discourse." In *Feminism/Postmodernism*, ed. Nicholson, pp. 324–40.

———. "Imitation and Gender Insubordination." In *Inside/Out*, ed. Diana Fuss, pp. 13–31.

Butler, Judith, and Joan Scott, eds. *Feminists Theorize the Political*. New York: Routledge, 1992.

Byerman, Keith. "Women's Blues: The Fictions of Toni Cade Bambara and Alice Walker." In *Fingering the Jagged Grain: Tradition and Form in Recent Black Fiction*. Atlanta: Univ. of Georgia Press, 1985. Rpt. in *Alice Walker: Modern Critical Views*, ed. Bloom, pp. 59–66.

Callahan, John. *In the African-American Grain: The Pursuit of Voice in Twentieth-Century Black Fiction*. Urbana: Univ. of Illinois Press, 1988.

Canby, Vincent. "From a Palette of Clichés Comes 'The Color Purple.'" *New York Times*, Jan. 5, 1986.

Carby, Hazel. *Reconstructing Womanhood: The Emergence of the Afro-American Woman Novelist*. New York: Oxford Univ. Press, 1987.

———. "White Woman Listen! Black Feminism and the Boundaries of Sisterhood." In *The Empire Strikes Back: Race and Sexism in 70's Britain*. London: Hutchinson, 1982.

Case, Sue-Ellen. *Performing Feminisms: Feminist Critical Theory and Theatre*. Baltimore: Johns Hopkins Univ. Press, 1990.

Chase, Richard. "The Brontë's, or Myth Domesticated." In *Forms of Modern Fiction*, ed. William V. O'Connor. Minneapolis: Univ. of Minnesota Press, 1948. Pp. 102–13.

Chambers, Ross. *Room for Maneuver: Reading (the) Oppositional (in) Narrative*. Chicago: Univ. of Chicago Press, 1991.

———. *Story and Situation: Narrative Seduction and the Power of Fiction*. Minneapolis: Univ. of Minnesota Press, 1984.

Chauncey, George, Jr. "Christian Brotherhood or Sexual Perversion? Homosexual Identities and the Construction of Sexual Boundaries in the World War I Era." In *Hidden from History*, ed. Duberman, Vicinus, and Chauncy, pp. 294–317.

Chodorow, Nancy. *The Reproduction of Mothering: Psychoanalysis and the Sociology of Gender*. Berkeley: Univ. of California Press, 1978.

Christ, Carol T. "Imaginative Constraint, Feminine Duty, and the Form of Charlotte Brontë's Fiction." *Women's Studies* 6(3) (1979): 287–96.

Christian, Barbara. *Black Women Novelists*. Westport: Greenwood Press, 1980.

———. "De-Visioning Spielberg on Walker, *The Color Purple*, The Novel and the Film," unpublished ms.

Cixous, Hélène. "The Laugh of the Medusa." *Signs* (Summer 1976). Reprinted in *New French Feminisms*, ed. Marks and Courtivon, pp. 245–64.

Cixous, Hélène, and Catherine Clement. *The Newly Born Woman*. Trans. Betsy Wing. Minneapolis: Univ. of Minnesota Press, 1986.

Clayton, Jay. "The Narrative Turn in Recent Minority Fiction." *American Literary History* 2(3) (Fall 1990): 375–93.

———. *The Pleasures of Babel: Contemporary American Literature and Theory*. New York: Oxford Univ. Press, 1993.

Clements, Marcelle. Review of "Madison County." *Ms.* 7, no. 2 (Sept./Oct. 1995): 88.

Cohen, Barry M., Esther Giller, and Lynn W., eds. *Multiple Personality Disorder from the Inside Out*. Baltimore: Sidran Press, 1991.

Collins, Gina Michelle. "*The Color Purple*: What Feminism Can Learn from a

Southern Tradition." In *Southern Literature and Literary Theory*. Ed. Jefferson Humphries. Athens: Univ. of Georgia Press, 1990, pp. 75–87.

Cott, Nancy F. "Feminist Theory and Feminist Movements: The Past Before Us." In *What Is Feminism*, ed. Mitchell and Oakley, pp. 49–62.

———. *The Grounding of Modern Feminism*. New Haven: Yale Univ. Press, 1987.

Craig, C. Armour. "The Unpoetic Compromise: On the Relation Between Private Vision and Social Order in Nineteenth-Century English Fiction." In *Society and Self in the Novel*. Ed. Mark Schorer. New York: Columbia Univ. Press, 1956.

Crapanzano, Vincent. "On Dialogue." In *The Interpretation of Dialogue*, ed. Maranhão, pp. 269–91.

Culler, Jonathan. *Structuralist Poetics: Structuralism, Linguistics, and the Study of Literature*. Ithaca: Cornell Univ. Press, 1975.

David, Deirdre. *Rule Britannia: Women, Empire, and Victorian Writing*. Ithaca: Cornell Univ. Press, 1995.

Davis, Charles T., and Henry Louis Gates, Jr., eds. *The Slave's Narrative*. New York: Oxford Univ. Press, 1985.

Dearborn, Mary. *Pocahontas' Daughters: Gender and Ethnicity in American Culture*. New York: Oxford Univ. Press, 1986.

de Lauretis, Teresa. *Alice Doesn't: Feminism, Semiotics, Cinema*. Bloomington: Indiana Univ. Press, 1984.

———. "Film and the Visible." In *How Do I Look?: Queer Film and Video*. Ed. Bad Object-Choices. Seattle: Bay Press, 1991. Pp. 223–76.

———. "Sexual Indifference and Lesbian Representation." In *Performing Feminisms*, ed. Sue-Ellen Case, pp. 17–39.

Delmar, Rosalind. "What Is Feminism?" In *What Is Feminism?*, ed. Juliet Mitchell and Ann Oakley, pp. 8–33.

Denby, David. "Purple People-Eater." *New York* Jan. 13, 1986.

Dews, Peter. *Logics of Disintegration: Post-Structuralist Thought and the Claims of Critical Theory*. London: Verso Press, 1987.

Diamond, Arlyn, and Lee R. Edwards, eds. *The Authority of Experience*. Amherst: Univ. of Massachusetts Press, 1975.

Diawara, Manthia. "Black Spectatorship: Problems of Identification and Resistance." In *Black American Cinema*. New York: Routledge, 1993. Pp. 211–20.

Dinesen, Isak. "The Blank Page." In *The Last Tales*. New York: 1957. Reprinted in *The Norton Anthology of Literature by Women*. Ed. Sandra M. Gilbert and Susan Gubar. New York: W.W. Norton, 1985. Pp. 1418–23.

Doriani, Beth Maclay. "Black Womanhood in Nineteenth-Century America: Subversion and Self-Construction in Two Women's Autobiographies." *American Quarterly* 43(2) (June 1991): 199–222.

Duberman, Martin, Martha Vicinus, and George Chauncy, Jr., eds. *Hidden from History: Reclaiming the Gay & Lesbian Past*. New York: Meridian, 1990.

Du Bois, W. E. B. "Criteria of Negro Art." *The Crisis* (Oct.1926): 290–97. Reprinted. in *W. E. B. Du Bois: Writings*. New York: Library of America, 1986. Pp. 993–1002.

duCille, Ann. *The Coupling Convention: Sex, Text, and Tradition in Black Women's Fiction*. New York: Oxford, 1993.

DuPlessis, Rachel Blau. "For the Etruscans." In *The Future of Difference*, ed. Eisenstein and Jardine. Reprinted in *The New Feminist Criticism*, ed. Showalter, pp. 271–91.

————. *Writing Beyond the Ending: Narrative Strategies of Twentieth-Century Women Writers*. Bloomington: Indiana Univ. Press, 1985.

Early, Gerald. "*The Color Purple* as Everybody's Protest Art." *Antioch Review* (Winter 1992): 399–412.

Echols, Alice. *Daring to Be Bad: Radical Feminism in America, 1967–1975*. Minneapolis: Univ. of Minnesota Press, 1989.

Eisenstein, Hester, and Alice Jardine, eds. *The Future of Difference*. Boston: G. K. Hall, 1981.

Evans, Sara. *Personal Politics: The Roots of Women's Liberation in the Civil Rights Movement and the New Left*. New York: Vintage, 1980.

Faludi, Susan. *Backlash: The Undeclared War Against American Women*. New York: Crown, 1991.

Farwell, Marilyn R. "Heterosexual Plots and Lesbian Subtexts: Toward a Theory of Lesbian Narrative Space." In *Lesbian Texts and Contexts: Radical Revisions*. Ed. Karla Jay and Joanne Glasgow. New York: NYU Press, 1990. Pp. 91–103.

Felski, Rita. *Beyond Feminist Aesthetics: Feminist Literature and Social Change*. Cambridge: Harvard Univ. Press, 1989.

Ferris, William. "The Arts and Black Development." *Negro World*, April 30, 1921.

Fetterley, Judith. "Reading About Reading: 'A Jury of Her Peers,' 'The Murders in the Rue Morgue,' and 'The Yellow Wallpaper.'" In *Gender and Reading*, ed. Flynn and Schweikart, pp. 147–65.

Findlen, Barbara, ed. *Listen Up: Voices from the Next Feminist Generation*. Seattle: Seal Press, 1995.

Finke, Laurie A. *Feminist Theory, Women's Writing*. Ithaca: Cornell Univ. Press, 1992.

Fish, Stanley. *Is There a Text in This Class? The Authority of Interpretive Communities*. Cambridge: Harvard Univ. Press, 1980.

Flax, Jane. *Thinking Fragments: Psychoanalysis, Feminism, and Postmodernism in the Contemporary West*. Berkeley: Univ. of California Press, 1990.

Flynn, Elizabeth A., and Patrocinio Schweikart, eds. *Gender and Reading: Essays on Readers, Texts, and Contexts*. Baltimore: Johns Hopkins Univ. Press, 1986.

Foucault, Michel. *The History of Sexuality*. Vol. 1, *An Introduction*. New York: Vintage, 1980.

Fox-Genovese, Elizabeth. "To Write My Self: The Autobiographies of Afro-American Women." In *Feminist Issues*, ed. Benstock, pp. 161–80.

Fraser, Nancy. "False Antithesis: A Response to Seyla Benhabib and Judith Butler." In *Feminist Contentions*, ed. Benhabib et al.

————. *Unruly Practices: Power, Discourse, and Gender in Contemporary Social Theory*. Minneapolis: Univ. of Minnesota Press, 1989.

Freedman, Estelle B., et al. *The Lesbian Issue: Essays from Signs*. Chicago: Univ. of Chicago Press, 1985.

Freud, Sigmund. "Beyond the Pleasure Principle." Reprinted in *The Standard Edition*, vol. 18, pp. 7–64.

————. "The Ego and the Id." Reprinted in *The Standard Edition*, vol. 19, pp. 3–66.

————. "Family Romances." Reprinted in *The Standard Edition*, vol. 9, pp. 237–41.

————. "The Interpretation of Dreams." Reprinted in *The Standard Edition*, vols. 4 and 5.

———. "An Outline of Psychoanalysis." Reprinted in *The Standard Edition*, vol. 23, pp. 144–207.

———. *The Standard Edition of the Complete Psychological Works of Sigmund Freud*. Trans. James Strachey. London: Hogarth Press, 1973.

Froula, Christine. "The Daughter's Seduction: Sexual Violence and Literary History." *Signs* 11(4) (Summer 1986): 621–44.

Frye, Joanne. *Living Stories, Telling Lives: Women and the Novel in Contemporary Experience*. Ann Arbor: Univ. of Michigan Press, 1986.

Frye, Northrop. *Anatomy of Criticism: Four Essays*. New York: Atheneum, 1968.

Fuss, Diana. *Essentially Speaking: Feminism, Nature and Difference*. New York: Routledge, 1989.

———. "Fashion and the Homospectatorial Look." *Critical Inquiry* 18 (Summer 1992).

———. *Identification Papers*. New York: Routledge, 1995.

———, ed. *Inside/Out: Lesbian Theories, Gay Theories*. New York: Routledge, 1991.

Gadamer, Hans-Georg. *Truth and Method*. New York: Crossroads, 1982.

Gallop, Jane. *The Daughter's Seduction: Feminism and Psychoanalysis*. Ithaca: Cornell Univ. Press, 1982.

———. ed. *Pedagogy: The Question of Impersonation*. Bloomington: Indiana Univ. Press, 1995.

———. "Snatches of Conversation." In *Women and Language in Literature and Society*, ed. McConnel-Ginet, Borker, and Furman, pp. 274–83.

Garber, Eric. "A Spectacle in Color: The Lesbian and Gay Subculture of Jazz Age Harlem." In *Hidden from History*, ed. Duberman, Vicinus, and Chauncy, pp. 318–31.

Gardiner, Judith Kegan. "Empathic Ways of Reading: Narcissism, Cultural Politics, and Russ's *Female Man*." Unpublished ms.

———. *Rhys, Stead, Lessing, and the Politics of Empathy*. Bloomington: Indiana Univ. Press, 1988.

Gates, Barbara Timm, ed. *Critical Essays on Charlotte Brontë*. Boston: G. K. Hall, 1990.

Gates, Henry Louis, Jr., ed. *Black Literature and Literary Theory*. New York: Methuen, 1984.

———. *Figures in Black: Words, Signs and the "Racial" Self*. New York: Oxford Univ. Press, 1987.

———, ed. *Reading Black, Reading Feminist*. New York: Meridian, 1990.

———. *The Signifying Monkey: A Theory of African-American Criticism*. New York: Oxford Univ. Press, 1988.

———. "Writing 'Race' and the Difference It Makes." *Critical Inquiry* 12(1) (Autumn 1985): 1–20.

Gates, Henry Louis, Jr., and Kwame Anthony Appiah, eds. *Alice Walker: Critical Perspectives, Past and Present*. New York: Amistad, 1993.

Genovese, Eugene D. *The World the Slaveholders Made*. New York: Vintage, 1971.

Giddens, Anthony. *The Constitution of Society: Outline of a Theory of Structuration*. Berkeley: Univ. of California Press, 1984.

———. *Modernity and Self-Identity: Self and Society in the Late Modern Age*. Stanford: Stanford Univ. Press, 1991.

———. *The Transformation of Intimacy: Sexuality, Love & Eroticism in Modern Societies*. Stanford: Stanford Univ. Press, 1992.

Giddings, Paula. *When and Where I Enter: The Impact of Black Women on Race and Sex in America*. New York: Bantam, 1984.

Gilbert, Sandra M., and Susan Gubar. *The Madwoman in the Attic: The Woman Writer and the Nineteenth-Century Literary Imagination*. New Haven: Yale Univ. Press, 1979.

———. *No Man's Land: The Place of the Woman Writer in the Twentieth Century*. 3 vols. New Haven: Yale Univ. Press, 1988, 1989, 1994.

———, eds. *Shakespeare's Sisters: Feminist Essays on Women Poets*. Bloomington: Indiana Univ. Press, 1979.

Gilligan, Carol. *In a Different Voice: Psychological Theory and Women's Development*. Cambridge: Harvard Univ. Press, 1982.

Gilman, Charlotte Perkins. "The Yellow Wallpaper." *New England Magazine* (May 1892). Reprinted in *The Captive Imagination*, ed. Golden, pp. 1–42.

Gilroy, Paul. *The Black Atlantic: Modernity and Double Consciousness*. Cambridge, Mass.: Harvard Univ. Press, 1993.

Girard, René. *Deceit, Desire, and the Novel: Self and Other in Literary Structure*. Trans. Yvonne Freccero. Baltimore: Johns Hopkins Univ. Press, 1972.

Glaspell, Susan. "A Jury of Her Peers." *Everyweek*, March 5, 1917. Reprinted in *Images of Women in Literature*. Ed. Mary Anne Ferguson. Boston: Houghton Mifflin, 1973. Pp. 370–85.

Glickman, Marlianne. "LeeWay" (interview with Spike Lee). *Film Comment*, Oct. 1986.

Goffman, Erving. *Forms of Talk*. Philadelphia: Univ. of Pennsylvania Press, 1981.

———. *Frame Analysis: An Essay on the Organization of Experience*. New York: Harper & Row, 1974.

Golden, Catherine, ed. *The Captive Imagination: A Casebook on* The Yellow Wallpaper. New York: Feminist Press, 1992.

———. "One Hundred Years of Reading 'The Yellow Wallpaper.'" In *The Captive Imagination*, ed. Golden, pp. 1–23.

———. "The Writing of 'The Yellow Wallpaper': A Double Palimpsest." In *The Captive Imagination*, ed. Golden, pp. 296–306.

Gooding-Williams, Robert, ed. *Reading Rodney King, Reading Urban Uprising*. New York: Routledge, 1993.

Grahn, Judy. *The Common Woman*. Oakland: Woman's Press Collective, n.d.

Greene, Gayle and Coppélia Kahn, eds. *Changing Subjects: The Making of Feminist Literary Criticism*. London: Routledge, 1992.

Gubar, Susan. "'The Blank Page' and the Issues of Female Creativity." In *Writing and Sexual Difference*, ed. Abel, pp. 73–93.

———. "Sapphistries." In *The Lesbian Issue*, ed. Freedman et al., pp. 91–110.

Gwin, Minrose C. "Green-Eyed Monsters of the Slavocracy: Jealous Mistresses in Two Slave Narratives." In *Conjuring*, ed. Pryse and Spillers, pp. 39–52.

Habermas, Jürgen. *Der Philosophisce DisKurs der Moderne*. Frankfurt, 1985.

———. *The Theory of Communicative Action*. Vol. 1, *Reason and the Rationalization of Society*. Vol. 2, *Lifeworld and System: A Critique of Functionalist Reason*. Both trans. Thomas McCarthy. Boston: Beacon Press, 1981, 1987.

Hall, James C. "Towards a Map of Mis(sed) Reading: The Presence of Absence in *The Color Purple*." *African-American Review* 26(1) (Spring 1992): 89–97.

Haney-Peritz, Janice. "Monumental Feminism and Literature's Ancestral House: Another Look at 'The Yellow Wallpaper.'" *Women's Studies* 12(2) (1986): 113–28. Reprinted in *The Captive Imagination*, ed. Golden, pp. 261–76.

Haraway, Donna. "A Manifesto for Cyborgs." In *Feminism/Postmodernism*, ed. Nicholson, pp. 190–233.

Harding, Sandra. "The Instability of the Analytical Categories of Feminist Theory." *Signs* 11(4) (Summer 1986): 645–64.

Harris, Trudier. "On *The Color Purple*, Stereotypes, and Silence." *Black American Literature Forum* 18(4) (Winter 1984): 155–61.

———. "From Victimization to Free Enterprise: Alice Walker's *The Color Purple*." *Black American Literature Forum* 14(1) (1986): 1–17.

Hart, Lynda, and Peggy Phelan. *Acting Out: Feminist Performances*. Ann Arbor: Univ. of Michigan Press, 1993.

Hartsock, Nancy. "Rethinking Modernism: Minority vs. Majority Theories." *Cultural Critique* 7: "The Nature and Context of Minority Discourse II," special issue. Ed. Abdul JanMohammed and David Lloyd, pp. 187–206.

Hedges, Elaine R. "Afterword to 'The Yellow Wallpaper.'" New York: Feminist Press, 1973. Reprinted in *The Captive Imagination*, ed. Golden, pp. 123–40.

———. "'Out at Last'? 'The Yellow Wallpaper' After Two Decades of Feminist Criticism." In *The Captive Imagination*, ed. Golden, pp. 319–33.

———. "Small Things Reconsidered: Susan Glaspell's 'A Jury of Her Peers.'" *Women's Studies* 12 (1986): 89–110.

Heilbrun, Carolyn G. "Critical Response II: A Response to *Writing and Sexual Difference*." In *Writing and Sexual Difference*, ed. Abel, pp. 291–97.

Hemenway, Robert E. *Zora Neale Hurston: A Literary Biography*. Urbana: Univ. of Illinois Press, 1977.

Hemingway, Ernest. *In Our Time*. New York: Scribner's, 1925.

Henderson, Mae Gwendolyn. "*The Color Purple*: Revisions and Redefinitions." *Sage: A Scholarly Journal on Black Women* 2(1) (Spring 1985).

———. "Speaking in Tongues: Dialogics, Dialectics, and the Black Woman Writer's Literary Tradition." In *Changing Our Own Words*, ed. Wall, pp. 16–37.

Henelly, Mark M., Jr. "*Jane Eyre*'s Reading Lesson." *ELH* 54(4)(Winter 1984): 693–717.

Henley, Nancy M. *Body Politics: Power, Sex, and Nonverbal Communication*. Englewood Cliffs: Prentice-Hall, 1977.

Henley, Nancy M., and Barrie Thorne. *She Said/He Said: An Annotated Bibliography of Language, Speech, and Nonverbal Communication*. Pittsburgh: Know, 1975.

——— and ———. "Womanspeak and Manspeak: Sex Differences and Sexism in Communication, Verbal and Nonverbal." In *Beyond Sex Roles*. Ed. Alice Sargent. St. Paul, Minn.: West Publishing, 1976. Pp. 201–218.

——— and ———, eds. *Language and Sex: Difference and Dominance*. Rowley, Mass.: Newbury House, 1975.

Henley, Nancy M., Chris Kramarae, and Barrie Thorne. *Language, Gender and Society*. Rowley, Mass.: Newbury House, 1988.

Herman, Sondra R. "Loving Courtship or the Marriage Market? The Ideal and its Critics, 1871–1911." *American Quarterly* 25(2) (May 1973):235–52.

Hermann, Anne. *The Dialogic and Difference: "An/Other" Woman in Virginia Woolf and Christa Wolf*. New York: Columbia Univ. Press, 1989.

Herndl, Diane Price, and Robyn Warhol, eds. *Feminisms*. New Brunswick: Rutgers Univ. Press, 1991.

Hine, Darlene Clark, ed. *Black Women in United States History.* 4 vols. New York: Carlson, 1990.

———. *Black Women's History, Theory and Practice.* 2 vols. New York: Carlson, 1990.

Hirsch, Marianne and Evelyn Fox Keller, eds. *Conflicts in Feminism.* New York: Routledge, 1990.

Hite, Molly. "Romance, Marginality, Matrilineage: Alice Walker's *The Color Purple* and Zora Neale Hurston's *Their Eyes Were Watching God.*" *Novel: A Forum on Fiction* 22(3) (Spring 1989): 257–73.

Hite, Shere. *Women and Love: A Cultural Revolution in Progress.* New York: Knopf, 1987.

Hole, Judith, and Ellen Levine, eds. *Rebirth of Feminism.* New York: Quadrangle, 1971.

Holloway, Karla F.C. *The Character of the Word: The Texts of Zora Neale Hurston.* New York: Greenwood Press, 1987.

Holquist, Michael. *Dialogism: Bakhtin and His World.* London: Routledge, 1990.

Homans, Margaret. *Bearing the Word: Language and Female Experience in Nineteenth-Century Women's Writing.* Chicago: Univ. of Chicago Press, 1986.

hooks, bell. *Talking Back: thinking feminist, thinking black.* Boston: South End Press, 1989.

Horne, Karen, and Helen Wussow, eds. *A Dialogue of Voices: Feminist Literary Theory and Bakhtin.* Minneapolis: Univ. of Minnesota Press, 1994.

Howard, Lillie P., ed. *Alice Walker and Zora Neale Hurston: The Common Bond.* Westport: Greenwood Press, 1993.

Huffer, Lynne. "Luce *et veritas*: Toward an Ethics of Performance." *Yale French Studies* 87 (1995). Special issue: "Another Look: Another Woman: Retranslations of French Feminism," ed. Huffer.

Huggins, Nathan Irvin, ed. *Voices from the Harlem Renaissance.* New York: Oxford Univ. Press, 1976.

Hughes, Langston. "The Negro Artist and the Racial Mountain." *The Nation* (June 1926). Reprinted in *Voices from the Harlem Renaissance,* ed. Huggins, pp. 305–9.

Hull, Gloria T. *Color, Sex, and Poetry: Three Women Writers of the Harlem Renaissance.* Bloomington: Indiana Univ. Press, 1987.

———. "'Lines She Did Not Dare': Angelina Weld Grimké, Harlem Renaissance Poet." In *The Lesbian and Gay Studies Reader,* ed. Abelove, Barele, and Halperin, pp. 453–66.

Hull, Gloria T., Patricia Bell Scott, and Barbara Smith, eds. *All the Women Are White, All the Blacks Are Men, But Some of Us Are Brave: Black Women's Studies.* New York: Feminist Press, 1982.

Hurston, Zora Neale. "Characteristics of Negro Expression." In *The Negro.* Ed. Nancy Cunard. New York: Ungar, 1970.

———. *Mules and Men.* Bloomington: Indiana Univ. Press, 1978.

———. *Their Eyes Were Watching God.* Urbana: Univ. of Illinois Press, 1978.

Irigaray, Luce. *Speculum of the Other Woman.* Trans. Gillian C. Gill. Ithaca: Cornell Univ. Press, 1985.

———. *This Sex Which Is Not One.* Trans. Catherine Porter. Ithaca: Cornell Univ. Press, 1985.

Iser, Wolfgang. *The Implied Reader: Patterns of Communication in Prose Fiction from Bunyan to Beckett.* Baltimore: Johns Hopkins Univ. Press, 1974.

Jacobs, Harriet A. *Incidents in the Life of a Slave Girl, Written by Herself.* Ed. Jean Fagan Yellin. Cambridge, Mass.: Harvard Univ. Press, 1987.

Jacobus, Mary. "An Unnecessary Maze of Sign Reading." In *Reading Women: Essays in Feminist Criticism.* New York: Columbia Univ. Press, 1986. Reprinted in *The Captive Imagination,* ed. Golden, pp. 277–95.

James, Deborah, and Sandra Clarke. "Women, Men, and Interruptions: A Critical Review." In *Gender and Conversational Interaction,* ed. Tannen, pp. 231–80.

James, Deborah, and Janice Drakich. "Understanding Gender Differences in Amount of Talk: A Critical Review of Research." In *Gender and Conversational Interaction,* ed. Tannen, pp. 281–312.

Jameson, Fredric. *Marxism and Form: Twentieth Century Dialectical Theories of Literature.* Princeton: Princeton Univ. Press, 1971.

———. *The Political Unconscious: Narrative as a Socially Symbolic Act.* Ithaca: Cornell Univ. Press, 1981.

James, Henry. *The Bostonians.* Harmondsworth, Middlesex, England: Penguin, 1985.

Jauss, Hans Robert. *Question and Answer: Forms of Dialogic Understanding.* Ed. and trans. Michael Hays. Minneapolis: Univ. of Minnesota Press, 1989.

———. *Toward an Aesthetic of Reception.* Trans. Timothy Bahti. Minneapolis: Univ. of Minnesota Press, 1982.

Jay, Karla, and Joanne Glasgow. *Lesbian Texts and Contexts: Radical Revisions.* New York: NYU Press, 1990.

Johnson, Barbara. "Metaphor, Metonymy and Voice in *Their Eyes Were Watching God.*" In *Black Literature,* ed. Gates, pp. 205–19.

———. "Thresholds of Difference: Structures of Address in Zora Neale Hurston." *Critical Inquiry* 12(1) (Autumn 1985): 278–89.

Johnson, James Weldon. "Race Prejudice and the Negro Artist." *Harper's* (Nov. 1928).

Jones, Ann Rosalind. "Imaginary Gardens with Real Frogs in Them: Feminist Euphoria and the Franco-American Divide, 1976–88." In *Changing Subjects: The Making of Feminist Literary Criticism.* Ed. Coppélia Kahn and Gayle Greene. London: Routledge, 1992. Pp. 64–82.

Joplin, Patricia Klindienst. "The Voice of the Shuttle Is Ours." *Stanford Literature Review* 1(1) (Spring 1984): 25–53.

Kahn, Coppélia. *Warriors, Wounds & Women: The Sexual Politics of Shakespeare's Roman Works.* Forthcoming, Routledge, 1996.

Kamuf, Peggy and Nancy K. Miller. "Parisian Letters: Between Feminism and Deconstruction." In *Conflicts in Feminism,* eds. Hirsch and Keller pp. 121–133.

Kaplan, Carla. "The Language of Crisis in Feminist Theory." In *"Turning the Century": New Directions in Feminist Criticism.* Ed. Glynis Carr. Lewisburg: Bucknell Review Press, 1992. Pp. 68–89.

Kaplan, Cora. *Sea Changes: Culture and Feminism.* London: Verso, 1986.

Kauffman, Linda S. *Special Delivery: Epistolary Modes in Modern Fiction.* Chicago: Univ. of Chicago Press, 1992.

Kennard, Jean. "Convention Coverage or How to Read Your Own Life." *New Literary History* 13(1) (1981): 69–88. Reprinted in *The Captive Imagination,* ed. Golden, pp. 168–90.

Kolodny, Annette. "Dancing Through the Minefield: Some Observations of the Theory, Practice, and Politics of a Feminist Literary Criticism." *Feminist Studies* 6(1) (Spring 1980): 1–25.

———. "A Map for Rereading; Or, Gender and the Interpretation of Literary Texts." *New Literary History* 11(3) (1980). Reprinted in *The Captive Imagination*, ed. Golden, pp. 149–67.

———. "Turning the Lens on 'The Panther Captivity': A Feminist Exercise in Practical Criticism." In *Writing and Sexual Difference*, ed. Abel, pp. 159–75.

Kristeva, Julia. *Desire in Language: A Semiotic Approach to Literature and Art.* Ed. Leon S. Roudiez. New York: Columbia Univ. Press, 1980.

———. "Woman Can Never Be Defined." In *New French Feminisms*, ed. Marks and Courtivron, pp. 137–41.

Kubitschek, Missy Dehn. "'Tuh de Horizon and Back': The Female Quest in *Their Eyes Were Watching God.*" *Black American Literature Forum* 17(3) (Fall 1983). Reprinted in *Zora Neale Hurston's Their Eyes Were Watching God.* Ed. Harold Bloom. New York: Chelsea House, 1987.

Lakoff, Robin. *Language and Woman's Place.* New York: Harper and Row, 1975.

Langbauer, Laurie. *Women and Romance: The Consolations of Gender in the English Novel.* Ithaca: Cornell Univ. Press, 1990.

Lanser, Susan Sniader. "Feminist Criticism, 'The Yellow Wallpaper,' and the Politics of Color in America." *Feminist Studies* 15(3) (Fall 1989): 415–41.

———. *Fictions of Authority: Women Writers and Narrative Voice.* Ithaca: Cornell Univ. Press, 1992.

———. *The Narrative Act: Point of View in Prose Fiction.* Princeton: Princeton Univ. Press, 1981.

Lazarre, Jane. "'Charlotte's Web': Rereading *Jane Eyre* over Time." In *Between Women.* Ed. Carol Ascher. Boston: Beacon Press, 1984. Pp. 221–35.

Lévi-Strauss, Claude. *The Elementary Structures of Kinship.* Boston: Beacon Press, 1969.

———. *Tristes Tropiques.* Paris, 1955.

Lewis, David Levering. *When Harlem Was in Vogue.* New York: Oxford Univ. Press, 1979.

Leys, Ruth. "The Real Miss Beauchamp: Gender and the Subject of Imitation." In *Feminists Theorize the Political*, ed. Butler and Scott, pp. 167–214.

Light, Alison. "Fear of the Happy Ending: *The Color Purple*, Reading and Racism." In *Plotting Change: Contemporary Women's Fiction.* Ed. Linda Anderson. London: Edward Arnold, 1990.

Lionnet, Françoise. *Autobiographical Voices: Race, Gender, Self-Portraiture.* Ithaca: Cornell Univ. Press, 1989.

Locke, Alain. "Art or Propaganda?" *Harlem* 1 (Nov. 1928). Reprinted in *Voices from the Harlem Renaissance*, ed. Huggins.

Lorde, Audre. *Sister Outsider.* Freedom, Calif.: Crossing Press, 1984.

Lubiano, Wahneema. "Constructing and Reconstructing Afro-American Texts: The Critic as Ambassador and Referee." *American Literary History* 1(2) (Summer 1989): 433–47.

Lugones, Maria C. and Elizabeth V. Spelman. "Have We Got a Theory for You! Feminist Theory, Cultural Imperialism and the Demand for 'The Woman's Voice.'" *Women's Studies International Forum* 6:6 (1983).

Luhmann, Niklas. *Love as Passion: The Codification of Intimacy.* Cambridge: Harvard Univ. Press, 1986.

Lyotard, Jean-François. *Just Gaming.* Trans. Wlad Godzich. Minneapolis: Univ. of Minnesota Press, 1985.

McConnell-Ginet, Sally, Ruth Borker, and Nelly Furman, eds. *Women and Language in Literature and Society*. New York: Praeger, 1980.

McDowell, Deborah E. "'The Changing Same: Generational Connections and Black Women Novelists." *New Literary History* 18(2) (Winter 1987): 281–302. Reprinted in *Reading Black*, ed. Gates, pp. 91–115. Also reprinted in *Alice Walker: Modern Critical Views*, ed. Bloom, pp. 135–51.

———. Introduction to *Quicksand* and *Passing*. By Nella Larsen. New Brunswick: Rutgers Univ. Press, 1986.

———. "Reading Family Matters." In *Changing Our Own Words*, ed. Wall, pp. 75–97.

McKay, Nellie. "'Crayon Enlargements of Life': Zora Neale Hurston's *Their Eyes Were Watching God* as Autobiography." In *New Essays on Their Eyes Were Watching God*. Ed. Michael Awkward. Cambridge, Eng.: Cambridge Univ. Press, 1990.

Mailloux, Steven. *Interpretive Conventions: The Reader in the Study of American Fiction*. Ithaca: Cornell Univ. Press, 1982.

Maranhão, Tullio, ed. *The Interpretation of Dialogue*. Chicago: Univ. of Chicago Press, 1990.

Marcus, Jane. "Alibis and Legends: The Ethics of Elsewhereness, Gender, and Estrangement." In *Women's Writing in Exile*, ed. Broe and Ingram, pp. 269–94.

———. "Daughters of Anger/Material Girls: Con/Textualizing Feminist Criticism." *Women's Studies* 15 (1988): 281–308.

———. "Sapphistry: Narration as Lesbian Seduction in *A Room of One's Own*." In *Virginia Woolf and the Languages of Patriarchy*. Bloomington: Indiana Univ. Press, 1987. Pp. 163–87.

———. "Still Practice, A/Wrested Alphabet: Toward a Feminist Aesthetic." In Marcus, *Art & Anger: Reading like a Woman*. Columbus, Ohio: Ohio State Univ. Press, 1988. Pp. 215–49.

———. "Storming the Toolshed." In *Art & Anger*, pp. 182–200.

Marcuse, Herbert. "The Affirmative Character of Culture." In *Negations*. Trans. Jeremy J. Shapiro. Boston: Beacon, 1968.

———. *Eros and Civilization: A Philosophical Inquiry into Freud*. Boston: Beacon, 1955.

Marks, Elaine, and Isabelle de Courtivon, eds. *New French Feminisms: An Anthology*. New York: Schocken, 1981.

Mayne, Judith. "A Parallax View of Lesbian Authorship." In *Inside/Out*, ed. Fuss, pp. 173–83.

Meehan, Johanna, ed. *Feminists Read Habermas: Gendering the Subject of Discourse*. New York: Routledge, 1995.

Meese, Elizabeth A. *Crossing the Double Cross: The Practice of Feminist Criticism*. Chapel Hill: Univ. of North Carolina Press, 1986.

Meyer, Susan, "Colonialism and the Figurative Strategy of *Jane Eyre*." *Victorian Studies* 33 (Winter 1990): 247–68.

Michie, Helena. *Sororophobia: Differences among Women in Literature and Culture*. New York: Oxford Univ. Press, 1992.

Miller, Nancy K. "Arachnologies: The Woman, the Text, and the Critic." In *The Poetics of Gender*. New York: Columbia Univ. Press, 1986.

———. "Emphasis Added: Plots and Plausibilities in Women's Fiction." *PMLA* 96(1) (Jan. 1981). Reprinted in Miller, *Subject to Change*.

―――. *Subject to Change: Reading Feminist Writing*. New York: Columbia Univ. Press, 1988.

Milloy, Courtland. "A 'Purple' Rage over a Rip-Off." *Washington Post*, Dec. 24, 1985.

Mitchell, Juliet, and Ann Oakley, eds. *What Is Feminism: A Re-Examination*. New York: Pantheon, 1986.

Modelski, Tania. *Feminism Without Women: Culture and Criticism in a "Post-feminist" Age*. New York: Routledge, 1991.

―――. *Loving with a Vengeance: Mass-Produced Fantasies for Women*. New York: Methuen, 1984.

Moers, Ellen. *Literary Women: The Great Writers*. Garden City: Doubleday, 1976.

Moglen, Helene. "*Jane Eyre:* The Creation of a Feminist Myth." In Moglen, *Charlotte Brontë: The Self Conceived*. New York: Norton, 1976.

Moi, Toril. *Sexual/Textual Politics: Feminist Literary Theory*. New York: Methuen, 1985.

Moraga, Cherrie, and Gloria Anzaldúa, eds. *This Bridge Called My Back: Writings by Radical Women of Color*. Watertown, Mass.: Persephone, 1981.

Munt, Sally, ed. *New Lesbian Criticism: Literary and Cultural Readings*. New York: Columbia Univ. Press, 1992.

Naylor, Gloria. "Love and Sex in the Afro-American Novel." *Yale Review* 78(1) (Autumn 1988): 19–31.

―――. *Mama Day*. New York: Ticknor & Fields, 1988.

"The Negro in Art: How Shall He Be Portrayed?" Symposium in *The Crisis*, 1926.

Nelson, Dana. *The Word in Black and White: Reading "Race" in American Literature, 1638–1867*. New York: Oxford Univ. Press, 1992.

Nicholson, Linda J., ed. *Feminism/Postmodernism*. New York: Routledge, 1990.

―――. "Introduction." In Benhabib, ed., *Feminist Contentions*.

O'Brien, Sharon. "'The Thing Not Named': Willa Cather as a Lesbian Writer." *Signs* 9(4) (Summer 1984): 576–99. Reprinted in *The Lesbian Issue: Essays from Signs*, ed. Freedman et al., pp. 67–90.

Olney, James. "'I Was Born': Slave Narratives, Their Status as Autobiography and as Literature." In *The Slave's Narrative*, ed. Davis and Gates.

Olsen, Tillie. *Silences*. New York: Delacorte, 1978.

Ostriker, Alicia S. "Thieves of Language: Women Poets and Revisionist Mythmaking." In *Stealing the Language: The Emergence of Women's Poetry in America*. Boston: Beacon, 1986. Pp. 210–38.

Parker, Andrew and Eve Kosofsky Sedgwick, eds. *Performativity and Performance*. New York: Routledge, 1995.

Pateman, Carole. *The Disorder of Women: Democracy, Feminism and Political Theory*. Stanford: Stanford Univ. Press, 1989.

―――. *The Sexual Contract*. Stanford: Stanford Univ. Press, 1988.

Peacock, John. "When Folk Goes Pop: Consuming *The Color Purple*." *Film Literature Quarterly* 19(3) (1991): 176–79.

Perera, Suvendrini. *Reaches of Empire: The English Novel from Edgeworth to Dickens*. New York: Columbia Univ. Press, 1991.

Peters, Joan D. "Finding a Voice: Towards a Woman's Discourse of Dialogue in the Narration of *Jane Eyre*." In *Studies in the Novel*. 23(2) (Summer 1991): 217–36.

Peterson, Carla L. "Capitalism, Black (Under)development, and the Production of the African-American Novel in the 1850s." *American Literary History* 4(4) (Winter 1992): 559–83.

———. *The Determined Reader: Gender and Culture in the Novel from Napoleon to Victoria*. New Brunswick, N.J.: Rutgers Univ. Press, 1986.

Peterson, Linda H. *Victorian Autobiography: The Tradition in Self-Interpretation*. New Haven: Yale Univ. Press, 1986.

Phelan, Peggy. *Unmarked: The Politics of Performance*. London: Routledge, 1993.

Poovey, Mary. *Uneven Developments: The Ideological Work of Gender in Mid-Victorian England*. Chicago: Univ. of Chicago Press, 1988.

Pryse, Marjorie. "Zora Neale Hurston, Alice Walker, and the 'Ancient Power' of Black Women." In *Conjuring*, ed. Pryse and Spillers, pp. 1–24.

Pryse, Marjorie, and Hortense Spillers, eds. *Conjuring: Black Women, Fiction, and the Literary Tradition*. Bloomington: Indiana Univ. Press, 1985.

Putnam, Frank W., M.D. *Diagnosis and Treatment of Multiple Personality Disorder*. New York: Guilford Press, 1989.

Rabinowitz, Peter J. *Before Reading: Narrative Conventions and the Politics of Interpretation*. Ithaca: Cornell Univ. Press, 1987.

Radway, Janice. *Reading the Romance: Women, Patriarchy, and Popular Literature*. Chapel Hill: Univ. of North Carolina Press, 1984.

"Redstocking Manifesto." In *Voices from Women's Liberation*, ed. Tanner, pp. 109–11.

Rhys, Jean. *Wide Sargasso Sea*. Harmondsworth, Middlesex, London: Penguin, 1960.

Rich, Adrienne. *Blood, Bread, and Poetry: Selected Prose, 1979–1985*. New York: Norton, 1986.

———. "Compulsory Heterosexuality and Lesbian Existence." *Signs* 5(4) (1980): 631–60.

———. "Diving into the Wreck." In *Diving into the Wreck: Poems, 1971–1972*. New York: W. W. Norton, 1973.

———. *The Dream of a Common Language: Poems 1974–1977*. New York: W. W. Norton, 1978.

———. *On Lies, Secrets, and Silence: Selected Prose, 1966–1978*. New York: W. W. Norton, 1979.

———. *Poems: Selected and New, 1950–1974*. New York: W. W. Norton, 1975.

———. "The Temptations of a Motherless Woman." In Rich, *On Lies*, pp. 89–106.

———. "When We Dead Awaken: Writing as Re-Vision." *College English* 34(1) (Oct. 1972). Reprinted in Rich, *On Lies*, pp. 33–49.

Riley, Denise. *Am I That Name? Feminism and the Category of "Women" in History*. New York: Macmillan, 1988.

Robbins, Bruce. "Death and Vocation: Narrativizing Narrative Theory." *PMLA* 107(1) (Jan. 1992): 38–50.

———. *Secular Vocations: Intellectuals, Professionalism, Culture*. London: Verso, 1993.

Roof, Judith. *A Lure of Knowledge: Lesbian Sexuality and Theory*. New York: Columbia Univ. Press, 1991.

Rorty, Richard. *Philosophy and the Mirror of Nature*. Princeton: Princeton Univ. Press, 1979.

Royster, Philip M. "In Search of Our Fathers' Arms: Alice Walker's Persona of the Alienated Darling." *Black American Literature Forum* 20(4) (1986): 347–70.

Rubin, Gayle. "The Traffic in Women: Notes Toward a Political Economy of Sex." In *Toward an Anthropology of Women*. Ed. Rayna Reiter. New York: Monthly Review Press, 1975.

Sadoff, Diane. "Black Matrilineage: The Case of Alice Walker and Zora Neale Hurston." *Signs* 11(1) (1985): 4–26.

Salem, Dorothy. *To Better Our World: Black Women in Organized Reform, 1890–1920*. New York: Carlson, 1990.

Schenck, Celeste, and Bella Brodzki, eds. *Life/Lines: Theorizing Women's Autobiography*. Ithaca: Cornell Univ. Press, 1988.

Scholes, Robert. *Fabulation and Metafiction*. Urbana: Univ. of Illinois Press, 1979.

Schuyler, George. "The Negro-Art Hokum." *The Nation* 122 (June 1926). Reprinted in *Voices from the Harlem Renaissance*, ed. Huggins, pp. 309–12.

Schweickart, Patrocinio. "Reading Ourselves: Toward a Feminist Theory of Reading." In *Gender and Reading*, ed. Flynn and Schweikart, pp. 31–62.

Scott, Joan W. "The Evidence of Experience." In *The Lesbian and Gay Studies Reader*, ed. Abelove, Barele, and Halperin, pp. 397–415.

Searle, John R. *Speech Acts: An Essay in the Philosophy of Language*. Cambridge, Eng.: Cambridge Univ. Press, 1969.

Sedgwick, Eve Kosofsky. *Between Men: English Literature and Male Homosocial Desire*. New York: Columbia Univ. Press, 1985.

———. *Epistemology of the Closet*. Berkeley: Univ. of California Press, 1990.

———. *Tendencies*. Durham: Duke Univ. Press, 1993.

———. "Queer Performativity: Henry James's *The Art of the Novel*." *GLQ: A Journal of Lesbian and Gay Studies* 1:1 (1993): 1–16.

Sedgwick, Eve Kosofsky, and Andrew Parker, eds. *Performativity and Performance*. New York: Routledge, 1995.

Sennett, Richard. *The Fall of Public Man: On the Social Psychology of Capitalism*. New York: Vintage, 1974.

Shockley, Ann Allen. *Afro-American Women Writers, 1746–1933*. New York: New American Library, 1988.

Showalter, Elaine. "Literary Criticism." Review Essay. *Signs* 1 (Winter 1975): 435–60.

———. *A Literature of Their Own: British Women Novelists from Brontë to Lessing*. Princeton: Princeton Univ. Press, 1977.

———, ed. *The New Feminist Criticism*. New York: Pantheon, 1985.

———. *Sister's Choice: Tradition and Change in American Women's Writing*. New York: Oxford Univ. Press, 1991.

Shreve, Anita. *Women Together, Women Alone: The Legacy of the Consciousness-Raising Movement*. New York: Viking, 1989.

Silver, Brenda R. "The Reflecting Reader in *Villette*." In *The Voyage In: Fictions of Female Development*. Ed. Elizabeth Abel, Marianne Hirsch, and Elizabeth Langland. Hanover: Univ. Press of New England, 1983. Pp. 90–111.

Singer, Irving. *The Nature of Love*. Vol. 2, *Courtly and Romantic*. Chicago: Univ. of Chicago Press, 1984.

Smith, Barbara. "*Color Purple* Distorts Class, Lesbian Issues." *Guardian*, Feb. 19, 1986.

———, ed. *Home Girls: A Black Feminist Anthology*. New York: Persephone Press, 1983.

———. "Toward a Black Feminist Criticism." In *The New Feminist Criticism*, ed. Showalter, pp. 168–85.

Smith, Barbara Herrnstein. "Contingencies of Value." *Critical Inquiry* 10(1) (Sept. 1983). Reprinted in *Canons,* ed. Robert von Hallberg, pp. 5–39. Chicago: Univ. of Chicago Press, 1984.

Smith, Dinitia. Review of *The Color Purple. The Nation,* Sept. 4, 1982. Reprinted in *Alice Walker: Critical Perspectives,* ed. Gates and Appiah, pp. 19–21.

Smith, Valerie. *Self-Discovery and Authority in Afro-American Narrative.* Cambridge, Mass.: Harvard Univ. Press, 1987.

Smitherman, Geneva. *Talkin and Testifyin: The Language of Black America.* Boston: Houghton Mifflin, 1977.

Snitow, Ann, Christine Stansell, and Sharon Thomson, eds. *Powers of Desire: The Politics of Sexuality.* New York: Monthly Review Press, 1983.

Spacks, Patricia. *The Female Imagination.* New York: Knopf, 1975.

———. *Gossip.* New York: Knopf, 1985.

Spender, Dale. *Man Made Language.* London: Routledge and Kegan Paul, 1980.

Spillers, Hortense J. "A Hateful Passion, a Lost Love." In *Feminist Issues,* ed. Benstock, pp. 181–207.

Spivak, Gayatri Chakravorty. "Three Women's Texts and a Critique of Imperialism." *Critical Inquiry* 12 (Autumn 1985).

Stanton, Domna C. "Language and Revolution: The Franco-American Disconnection." In *The Future of Difference,* ed. Eisenstein and Jardine, pp. 73–87.

Steiner, George. "Eros and Idiom." In *On Difficulty and Other Essays.* New York: Oxford Univ. Press, 1978.

Stepto, Robert. "Distrust of the Reader in Afro-American Narratives." In *Reconstructing American Literary History.* Ed. Sacvan Bercovitch. Cambridge, Mass.: Harvard Univ. Press, 1986. Pp. 300–322.

———. *From Behind the Veil: A Study of Afro-American Narrative.* Urbana: Univ. of Illinois Press, 1979.

Stimpson, Catherine. "Zero Degree Deviancy: The Lesbian Novel in English." In *Where the Meanings Are: Feminism and Cultural Spaces.* New York: Methuen, 1988. Pp. 97–110.

Tannen, Deborah. *Conversational Style: Analyzing Talk Among Friends.* Norwood, N.J.: Ablex, 1984.

———, ed. *Gender and Conversational Interaction.* New York: Oxford Univ. Press, 1993.

———. *Talking Voices: Repetition, Dialogue, and Imagery in Conversational Discourse.* Cambridge, Eng: Cambridge Univ. Press, 1989.

———, ed. *That's Not What I Meant! How Conversational Style Makes or Breaks Relationships.* New York: Ballantine, 1986.

———, ed. *You Just Don't Understand: Women and Men in Conversation.* New York: Ballantine, 1990.

Tanner, Leslie B., ed. *Voices from Women's Liberation.* New York: New American Library, 1970.

Tanner, Tony. *Adultery in the Novel: Contract and Transgression.* Baltimore: Johns Hopkins Univ. Press, 1979.

Tate, Claudia. *Domestic Allegories of Political Desire: The Black Heroine's Text at the Turn of the Century.* New York: Oxford Univ. Press, 1992.

Taylor, Charles. *Multiculturalism and "The Politics of Recognition."* Princeton: Princeton Univ. Press, 1992.

———. "The Politics of Recognition." In *Working Papers and Proceedings of the Center for Psychosocial Studies.* Chicago: Center for Psychosocial Studies, 1992.

———. *Sources of the Self: The Making of the Modern Identity.* Cambridge, Mass.: Harvard Univ. Press, 1989.

Terborg-Penn, Rosalyn. "Discontented Black Feminists: Prelude and Postscript to the Passage of the Nineteenth Amendment." In *Decades of Discontent: The Women's Movement, 1920–1940.* Ed. Lois Scharf and Joan M. Jensen. Boston: Northeastern Univ. Press, 1983. Pp. 261–78.

The Lesbian Issue. Signs 9(4) (Summer 1984). Reprinted (with additions) as *The Lesbian Issue: Essays from Signs.* Ed. Estelle B. Freedman, Barbara C. Gelpi, Susan L. Johnson, and Kathleen M. Weston. Chicago: Univ. of Chicago Press, 1985.

Tillotson, Kathleen. *Novels of the 1840s.* New York: Oxford Univ. Press, 1967.

Tompkins, Jane P., ed. *Reader-Response Criticism: From Formalism to Post-Structuralism.* Baltimore: Johns Hopkins Univ. Press, 1980.

Treichler, Paula A. "Escaping the Sentence: Diagnosis and Discourse in 'The Yellow Wallpaper.'" In *Feminist Issues,* ed. Benstock, pp. 62–78. Reprinted in *The Captive Imagination,* ed. Golden, pp. 191–210.

Turan, Kenneth. "Movies." *California Magazine,* Feb. 11, 1986.

Turner, Darwin T. *In a Minor Chord.* Carbondale: Southern Illinois Univ. Press, 1971.

Turner, Victor. *The Anthropology of Performance.* New York: PAJ Publications, 1986.

Vance, Carole S., ed. *Pleasure and Danger: Exploring Female Sexuality.* New York: Monthly Review Press, 1983.

V-Girls, The. "Daughters of the Revolution." *October* 71 (Winter 1995): 121–40.

Vincent, Theodore G., and Robert Chrisman, eds. *Voices of a Black Nation: Political Journalism in the Harlem Renaissance.* San Francisco: Ramparts Press, 1973.

Wald, Priscilla. "'Becoming Colored': The Self-Authorized Language of Difference in Zora Neale Hurston." *American Literary History* 2(1) (Spring 1990): 79–100.

Walker, Alice. *The Color Purple.* New York: Simon & Schuster, 1982.

———. "A Conversation with Sharon Wilson." *Kalliope* 6 (1984). Reprinted in *Alice Walker: Critical Perspectives,* ed. Gates and Appiah, pp. 319–25.

———. *In Search of Our Mothers' Gardens: Womanist Prose.* New York: Harcourt, Brace, Jovanovich, 1983.

Wall, Cheryl A., ed. *Changing Our Own Words: Essays on Criticism, Theory, and Writing by Black Women.* New Brunswick: Rutgers Univ. Press, 1989.

———. "Introduction: Taking Positions and Changing Words." In *Changing Our Own Words,* ed. Wall, pp. 1–15.

Wallace, Michelle. "Blues for Mr. Spielberg." *Village Voice,* March 18, 1986.

Warner, Michael. "Homo-Narcissism; Or, Heterosexuality." In *Engendering Men,* ed. Boone and Cadden, pp. 190–206.

Washington, Mary Helen. Foreword to *Their Eyes Were Watching God.* New York: Harper and Row, 1990. Pp. vii-xiv.

———. "'I Love the Way Janie Crawford Left Her Husbands': Hurston's Emergent Female Hero." In *Invented Lives: Narratives of Black Women, 1860–1960.* New York: Doubleday, 1987. Pp. 237–54.

Weisberg, Richard H. "Family Feud: A Response to Robert Weisberg on Law and Literature." *Yale Journal of Law and Humanities* 1:1 (Dec. 1988).

Williams, Carolyn. "'Trying to Do Without God': The Revision of Epistolary Address in *The Color Purple*." In *Writing the Female Voice: Essays on Epistolary Literature.* Ed. Elizabeth C. Goldsmith. Boston: Northeastern Univ. Press, 1989. Pp. 273–85.

Williams, Patricia J. "On Being the Object of Property." *Signs* 14(1) (1988): 5–24.

Williams, Raymond. *The English Novel: From Dickens to Lawrence.* London: Chatto & Windus, 1970.

———. "Forms of English Fiction in 1848." In *Writing in Society.* London: Verso, n.d. Pp. 150–65.

———. *Keywords: A Vocabulary of Culture and Society.* New York: Oxford Univ. Press, 1983.

Willimon, William H. "Seeing Red over *The Color Purple*." *Christian Century,* April 2, 1986.

Willis, Susan. *Specifying: Black Women Writing the American Experience.* Madison: Univ. of Wisconsin Press, 1987.

Wittig, Monique. "One Is Not Born a Woman." *Feminist Issues* 7(4) (Winter 1981).

Woolf, Virginia. "*Jane Eyre* and *Wuthering Heights*." *The Common Reader.* New York: Harcourt, Brace, Jovanovich, 1925.

———. *The Pargiters: The Novel-Essay Portion of "The Years."* Ed. Mitchell A. Leaska. New York: Harcourt, Brace & World, 1978.

———. *A Room of One's Own.* New York: Harcourt, Brace & World, 1929.

Wright, Richard. "Between Laughter and Tears." Review of *Their Eyes Were Watching God. New Masses,* Oct. 5, 1937, pp. 22–25.

Wyatt, Jean. "A Patriarch of One's Own: *Jane Eyre* and Romantic Love." *Tulsa Studies in Women's Literature* 4 (2) (1985): 199–216.

Yaeger, Patricia. *Honey-Mad Women: Emancipatory Strategies in Women's Writing.* New York: Columbia Univ. Press, 1988.

Yeazell, Ruth Bernard. "More True Than Real: Jane Eyre's 'Mysterious Summons.'" *Nineteenth-Century Fiction* 29 (1974): 127–43.

Yellin, Jean Fagan. Introduction to *Incidents in the Life of a Slave Girl,* by Jacobs, pp. xiii-xl.

———. "Text and Contexts of Harriet Jacobs' *Incidents in the Life of a Slave Girl, Written by Herself*." In *The Slave's Narrative,* ed. Davis and Gates.

———. "Written by Herself: Harriet Jacobs' Slave Narrative." *American Literature* 53(3) (Nov. 1981): 479–86.

Young, Iris Marion. *Justice and the Politics of Difference.* Princeton: Princeton Univ. Press, 1990.

———. *Throwing like a Girl and Other Essays in Feminist Philosophy and Social Theory.* Bloomington: Indiana Univ. Press, 1990.

Zimmerman, Bonnie. "What Has Never Been: An Overview of Lesbian Feminist Criticism." In *The New Feminist Criticism,* ed. Showalter, pp. 200–224.

Index